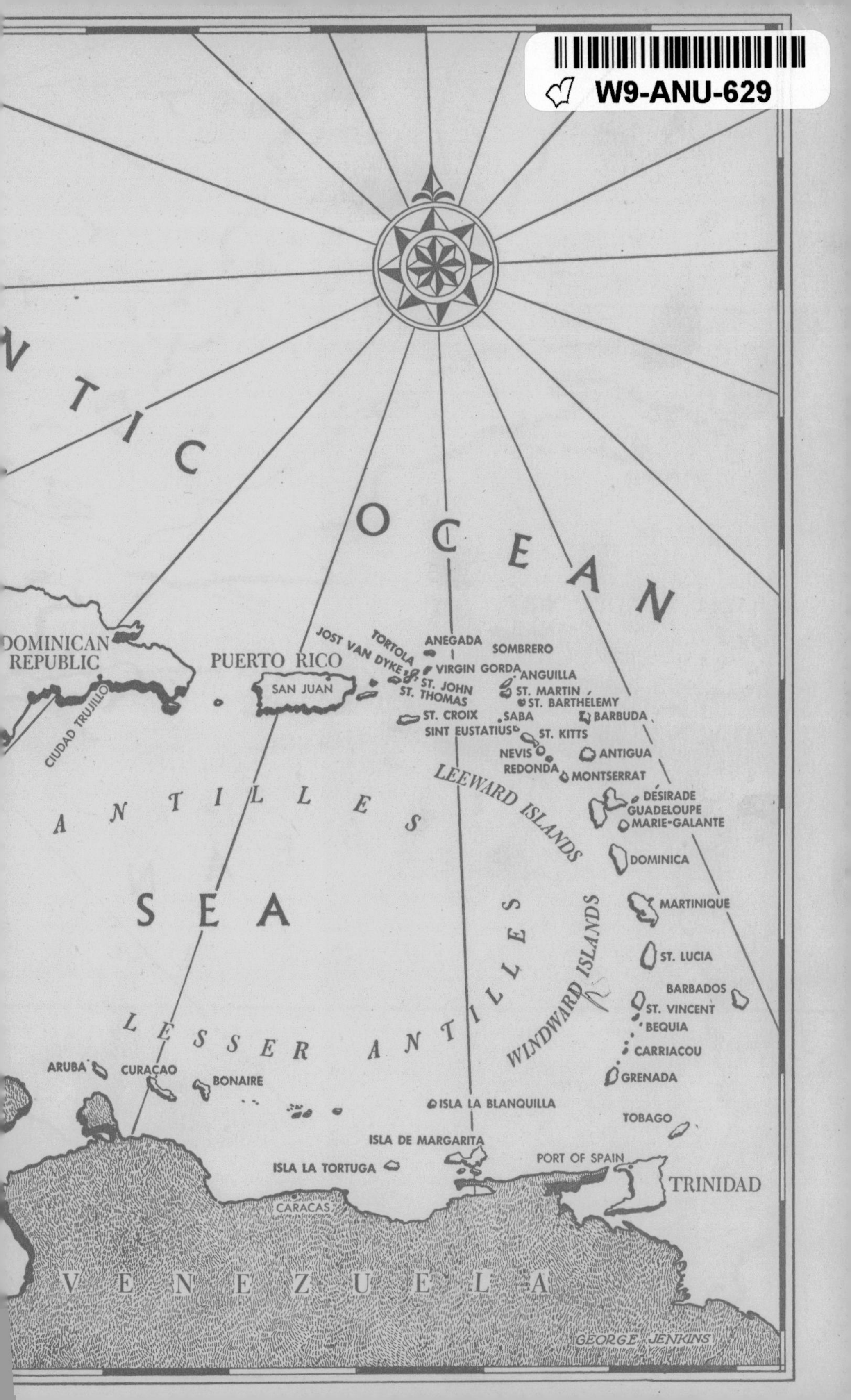

W9-ANU-629
NTIC
OCEAN
DOMINICAN REPUBLIC
CIUDAD TRUJILLO
PUERTO RICO
SAN JUAN
JOST VAN DYKE
TORTOLA
ANEGADA
SOMBRERO
VIRGIN GORDA
ANGUILLA
ST. JOHN
ST. THOMAS
ST. MARTIN
ST. BARTHÉLEMY
ST. CROIX
SABA
BARBUDA
SINT EUSTATIUS
ST. KITTS
NEVIS
ANTIGUA
REDONDA
MONTSERRAT
LEEWARD ISLANDS
DÉSIRADE
GUADELOUPE
MARIE-GALANTE
ANTILLES
DOMINICA
SEA
MARTINIQUE
WINDWARD ISLANDS
ST. LUCIA
BARBADOS
ST. VINCENT
BEQUIA
LESSER ANTILLES
CARRIACOU
ARUBA
CURAÇAO
BONAIRE
GRENADA
ISLA LA BLANQUILLA
TOBAGO
ISLA DE MARGARITA
PORT OF SPAIN
ISLA LA TORTUGA
TRINIDAD
CARACAS
VENEZUELA
GEORGE JENKINS

ESCAPE TO THE WEST INDIES

Bradley Smith

ESCAPE TO THE WEST INDIES

A Guidebook to the Islands of the Caribbean

with photographs by the author

New York, 1956, Alfred A Knopf

L.C. catalog card number: 55–9291

THIS IS A BORZOI BOOK,
PUBLISHED BY ALFRED A. KNOPF, INC.

Manufactured in the United States of America. Published simultaneously in Canada by McClelland and Stewart Limited.

FIRST EDITION

FOR

Sharon, Michael, Terrence, Steven, Susan, Nancy,

and especially Adele

INTRODUCTION *and* ACKNOWLEDGMENTS

I escaped to the West Indies for the first time after a bleak, gray, ice-slippery Connecticut winter. The first exploratory trip I made alone, but ever since then my family has escaped with me. We have found the islands warm, sunny, and healthy, and with a few exceptions comfortable and inexpensive.

Most of all, they are full of easy-going people; it was this make-our-house-your-home attitude which made the writing of this book possible. For no one writes a book alone, least of all this kind of book. As I journeyed from one sun-bright shore to another, there were friends, or friends of friends, to help out with a story, a dinner (and a recipe), or more of those wonderfully relaxing West Indian drinks.

It was over the excellent rum punches served by Sir Errol and Lady Dos Santos, distinguished citizens of England and Trinidad, that the book was actually launched. Sir Errol witnessed my signature to the contract, then took me to a "jump-up" at Port of Spain's Country Club, where he personally demonstrated what a jump-up really was. Also in Trinidad, John Rahr of British West Indian Airways and wife Joan fed me information and Trinidad delicacies. Donald Bain of the Tourist Board drove me about and showed me the night life. Winston Minshell, a fine artist, counseled, advised, and drank with me at his Art Center. I was especially grateful for the opportunity to meet the artists of Trinidad and to see their work.

But though the contract was signed in Trinidad, the book really started in New York when Mary Hamman of *Life*'s Modern Living Department suggested that we plan a color essay about the small, off-the-tourist-track islands of the Lesser Antilles. Patsy Parkin of the research staff consulted maps, talked to consulates, airlines, and shipping companies, and wrote a general script. Maitland Edey, Mary, Patsy, and I worked out the details. Ray Mackland, Picture Editor, assigned me to do the story because I had already visited all the larger islands and had an intense interest in the small ones. This resulted in the picture essay "West Indies Escape" (*Life*, January 11, 1954). This was the beginning, but the fact that the book was written is owing mostly to my interested and knowing assistant, Ruth Hoagland. Without Ruth's energy and initiative the information in the back of the book could never have been assembled. Two others were key factors in the book's development. George Jenkins, a great designer and a good friend, assembled and edited hundreds of pictures. If Herbert Weinstock had not been both good-humored and psychic about keeping track of me all over the Caribbean and the United States, our author-editor communication could never have been maintained.

I moved the family into a beach house in Jamaica, between Montego Bay and Falmouth. From there my camera assistant, Myles De Russey, and I traveled up and down Jamaica, learning history and customs from Walter Fletcher, the patriach of Montego, and C. Bernard Lewis, the scholarly director of the Institute of Jamaica in Kingston. I owe a very special debt to the Institute, for I did most of my early historical research in their excellent library. There I found translations of Père Labat, Moreau de St.-Méry, Bartolomé de Las Casas, the letters and journals of Columbus, and early editions of Peter Martyr's and Bryan Edwards's works, to mention just a few. Mr. Lewis was also kind enough to fill out a very elaborate questionnaire regarding the physical and social aspects of the island. Dr. Ian MacKay of the University of the West Indies was my companion on an adventurous tour from the Blue Mountains to Port Antonio. Other University people who gave me essential information were Garth Underwood of the Department of Zoology, the greatest authority in the world on lizards, and G. F. Asprey, the well-known botanist. Robert Verity, the Supervisor of Junior Centers, Art, and Music Activity, discussed the current culture among young people in Jamaica and showed me the interesting primitive paintings done by "his children." No less interesting was the contribution of Kingston's Chief of Police, who showed me the city's life between dusk and dawn.

I remember hard-driving, pleasure-loving Mickey Nation and his distinguished father, Judge Nation, in Montego Bay the Ewen Brothers of Casa Blanca, Carmen de Lisser of Sunset Lodge and especially Matt Archibald of the Montego Beach, all for their stimulating conversation against a background of slow-moving days and whisper-soft nights.

In the near-by Cayman Islands the Greenall family of Galleon Beach helped me gather information, as did Ertis Ebanks, taxi-driver extraordinary, guide, philosopher, and, by his own admission, "the best damn conch-diver in the Caribbean."

In Cuba everyone was helpful, and the tourist police were so well organized that travel was swift and easy. One person stands out, though: Señora Marguerita La Rosa, the attractive owner of Casa La Rosa at Varadero Beach, who gave much time to helping me understand the many-faceted Cuban personality. At every airport I was warmly greeted and the facilities of Pan American World Airways were put at my disposal. For this exceptional service my thanks to all their personnel, and especially to Caribbean publicity chief Roger Wolin.

In Haiti, I was triply fortunate. My friend Roger Coster, a great photographer, resident of Port au Prince and owner of the Hotel Olaffson, with his attractive wife, introduced me to that fascinating city. He also introduced me to DeWitt Peters, director of the Haitian Art Center, who in turn showed me some of the architectural gems of the countryside and then, trying to be even more helpful, introduced me to a young artist, thereby unwittingly almost getting me killed when the young man took me to a real Voodoo rite. I admit that I should not have been there at all, especially not with my cameras; one of them was broken by a wildly indignant dancer, and for a time it looked as if we would both be stoned by the excited group. But it was all my fault.

Lon Southerland of Southerland Tours helped me to get around the countryside smoothly. I also learned a great deal from my friend Selden Rodman, author of *Haiti the Black Republic* and director of the great primitive mural project in the Episcopal Cathedral.

In Puerto Rico I owe much to O. L. Sands, Chief of Aviation of the Puerto Rico Transportation Authority, and to his son Ralph of the Couture Car Rental Bureau. Through Sammy Negron, I ate the wonderful shrimp of Ponce at the Ponce Men's Club, which is the ultimate in male privacy; it can be reached only by boat. At Mayagüez, Rafael Izquierdo taught me about turtle steaks cut from the Carey, an almost unbelievably tender and delicately flavored sea food.

In the Dominican Republic, Ben Carruthers and Horacio Vicioso were hospitable, and in St. Thomas, Jonel Jorgulesco, of New York and St. Thomas, briefed me on the island and introduced me to some fascinating characters; Lind Weber of Bluebeard's Castle flew a messenger to San Juan, P.R., and back one afternoon to pick up some camera equipment for me, proving that all things are possible in the Virgins. At St. John, Mr. and Mrs. Ron Morrisette risked their lives and mine on the steep Jeep slopes and in climbing the sheer rock cliffs of the near-by British Virgins. St. Croix was made even more pleasant than usual by Mary Millar, who dragged my willing feet from one end of the island to the other.

In the Netherlands island of Saba and in Sint Maarten and Sint Eustatius, Mr. Leonard Bouman of the Netherlands Tourist Board deserves my thanks, as do the Saba men who landed me on the rocky shore. In Curaçao, Dr. Ch. Engels and wife Lucilla, leaders of the art movement there and fine painters themselves, led me into the midst of culture and good conversation on the island. The head of the Tourist Board Mr. Philip J. Evertsz gave freely of his time, gallantly overindulging with me in the great Dutch cuisine and the accompanying Holland gin and curaçao liqueur. In Aruba, Mr. Ernest Bartels, Secretary of the Tourist Board and Mr. Vergeer, promoter and enterprising innkeeper, did much to make my stay interesting. In Bonaire, where the fish are six feet long and the cactus thirty feet tall, everybody was excited about my visit and stood by with information and helpful suggestions.

My friends in the French islands are too many to name, and too cosmopolitan not to agree with my choice when I mention only a few whom I will never forget: Mario and Umberto Petreluzzi and their friend M. Dain, bulwarks of culture in Guadeloupe, and young Georges Barbitteau, who acted as my translator and guide. In Martinique, Roger Albert, parfumeur extraordinaire, and Dr. Rose Rosette, agricultural expert and authority on early African dances, entertained me as only Martiniquans can. Rémy de Hænen, the high-flying Conseiller General of St. Barthélemy, whisked me through the clear Caribbean skies and served wonderful meals at his tiny beach house on St. Barts.

Now for the interesting and helpful Britishers: In Antigua, Hay Bryson and Happy Ward made me welcome; later one of *Life*'s editors, Hugh Moffett, made his notes on the island available. In St. Kitts, Acting Administrator Lloyd Matheson taught me much about education, history, and housing. On the near-by island of Nevis, Mrs. Mary Pomeroy drove me about, and with her excellent larder rescued me from the canned diet I had been sailing with.

In Dominica, Messrs. Lindo and Aird, and Mrs. Lennox Napier could not have been more hospitable. I am especially indebted to Mrs. Napier, author, legislator, and mistress of one of the most delightful homes in the West Indies. I arrived at her house hungry, tired, and confused about how to get to the Carib country. She fed me, put me up in a restful room lined with good books, and clarified my thinking about the geography of the island. But I could never have reached the Carib country without the help of Nicholas Taylor and his father, anthropologist Douglas Taylor, author of *The Caribs of Dominica* and *The Black Caribs of British Honduras.* Taylor lived with the Caribs for many years, and knows them better than any other living man. He lent me his son Nikko as guide and interpreter for the trip to Battaka in the middle of the Carib Reservation.

In Barbados, the most British island of the Lesser Antilles, I made many friends on many visits. The George Huntes, publishers of *The Bajan,* are walking encyclopedias of information about the Crown Colony. Fred Goddard introduced me to the cooling spiced drink of Barbados, the Sangaree; Charlie Taylor of the Hotel Royal-on-Sea discussed native cooking; Frank Collymore told me about the theater and The "Bajan" dialect; Neville Connell of the Barbados Museum was always available for advice. Ronald and Marietta Tree gave me a place to lie on their beach and nourished me with tea, ideas, and an occasional dollop of whisky. Mrs. Eileen Robinson, the gracious proprietress of Bagshot House, made perhaps the most unusual contribution of all: she took a fifteen-year-old son off my hands at a time when my wife and I had to be off for Puerto Rico and his school (Lodge in Barbados) had not yet opened.

In St. Vincent there are friends whom I had better mention or not go back, and go back I intend to, every winter. They are Gerald and Jeanne Palmer, my favorite islanders, and managers of Sugar Mill Inn; "Marse Fred" Hazell, a great drinking companion; Cyril and Hazel de B. Barnard, gracious hosts of Orange Hill Plantation, and their neighbors at Montague House, Ian and Vivian Child, who have three times led me on an adventurous climb up the volcano. Then there is Alec (the Hon. E. A. C.) Hughes, recently appointed Counsel to St. Vincent under the new Constitution of 1956, and his pretty wife,

Peggy. Finally there are Winston Lewis, editor of the *Vincentien*, Police Band Leader, and the life blood of St. Vincent's tiny radio station; and Vin Sprott, singer, composer, pianist, and Public Relations Officer for the island.

Just a few miles north of St. Vincent is St. Lucia. Harold Simmons, its outstanding artist, and its distinguished poet, Derek Walcott, were interesting and helpful. I especially enjoyed my visit to Pigeon Island, where Mrs. Josette Legh entertained me by allowing me to make and serve the drinks.

In Grenada, Louis Law, whom I first met in Antigua, has kept me posted on current conditions in the island, and young David Otway spent days and sleepless nights trying to assure my getting all the pictures and information I wanted.

In the slow-moving island of Tobago, I learned about Arawak-Carib culture and artifacts from Tom Cambridge, then the warden; about geography and history from Commander and Mrs. Jack Crooks of the Blue Haven. So the circle of Caribbean friends is complete, and we are geographically back at Trinidad, where this book started. To all of you, and all the others, thanks again—and cheers.

BRADLEY SMITH

Sugar Mill Inn
St. Vincent, B.W.I.

Contents

Part III *Independent Islands*

Part IV *Netherlands West Indies*

Part V *United States West Indies*

Part VI *Venezuelan Island*

Appendix: Tabular Information for Tourists, Travelers, and Prospective Settlers

ESCAPE TO THE WEST INDIES

WHAT EVERY TRAVELER SHOULD KNOW ABOUT THE CARIBBEAN

Your Health

Travel throws everyone off balance. Tension increases. Nerves become easily frayed. First rules: relax! enjoy yourself! don't rush! don't worry! Make reservations early—get to the airport or dockside well before departure time. Be prepared for delays and changes in schedules and routings. Take along Dramamine for airsickness or seasickness especially for island-to-island schooner trips.

Don't upset your stomach by a sudden surfeit of tropical fruits and juices. Your system is not used to it. Take it easy on the rum the first few days, for the combination of too much fruit, too much rum, and too much tension is often responsible for the diarrhea usually blamed on the water. A small bottle of paregoric is useful.

The sun in the Caribbean is both beneficent and baleful. Wear a hat, and take a siesta as the sensible residents do. Don't try for a two-day deep tan or you'll wind up baked and feverish. If you play tennis or engage in other active sports, a salt tablet will help keep up your energy. Wear long sleeves and slacks when on long fishing or sailing trips. Many people find sunglasses an essential to prevent glare headaches.

Rain comes often and suddenly in the West Indies, and can be unpleasant and chilling. A pocket-size plastic raincoat and foldaway rain hat are essential.

Some islands have *some* malaria. If you expect to visit them, ask your doctor to prescribe Arelin pills for ten days before you set out. On trips that will take you to the undeveloped interior of an island, it is always best to have typhoid shots in addition to the required smallpox vaccination. The United States islands and others also require yellow-fever certificates for travelers going to certain parts of South America.

Even the smallest islands have medical facilities. Doctors are good, and are especially familiar with disorders peculiar to the Caribbean.

Your Money

For some unaccountable reason money seems to become more important as soon as you start your trip. This may be because the currency is unfamiliar. Remember that goods and services are always as cheap or cheaper than in the United States. Take the trouble to familiarize yourself with the currency. Carry plenty of small change—but not pennies—for tipping. When in doubt, don't tip at all. Ten per cent is always adequate. Don't give to beggars. All islands are trying to find a means of caring for their poor. Support of the beggar population by tourists only increases its numbers.

Some merchants and individuals in a few islands will buy United States dollars at higher than the standard rate. You stand to make very little on these transactions in the West Indies, and will lose more time finding the contact than the small profit is worth.

The recommended hotels, restaurants, and large merchants have a reputation for honesty. Check your account carefully, but don't expect to be cheated—few travelers are. If you ask an islander to pose for a picture, tell him in advance how much you will give him—otherwise he may demand a dollar or more. Ten to twenty-five cents is the usual fee. If you photograph groups, try to do it from a distance or when they are unaware of it. Most natives resent intrusion on their privacy, so make arrangements in advance or be invisible.

Travelers' checks in small denominations are the safest and most convenient way to carry money, and are accepted on almost every island. Banks and hotels are the best places to cash them.

When buying to bring back to the States, keep weight and bulk in mind as well as price. The United States allows residents who have been out of the country for longer than forty-eight hours to bring in $200 worth of purchases duty-free. Residents who are out of the country for an additional twelve or more days may bring in an additional $300 worth of purchases duty-free, making a total allowance of $500 per person. This means $1,000 for two people. Few bring back this much, but many buy things far too big to transport, and others lose the saving by paying excess weight across the United States when they return. Keep an accurate record of (and the receipts for) all purchases you make. You will need them when filling out your Customs Declaration. Be careful, too, of certain trade-marked items that may not be brought into the United States. Some brands of perfumes, watches, and cameras are on the restricted list.

Your Time

It is easy to waste a lot of pleasant holiday time in transit and wind up feeling like a displaced person. Don't try to see a new place or a new island every day. The extra packing and unpacking uses up time. Explore and enjoy one spot before rushing to another.

Letters of introduction are time-savers, and islanders appreciate them. If you have introductions, use them and let your new friends show you around. Don't pass up guided tours. They are one of the best ways to get orientated. Later take a map along and go exploring on your own. The siesta is not a time-waster—you'll have more fun and feel better for the heat-of-the-day rest period.

Your Children

All children are good travelers, and West Indies airlines and cruise ships cater to them. Hotels, large and small, are well equipped to handle them, and nursemaids and baby-sitters are cheap and dependable. Most islands have a private day school for children up to twelve years. When on a trip for several weeks or a month, some parents take schoolbooks along and conduct classes for an hour or two on the beach or hotel veranda. Canned baby foods (and most other United States canned goods) are available on all except the most remote islands, and even on Saba. There are plenty of eggs, chickens, canned and powdered milk, fruit, and cereal. The Caribbean is an ideal holiday area for children.

Your Clothing and Accessories

Keep them at a minimum. If you take off from Florida, New Orleans, or San Juan, make a last-minute check. Take out all nonessentials and mail them home. Some travelers going to the islands in the winter check their topcoats in Miami or San Juan to be picked up on the way back.

BASIC LIST FOR WOMEN: Sneakers, walking-shoes, evening sandals, hose (you will rarely wear them). Simple cotton dresses for the daytime, gay ones for cocktails. At least two summer evening dresses. Two or three bathing-suits (you'll live in them). Shorts are optional, but cotton slacks are useful for fishing trips and mountain-climbing. A scarf, a lightweight sweater or jacket, an evening wrap, a foldaway plastic raincoat and hat, and a pocket flashlight. Don't take too many dresses or scarves. Materials are inexpensive, and so are dressmakers in the islands.

BASIC LIST FOR MEN: Sneakers, walking-shoes, dancing-shoes, white or tan Bermuda shorts, calf-length socks, lightweight cotton (nylon is too hot), not-too-gay sport shirts, a lightweight dark suit, a white linen suit (it can double as a summer formal), lightweight slacks and jacket. White dinner jacket and black trousers with accessories, two pairs of bathing-trunks, plastic foldaway raincoat and hat, pocket flashlight, electric shaver with variable transformer for different types of current and a set of foreign plugs for different types of sockets. A safety razor and blades for emergencies.

Your Fun

Be careful of the car you rent. Exploring an island can be fun, but missing connections because of a flat tire or a slipping clutch is not. Rent only from reputable dealers. Check the tires and spare, and learn how to change them; foreign cars are tricky. Give the car a trial spin.

Travelers often miss the really interesting off-beat places. These are the churches where some of the best West Indian music can be enjoyed; the art exhibits where primitives rub frames with moderns to indicate the cultural development of the island; and the museums and botanical gardens.

Check on sailings of local motor launches that carry mail, supplies, and sometimes passengers from one coastal town to another. It is an inexpensive way to see places seldom visited by travelers. Another adventure is a fishing trip on a native schooner or an inexpensive but rough island-to-island trip.

It is inadvisable and occasionally dangerous to go looking for the kind of night life "the tourist does not see." It does not exist, and what passes for this type of entertainment affords views only of hungry prostitutes, dancers more shabby and amusing than lewd, and indifferent musicians. Generally, the best entertainment is found in the best-known places.

Your Manners

Don't throw opinions or money around recklessly. Most travelers to the Caribbean become experts on race relations a day or so after their arrival even though they have never been interested in the subject at home. Islanders also resent over-tipping and over-paying generally. Remember that it is their country and you are a guest: don't expect to be treated as a member of the family. Most islanders, while friendly and eager to be helpful, tend toward European rather than American social customs. You are welcome in the clubs and hotels, but few inlanders invite you to their homes. They are pleased when you try to speak their language: French in Haiti, Martinique, and Guadeloupe; Spanish in Cuba, the Dominican Republic, Puerto Rico, and Margarita.

Don't get angry with the Customs, Immigration, and Health officers. Remember that the United States Customs are among the most difficult in the world and that islanders have much more trouble entering your country than you do theirs. Have proper identification, health certificates, and tourist card (if required) ready. Be helpful, and don't attempt to show how important you are. If you are a V.I.P., everyone will know it. If not, nothing you say will convince them.

Your Photography

When selecting a camera for Caribbean travel, consider these points. It must be light in weight, take a number of pictures before reloading, be easy to load in daylight, and use a popular size of color or black-and-white film. It should also take interchangeable lenses to allow for telephoto close-ups distances away from the subject. 35 mm. cameras such as the Leica, Contax, Nikon, Canon, or Eastman 35 fill these requirements. It is not necessary to buy the most expensive model, but it is important to have a telephoto lens—preferably an 85 or 135 mm.—with you in addition to the standard lens that comes on the camera. This type of camera will yield color transparencies that may be projected or inexpensively printed in color. They may also be used for black-and-white, preferably with a fairly slow fine-grained film.

If you take a foreign camera or lens with you, register them with the United States Customs at your point of departure, obtaining a receipt enabling you to bring them back in without paying duty.

Accessories should include a gadget bag of fairly rigid and relatively waterproof construction, a skylight filter for color pictures in the shade or on dull days, lens shades, and a packet of lens tissues for cleaning salt spray, fog, or dust off the lenses. An exposure meter is useful in islands where the light conditions range from dazzling sunshine to deep shadow. Unless you have used a meter, give yourself some lessons, carefully following the instructions, and take a sample roll of film before leaving on your trip.

Most common faults of amateur photographers are traceable to lack of planning the pictures, and to excitement and tension while taking them. First, look at the scene and decide whether you will want to project or print it later. Then look through the view-finder to see if it fills the frame, or if you should move closer (use the telephoto lens) or farther back. Try to show how the island, its people, and its scenery look to *you.* Be personally selective. Even when you are photographing your friends, wife, husband, or children in colorful surroundings, it is best for them to be engaged in a typical situation rather than posed stiffly in the center of the scene.

Carry all the film you expect to use on the trip. While some may be available, it is likely to be out of date in the smaller islands. This means that heat or moisture may have affected it. Your film supply will keep well in the unopened packing. Beat the heat and moisture after exposing the rolls by putting them into a small coffee can one-third full of rice and sealing it with Scotch tape. Don't put film or camera in the trunk of your car or in the glove compartment. Both get too hot, and may cause color changes in the film.

Flash bulbs are usually available, but there are few places you will want to use them. Almost any picture can be taken by putting the camera on a table, chair, or window sill and making a time exposure.

Black-and-white pictures of islands are disappointing, as is the local processing of negatives. It is always best to bring undeveloped film back or take along one of the new Polaroid Land cameras (and a stock of the special film for it) and get your finished picture one minute after taking it. The Polaroid Land is highly recommended as a second camera.

Movie cameras should be checked mechanically before starting out—they cannot be repaired in the islands. Carry a stock of film—8 mm. is handier to carry than 16 mm. A lightweight tripod that telescopes into a small size is almost an essential for good movies. Again, plan the individual pictures carefully. See that the action and composition are interesting to eye and mind, and check exposures carefully.

Finally, remember that the islands are not a circus with sideshows for your benefit. Try to think how you would feel if everyone passing your home whipped out a camera and took pictures of you mowing the lawn, playing with your children, or doing your marketing. Ask permission before shooting, and respect the privacy of those citizens who don't want to be recorded on film.

Your Swimming (Snorkeling—Spear-fishing)

The water of the Caribbean is warm and clear, and offers ideal swimming, snorkeling, and spear-fishing. Take quick-drying nylon suits, a pair of swim fins, and (optionally) a face mask and snorkel for undersea observation. Be sure to use the full foot-heel-and-toe type of swim fins or wear sneakers in the water whenever there is danger of coral cuts or spiny sea urchins. Face masks and snorkels (tubes that allow you to breathe with your head in the water) should be carefully fitted, or they will leak.

Underwater photography is possible through the glass bottom of a sightseeing boat or with one of the waterproof camera cases made for this purpose. Remember that things look about one-third larger under water. If the sun is shining brightly through the water and is reflected by the coral, exposures are usually just slightly under the exposure above the surface. An amateur photographing underwater scenes should go down for a preliminary survey, estimate the distance of coral, person, or fish, come up to set camera, then submerge for the exposure. Surface again to wind and reset camera.

Possibly the finest spear-fishing in the world is to be found in the warm, lucid waters of the Caribbean. Expert spear-fishermen who will give lessons are available in almost every island. Some of them furnish equipment, but, to be on the safe side, take your own along.

Part One

BRITISH WEST INDIES

SAINT VINCENT: *Cricket game on the savanna before the cathedral, Kingstown.*

ANTIGUA: *The dazzling white sand beach of the Mill Reef Club.*

ANTIGUA

With the exception of Barbados, this is the most intensely English and most accessible of the British islands in the Lesser Antilles. It is forty-nine miles east of Nevis and forty miles north of Guadeloupe. It also has the most highly developed beaches and hostelries. Its surface is flat enough to be almost entirely planted in sugar cane and cotton. A few hills rise high enough (Boggy Peak to 1,319 feet) to break the monotony of the landscape, but not so high as to milk the clouds of their accumulated moisture.

The resulting lack of rainfall is a mixed blessing. Antigua looks and is dry, especially in winter. Yet the Tourist Board is able to advertise "sunshine every day" and deliver it. Enough water for household use is caught in the catchments, but not enough to propagate the many tropical plants and trees with which the more mountainous islands are endowed. Because of its very flatness, Antigua can boast more and better beaches than her rugged neighbors.

It has been said that Antigua is too British. It can also be said that Britishness is one of the island's greatest assets. The English heritage has caused two famous names to be emblazoned throughout the island: that of Lord Nelson, who lived and labored at English Harbour as the captain in charge, and that of the Duke of Clarence, later William IV, who built Clarence House on Shirley Heights overlooking English Harbour and Nelsons Dockyard.

For nearly one hundred years this area was the scene of a continuous sea struggle among Britain, Spain, Portugal, France, and Holland. Privateers and pirates preyed on shipping. Following the American Revolution, Great Britain continually attempted to restrict trade between her colonies and the United States. So English Harbour became an important British navy base with extensive facilities.

Even today it is visually stunning in its impact. The entire area is best seen from Shirley Heights, above the harbor. From there an almost perfectly circular harbor, completely hidden and protected from the open roadstead, can be seen. Much of Nelsons Dockyard is visible, too, though from this distance it looks like a toy naval base. The ruins of the barracks of the fort that protected this area are also on the heights. There are long lines of decaying walls, arches, and gun emplacements. The dockyard itself is a magnificent monument to Hood, Rodney, Nelson, and the British sailors of the eighteenth century. As His Majesty's ships were refitted here, there were a mast house, a cooper, a lumber store, and refitting shops. There were also the admiral's house and a boathouse that lost its superstructure in a hurricane decades ago. Indeed, the entire base was disintegrating until 1951, when the Society of the Friends of English Harbour was formed to preserve the buildings. If they keep up the effort, and if contributions continue to come in, they will maintain a noble relic of the early naval wars.

The approach to the dockyard is past a small village still called English Harbour. On the road is a vast water catchment used now by the villagers, but the names of the sailors and ships carved and written there are those of the eighteenth and nineteenth centuries. Going through the dockyard gates under an ancient bell is like walking back two hundred years. On every side are reminders of its golden days. Old cannon are sunk into the ground. Huge caldrons used for boiling pitch are scattered about. A large sundial is mounted near the center, and a giant anchor lies alongside a great stone block. The sensation is that of walking in historic footsteps.

Best preserved of all the buildings is the admiral's house, where Nelson lived with his bride, the widow Nisbet, who came from the near-by island of Nevis. The house is largely unrestored, but in excellent condition. Walking through it, one receives the impression that Nelson has just stepped out and will return shortly. A bust of him, patch over one eye, stands outside the entrance; it was once a ship's figurehead. Behind the house is the old kitchen, whose big ovens are still used occasionally during celebrations by the near-by villagers. The entire naval station is alive with memories.

But it is also alive as one of the great international gathering-places for world-traveling yachtsmen. It is common to see from four to six yachts of varying sizes flying the colors of England, South Africa,

Australia, or the United States tied up in the dockyard. Some are refitting, as did Nelson's ships. Many have husbands, wives, and even children painting, chipping, and polishing. Others are simply enjoying the sunny, beautiful anchorage and the good company of fellow yachtsmen. A number of these seafaring wanderers use English Harbour as an address and pick up their accumulated mail every few months. The dockyard is also home base for the fleet of charter yachts operated by Commander V. E. B. Nicholson, formerly of the Royal Navy, and his two seafaring sons. Their vessels may be chartered for seven-, fourteen-, or twenty-eight-day cruises up and down the small islands.

This is an ideal way to see the islands, and for a group of four or five sharing the expenses it costs only about $150 per person per week. This includes food, drink, spacious quarters with hot and cold baths, plenty of ice, interesting ports of call, and a captain and crew at your personal disposal. Arrangements can be made to have the chartered trip start at almost any of the islands of the Lesser Antilles, allowing the charterer to be picked up at any spot to which he would like to fly.

The best sailing in these islands is not, as might be supposed, in the popular winter months. Actually the weather is ideal in May, June, July, November, and December, when the trade winds are light but constant and the yachts carry light-weather canvas. During these months the seas are as smooth as glass. The weather is cooler—and sailing can be very pleasant—from January to April, but the seas are somewhat rougher in the passages among the islands.

On these cruises it is not even necessary to be completely out of touch with the outside world, though that too can be arranged. A radio-telephone service is maintained from English Harbour, and messages can be relayed to and from the Nicholson yachts. A very popular feature of these cruises is the opportunity of the charterer, his family, or his friends to study navigation with experts. Another is the use of the motor boat and dinghy for shore picnics and exploratory journeys up the island rivers.

After leaving English Harbour, a trip to Clarence House, built by Prince William Henry, is indicated. The house is in perfect condition, and is used by the present governor of the Leeward Islands as his country home. There is a fine view of the dockyard and it is a particularly good place from which to photograph the area.

In direct contrast to the memorials to Nelson and King William are a series of modern enterprises developed by two twentieth-century gentlemen who have teamed up to give the island a new look. They are

"Happy" Ward, a distinguished architect with a flair for spear-fishing, and Clare Johnson, his contractor-partner. Both are busy United States types who build fine homes and tourist facilities on the tropical dream-sites so abundant along the Antigua shoreline. Their work has been called Antigua Modern. The big difference between the Ward-Johnson type of building and earlier Antigua structures lies in the combination of seclusion with utility, accessibility to beach, breeze, and view.

These two men were responsible for outfitting the Mill Reef Club, located on an ideal stretch of beach at the southeast corner of the island. The Club evolved when they first built homes for several wealthy Americans who combined to purchase the land, form a club, and build a sumptuous clubhouse to take care of friends and relatives of members. While not actually a millionaires' club, it is made up of wealthy and prominent men and women who like to combine warm winters with a high degree of seclusion. The clubhouse is operated on a commercial basis and charges (for the Caribbean) higher than average rates. Only visitors properly introduced by a member are admitted. The generally excellent food is served in dining-room or beach house. Tipping is prohibited, but a percentage is added to the bill. Inside the door of each room is a small placard that reads in part: "Dress: Gentlemen are requested to wear jackets at dinner, and shirts in the bar and beach house. We suggest ladies do not wear slacks or shorts in St. John. Snakes, etc.: There are no snakes or dangerous insects in Antigua. The lizards are entirely harmless and are great insect destroyers."

For those travelers who lack a key to the Mill Reef Club there is the new White Sands Hotel on Hodges Bay. This colorful cluster of tropic-pink plaster buildings, also constructed by Ward and Johnson, is laid out in four groups of four cottages each. The dining-room and patio bar are in the home of the owners, the Stanley J. Hawleys. For the towering, drafty, old-fashioned Antigua Beach Hotel, Ward and Johnson have erected a string of beach cottages that are a great improvement over the hotel's distinctly dated bedrooms.

Probably the most notable gathering-place for natives and visitors at cocktail time is the Pelican Club, presided over by bartender Dublin. From a reclining chair in the sunny patio it is very pleasant to look through a Scotch Mist and see the native sailboats working the reef for fish—sturdy Antigua boys with face-plate and spear out for a marketable lobster or any hapless fish that ventures in over the reef.

Less than half a mile out from this point stands Prickly Pear Island. It is an alluring spot half covered with prickly pears, and has many coral caves into which the sea thunders. On the far side an angler can cast to the deep water outside the reef and be prepared for a strike. On the near side the coral slopes gently into the sea in a reef that continues close to the surface for nearly a mile. This particular reef is recommended for the neophyte skin-diver: he can proceed along it for at least a city block without going beyond his depth, all the while observing the face of the coral wall, in and out of which dart the gay-colored fish of the West Indies.

Antigua has one city, St. John's, a rather dingy place of long streets and low, white, seemingly empty buildings. There are few people on its streets at any time of day, and the sun beats down mercilessly against the gleaming white structures. The liveliest spot is either the market located near the docks or the bus station where long lines of Antiguans wait to travel to their homes all over the island. For lunch in town try the Kensington Guest House, a dark, cool oasis where good drinks and excellent food are served. It also offers accommodations for visitors. Another interesting spot in Antigua is the Lord Nelson Club, not far from the Antigua Beach Hotel. It is on the sea looking eastward to Long Island, where bonefish, the prize of sophisticated anglers, clutter the sand-bottomed waters. The Lord Nelson, presided over by Nick Fuller of Toledo, Ohio, has a distinguishing attraction: a brace of slot machines definitely known to have paid off a few well-spaced nickels here and there over the years. The place jumps on Wednesday and Saturday nights during the season, when the steel band bends to its task. The steel-band musicians in Antigua have become so proficient that they are sure they are better than the Trinidadians who invented the bands. They are wrong.

There is, however, on the island one group of entertainers without a peer in the Caribbean. These are Negro maskers who dress as clowns and dance on the beach for visitors. Their dances, different from any others in the islands, seem to be derived from those of some unusual African group. An amazing whip dance is performed by two men, one of whom chases and lashes at the other, who dances skillfully out of range of the rawhide.

From a tourist standpoint, Antigua is in a critical stage of development. It is not recommended to those who insist on the very last word in service and entertainment. But it is ready for development, and it does have facilities for a considerable number of visitors. Some things are lacking. The British are reticent and do not make friends easily: social life is limited. It takes a while to find the right places to fish and to locate a guide, but a little inquiry uncovers the good places such as (at sunup or sundown) The Narrows east of the delightful village of Parham, opposite the island of Guana. It is claimed that a seven-foot barracuda holds sway over the waters there. Willoughby Bay might be best some afternoons, or Falmouth, if the Bay is too rough. In spring and summer the local fishermen go out to deep water, weight the line for big ones, and hope the sharks and barracudas will have left more than a fish-head when they reel in. After a good day's fishing, it is a fine feeling to cut through the phosphorescent water while it sparkles all around you in the early dark, as you hurry to get to the dock in time to dress the fish before nightfall. The fishing around Antigua can be very, very good.

ANTIGUA: *Women carry grasses for use in weaving baskets, mats, and handbags.*

ANTIGUA: *Two of the island's clowns, famous beach entertainers, perform the whip dance.*

ANTIGUA: *Nelsons Dockyard at English Harbour.*

BARBADOS

By far the most influential of the islands in the Lesser Antilles is the British Crown Colony of Barbados. Not large, its hilly terrain stretches only nineteen miles north and south, eleven miles east and west; it has through the force of the personality of its settlers become the cultural and resort center of the southeastern Caribbean.

Imagine a sugar-cane green, estate-house white island shaped like a teardrop. The apex points north, its broad base east and west. The south and west coasts offer fine sea bathing, distinctive resort hotels, and good shopping facilities. The eastern (windward) coast is constantly pounded by surf, and magnificent panoramas abound from the Chalky Mount district through Bathsheba down to Ragged Point lighthouse.

Easternmost of the Caribbean islands, Barbados lies 95 miles due east of St. Vincent, 200 miles northeast of Trinidad, and 600 miles southeast of San Juan, Puerto Rico. Plane service from the States, through Bermuda and San Juan, is regular and rapid. From the south, planes fly from Trinidad on daily schedules.

Each island in the Caribbean reflects a personality, and Barbados has a unique aura. For generations the plantation system has dominated the social and economic life, and because it has been a British possession ever since it was colonized in 1627 it is by far the most "English" island of them all. Indeed, some Britishers have expressed the opinion that Barbados is even more British than England. The Barbadian leaving on a holiday for Great Britain invariably speaks of going home.

Barbados was first occupied by Arawak Indians who left evidence of their occupation in the form of weapons and tools made of shells. But before the first Englishmen arrived, a Portuguese seaman, Pedro a Campos, stopped there long enough in 1536 to leave some hogs to breed so that he might put in again when in need of fresh meat. It is also believed that he named the island Bernardo, for it is so noted on maps of the sixteenth century. The Arawaks had left before his arrival, driven away by the migratory Caribs or enslaved and exported by transient Spaniards to work in the mines of Hispaniola. When British captain John Powell landed from his ship, *The Olive Blossom,* in 1625, he found the island deserted. Setting up a cross, he also inscribed on a near-by tree: "JAMES K. of E. and this island." On this spot in 1627 the first British settlers cleared the brush away, erected wooden houses, and hunted out the wild hogs left by the Portuguese.

The name of the first settlement has been changed from Jamestown to Holetown. The location is midway between Harrison Point and Carlisle Bay on the west coast of the island. The first visitors must have been greatly impressed by the dazzling beaches sloping gently into the translucent blue-green waters. For the spot of the first community is one of the finest resort areas in the islands. Today north and south of Holetown are modern hostelries such as the Coral Reef, Colony Club, Paradise Beach Club, and Four Winds. Back from the beach the land rises in gentle hills culminating in Mount Hillaby, 1,104 feet above sea level, the highest point on the island.

From a plane flying into Barbados across Carlisle Bay and the rolling hills to Seawell Airport, the terrain looks much like that of the green hills of Devon in England, and Barbadians are proud of this similarity. Checkerboard patterns indicate extensive sugar estates, with mills and an estate house in each large square. At Seawell Airport the whitecaps of the turbulent surf are visible from one side of the plane, the undulating hills of sugar cane from the other.

More exciting than entering the island by plane is arriving by ship. Carlisle Bay is a neat semicircle of pastel houses leading into an inner harbor and careenage, where lighters from the big cruise ships, freight ships, and inter-island schooners take on and discharge passengers and cargo.

The careenage docks are an ever-changing, always interesting sight. Sailing vessels from St. Vincent, St. Lucia, Martinique, and Dominica tie up almost in the center of the city of Bridgetown. Small yawls and yachts skim in and out of this convenient inner harbor. Higglers (peddlers) weave through the cargoes and dockside workers, selling laces, fruits, notions, and bread. A very special drink called Mauby is sold by elderly women who wend their way along the dock, carefully balancing small kegs on their heads. The unique liquid is dispensed by holding a cup at waist level and catching the liquid as it pours from the spigot on the keg. The same cup is used over and over again. Mauby is an ancient Barbadian concoction made of a boiled bark flavored with unrefined sugar. A coffee-colored liquid with a clean, astringent taste, it is quite refreshing. The dock workers say it has medicinal properties.

The tall masts swaying in the careenage, the vivid colors of the lighters, and the pungent smells of the cargoes create a picture of island life as it must have been when Nelson's ships visited here. To heighten the effect, even today the harbor police dress as Nelson's sailors did. They wear bell-bottomed trousers, white pull-over shirts with triangular neckerchiefs, and flat straw boaters with black bands.

Most of Barbados is highly picturesque, and the costumes of the higglers—the biscuit man with his red cap and a bugle to attract attention, the market women balancing objects ranging from an entire notions counter to one orange on their heads—make excellent pictures. Be careful, though—make arrangements for photographs in advance or do it without the subjects' knowledge. These people do not like to be photographed except for profit. Everyone enjoys photographing the Barbados policemen in their spotless white jackets and hats and blue trousers that have a brilliant red stripe down the side. They stand on their platforms under a green or black umbrella directing the continuous stream of automobiles, burro carts, pushcarts, and trucks in the center of the narrow thoroughfare, and offer unlimited picture possibilities. All the policemen of the island are well trained, polite, and eager to be of help to travelers. The regimental bandsman, too, with his baggy blue pants and bolero jacket of cerise and gold, is a highly photogenic sight.

The city of Bridgetown begins at the careenage and extends back toward the east, south, and west along the coast. A landmark for travelers is Nelson's statue in Trafalgar Square, just off the careenage. Barbadians—or Bajans, as they like to call themselves—are inordinately proud of the fact that they erected the statue to Admiral Nelson in 1813, twenty-seven years before one was erected in London's Trafalgar Square. Because Barbados was at that time, and still is, largely dependent on its sugar markets, the Bajans were particularly pleased that Nelson's victory had broken Napoleon's blockade, which had been so effective against island exports to European countries.

Starting at the statue, it is a short, pleasant walk across Broad

Street, the shopping center of the entire island. During the winter season the street teems with taxis, their drivers standing beside them waiting for a fare. No one is expected to walk anywhere, but the shopping district extends for only a few blocks and can best be visited on foot. In the Women's Self-Help Association will be found carved wooden replicas of different types of workers on the island: the Mauby-seller, her keg on her head and arm extended with cup to receive the liquid; the harbor police in their Nelson costume; various lace- and produce-sellers carefully done, complete to the baskets on their heads.

But souvenirs are not the only items that may be bought. Cameras, films, Wedgwood china, tobacco, perfume, Royal Doulton figurines, long-playing classical or jazz records, phonographs, British shoes, cashmere sweaters, gloves, and Irish linens are available at prices that may be slightly higher than at some other islands. The selection, however, is much wider. It is also possible to arrange to have summer suits tailored in the British tradition at lower than stateside or British prices.

While English imports constitute excellent buys and a most complete stock can be found on the island, the import houses get a great deal of competition from native craftsmen. Small shops offer Bajan-designed and executed skirts and blouses, and men's shirts that are distinctive and reasonably priced. Expert craftsmen produce a great many costume jewelry pieces from tortoise shell, metal, and pottery. As in many of the islands, there is a wide range of basketry, ranging from the small cane lily baskets used as women's pocketbooks to larger functional baskets. Broad Street also offers four banks, airlines offices, and three restaurants, and the American Consulate is near by.

No island in the Lesser Antilles has a more creative literary group than Barbados. Two magazines are published. *The Bajan*, a monthly, prints well-researched and interesting articles about Barbados and surrounding islands, as well as poems and short stories. *Bim*, published twice a year, is an *avante-garde* literary magazine of extraordinary merit. It publishes essays, short stories, and poetry, and occasionally reproduces original drawings and photographs. Barbadians on every level are constantly developing a more picturesque language, which *Bim* reports. Besides its active literary group, the island also has active amateur theater groups producing classical and modern plays.

It is a great pleasure to find a museum as well organized as the one on this island. Its art galleries are spacious, and exhibitions of contemporary art from Barbados and the surrounding islands reveal much about the culture of the British West Indies. In addition to art exhibitions there is a unique display of the large and small fish of the Caribbean encased in glass with backgrounds so natural that the fish appear to be swimming under the sea. The museum also sells a series of pamphlets and well-written booklets covering the early history of Barbados, folk tales of the island, and—of special interest to the United States visitors—a pamphlet describing the visit to Barbados of George Washington in 1751.

Washington was then only nineteen years of age, but had been working as a surveyor for over three years. He went to Barbados, the only foreign country he ever visited, to accompany his half-brother, Lawrence, who had developed tuberculosis in Virginia. Barbados was selected for its mild climate and because of its close ties with the mainland colonies—ships sailed regularly from the Potomac River, and the Washingtons had friends and relatives on the island. Shortly after they arrived, George contracted smallpox—then prevalent on the island, now completely wiped out. Some historians have suggested that this might have been lucky, for the mild case he got immunized him from the virulent attacks that later struck the Colonial army during the Revolutionary War. A house on Upper Bay Street in Barbados is called Washington's house, but the island's historians have found no evidence to support its claim to be the residence he occupied. That he enjoyed his visit is evident from his journals: ". . . and were perfectly enraptured with the beautiful prospects which on every side presented to our view—the fields of cane, corn, fruit trees, etc. in a delightful green." George returned to the United States after about two months, leaving Lawrence to undergo further treatment.

At the time Washington visited Barbados, sugar had become the important crop of the island and almost every available foot of soil was used for its cultivation. There was a brisk trade between the mainland colonies and Barbados in sugar, rum, and slaves. This trade had existed for almost a hundred years in some form, and it is interesting to read in Richard Ligon's *A True and Exact History of The Island of Barbadoes 1647–1650:* "When they [slaves] are brought to us, the Planters buy them out of the Ship, where they find them stark naked, and therefore cannot be deceived in any outward infirmity. They choose them as they do Horses in a Market; the strongest, youthfullest, and most beautifull, yield the greatest prices. Thirty pound sterling is a price for the best man Negre; and twenty five, twenty six, or twenty seven pound for a Woman; the children are at easier rates. And we buy them so, as the sexes may be equall; for if they have more men than women, the men who are unmarried will come to their Masters, and complain, that they cannot live without Wives, and desire him they may have Wives. And he tells them, that the next ship that comes, he will buy them Wives, which satisfies them for the present; and so they expect the good time: which the Master performing with them, the bravest fellow is to choose first, and so in order, as they are in place; and every one of them knowes his better, and gives him the precedence."

Rum was exported to England from the colonies, and the Bajans soon developed the great reputation they still enjoy for the production of fine light rums. One of the early West Indian drinks, the Sangaree, was noted in 1694 by Father Labat, a traveling French priest. He said: "It is one of the two or three drinks invented by the English whose use and abuse was attributed to the French." In the early days the Sangaree, which preceded rum as a favorite drink, was made of Madeira wine with sugar, lime juice, powdered clove, nutmeg, and a piece of burned toast. After the liquid had absorbed the flavor of the ingredients, it was strained and served. The recipe throughout the next two hundred and fifty years varied, and at the Bridgetown Club in Barbados today is as follows: a half-pint tumbler of cracked ice, one wineglass of Madeira, one-half teaspoon simple syrup, one-half teaspoon curaçao or benedictine. Fill glass with soda, add slice of lime, stir until cold, and sprinkle grated nutmeg on top.

From the earliest days of sugar-grinding, rum was an important by-product. Ligon writes in 1647: "And as this drink is of great use, to cure and refresh the poor Negres, whom we ought to have a speciall care of, by the labour of whose hands, our profit is brought in; so is it helpfull to our Christian Servants too; for, when their spirits are exhausted, by their hard labour, and sweating in the Sun, ten hours every day, they find their stomacks debilitated, and much weakened in their vigour every way, a dram or two of this Spirit, is a great comfort and refreshing to them. This drink is also a commodity of good value in the Plantation; for we send it down to the *Bridge*, and there put it off to those that retail it. Some they sell to the Ships, and is transported into foreign parts, and drunk by the way. Some they sell to such Planters, as have no Sugar works of their owne, yet drink excessively of it. . . ." Barbados rum punch is made with lime juice, sugar, and ice. Nutmeg on top is optional. Today rum is the tourist and the native drink—most white Barbadians prefer Scotch.

An interesting etching made in 1803 caricatures the West Indian planter of that period. He is pictured seated in a comfortable chair, his feet propped on a stool, with a slave holding a large umbrella over his head. On the floor near him are a series of five-gallon kegs marked Royal Punch, Sangaree, and Rum. A small Negro boy is approaching him with a gigantic glass of liquor. Under a coconut palm another slave is brushing flies away from a picnic lunch consisting of roast pig, fish, and fowl. In the distance a third slave is driving a flock of birds toward the planter, who has his gun in his left hand. The caption reads: "Make haste with the Sangaree, Quashee, and tell Quacko to drive the birds up to me. I am ready."

Bridgetown is a good place to start a quick tour around Barbados. The Tourist Board and most shops sell excellent pictorial maps as well as auto and bicycle maps. They are easy to follow and indicate the best routes to the most interesting places on the island. Taxis or bicycles offer the best means of exploring Barbados. Taxi prices, controlled by the government, are quite reasonable. It is customary to use the same driver during your entire stay on the island, and by some magic or inner vision your driver invariably shows up at the time he is needed. The disadvantage of this system is that the driver spends many hours waiting while the visitor explores, but the advantage is that there is only one man to tip. As one becomes acquainted with the driver, it is possible to learn a good deal from him about the island.

Roads in Barbados are mostly paved and good, though narrow in many places. Unless the visitor is familiar with driving on the left on narrow roads, it is safer to employ a chauffeur. Cars without drivers are available, and drivers' licenses are easy to acquire.

If a one-day stop on Barbados is planned, a trip to the east coast, which includes a drive along Highway 7 to Christ Church six miles from Bridgetown then across to Highway 6 and Sam Lord's Castle, is indicated. This is one of the great estate houses in the West Indies, and was built by Sam Lord in 1830. The white stone building is truly a castle, with beautifully planned gardens; the entire grounds are guarded by a wall. Built upon a terrace overlooking the Atlantic, it stands above a long beach fringed with coconut palms. Furnishings date back to the 1800–30 period and are matchless antiques. The ornate plaster work of the ceilings in the reception rooms was executed by an Italian artist especially imported for this work.

Tales of Sam Lord's exploits make fascinating reading. It is said that he cruelly ill-treated his wife and sometimes locked her in the dungeon of the castle. There are many tales of his having wrecked ships on the reefs along the bay near the castle by fixing lighted lanterns in the coconut trees. At night the swaying of the lights in the wind looked to ships' captains like vessels lying at anchor in a harbor. Lord and his well-trained slaves were ready to take over any ship wrecked against the reefs, salvaging its cargo and sometimes murdering any of the crew who escaped drowning.

The castle Sam Lord built has become a distinguished inn. There are twelve exquisite bedrooms in the main house. The master bedroom, that of murderous old Sam Lord himself, has his own mahogany fourposter bed and richly carved wardrobe. It is possible to have an excellent luncheon during your visit, but reservations should be made the day before. Like many Barbados hostelries, Sam Lord's is operated as a club so that the management may select its clientele.

Like all the West Indies, Barbados has a distinct caste and color problem. Because the island's economy was based on slave labor for so many generations, there is little social and economic mixing between blacks and whites. To the short-term visitor it seems to be an island of two distinct color groups. Yet this is not true. Many white Barbadians hold liberal political and social views and work toward a more democratic society. The mulatto population of Barbados has increased continually during the past two hundred years, and many distinguished families socially acceptable everywhere belong to this group. Negroes are prominent in politics, the professions, and athletics. Yet, just as in most of the world, the farm laborers do not mix socially with the leading professional men, nor the Bridgetown merchants with the fishermen from the villages. This is not to say that Barbados is not highly color-conscious—it is. But it is less so than the southern states of the United States or even some parts of England.

An important contributing factor to the caste system in Barbados is the wide economic differences among agricultural workers, domestic servants, fishermen, peddlers, government employees, merchants, and professional men. With no factories and no large industrial class, it is difficult for the agricultural or domestic worker to advance toward increased earnings and a better social and economic position.

The traveler arriving in Barbados will find introductions to residents of the island useful. Family and connections make a real difference in the social life of the island. Like Virginians, Barbadians have a great deal of respect for good manners and established social customs. But most travelers won't want to be bothered with the social life of the islanders. Barbados is an ideal place to rest, swim, golf, sightsee, and fish. Time slips by very quickly, and it is easy to ignore everything except the sand, the sun, and the sea.

One kind of fishing that is distinctly Barbadian should be tried. The clear waters around the island abound in the flying fish. A day's outing in a small power launch will yield great sport as well as a good catch of these swift, glittering fish with wings. Power launches ranging from twenty-one to twenty-seven feet are safe and inexpensive to rent. It is not advisable to go in the small sailboats used by the native fishermen: they are uncomfortable and have a tendency to bounce one about too much, offer no toilet facilities, and are precariously balanced. Arrangements should be made to include bait and tackle when the launch is rented. Even non-fishermen will find the flying-fish cruise exciting. Sometimes a hundred or more fish at one time leap and play around the boat.

One of the island's great sights is watching the commercial flying-fish fleet return with its catch in the early afternoon. The gray-white sails appear as tiny flecks of light upon the cerulean sea, hardly distinguishable from the whitecaps. The triangular sails take shape, the hulls like cigar-shaped corks bob in the breeze. The little craft stay close together, and the pattern in the distance is like a flock of geese skimming the horizon. When they near shore, especially if there is a great demand for fish, one of the fishermen will tie a sackful around his neck and slip over the side of the boat. It will take him five to fifteen minutes to swim ashore with his catch, but he will arrive before any of the others can reach land. The best place to see the fleet come in is Tent Bay, near Bathsheba on the east coast.

The flying fish is a delicacy comparable to the moro crabs of Cuba, the turtles of the Cayman Islands, and the langouste of St. Lucia. Just to eat them is worth a trip to Barbados. They are served boiled, fried, and baked, and are delicious stuffed. The flesh is moist and flaky and has a nut-sweet, delicate taste.

Sport fishing is deservedly popular too. The waters abound in kingfish averaging from thirty-five to sixty pounds (the record catch is 104 pounds). Green dolphin, bonito, and wahoo are also plentiful. Because sport fishing is relatively new, proper tackle is not always available and it is a good plan to bring favorite rods and reels and line along. Be sure to have dark glasses, plenty of suntan oil, a wide-brimmed hat, a long-sleeved shirt, and long trousers. The sun can be dangerous.

There is much spear-fishing in the calm waters off the west coast. Native fishermen with home-made equipment take their living out of the sea by spearing chub, mackerel, and giant crayfish. Visitors and young Barbadians are flocking to this reef-protected leeward coast with snorkel masks and modern spear guns. Also located in this area near the Coral Reef Club is the newly constructed Bellairs Research Institute of McGill University of Montreal. The Institute plans a detailed analysis of the animals and plants in the waters around the island. They selected Barbados for their studies because of the widespread coral reefs around the island. They are bringing to the area advanced techniques for underwater exploration which should stimulate the use of aqualungs and other undersea equipment by both sportsmen and students.

The visitor with enough time to spend will enjoy the Barbados race course, the Rockley Golf Club (nine holes), the numerous lawn-tennis courts, polo games, and the wealth of good cricket matches.

Every British island plays cricket, but on Barbados the game is almost a religion. During the annual test matches every radio is tuned in, and over half the population goes out to the games. No conversation seems to exist except about cricket. Most business comes to a dead stop.

Highway 1 from Bridgetown to Speightstown leads into the parish of St. Peter, where at least two early eighteenth-century estate houses may be seen. Farley Hill, the oldest in the area, is fast falling into disrepair, and the tall traveler's-tree palms are growing close to its arched and shuttered windows. Near-by Alleynedale Hall is another of the great plantation houses. In addition to being an architectural triumph, it has the distinction of a ghost that haunts its second floor, opening and closing doors mysteriously. This is said to be the ghost of William Tyrell, who committed suicide many years ago and is buried in the cellar. A few miles east is Nicholas Abbey, a sprawling white plantation house trimmed in red.

After seeing the early estates, it is easy to visualize the pattern of life which existed during the eighteenth century. In this same district, called Scotland, live the few blond, blue-eyed descendants of the early indentured white servants. Although they are called "red legs"—a term originated in England to describe bare-legged Scotsmen—only a portion of these people's ancestors came from Scotland. Many came from English prisons, others were Cromwell's prisoners, and still others were deported and sold into bondage after Monmouth's unsuccessful rebellion against James II. Almost from the beginning of colonization in Barbados, prisoners were shipped to the island to work on plantations. The flow was greatly accelerated when sugar production began about 1640. Ligon in his history of Barbados writes: "Labour for the settlement of the British West Indies had come in the first years from Britain. Thousands of poor men and women were ready to bind themselves as servants for five or seven years in exchange for free passage to the West Indies, and a portion of land or a small sum of money at the end of the period of bondage, while the master undertook to maintain them during the years that they were indentured to him."

Although some Bajan families send their children to school in England, the island offers a well-integrated primary-school system that has a higher percentage of attendance than any of the other British West Indies school systems. It also boasts Codrington College, a theological school affiliated with Durham University.

Driving through the hills from Codrington College back toward Bridgetown, one sees a surprising statue of a giant lion rampant against a green hillside. This famous lion of Gun Hill was carved out of the limestone by Colonel Henry John Wilkinson in the nineteenth century. Although not an outstanding work of art, it is a unique landmark.

The oldest folk song of the island tells something of its early romantic history. It concerns a British sailor named Inckle who had a romance with an Indian maiden named Yarico. Inckle, while exploring a near-by island, became separated from his companions and was rescued by Yarico, who hid him from the hostile Indians and fed him until rescuers came to take the two to Barbados. There the young man soon forgot her kindness and sold her as a slave. One version says that Yarico consoled herself with a lover, became pregnant, and "walked down to a wood and there by the side of a pond, brought herself abed of a lusty boy, frolicsome and lively." Yarico's Pond may be found on Barbados.

Although Bajans like to sing, there is little music on the island after dark. An occasional Calypso or steel-band group, its music borrowed from Trinidad, performs in the night clubs. But, unlike most British islands, Barbados has at least three pleasant places to dine and dance after dark. In keeping with the personality of the island, they offer good food—especially steaks, dolphin, and flying fish—mediocre stateside or English dance music, and a pleasing, respectable West Indian atmosphere.

BARBADOS: *This rock-strewn cove has white sand and calm, clear water.*

BARBADOS: *Sugar is still king: an overseer supervises the loading of a cane trailer.*

BARBADOS: *On Broad Street, one of Bridgetown's busiest intersections.*

BARBADOS: *The careenage. Harbor policemen are still garbed as in the days of Admiral Nelson.*

BRITISH VIRGIN ISLANDS

These almost unknown islands are excellent inexpensive resort spots located only a few miles east and north of the American Virgin Islands and sixty miles east of Puerto Rico. Even more numerous than the United States Virgins, the thirty-six British Virgin Islands are all small. The largest, Tortola (Turtle Dove), is almost the size of St. Thomas. Among the smallest is Dead Man's Chest (off Peter Island), the rocky cay where buccaneer Edward Teach ("Blackbeard") playfully marooned fifteen insubordinate pirates just to prove that, no matter how tough you are, you cannot survive without food or water.

Tortola (population 7,000), the seat of the government, is a rough, sharply sloped island with hillocks that rise up to 1,780 feet. Very little of the island is flat, and it is covered with dense brush except for the high forested sections, small farm livestock pastures, and sugar-cane patches. Few except yachtsmen and treasure-hunters visit Tortola, but charter boats and motor launches from St. Thomas anchor off the village of Road Town every day. This town is the capital of the British Virgin Islands.

Tortola has one thing in common with St. John—there are almost no motor roads. But two venerable taxis have somehow been imported. There are about sixty miles of mule tracks, but only some five miles of automobile road. Exploring by mule or horseback comes under the heading of high adventure, and very few travelers have tried it.

It is possible to spend a week or two at one of the two guesthouses at Road Town, and not only to explore the trails and ruins, but to go out to the almost perfect beaches a mile or so from town. None of these beaches has been developed, and they have no places to dress and no available fresh water. Living in Road Town is extremely inexpensive, and it is possible to arrange transportation to the beaches.

It is surprising that on this British possession the currency in use is that of the United States. This is because of the continuous migration of the residents of Tortola to St. Thomas in search of work. Many of the able-bodied men succeed in getting jobs on the docks, leaving the older men and women to work the farms back on Tortola. Because there is little official marriage on this island or St. Thomas, many men have families on both sides, which complicates the citizenship set-up considerably. Residents of Tortola are eager to go to St. Thomas because there is more work opportunity and because St. Thomas pays three to four times as much for domestic servants and dock workers.

Tortola itself has very little money of any kind, and because there are so few taxes to collect, about one half of the total income of the island comes from stamp sales to philatelists all over the world. There are opportunities in Tortola now for stock-raising. There is enough pasture land, but so far not enough good breeding-stock. It would also be possible to make money in truck farming, for St. Thomas would be a ready market. At present, coconuts, fish, and about three thousand head of cattle a year are exported.

The island was settled in 1740, and at one time had a goodly number of small, profitable sugar estates. But when sugar prices went down, the planters went down with them. Most of them migrated back to Europe, leaving the plots of land to their slaves. This accounts for the fact that almost all the land is owned by Negroes who work it. Much of it is divided into small plots; no estates survive as such.

Although there is not much shopping to be done in Road Town, there is one small shop with a big name. It calls itself the London Shop and, among other things, has for sale magnificent straw hats that can be purchased for a dollar and are excellent for shading the face and shoulders on schooner trips from island to island. But Road Town is a drab, uninteresting little place where the electricity goes on for just six hours every evening. There is no telephone, cable, or wireless, no newspaper, and not even a club—which in a British island is incredible.

In spite of the fact that Tortola is primitive, it has a doctor, a hospital, and a small laboratory. Malaria is rare, but water and milk must be boiled and regular typhoid inoculations are recommended. The *British Information Service Bulletin*, under "Educational Facilities," writes: "There are no schools suitable for English children."

The other islands of the British Virgins have been explored mostly by yachtsmen or holiday sailors out of St. Thomas or St. Croix. They are delightful to sail in, for it is possible to explore them for days on end without ever going out into the open sea. The fishing is good, and the same fish found in the United States Virgin Islands abound here. Favorite stops through the islands are Virgin Gorda, a square mountain of an island full of huge boulders with rocks tumbled all about and deep pools and caves around one side. There are also ruins of ancient baths cut out of granite blocks. It is an excellent place for spear-fishing and snorkeling. The water is deep and clear, and some of the treasure caves can be explored with a guide. Another favorite spot is called Fallen Jerusalem. Here the rock formations are like the ruins of a great city. A similar formation in Arizona is called the Holy City, and it also somewhat resembles the white cliffs of the Missouri River in Montana. Norman Island, another stop, makes the claim that Robert Louis Stevenson used it as the locale for *Treasure Island*. This could certainly be true, but the claim is also made by a number of other islands. Jost Van Dyke is a comparatively large island where a Quaker colony flourished in the eighteenth century. A square replica of it, called Little Jost Van Dyke, is located just behind it.

Not the smallest, but the most interesting viewed from the air, is Sombrero, shaped precisely like a Spanish hat with a forty-foot crown and a broad brim. Located in Anegada Passage, it is twenty miles north of Dog Island (the early sailors said it barked), thirty miles northeast of Anguilla (Snake Island), and about sixty miles west of Anegada, most northerly of the British Virgins. Anegada, the most isolated of the group, is surrounded by submerged reefs; a heavy mist shrouds the coastline.

One of these British Virgin Islands is owned by a group of American sportsmen. Called 'Guana, it has lovely green hills and excellent white sand beaches. It is an exclusive private club whose members are devoted to hunting, swimming, big-game fishing, and comfortable roughing-it. There is a large main clubhouse with sleeping quarters for twenty members and guests. Each house or apartment of the twenty houses has been decorated and furnished by a specific member of the club, and is reserved for him. As all the members are rarely on the island at one time, paying non-members are permitted to reserve the unoccupied space. Applications, made well in advance, for accommodations should be addressed to the 'Guana Club, Charlotte Amalie, St. Thomas, United States Virgin Islands. There is a good dining-room, with most of the food either grown locally or coming directly out of the sea. The club runs a motor cruiser between St. Thomas and the island and can pick up members or friends if given enough notice.

Yachtsmen know these islands well as excellent places to sail. Trade winds blow over them, and the weather is almost always ideal.

CAYMAN ISLANDS

The latest bid for resort status comes from a flat scrub of an island with some of the finest beach frontage in the Caribbean. Although there are three Cayman islands—Grand Cayman, Little Cayman, and Cayman Brac—and all are under British rule, only Grand Cayman has developed resort facilities for visitors.

This strange island has more white natives of European descent than Negroes, no income or real-estate taxes, more churchgoers and a higher per-capita liquor-consumption than most other islands, and at least one-third more women than men.

Grand Cayman is located two hundred miles south of Cuba and one hundred and eighty miles northwest of Jamaica. From November to May its weather could not be better. Days are warm, the humidity is low, and there is a constant breeze. In midsummer (May to October) the sun bears down, but even then the heat is not unbearable and can be compared with that during the same months in the midwestern states, except that Grand Cayman boasts the trade winds. The summer months bring a major problem, though—mosquitoes, which sometimes arrive in swarms. The government has a control program and sprays swamps continually in the hope that someday the pests will be entirely eradicated.

A thatched open-sided waiting-room, cooled by the breezes, stands next to the airport. It is usually crowded with some of the six thousand islanders watching the planes land and take off. Next to this primitive waiting-room is the Customs and Air Control Building. Two airlines serve Grand Cayman: B.W.I.A. (British West Indian Airways), which flies from Miami to Jamaica and Cayman, and

LACSA (Lineas Aéreas Costarricenses, S.A.), which flies from Panama to Costa Rica, Grand Cayman, and Miami.

From the air, Grand Cayman's fine beaches are strips of gleaming white separating the pale-blue sea from the deep-green scrub, trees, and undergrowth. The outline of its flat terrain is shaped like a buttonhook twenty-two miles long by eight miles wide at the widest point, with the curve of the northern sound cutting deep into the western portion.

Grand Cayman can be reached by sea as well as by air. One steamer, the *Caymania* (750 tons), goes to Jamaica and Belize (British Honduras) every three weeks. Two smaller steamers make regular trips from Tampa, Florida. Fares are considerably lower than by air, but the trip can be rough, and accommodations are only fair at best. One of these ships, the *Merco*, also stops at Cayman Brac and Little Cayman once each month. The *Merco* can be boarded at Grand Cayman or Kingston, or on the United States mainland by travelers who wish to see these little islands.

The people of Grand Cayman are unique in the Caribbean. The white population is probably descended from early buccaneers or marooned sailors, and a few British colonists insist on drawing a strong color line with regard to intermarriage. This has resulted in continuous inbreeding, and while there are several leading families—notably the Bowdens, Edens, Merrens, and Ebanks—it has been said that if they were traced back far enough they would all belong to one family. They all have a tendency toward unusually ruddy, very thin skin. Surprisingly enough for a small, peaceful island, the major diseases are hypertension and anxiety neuroses.

Religion plays a large part in the social and even the economic life of the island. The three churches are in continuous rivalry. There is some kind of service every night, and the only competition given the churches by night life comes from a small cinema in Georgetown, the island's leading village; Captain Ben's bar, which has a small room for ladies; and the hotel bars and cocktail lounges. The island is so religious, however, that not all of the hotels serve liquor. Each church group operates its own secondary school, the Presbyterian High School being the only one offering a course to prepare students for college. There is only one newspaper, a monthly religious sheet called *The Gospel of the Kingdom.* It is replete with moral platitudes and carries almost no local news. Some of the religious bans have turned out to be blessings in disguise. One group frowns upon the wearing of ties or jackets by men—all this is vanity, they say. It certainly results in the men looking and being much cooler on their semi-tropical island. Another group condemns the semi-transparent blouses worn by women all over the world. These are reviled as "see-more blouses." Drinking is frowned upon in theory, as is illegitimacy, but many church people are seen tipsy and even more support "outside" children.

Most Caymanians have a great affection for the United States and, though British subjects, feel a close affinity to stateside customs. They do not want to be known as West Indians. Their admiration for the material progress of the United States is boundless. One excellent example is the use of the word "nylon" as a superlative to describe anything very fine or very pretty. When speaking of a new baby, especially a blond one, they say: "It's a real nylon baby." Or, if you happen to be late for breakfast: "You will get no nylon breakfast this morning."

Caymanians are highly independent people. Almost all own their own homes, keep them neat, and tend flower beds when they will grow in the sandy soil around the white wooden houses. They take life easy, for the most part, and would rather do without good roads than have higher taxes. Consequently, there are about forty miles of narrow, bumpy thoroughfares around part of the island. The economy is based primarily upon checks sent home by the Cayman men, who go to sea between the ages of twenty and fifty. As a result of this exodus, a great many extra women remain on the island. Other methods of supporting the island come from the sale of postage stamps (some Cayman issues are very rare, all are popular), an annual head tax of $1.10 on each male citizen, and a fifteen-per-cent duty on imports. Rope made by the women and children is sold by the government. It is an excellent thatch rope with high resistance to salt water, and all of it is purchased by the Jamaica fishing industry. Out in the countryside, children from six to twelve can be seen winding the long strands with primitive and makeshift equipment.

But the most interesting occupation on Grand Cayman is the hunting of the giant green turtle. When Columbus came to these islands, he called them Las Tortugas because of the great number of turtles along the shore. These are gone now, and the turtle industry has had to reach out into the waters of Nicaragua. Men who do not take jobs on United States or South American vessels sign up with the local skipper of a schooner and go out to bring back these turtles, which weigh up to six hundred pounds. The work is done on a co-operative basis: the captain furnishes the boat; the crews do the work and pay for their own supplies. The Nicaraguan government receives a royalty for the use of its waters. Turtles are caught alive and brought back to Cayman, where they are put in large wire-mesh pits known as turtle-crawls. The initials of the owner are carved on the underside of the shells so that they can be identified later. A visit to the turtle-crawls provides one of the most unusual sights in Grand Cayman, and a turtle fisherman should be taken along so that he can take one of the monsters out of the crawl and show you the carved initials. The men show no fear of these large green or hawkbill varieties, pulling them out and wrestling with them on the edge of the pits.

The hawksbill is valued primarily for its back. Very intricate and delicate shellwork on such things as combs, wristwatch bands, and pins is done on both Grand Cayman and Cayman Brac. Most of the green turtles are shipped to the United States, but many of them go into delicious local turtle soup and turtle steaks.

The fishing off Grand Cayman is excellent, though not particularly well organized. It is best to bring your own tackle to catch the blue marlin, sailfish, kingfish, queenfish, and barracuda.

Lobster (langouste) progging is a great sport. Start out in the morning for Rum Point with a group and a guide. It is a two- to three-hour trip, depending upon how much fishing is done along the way. The route to Rum Point leads along the reef that almost completely surrounds Grand Cayman, where hundreds of langoustes lurk in the coral caves.

A glass-bottomed box is hung over the side of the boat, and the langoustes can be spotted lying motionless or moving very slowly in the still, shallow waters. When a langouste is sighted, a long stick with two prongs is pushed rapidly through the water and the crustacean is caught between the prongs. Such expeditions are fun, and can be highly recommended, as the langoustes are so plentiful that everyone in the party can successfully bring one or more to the surface. It is also probable that some fish will be caught by trolling along the reefs.

Arriving at Rum Point, the guide quickly makes a fire and puts a large pot of sea water on to boil. When it starts bubbling, the three- to five-pound langoustes are popped in and cooked for twenty-five minutes. The guide usually brings along a small bottle of vinegar, and a tablespoon or two of it added to the water tenderizes the langouste meat. When they are cooked, they are taken from the pot and the tails removed and broken open. When a little butter and salt is added, the most delicious possible lunch, all directly out of the sea, is ready.

Rum Point, a sparse, sandy beach, is a good spot for swimming and picnicking. On such an expedition, many giant conch shells are usually pulled in. They make excellent souvenirs to take home, and the conch inside makes a very tasty dish. First the shell must be broken and a knife inserted to cut the muscle that fastens the creature to its shell. This break can be very small, and will not injure the shell seriously. The conch is taken out and thoroughly pounded to tenderize it. Then it is carefully peeled and boiled. At this point, a great many natives say, it is at its best and can be eaten with a little lime juice. Other recipes call for grinding it into small pieces and frying with salt pork, or dicing it and stewing it in coconut milk. The hotels sometimes serve conch cocktail: cold cooked diced conch.

In addition to the deep-sea fishing and lobster-progging, the spear-fishing around Cayman is becoming an important activity. There is a good instructor, and fish abound in the coral coves that line the reefs. It is a good idea to bring your own equipment, though some can be purchased on the island.

The hotels on Grand Cayman are attractive and well designed. Two of them have swimming pools, and two others, on West Bay, have magnificent beaches. Food is generally good, and the more expensive hotels feature imported chefs and French and Italian cuisine. The others stick to stateside and local dishes—the fish stew is outstanding, if heavy. There are plenty of fresh vegetables, flown in from Florida. There is enough fertile soil on Cayman to raise vegetables, but the native population does not seem interested in this type of pursuit: they have followed the sea too long. There is a definite shortage of local meat, and a small cattle industry could be very profitable.

The pride of the island is a new yacht club located between Georgetown and West Bay. There are a fairly good harbor for small boats, a cocktail lounge, bar, and altogether pleasant surroundings for visitors.

The biggest celebration in Grand Cayman occurs at Christmastime. There is a Christmas parade of decorated trucks and cars, with all the island's pretty girls riding on them. Santa Claus passes out presents under a big tree, and there is something highly incongruous about this and the line of perspiring children singing "White Christmas." But the Caymanians take Christmas seriously, and for weeks beforehand, parties, dances, and church bazaars are held. Finally all the families in the island can be seen storing buckets of white sand around their houses. On Christmas Eve during the night the mother or father takes this sand and carefully spreads it over the entire yard to make it look as though snow had fallen when Christmas morning dawns and the children run to the windows.

Another interesting sight on Grand Cayman is a desolate area called Hell. Acres of jagged, sharp edges of igneous rock rise up, and there is not an inch of soil. It is almost impossible to walk here, for the sharp rocks are from four to seven feet high. A million points of gray, green, and red give an impression of complete unreality, like a visit to Mars. A barefoot boy, unafraid of the jagged rocks, will guide you around the edge of this cold and forbidding area, break off a piece of rock, and strike it against another. It gives off a sharp ringing sound that can be heard for great distances.

CAYMAN ISLANDS: *Giant turtles are kept in pens; owners' initials are carved on the belly.*

CAYMAN ISLANDS: *Langouste, minutes out of the sea,*
are boiled in sea water at Rum Cay, Grand Cayman.

CAYMAN ISLANDS: *Spear-fishing off the islands ranks with the best in the Caribbean.*

DOMINICA

From the deserted beaches of golden or black volcanic sand, through the steaming jungles up to the great rain forests, then finally to the cloud-drenched peaks, this is an unexplored and mysterious island. It is still remote, separated from the world and neighboring islands by a lack of transportation. The beauty and dark dignity of the mountains (the highest, Morne Diablotin, rises to 4,747 feet) can be seen clearly from Martinique, thirty miles south, or Guadeloupe thirty miles north—for this British island is located midway between these French islands. It is these mountains that have caused the lack of communication and travel to Dominica; their jagged edges have blocked the construction of a practical airstrip, and their steep grades and thick forests have made it impossible to build a road across the island.

Yet the interested traveler can explore this wild, beautiful, and unspoiled land. The fastest way to get there is by the twice-weekly amphibian plane from Martinique. Occasionally, ships call directly, but it is easier to go to Martinique or Guadeloupe and sail on one of the small schooners to Dominica's harbor of Roseau, or to the quiet harbor of Portsmouth. This is a lovely bay, with but few houses near the dock, for Portsmouth can scarcely be called a town. Its appearance is that of a ghost village in the United States desert, but with dank, jungle foliage close behind it. It is possible to land in Portsmouth's Prince Rupert Bay, pass briefly through customs, and take the government launch to Roseau without being conscious of the town at all.

Prince Rupert Bay, however, is worth more than passing notice. It offers excellent anchorage for small boats. Because it is in the direct line of the trade winds, there is almost always a cool breeze. It was here in 1953 that Anne Davidson, an adventurous English girl, made her first landfall after crossing the Atlantic alone in her tiny boat, the *Plymouth*. Her route was the one pioneered by Columbus on his second voyage in 1494.

Here, too, on Christmas 1674, occurred the greatest act of treachery in the history of the West Indies. On that day Philip Warner, son of Sir Thomas Warner, the first Governor of St. Kitts—credited with being the first great colonizer of the West Indies—led a group of three hundred men to raid the Caribs on the windward side of Dominica. To help him in this assignment he asked and received aid from his half-brother Carib Warner, son of Sir Thomas and a Carib woman of the island. The brothers were successful in their raid against the Caribs on the windward side, and Carib Warner led his Carib group to the leeward side. To celebrate the victory Philip invited his dusky brother, together with sixty men, women, and children, aboard the ship. They were given much to drink and late at night were all murdered. And then, as Douglas Taylor, anthropologist and authority on the Caribs, writes, "a grown-up son of Carib Warner, learning of his father's fate, came on board later and exposing his throat, asked to suffer the same death—a wish that was promptly granted." Today in the hills high above Prince Rupert Bay are the last few remaining pure Carib Indians in the world. On the reservation live about six hundred members of this dying race. Of this group perhaps fifty are of pure "red" Carib descent. Few travelers have visited their mountain retreat, but it is a safe and not too difficult trip for the adventurous.

Start by spending a day in Portsmouth, where arrangements can be made for a car. It is twenty-one miles from Portsmouth to Petit Marigot, where a stop is made to rest and have lunch before proceeding to Hattan Gardens. At this point a guide ready to carry a pack will meet you and lead the way up the five-mile trail to Battaka, one of the Carib villages. Near Portsmouth the road is lined with coconut groves. It goes through the village of Calibishie near the lovely home of Mrs. Lenox Napier, a writer who now makes her home in Dominica, is a member of the island's House of Representatives, and has a continuing interest in the problems of the Caribs.

The sea in this area is rough and beats wildly against the high red rocks that line the steep shoreline. The scenery is not unlike that of the Pacific coast of the United States, though even more impressive.

While stopping at Petit Marigot, pick up a supply of raw rum and tobacco to take along as gifts for the Indians. They are particularly fond of rum—a failing that has contributed considerably to their lack of development, for they have been known to trade almost any possession for rum. The tiny store at Petit Marigot supplies it in kegs, drawing it off into quart bottles as it is purchased. The rum comes in two grades, new and old. The Caribs are delighted with either.

It is possible to stay overnight in Petit Marigot at a guesthouse called Winstons, but this is not recommended except to hardy travelers. The house has two bedrooms; the term is used loosely. They are crude, unpapered, unpainted wooden rooms without toilet or bath facilities, and have no screens in their open windows. Mosquito netting is supplied, as are a washbasin and pitcher. The rest-house is lighted by two kerosene lamps. All in all, it is highly unprepossessing. On the other hand, the food at Winstons, while ordinary, is not always dull. If the visitor is lucky enough to get a calaloo made in the Dominican style, it can be a very exciting meal indeed. Calaloo is made of river crabs cracked up and lightly sautéed in oil. Spinach and dasheen leaves are washed and boiled with green bananas, lime juice, bay leaf, salt, and pepper until tender. The crabs are then added. It is a delicious stew.

The meeting-place at Hattan Gardens looks quite unlike the beginning of a rendezvous with a vanishing race. From the broad glade under the large gommier trees a steep, narrow trail leads through the forest. The trip can be made by horseback, but this is not recommended unless you have seen the horse and are an experienced horseman. The loose stones and numerous muddy spots make horseback going more difficult than foot travel. It is a two-hour walk with little to be seen along the way except flora. There is the tall latanier tree; the Caribs make hats and brooms from its fibrous leaves. The yanga palm is used for thatching Carib huts. Flowers include the rain-forest vine and the roku, a flower bearing red-seeded fruit that the Indians use for dyeing basket fibers.

Although there have been many changes in the way Caribs live since the time they repulsed Columbus's men on the beaches in 1493, none of the changes is visible to the visitor today. Huts, for the most part, are of local timbers with thatched roofs. The visitor might see an ajoupa, a quickly built hut used when hunting or traveling overnight—it can be put up in an hour and offers complete protection against tropical rain. The Carib home is surrounded by a well-worn yellow clay yard, and the kitchen is usually a small thatched building near the main house. It is interesting that these homes and kitchens are kept spotlessly clean; each of the few items used for the preparation of food is carefully put away.

The physical appearance of this disappearing race is remarkable. They are people of average stature, small-boned, with long, delicate hands and feet, perfectly straight hair, and a physiognomy somewhat like that of the northern Chinese. They are particularly proud of their small eyes, which slant slightly. The women are very handsome, but quite shy, and it is unusual to see a pure-blooded Carib woman close enough to talk to for any length of time. The men, too, are attractive, having straight hair and lean, muscular bodies.

Life in the village moves much as it did hundreds of years ago. The men fell the gommier trees to make canoes. These are dug out and filled with stones and water to make the trunks swell. Small fires are kept burning on either side during this process. After the spreading, the ribs and thwarts are inserted. Later the sides are built up with boards to make a handsome, seaworthy craft. These canoes are no longer paddled, being rigged with square sails that carry the craft along rapidly before the wind.

Near the canoe-maker there will probably be a group of men making various types of the famous Carib baskets. One fine, beautiful, rainproof type, made only by the men, is woven in every possible size from very tiny baskets to large suitcases. They are made from the larouman plant and are actually two baskets in one. The inner one is sewed to the outer one with strong homemade thread. The two baskets are separated by a rainproof layer of balisier leaves. Lesser baskets are made by the Carib women.

Another important activity in the Carib village is the making of cassava flour. This is prepared from the manioc root, which is the number-one crop plant of the Carib and is still well known in the other Windward Islands. The Indians discovered that this poisonous root could be made non-poisonous by proper preparation. They remove the outer skin by scraping and grating. The tuber is then squeezed in order to remove the poisonous juice, and the pulp is dried. The resulting meal, after being beaten into a fine powder, is used to make cassavas, large flat pancakes that replace bread.

But the Caribs do not enjoy entertaining visitors, and unless the traveler is accompanied by a guide known to them and comes bearing gifts, he may see no Caribs at all. It is very easy for them to vanish into the woods or into their houses as the visitors pass by the seemingly deserted village.

These Indians have a difficult time earning cash to buy rum. A Carib man will work for weeks, sometimes months, on a group of baskets. He then ties the huge pile into a knapsack-like arrangement on his back and staggers down the hill toward the villages to sell them. His prices are high at the first store, but as his load gets lighter and he becomes more eager for his rum, he lowers them. By the time he has reached the last village near Petit Marigot or even Portsmouth, the baskets are sold for very little.

The trip down the west coast from Portsmouth to Roseau on the government launch takes about four hours. There is little to see except an occasional fishing boat and the towering mountains. The mail boat sometimes makes a stop or two at a tiny village like the one called Massacre because the Caribs once wiped out a French settlement here. At Roseau there is little activity around the docks. This is not one of the better harbors of the West Indies, and very few large boats put in. The capital itself is attractive in a quiet, unworldly way. The narrow streets have overhanging galleries. Houses have odd shapes, some being built like tiny French chalets. Business houses, as in most islands, have incredibly dull façades made of two large doors opening into a plain dark interior. There is an excellent drugstore operated by a gentleman interested in photography, so there is usually film on hand. Near Roseau is perhaps the most beautiful botanical garden in all the West Indies.

Dominica has no organized fishing facilities for visitors, though there are many fish in these waters. The same is true of sailing facilities. The entire island, of course, turns off its lights very early in the evening. There are few dances and no night life of any kind.

The island is distinguished not only as the home of the last of the Caribs, but also as the home of a highly distinctive method of weaving carpets of fibers. The Convent of Roseau has approximately one hundred young girl students who help to earn their way by weaving the large floor mats that are used throughout the Caribbean islands. These girls do not want to go into domestic service, and there is little other opportunity for them in Dominica, so they continue to weave carpets. There are a number of unusual designs and the carpets are reasonable in cost. Many visitors have them shipped back to the States or to England. They rate as one of the best buys in the islands.

A few miles outside Roseau is the Morne Valley, where the Roses Lime Juice Company operates a lime-tree plantation. From the top of the hill it is possible to look down into this tremendous valley and see the delicate lime trees completely protected by a high row of eucalyptus trees. In the background lurk the soft, misty, rain-drenched mountains.

Another excellent trip out of Roseau is a picnic to the waterfall four miles from the city. Everyone there knows the long, thin column that tumbles some sixty feet out of the mountain. It is a difficult climb to the picnic spot beneath the falls, but well worth it. It is a good plan to take along a machete, for it may be necessary to cut your way through some of the brush.

DOMINICA: *Waterfall and picnic grounds near Roseau.*

DOMINICA: *Directly descended from the Carib-Arawaks who fought Columbus's men, this girl is one of less than twenty-five surviving pure members of her race.*

DOMINICA: *The last of the Caribs still weave traditional baskets on their reservation at Salybia.*

DOMINICA: *Coconut forests lead up to the Carib reservation; an Indian sleeps under the trees.*

DOMINICA: *On the Carib reservation, an Indian fashions a traditional canoe.*

GRENADA

The land-locked harbor of St. George's, Grenada, is considered the most beautiful in all the Caribbean. Golden-green wooded hills bathed in almost constant sunlight, gleaming beaches, and a warm-to-hot climate make this small island an attractive place to visit. It is the southernmost of the Windward group.

Columbus viewed the island as he sailed to Trinidad, eighty-five miles to the south, on August 15, 1498. He named it Concepción. Perhaps because he knew it was well populated by the warlike Carib Indians, he avoided it and sailed east along the Venezuelan coast. Today Grenada (pronounced Gra-*nay*-dah) is the first stop on British West Indian Airways north from Trinidad. Grenada is separated from St. Vincent, seventy-five miles north, by a chain of volcanic islands and cays called the Grenadines.

The Caribs prevented first the English, then the French settlers, from establishing colonies for one hundred and fifty years after Columbus sailed by. Surprisingly, they then sold it to a band of two hundred French adventurers for a few metal knives (they had only shell tools), some hatchets, a few hundred glass beads, and—as it is told in Grenada—two bottles of brandy for the chief.

It was quite a buy for the French. The island measured twelve by twenty-one fertile miles. Well watered, its slopes were not too steep to cultivate. The surrounding sea and interior rivers were alive with fish. The climate, because of the high green mountains and the constant trade winds, was warm and dry in winter, hot and breezy in summer.

All these natural assets are still there, but a great many others have been added. The beaches meant little to the early settlers. Now they are among the island's great attractions. Add good roads, a solid economy based on spices, a superlative harbor and careenage, and you have Grenada today. Only two things are lacking. One is better accommodations for visitors. The islanders have been working toward this, but, while there are enough rooms available, they have not yet learned what the traveler wants. Water pressure goes down to a trickle and sometimes stops altogether. Service is incredibly slow. Menus are often dull, with the so-called British food that most Englishmen of good taste have deplored for generations. The second element lacking is development of the marvelous shoreline. Grenada is blessed with three of the really fine beaches of the West Indies. Grand Anse is a half-mile sweep of oyster-white sand fringed with coconut palms. Point Saline is a peninsula on the southwesternmost tip of the island with a clean blue-black beach of volcanic sand on one side of the road and a stretch of pure-white surf-washed sand on the other. Levera Beach, on the north, is the most beautiful of all, though not the best for swimming because of its rough surf. Yet only at Grand Anse Beach is there a clubhouse of any sort, or dressing-rooms. Even there facilities are inadequate. But these are minor drawbacks compared with the advantages offered by this spice island, and they should not deter the visitor.

Throughout its entire history, Grenada has been a restless island. Although the French occupied the first permanent settlement, the Caribs soon regretted the quick sale of their island and began hostilities. The French, with comparatively modern weapons against the flint hatchets and wooden spears of the Indians, pushed them back to Le Morne des Sauteurs (Leapers' Hill). Here the last defenders of the northern part of the island leaped off the cliff into the sea, breaking their bodies against the rocks rather than endure capture by the French. Today Le Morne des Sauteurs has a highly dramatic impact upon the viewer. Although a children's school and a church stand near the cliff, the steep edge of the promontory may still be seen, and a long path leads down to the jagged rocks at the bottom. This uprising ended the resistance of the Indians. The remaining bands were rounded up, and men, women, and children put to the sword. A few escaped to the hills and, adding the savage Carib blood to that of the Negro slaves, seem to have tempered the personalities of the natives of the island today.

Near the town of Sauteurs is Levera Beach, where great rocks are strewn along the approach to the curve of pure-white sand that slopes gently into the water. Although the surf is strong, this has proved an excellent spot for spear-fishing.

A short distance out from the beach are Levera and Green Islands, where excellent shooting is enjoyed by underwater fishermen. Green Island, which has a good beach, can be rented in its entirety, including a house with bathroom, kitchen, bedroom, and living-room. There is no electricity, but adequate oil lamps are provided. The rent is low, and applications should be made well in advance because it is very popular as a summer or winter resort with both West Indians and visitors.

Pearls Airport on the eastern side of the island is the only landing-strip. As one reaches Grenada by air, Green and Levera Islands are visible below. The drive from the airport diagonally across the island to St. George's, Grenada's capital and only city, is unusual and interesting. The road winds along the coast through Grenville, a small marketing and fishing village where travelers who enjoy taking pictures can spend a profitable hour. Past Grenville the route winds through the ridges of the green hills. Magnificent vistas of the interior flash by. Large patches of flaming immortelle trees against the green mountains dominate the view. If you are lucky, you may see the brown hummingbird locally called the doctor bird, with its brown-and-green body and very long bill—this very rare variety is believed to be unique to Grenada, and few are found even there—or, high in the hills near the Grand Etang mountain lake, the Mona monkey, originally from Africa.

Eighteen hundred feet up, the Grand Etang is a small lake so calm that it looks like a sheet of ice on top of a mountain. It lies in an extinct volcanic crater. On the lakeshore is a government resthouse that may be rented by the day or week. Because this area is isolated from both St. George's and Grenville and is almost always too cool except during the summer months, it is not recommended to visitors as a place to stay.

The road leading from the Grand Etang to St. George's goes through hilly, jungle-like terrain. Along the way, noisy blackheaded pripri birds keep up their constant whistling, and the larger gray-blue ramier bird is frequently seen. Grenada's varied fauna also include six varieties of bats, seven varieties of lizards, a few scorpions and tarantulas (although they are rare, it is not a bad idea to shake out your shoes before putting them on in the morning), and seven varieties of harmless snakes. Its mountains are bright with tropical and semi-tropical flowers. It is known as the island of spices, and cinnamon, bayberry, vanilla, ginger, and nutmeg grow on the fecund slopes on both sides of the north-south road. In addition to these trees Grenada has many roots used by the natives for their medicinal properties. An odd and interesting plant called crab eyes is used for coughs and colds. Another called woman's tongue is said to be of particular value for nervous diseases. Wonder-of-the-world plant has leaves that are applied to wounds and boils. The chew stick is used, as the name implies, to clean the teeth, and also as a substitute for ginger in the making of ginger beer.

Although Grenada has been British since 1783, its magnificent port city of St. George's still wears a French look. Built by the French in 1732, it was originally called Port Louis. They constructed many of the old forts surrounding the city today. Now St. George's combines the clean, well-scrubbed look of the British with many buildings showing architectural details dating back to the French occupation in the eighteenth century. Almost all the houses are of brick or stone. St. George's in its early years was destroyed by fire three times; finally an ordinance was passed forbidding the construction of wooden houses.

From the vantage point of the Hotel Santa Maria, St. George's looks like a toy European city, with tiny red and white iridescent buildings dotting the hills and a long curve of pastel pink, lavender, and orange commercial buildings seemingly floating on the edge of the blue waters of the Careenage. Its narrow streets are crowded from early morning until noon with noisy, busy, good-humored Grenadians. They speak rapidly in the French rather than the English manner and use island slang that sounds meaningless to the visitor. "There goes a nice craffe" means that a good-looking girl is strolling by. In the case of a handsome male, they say: "There goes a big grain of man." They have a salty tongue and often combine French words with English slang. A big dance is spoken of as "fête for so."

The independent attitude of the natives was partially responsible for the successful shifting of Grenada's economy from comparatively unprofitable sugar to profitable spices. After slavery was abolished, the planters tried importing labor from Malta, Madeira, and the East Indies (twenty-five per cent of the East Indian coolies died in transit). They were not very successful, however, and the independent Negroes who had taken to the hills began cultivating their own "gardens." They planted cocoa in the shade of the immortelle trees and grew coffee and yams. From these small beginnings, the present economy based on spices began as white planters shifted from sugar to nutmeg, cocoa, and limes.

The cocoa plantations on the slopes are located near the main roads and can easily be visited by travelers. The nutmeg groves are often adjacent. Both cocoa and nutmeg grow best in deep, shady groves, and it is a fascinating sight to watch young Negro and mulatto women in bright cotton dresses picking up the yellow and red pods of the nutmeg—yellow on the outside, with the scarlet lacy-like membrane showing through where they have broken. Cocoa is dried in the sun and the long trays of chocolate-brown pods are turned with a rake while drying. Cocoa-polishing is still done mainly by hand, or, rather, by foot. It is put in a vat, and barefoot men tread on the pods in an operation similar to pressing grapes for wine in Europe. It has been found difficult to polish the smooth beans effectively and inexpensively by machine.

In some of the shops it is possible to buy palm-leaf baskets filled with all the spices of Grenada. They make an excellent take-home gift.

Except for a short stay of a week or two, living at the hotels and guesthouses is not a good idea. None is on the beach, and transportation is relatively expensive. By writing in advance to the Grenada Tourist Board you can make arrangements to rent a cottage near Grand Anse Beach or at Point Saline.

An outing particularly recommended is an all-day picnicking trip to Annandale Falls, where one can swim in the clear blue-green river water. Adventurous swimmers can plunge under the magnificent forty-five-foot falls that cascades over the golden-purple rocks. Dripping lianas hang down the rocks, their rope-like branches sprayed by the clear river water. Huge deep-green elephant's ears grow out of the rocks. The churning white water turns to pale green as it falls into the deep pool under the falls. On a hill overlooking the scene is a small cabin with two tiny rooms separated by a half-wall. It is not a very pleasant dressing-room, and most people prefer to change in the privacy of the near-by woods. Visitors must enter the Annandale Falls area through a gate with a watchman; a small fee is charged.

Grenada is an island of daylight. When the sun sets and the brief moment of twilight is gone, the island dies. Except for the dances at the hotels to excellent steel bands or a trip to the local movie, there is no night life. There is, however, almost always a breeze, and no night noises disturb the traveler's sleep.

GRENADA: *Steep, narrow streets lead through the center of St. George's.*

GRENADA: *The deep harbor of St. George's, where cruise ships can dock alongside the city.*

GRENADA: *The famous black sand beach.*

GRENADA: *A woodland cascade provides clear fresh-water swimming.*

GRENADA: *Beauty-contest winner and carnival queen.*

JAMAICA

From the air this massive island, one hundred and fifty miles long by fifty miles across, looks like a mountainous green continent. As a plane approaches Montego Bay, the dim outlines slowly become discernible. The reef with its deep-blue waters appears below, melting into paler and paler greens as you rush downward toward shore. It takes only a few moments to skim over the distance between reef and white sand. This beach, Jamaica's best, is called Doctor's Cave. It is unbelievably beautiful from the air, and all planes cross near it as they enter Jamaica through the resort town of Montego Bay.

The island of Jamaica (Indian, Xaymaca: sometimes translated as "isle of rivers") is located in the center of the Caribbean Sea. It is an island of great variety, with many white sand beaches, extensive green savannas, large areas of mangrove swamp and river delta, and a fantastic geological formation known as the Cockpit Country. The high peaks of the Blue Mountains reach up 7,402 feet into the clouds.

Over ninety per cent of its population of about one million and a half is of African descent. The rest is primarily European, East Indian, Chinese, and Syrian. The temperature ranges between 70 and 90 degrees, being very pleasant from January through April, warmer in the summer months (except in the mountains), and rainy in the autumn.

The landing at Montego Bay is thirty miles from Discovery Bay, where Columbus landed on his second voyage. The coastline has changed little since his day. It is possible to walk for miles along the beach, seeing no person or human habitation, but only green-blue-purple sea, golden sand, and pastel oceanside flora.

But it is not like this at the airport at Montego Bay. Here the atmosphere is gay, informal, and friendly. As the visitor steps from the plane, he is guided quickly into a small but efficient airport, handed a Planter's Punch to help while away the minutes as the Customs, Health, and Immigration officers complete their processing. By the time the tall rum drink is finished, the visitor is ready to board a waiting taxi and be off to one of the resort's fine hotels. This hotel community likes to think of itself as the "Riviera of the Caribbean," and with reason. The weather throughout the winter season is even better than that of the Mediterranean. It does not have as many available beaches, but Doctor's Cave is one of the finest in the world. The hotels are ultra-modern, comfortable, occasionally ornate, and—by West Indies standards—expensive. The atmosphere is that of the international society set, an aura that is deliberately and continuously promoted. This is an ideal vacation spot for the wealthy or semi-wealthy winter vacationer. The traveler of modest means who is willing to stay at a guesthouse or one of the smaller hotels can also have a pleasant time in and around the resort.

Three types of hotels are available in Montego Bay. First, the very expensive type, which features fine furnishings, imported foods flown in daily, continental atmosphere, a group of famous guests, some entertainment, and lots of privacy. The second, though almost as expensive, does not concentrate on food so much as on dancing, entertainment, and beach parties; it is the type of establishment a younger but not quite so wealthy traveler might enjoy. The third type includes the small hotels and guesthouses outside the social picture. These are inexpensive; their food is dull and British, their entertainment almost nonexistent. A quiet, restful vacation may be had in Montego by stopping at one of these inexpensive hotels and spending the perfect days at Doctor's Cave.

A small set of coincidences make Doctor's Cave an ideal beach: the sand is white and fine; the reef is located just the right distance from shore, keeping the surf from being rough and unwanted big fish from coming in; almond trees with orange-colored leaves grow along the beach, providing shade and contrast to the bright reflections; the hard-packed, coral-free sand has a gradual slope; and the gin-clear water has an unbelievable temperature of about 72 degrees the entire year.

In addition to these natural virtues, Doctor's Cave has spacious dressing-rooms, umbrellas, beach chairs and pads that may be rented for a few pennies a day, benches, picnic tables, waiters ready to serve snacks or drinks, a small bandstand, and even an exhibition gallery for an occasional art show. Admission charge to this beach is very moderate. It is operated as a private club, but all hotel guests are welcome.

An average day at one of the larger Montego Bay hotels begins with a tropical breakfast served in your room or on the outdoor dining-terrace. After breakfast most guests walk to Doctor's Cave for a morning sunbath or swim. After coming back to the hotel for lunch, many guests take a short nap, but some spend the afternoon sightseeing or shopping.

Interesting sightseeing in the area includes the large, ancient sugar estates called "Great Houses," which date back to 1750. Some are still standing and in good repair: Good Hope near the town of Falmouth, east of Montego Bay, and Tryall, which is in the opposite direction, toward the village of Lucea (pronounced Lucy). These magnificent estate houses have been converted into the Jamaican version of the dude ranch. While horses are available, they are not particularly important, and there is certainly no "wild west" atmosphere. The pace is quiet and leisurely with trips to the beach, picnics in the country, and fishing. A third "Great House" is Cinnamon Hill, which has a hurricane cellar. This was once the estate of Edward Barrett, father of Elizabeth Barrett Browning, and is now a private residence.

The most colorful and photogenic ruins near Montego Bay are those of Rose Hall, about twelve miles away. It is still operated as a sugar estate, though the great house has been in ruins for many years. The locale has served for a lurid novel called *The White Witch of Rose Hall,* which purports to be the intimate story of one Annee Palmer, said to have been a beautiful and tempestuous woman who murdered two of her husbands and an overseer, and who was finally murdered and dismembered by the last of her lovers. Many of the Negroes in the area believe that Rose Hall is haunted.

The house is still a magnificent structure, though much of the roof has caved in and all the delicate woodwork has long since been torn out. It lies at the end of a long narrow road with sugar cane growing high on either side. It is not the place for a picnic, but a pleasant hour of sightseeing may be spent here. Once a week a group of naked and semi-naked native boys drives hordes of Brahmin cattle into the sea in front of the plantation, to be cleansed of the parasites that infest them. The cattle will not go into the sea without a leader, so plantation mules are rounded up to lead them, and the boys push and swim alongside them in the water in a semicircle. The cattle are then led out glistening to be driven back to the plantation.

The town of Montego Bay itself is well worth half a day's exploration. It is a short walk and only a five-minute taxi ride from many of the hotels. On Saturday mornings farmers and their wives from the surrounding areas bring produce to the market. Although shopping is impossible in the hubbub of the market itself, it is exciting to walk through the clamorous shops run by East Indians, Chinese, and Syrians. A wide variety of British fabrics, Indian silver, and similar imports is sold, and it is an excellent place to order suits and dinner jackets from one of the many good tailors.

Fishing boats go to Bogue Islands, just off Montego Bay, where mangrove swamps shelter many fish, and where tiny oysters grow on the trees. Explore the coral reef in a glass-bottomed boat. Go snorkeling or spear-fishing. Rent a small sailboat. Visitors are welcome at the Montego Bay Yacht Club.

Perhaps the most interesting fishing expedition in Montego Bay is at night in one of the small boats with a Negro oarsman as captain and crew. He will row you out to the fishing grounds. There, seated in the dark, listening to the water lapping against the side of your boat, watching the lights of Montego Bay flicker, you will catch yellowtails and snappers. The only light in this tiny craft is the glow from a primitive rag lamp made by thrusting a cloth into a can or jar of kerosene. It burns with a smoky yellow flame for hours. Other little bright oases in the black sea can be picked out on the horizon.

Night at Montego Bay brings Calypso singers, West Indian dancers, and sensational fire-eaters, who are the descendants of the legendary "John Canoes" whose costumes and fire dances are in part derived from the Ashanti fire dances of Africa.

These entertainers come to the hotel piers after dinner, paddling long, flat-bottomed boats that also serve as theaters. Most of the singing done in Jamaica is more folk song than true topical, spur-of-the-moment Calypso of the Trinidad type. Although new songs are heard every year in Trinidad, and indeed almost every day, in Jamaica the old favorites are sung year after year. The older they get, the better they sound.

Unfortunately, much of the Jamaican entertainment at the hotels has become commercial. The singers try to give the American traveler what they think he wants, and it is impossible to avoid endless repetitions of "Rum and Coca Cola," a Trinidad Calypso of World War II, and "Take Her to Jamaica Where the Rum Comes From." But many of the ancient native songs—like "Linstead Market," with its gay melody and sad lyrics about a woman who carried her "ackee" (native vegetable) to market and couldn't sell even a "quatty" (one and one-half pence) worth, and who spent a miserable Saturday night without a customer—give a true picture of Jamaican folk music.

West Indian dancers who entertain at the hotels are often thin-shanked, awkward girls in short bloomers and bras who do routines resembling amateur night in Harlem (usually consisting of unskilled bumps and grinds) to the music of guitar, flute and drums.

It is difficult to find good dancers in Jamaica who can do the early African dances as modified by the West Indies. A few are trying to develop a true West Indian style, but they are seen rarely and mostly in and around Kingston. By far the best of the native dancers are the "John Canoes" who appear around Christmastime. Their grotesque costumes represent British subjects at the time of Elizabeth I. But the addition of fire is African. Wicks made of cloth saturated with kerosene project from their ankles, elaborate head-dresses, and midriffs. The wicks are lighted, and the dancers, on fire from head to foot, begin a slow, measured, traditional procession from one position to another. At a big performance one man is costumed as a horse with a papier-mâché head and calico body. At the climax of the dance he too will be lighted up and move nimbly about. Finally the fire-eaters take large mouthfuls of kerosene and spew forth flames that sometimes reach a distance of four feet. This demonstration, with the three-piece Calypso band playing "God Bless America" or "God Save the Queen," closes the show.

Native talent constitutes a very small part of the resort entertainment at Montego Bay. Large dance bands play rumbas, mambos, tangos, and stateside music at various hotels in the evening. For many years the custom of all hotels has been to make guests of other hotels welcome at their dances, and there is a dance somewhere in Montego Bay almost every night. This does not, however, mean a breakdown of the social system. The rich and the famous still associate with one another; the onetime tourists are also clannish; and much of the local population, especially the black, cannot afford to mix socially at all.

Just south of Montego Bay lies the wild, inaccessible Cockpit Country, the greatest possible contrast to the luxurious community.

It is so named because of its many precipitous hillocks and deep overgrown holes resembling giant cones and giving the impression of a nature-formed cockpit. This is one of the rare places where some of Jamaica's early timber still stands. Tall mahoe trees with delicately veined wood, broadleaf, cedar, and Spanish mahogany may still be found. This is also one of the rare places in Jamaica where the yellow snake, a large boa constrictor sometimes attaining a length of seven feet, is found. Occasionally a small (one- or two-foot) boa constrictor is seen. Neither of these attacks man; both are non-poisonous. The entire region is replete with shady glens and awe-inspiring, overhanging, moss-grown rocks. The terrain is one of the most difficult to traverse in the world. Exploration of the interior is so arduous that the visitor should plan a trip carefully in advance and give at least two weeks to the project.

This remote area is the country of the Maroons, a group of slaves who rebelled against their owners in the earliest days of slavery, when the Spanish held Jamaica. When the British, led by Admirals Penn and Venables, landed on the island with an overwhelming superior force in 1565, the Spanish, before relinquishing it, set the remainder of the slaves free. They quickly melted into the Cockpit Country and joined their friends. A tiny nation began to form. During the next generations they grew in number and became even better entrenched in their wilderness stronghold. The British tried to dislodge them by military force in 1734, but were badly beaten both by the wild country and by these independent, hard-fighting ex-slaves. A treaty signed under a tree that still stands guaranteed the Maroons their freedom and continued ownership of land in the area comprising the Cockpit Country.

But the second Maroon war broke out in 1795, and this time the British won the decision. They lost a great many men, however, while few Maroons were killed or wounded. To bring the war to a conclusion, the British imported sixty pairs of "maroon" hounds, huge mastiffs trained to hunt men. Although the Maroons were promised their freedom, the promise was forgotten, and five hundred of them were shipped to Nova Scotia to settle. They were later sent to Sierra Leone in Africa. The largest group of Maroons in the western part of the country had not joined in this second war, however, and to this day enjoys a degree of sovereignty decreed by the treaty of 1734. They operate their own schools and towns and have a chief, one of a line that stretches back to old Cudjoe, their first general.

The wild Maroon country is also known by the fascinating name of "Land of Look Behind" because of the continuous possibility of ambush in its early history. Villages in Maroonland carry such provocative names as Wait a Bit, Virgin Valley, Retirement, Friendship. One quite surprisingly is called Me No Sen—You No Com.

The Jamaican Negro has a happy faculty of creating vivid descriptive words for flora and fauna as well as for places. One example is the ever-present poinciana tree with its vivid scarlet flowers. In Jamaica it is colorfully called the Fancy Anna. A very hot local pepper is known as the "burn to hell." The clinging flower known as the sweetheart in Trinidad becomes the shame lady in Jamaica. A species of brown rat is known as Charley Price, named after Sir Charles Price, who imported them to kill off the cane-eating black rat. The best-known character in Jamaica is the John Crow, a vulture similar to the American turkey buzzard, named for a greatly disliked black-robed minister who officiated at the church at Port Royal in 1692. Curiously, the beautiful John Crow Mountains in the northeastern corner of the island also bear his name.

Travelers to Jamaica will find the Jamaican Negro superstitious. The fear of ghosts or duppies goes back to both African and early Arawak Indian beliefs. Peter Martyr, the first bishop of Jamaica, wrote in his *Historie of the West Indies* (1515) of the superstitions of the Arawaks:

> They are also subject to another kind of superstition: for they thinke that dead folks walke in the night, and eate the fruite called *Guannaba*, vnknowne vnto vs, & somwhat like vnto a Quinse: affirming also that they are couersant with liuing people: euen in their beddes, and to deceiue women in taking vpon them the shape of men, shewing themselues as though they would haue to doe with them: but when the matter commeth to actuall deed, sodainly they vanishe away. If any do suspect that a dead body lyeth by him, whe he feeleth any strag thing in the bed, they say he shall bee out of doubt by feeling of the bellie thereof: affirming that the spirites of dead men may take vpon them all the members of mans body, sauing onely the nauel. If therefore by the lacke of the nauel he doe perceiue that a dead body lyeth by him, the feeling is immediately resolued. They belleue verily, that in the night, and oftentimes in ther journeies, and expecially in common and high wayes, dead men doe meete

> with the liuing: Against whom, if any bee stout and out of feare, the fantasie vanisheth incontinently: but if anie feare, the fantasie or vision dooth so assaulte him and strike him with further feare, that many are thereby astonyshed, and haue the lymmes of their bodies taken.

But duppies do not appear only at night. They appear in the daytime, too, and are sometimes good and sometimes bad. The bad ones throw rocks at houses and frighten women and children. They even affect the garden. The duppy tomato has prickles unlike the normal ones. There are also misshapen duppy pumpkins and too-small duppy cucumbers. It is believed that duppies inhabit the ceiba or silk cottonwood, one of Jamaica's most beautiful trees.

A belief in spirits is reflected in the vestiges of the evil black magic of Obeah, a witchcraft cult brought from Africa, now prohibited by law. Such milder forms of witchcraft as "faith-healing" are practiced in the "balmyards," revival missions operated throughout the interior of the country. Each balmyard has a "mother" who practices healing and sells "bush" medicine. These missions are large huts of mud and wattles where regular religious meetings are held and where the poor, highly superstitious Negro is likely to go for treatment of real or imaginary ills.

By far the most interesting form of religion in Jamaica is Pocomania, a curious mixture of old-time Protestant revival meeting and African Obeah magic. Services of this unique sect are held legally, but in some sections there is a time limit and the more violent groups are discouraged by the constabulary. Meetings begin like many other religious gatherings; hymns are sung, and the "shepherd" (preacher) shouts a sermon castigating Satan, bringing out by simple example the virtues of being close to Christ and the Trinity.

Costume plays an important part in the ritual. The shepherd appears in colorful robes with a staff and headdress probably copied from colored pictures in the Bible. His assistants, a "mother" and a "governess," are also elaborately gowned, usually in white. After the sermon, the congregation strives for possession. They shout and sing for God to come into them. While singing and praying they suddenly begin a noise called "trumping." This is a deep, loud roar. As the roaring becomes louder, the shepherd is likely to start leaping as he shouts. The congregation growls and jumps with the shepherd. After a time, many fall to the ground and flail about, writhing and speaking in unknown tongues. Some Pocomania meetings attain this hypnotic condition by the continuous roaring of the people. Other groups use drums steadily beaten while the worshippers dance and shout. Certain Pocomania shepherds in recent years have turned to smoking ganga, a weed similar to marijuana. It is believed that they use it to improve their vocal ability and stamina. There is no question but that a considerable amount of ganga is grown in the Jamaica countryside and it is extremely difficult for the police to detect it because it grows quickly and can be easily hidden. It stimulates the strength of the user, at least temporarily, and allays hunger. Ganga has not been found only in the country: the police often find it growing inside the city limits of Kingston.

There are three ways to travel from Montego Bay to Kingston. The trip by plane takes less than thirty minutes and offers an air view of spectacular mountains and deep green valleys. The trip by train (a small diesel that stops frequently) is interesting and inexpensive, and offers a chance to mix with the local people and see over one hundred miles of picturesque countryside. It is the kind of train trip during which the engineer may stop to find out the cricket score at a local settlement or to chase a sleeping Brahman bull off the tracks.

The third way, the most expensive and time-consuming, is also the most rewarding. This is to rent an automobile at Montego Bay and drive along the coast and around the eastern point of the island to Kingston. A driver's license is necessary, and for this photographs must be taken, the director of the license bureau must be found to sign the application, and a visit to the courthouse must be made. It is then time to shop for a car. The available automobiles will be small and British—a good thing because the roads are narrow and gasoline expensive. It takes only a few moments to learn to drive one of these comfortable little cars.

The road winds along the coast through the dusty little town of Falmouth, the home of Antonio's, a famous place to shop for fabrics. It is located in an old two-story residence of the classic West Indian raised-cottage type. It is cool and dark inside, and the main shopping-room has an amazingly complete selection of woolens and cottons, but it is in the second room that you will be especially delighted. Here the walls are covered with a riot of bright materials; lavenders, pinks, chocolates, vivid reds, deep blue-purples fill every corner. These cotton prints are made in England for the African trade, but are diverted to Jamaica by Antonio. Prices are exceptionally low, and many remnants large enough for a skirt, dress, or vivid shirt are available. Antonio's can be highly recommended for the traveler's "take home" shopping.

From Falmouth to St. Ann's Bay the road runs along Jamaica's most historical shore. Dry Harbour, where Columbus landed on May 4, 1494, is now Discovery Bay. From Runaway Bay, just next door, the Spanish garrison escaped to Cuba after their defeat by the British. At St. Ann's Bay, a few miles farther along, Columbus on his fourth, final voyage spent a year with his wrecked caravels awaiting help from Española.

At St. Ann's Bay the road branches. To the south it rises over the foothills of the Dry Harbour Mountains and into the peaks of the high Blue Mountains. It is a short but hilly ride to Kingston. While it goes through beautiful country, it misses many of Jamaica's thrilling coastline experiences. The scenic route continues east straight along the coast, past fishing villages with crews in tiny sailboats taking off or returning with their catch. Along these beaches are copra plantations where coconuts are dried in the sun. Then comes the unexpected beauty of Dunn's River, where a stream of cascading pale-blue water falls into the salty blue sea. For a few pence a dressing-room is available, and it is possible to bathe in the ocean from a broad white sand beach and then climb up the gushing cascade of the river to let the clean, cool fresh water bubble over you. This is the only beach in the West Indies—and perhaps in the world—with a waterfall.

The road from Dunn's River leads through Fern Gully, and the temperature drops ten degrees as the car enters a wonderland of greens. The tree ferns in this lush gully are so large that they almost meet overhead; the golden sunlight is so filtered through the deep greens that there are only occasional flashes of chartreuse on the road.

Fern Gully is a garden of tropical ferns. Almost every variety can be found, and many tropical flowers grow intermingled with the lacy plants. Giant fernlike elephant's tongues grow here, as does the walking fern, which bends over so far that the tip forms a new root. The familiar maidenhair fern grows in the moist areas, with the stately tree ferns waving high above. There are also swamp fern and sword fern. This is literally a velvet forest, with every variety of fern from the midget one-cell fronds to the colossal many-branched trees.

After a swim in Dunn's River and the drive through Fern Gully, you can get an excellent lunch at the Tower Isle Hotel, sixty miles from Montego Bay and another sixty from the ideal overnight place, Port Antonio. Tower Isle is Jamaica's largest resort hotel. It has tennis courts, croquet, shuffleboard, and archery. Horses are available for riding around the countryside, and golf may be played at a near-by country club. Facilities are available for spear-fishing, surf-boating, water-skiing, and snorkeling. Sailboats and a deep-sea fishing boat may be hired. This area near the town of Ocho Rios abounds in excellent hotels.

The sixty miles from Ocho Rios to Port Antonio is along a fast, all-paved road. A few picturesque towns along the way break up the monotony of the beach: Port Maria, Annotto Bay, Buff Bay, Hope Bay, and St. Margaret's Bay. Finally the cluttered harbor of Port Antonio comes into view. A bustling village with crowded, narrow streets and very old buildings lines the port. From the village it takes only a few moments to reach the famous Tichfield Hotel, a sprawling structure once owned by cinema actor Errol Flynn.

Arrangements can be made here for Jamaica's most exciting scenic trip, rafting down the Rio Grande. It is also possible to make arrangements for the rafting trip in the town of Port Antonio or at Bonnie View, a small but excellent hostelry that overlooks the town, harbor, and palm-fringed Navy Island in the distance.

A driver for your car must be hired, for he will have to drive you to the rafting center near the village of Berrydale and then take the car to wait at the end of the trip near St. Margaret's, close to the mouth of the Rio Grande.

The first view of the raft is prepossessing. A group of flat bamboo poles lashed together with wire and a seat built across the back third make up the vessel. A brawny, black, gleaming athlete with a long rafting pole completes the picture. As visitors arrive at the rafting center, the raftsmen argue over which boatload will go out first. There is little brawling over which man will take the raft down, for an organization requiring the men to take trips in rotation has been formed. Each raft carries two or three passengers in addition to the raftsman, known as the captain.

The ideal costume for rafting is a bathing suit (so that you can go for a swim along the way) plus a long-sleeved cotton shirt to shield you from too much sun. It is a good plan to take a thermos of rum, brandy, or lemonade, and a packet of sandwiches. Although the trip lasts only a little over one hour, a picnic along the way can be very pleasant, and a couple of drinks of rum come in very handy in case a sudden rainstorm breaks. This frequently happens, as this area has the highest precipitation on the entire island.

When the little raft is shoved off, a group of boys between the ages of three and seven suddenly appears, playing simple tunes on reed pipes. They wade into the water as the raft moves out, continuing their serenade until the water reaches their necks. They expect, and usually receive, a shilling or two.

The early part of the trip is smooth. Long vistas are revealed as the river winds its way down through quiet fields. As the buoyant craft descends, the river becomes narrower. Yellow and orange bamboo groves grow high along the banks. The tamarind tree and coconut palm crowd close along the shores.

On each side of the river various phases of human activities glide by like a series of life-sized color slides seen through an incredibly brilliant projector. Intent women, skirts tucked high, search for tiny succulent river shrimp; young boys, apprentice raftsmen, move upstream, dragging the bamboo floats back to the starting-place. Sometimes, like Volga boatmen, they pull the rafts with ropes from a path alongside the riverbank. At other times they are forced by the contours of the bank to wade along, pushing the raft ahead of them.

Rafting along the Rio Grande has been going on for well over fifty years. No man among the raftsmen can actually remember when it started, but they will tell you that the oldest raftsman died many years ago. They take great pride in their operation of the fragile craft and have a reputation for never spilling a passenger into the water. The rafts are named after ocean liners.

As the river narrows, long liana vines hang down from the trees on either side. The raft floats lazily beneath them. Two great rocks appear in the river, and between them is a magnificent deep pool ideal for a swim. The raftsman stops while passengers dive off and swim around in the vivid blue, marvelously clear, fresh water. A short way down the river from here a peninsula juts out which is ideal for a picnic.

Then comes the exhilaration of shooting the rapids. Although by no means dangerous, it is very exciting. The little craft turns and whirls as the raftsman guides it between rocks through the channel. Spray jets back through the bamboo frame. Shortly after the rapids, the end of the trip is reached. A short walk up the bank to the waiting car, and the exciting experience of rafting down the Rio Grande is over. But it is possible to do it all over again the next day.

No visit to Jamaica is complete without a few days in the area of Kingston. This is the largest city and the capital of the island. The harbor, one of the six best in the world, has facilities permitting ocean liners to dock in the very heart of the city. As the big cruise ships come in, small, naked Negro boys dive off the dockside. They swim out toward the ship, pleading with the passengers to toss down a dime or a shilling. Tourist facilities are carefully geared to service the cruise passenger; a special police escort meets each incoming ship, and the Tourist Trade Development Board maintains a large office adjacent to the docks.

Because passengers land near King and Harbour streets, shopping is convenient. The retail stores on these streets normally close at two o'clock on Wednesdays, but when a cruise ship is in, they remain open all afternoon.

A shopping innovation that is fast making Jamaica one of the three chief buying centers in the Caribbean is the Free Port shop. Merchandise from all over the world is stored in bond; samples are displayed in the shop; and the traveler can buy without paying tax or duty. As far as visitors are concerned, Jamaica has become a "free port" and prices are as low as those in the Dutch and French islands, but stocks are more limited. Buyers are not permitted to pick up their merchandise, but must have it delivered to the boat or the airport in bond. No local citizen is allowed to buy free-port merchandise.

Kingston itself is unprepossessing, but has two outstanding places to visit. Within the ruins of Fort Charles, where Lord Nelson was once stationed, there is a plaque reading: "In memory of Admiral Horatio Nelson, 1758–1805. You who tread his footsteps; remember his glory." Nelson's quarterdeck, a portion of the fort which still remains, re-creates the atmosphere of the days when he paced along these ramparts behind the cannon facing out to sea. The fort is deserted except for an occasional visitor and a young Negro boy who knows the legends and acts as guide.

The point where Fort Charles is located is all that remains of the wicked and wealthy city of Port Royal, which was completely destroyed by a violent earthquake and tidal wave in 1692. Twenty-five hundred houses were razed and a large percentage of the population was lost. The wealth and wickedness that made Port Royal famous were derived from the piracy of its citizens. Here the treasure from captured vessels was divided and spent. Captain Henry Morgan, the pirate who later became Lieutenant Governor of Jamaica, amassed most of his wealth in Port Royal. It was generally believed throughout Jamaica that the terrible devastation of the city was brought on by its evil ways.

Before leaving Fort Charles, a visit to St. Peter's Church, also destroyed by the earthquake of 1692 but rebuilt in 1725, is indicated. Here some of the silver of Morgan the pirate has been preserved in an ancient press, or cabinet, dating from the same period. The key, almost as big as a man's hand, weighs over a half a pound. An ornate silver flagon with a whistle at the base enabled the Captain to summon servants when the flagon was empty. Here also is preserved a delicately proportioned wine chalice now used at communion ceremonies in the church.

Kingston's second-greatest attraction is the Institute of Jamaica, the cultural center of the city. The extensive museum contains an iron cage once used to imprison women slaves. A hook on top was used to hang the cage, and round iron bands enclosed the waist, head, hips, and legs. There are also leg shackles and steel necklaces constructed to keep slaves from escaping. The museum has very fine examples of Arawak tools—files and rasps made of coral, cups made of shells, flint knives—and of delicately shaped clay vessels.

The most unusual exhibit is a glass case containing the famous "shark papers." These documents, which were found in the belly of a shark in 1799, proved that the United States brig *Nancy*, which had been captured by the British, was actually giving aid to their enemies and was therefore a legitimate prize of war. The papers are still well preserved, along with the affidavit of the lieutenant who recovered them.

In addition to the museum, the Institute operates an art gallery and, in the annex across the street, has an art school and display room for Jamaica's children. A number of European and native painters work on the island, and the children, with the encouragement of the adults, show promise of developing a highly distinctive style of West Indian painting.

An outstanding experiment in education is in progress in the Mona district a few miles outside Kingston. The University College of the West Indies, opened in 1948, offers a university education to British and West Indians able to qualify. It is a branch of the University of London. It offers courses in medicine, science, and the liberal arts. Located in the foothills of the Blue Mountains seven miles from Kingston, with a ridge rising nearly two thousand feet behind the modern white buildings, it has one of the most beautiful campuses in the world. Modern buildings are functional as well as attractive. The side walls of classrooms are almost nonexistent, a plan allowing a breeze to sweep through almost as though the rooms were open under the cool shade trees. A view of hundreds of students ranging in color from white to black and wearing scarlet undergraduate gowns is an unforgettable sight. The bright gowns are a result of the request of the university that its academic dress might be copied after the fashion of St. Andrew's in Scotland. The request was granted.

Among its facilities the University College includes a hospital, a well-stocked library, and research equipment for science and medical departments. Expenses are borne by the British West Indian islands in proportion to their population. There is no color problem here. The undergraduates represent all the many nationalities that have built up the population of these islands: African, Chinese, Syrian, and varieties of European. There has never been a problem in race relationships; these groups have studied together harmoniously since the opening of the university.

After-dark entertainment in Kingston is limited to dances at private clubs, cocktail parties, motion-picture shows, and such public open-to-all night spots as the Glass Bucket and the Colony. These rowdy night clubs occasionally offer good native entertainers and second- or third-rate imported artists. Orchestras are loud and "hot," and the audience is usually over fifty-per-cent non-resident. Prices are reasonable, but food and service are poor. The Club Havana, a dine-and-dance hall on the outskirts of Kingston, is built in a circle with the center of the room open to the sky. It is lighted almost exclusively by moonlight, which means that near the tables it is very, very dark. The band beats out Jamaica Calypsos and sentimental stateside music, but specializes in the mambos, rumbas, and sambas of Cuba. The Chinese food is good and inexpensive.

The city has an undeserved reputation as an extremely dangerous place for tourists at night. It is true that in some sections, as in London, Paris, and New York, it is inadvisable for strangers to visit alone, but the efficient police force carefully notes and controls the vice-ridden areas. There is, however, a great deal of prostitution in Kingston caused by the hundreds of country girls who come to the city and are unable to find work. They have a saying: "Gel com to get wuk instead get pinkney [baby]." Most of these girls work out of small barrooms with brothels attached. Patrons are primarily the thousands of sailors who visit Kingston during the year. There is one major difference between the Jamaica prostitute and her sisters in the United States and Europe: she is quiet, reserved, and ladylike. She never solicits attention and is willing to dance or talk for a couple of drinks without suggesting that the relationship go any further. Her attitude is one of acquiescence. Unfortunately, the venereal-disease rate in Kingston is much higher than in the rest of the island.

At six in the morning, traffic begins to pour into Kingston over its limited highways. By noon the roads are crawling with cars, trucks, bicycles, wagons, pushcarts, and pedestrians. The most serious traffic pile-up is on the main artery leading to Spanish Town, once the capital of the island, known by the Spanish as Sant' Jago de la Vega.

Little of the Spanish influence remains. The most interesting sight is the odd memorial to a British sea hero, Admiral Rodney, who defeated the French when they set out to attack Jamaica. The statue is enclosed in an octagonal temple built in the Spanish Renaissance style. On either side a colonnade of Ionic columns supports a balustrade. The temple dome is surmounted by a cupola. But the statue itself is more amazing than its pink-and-white setting. Rodney is cast as a conqueror in Grecian toga and sandals, with his sword extended. The Cathedral of St. Catherine, oldest church on the island, has a floor covered with memorials to distinguished soldiers, planters, and governors, with interesting epitaphs.

The southwest area of the island, between May Pen (farms are known as pens) and Clarendon, includes Jamaica's richest fruit-growing section. Along the road orange, grapefruit, lime, and tangerine trees dominate the scenery. About fifty miles from Kingston on this route is Mandeville, an important resort for Jamaica's resident British population. Two thousand feet above sea level, it is always pleasantly cool. Because of its climate, it is popular in both summer and winter. Mandeville is typically British, with a village square that, except for the majestic royal palms, could be found in the English countryside. It is a quiet resort with a good golf club and picturesque bridle paths. There is no night life at all.

West of Mandeville, the Black River, Jamaica's largest, winds through fertile valleys down toward the alligator country. Actually Jamaica has no true alligators, but crocodiles are plentiful. They are similar to the Egyptian crocodile, having a long sharp nose and a smaller body than the American alligator. The terrapin, called the pond turtle in Jamaica, is also found in this region. The tortoise-shell ornaments made by the natives come from this turtle, not from a tortoise. During the mosquito season the anopheles and the stegomyia are plentiful along the coast. Jamaica is fortunate in not having any yellow fever for the stegomyia to carry. This southwest coastal area has great natural beauty, and contains some of the island's finest fishing-grounds. Tarpon, snapper, stone bass, and snook are abundant.

Because this section is a considerable distance from the points of entry to Jamaica, it has remained relatively unexplored. During 1954 exploration by the Basic Metals Corporation was begun at Negril (on the island's western tip) for oil and gas, and between Mandeville and Negril lie many of the bauxite deposits that have increased the prosperity of the island.

The coconut-palm beach at Negril is completely untouched by man; when developed, it should become one of the great resorts of the world. Between Negril and Green Island there is no road at present; the country is like a virgin forest preserve. Little white sand beaches are revealed in every cove. This is particularly true from Green Island around the coast through the villages of Lucea and Redding and on to Montego Bay, where this visit to Jamaica began.

JAMAICA: *The Royal Jamaican Band plays for an outdoor concert.*

Above: JAMAICA: *The ruins of Rose Hall, one of the most elaborate great houses.*
Below: JAMAICA: *The entire north shore has long beaches and lush foliage.*
Following pages: JAMAICA: *Montego Bay, with Doctor's Cave Beach in the background.*

MONTSERRAT

The natives of this small, rocky, but fertile island, almost all of African descent, speak English with a distinct Irish brogue; oversize frogs called crapauds are the greatest culinary delicacy; all the sugar is used to make rum; and prices are the lowest in the entire Caribbean.

Shaped like an arrowhead with the sharp tip pointed north, Montserrat is twenty-seven miles southwest of Antigua and about the same distance southeast of Nevis. Mountainous, Montserrat has adequate rainfall, and its hills, valleys, and coastal areas are green and fertile. High slopes and well-forested mountains dominate the terrain, with Chance Mountain (2,999 feet) the highest point.

Half of the land is under cultivation, mostly in sea-island cotton and tomatoes. There is a ready market for the cotton, but because there is no tomato-canning plant, this crop must be limited. A real opportunity awaits such a project, for tomatoes are grown easily and labor costs are low. Another interesting opportunity exists for a privately owned and operated electric plant to supply the island. The Government would arrange to subsidize such a project and would make unusual tax concessions. A few plantations run their own electric plants, but the lack of light and power has handicapped the island's development.

Over one hundred miles of roads stretch around the hills, but two thirds of them are little more than mule tracks or plantation roads suitable only for horses, mules, and jeeps. Horseback riding is a recommended and popular way to see the countryside. Rental of horses by the day or week is amazingly low, and good mounts are available.

The island's motor vehicles consist of a few jeeps and about one hundred and twenty-five passenger cars.

The town of Plymouth is a line of red-roofed stone and wood white buildings set against the high green plateau of St. George's Hill. On top of the hill the ruins of Fort St. George, once the defender of the island against the French, are overgrown by dense jungle foliage. The beach on the waterfront is black sand. A small pier where passengers are landed extends out into the clear, deep water. Large ships, freighters of Canadian National or Alcoa, anchor out in the open roadstead and unload cargoes into lighters to be rowed ashore.

A small airplane service reaches Montserrat, and the access by sea is an irregular motor-launch or freighter service from Antigua and St. Kitts; by yacht; or via the many trading schooners that sail from Guadeloupe, Antigua, and other near-by islands. The trip from Antigua is short and reasonably smooth, with the prevailing northeast trades blowing all the way.

Near the town of Plymouth is Government House, one of the most beautiful residences in the islands. Set in a bright garden of tropical flowers, with tamarind and flamboyant trees, the great house rises three stories, with graceful verandas in the plantation style across the first two. Elaborate double doors lead into a broad hallway and a living-room handsomely furnished with antiques. Spacious windows look out on the garden on two sides.

The brogue of the natives comes naturally; the island was settled by a group of Irishmen sent out by Oliver Cromwell. Twice it was captured by the French, once in 1664 and again in 1782, but in neither case did they hold it long, and since 1783 it has been British. Twenty-seven estates remain today, and many carry names reminiscent of Ireland: Galways, Fergus Mountain, and Sweeneys. Most of them grow sea-island cotton exclusively, but some have experimented with tomato crops, and others are trying the cultivation of pineapples.

The road across the island heads over steep hills and deep gulleys. Most of the 13,594 people are rarely seen, so the hillsides seem deserted. Occasional schools dot the slopes (3,000 children are enrolled in the twelve schools), and these long white buildings with their groups of pupils lined up in front for gymnastics or reciting their lessons under a tree add considerably to the charm of the rugged scenery.

On Saturday, which is clinic day as well as market day, scores of women, many of them pregnant, can be seen climbing the steep paths from their primitive dwellings to see the doctor or nurse, with small children being tugged along.

Medical service is good in Montserrat, with two doctors in attendance. The island also boasts a dentist and a visiting-nurse service. The small hospital is generally well equipped, but there is no X-ray equipment.

In Plymouth a cinema sometimes runs and sometimes flickers, and films are not the latest. The most popular sport of the Europeans on the island is tennis, while cricket is the big game of the native Negroes.

Another favorite sport is the hunting of the crapaud, the tender edible frog that sometimes grows as large as a small chicken. The natives use a loop of twine, going out at dusk, approaching from the rear, and dropping the loop in front of the frog. As it leaps forward, the loop closes. To skin and clean one takes only a minute.

There are two guesthouses that take up to six visitors each, but other residents will also take guests. It is possible to live in one of these homes for as little as fifty dollars a month, three meals included. Houses to rent or buy are hard to find, but servants are plentiful. To quote from one of the bulletins issued by the Government of Montserrat, "The number of servants varies according to the size of the family and the house and standard of living. The usual minimum is a cook and a housemaid-laundress. Cooks' wages vary from $8. to $20. a month with or without meals; butlers $20. a month; housemaids $2. to $4. a week; gardeners $4. to $5. a week; chauffeurs $6. a week; messenger boy or girl $1.60 to $2.40 a week. No white servants are employed." The prices quoted above are B.W.I. currency, which means deducting almost forty per cent to translate it into United States currency.

But remember that Montserrat is not ready for a large influx of travelers expecting the luxuries of the big islands. Beaches are undeveloped and range from white to black sand. There is no night life. But the slow tempo of plantation life on Montserrat, with picnics and parties, can be very pleasant indeed.

MONTSERRAT: *A crapaud, the giant frog served as a delicacy known locally as mountain chicken.*

MONTSERRAT: *Although slopes are steep, much of the land is arable. In the distance, romantic uninhabited Redonda.*

NEVIS

Once the most important health resort of the British West Indies, Nevis, though still possessing the natural advantages of good beaches, fine climate, and exceptional scenery, has come to be almost ignored by travelers.

The wide streets of Charlestown and Newcastle, long ago colorful with Regency beaus and their fashionable ladies, and noisy with the rumble of great carriages hurrying the aristocracy to the thermal baths, are now drab and empty. An occasional two-wheeled cart joggles down the street, and a black face may be seen peering from a window, but the glamour of this once-great health resort is gone.

Yet its rural beauty has not diminished. Seen across the waters from St. Kitts, it rises dark, blue-green from the sea, to culminate in the cloud-wreathed Nevis Peak (3,596 feet). We can readily believe that Columbus, ever ready with a name for an island, was reminded by the always present white clouds on this mountain of the snow-capped peaks of Europe and called it Nieve (meaning "snow" in Spanish). There is no record of its ever having snowed in Nevis, where even in winter the temperature ranges between seventy-five and eighty degrees. The late-summer and early-fall temperatures are slightly higher, but constant trade winds cool the island all year round.

Nevis is located two miles southeast of the long peninsula that juts out from St. Kitts, and is separated from it by a passage called The Narrows. The trip from Basseterre, St. Kitts, to Charlestown, Nevis, a distance of thirteen miles, takes two hours. A motor launch leaves daily (except Sunday) from Basseterre at three p.m. and returns from Charlestown the following morning. Once a week the launch makes the round trip in one day. Although large, it is always crowded with natives visiting between the two islands; it is best to arrive quite early to get a good seat. Ask the captain for a place where you won't get drenched by sea spray when the going gets rough. This motor launch, called the *Queen Elizabeth*, is the only way to travel to and from Nevis unless you charter a schooner, fishing boat, or yacht.

The launch docks at Charlestown, capital of Nevis and the only town (the others are villages at best) on this six-by-eight-mile, almost round island. The little port of Charlestown has a pier jutting out toward the open roadstead, and the dockside includes a small Customs building and a warehouse. Back of the docks is the quiet little town.

The streets are lined with two-story, red-roofed, white houses built of stone on the first floor, wood on the second. They have wide shuttered windows, usually closed, and long balconies, some of which are enclosed almost entirely by louvers. The streets are wide, completely clean, and usually deserted.

On the edge of town is a venerable stone wall with a gateway that joins it to a small stone-and-wood house. It is surrounded by coconut palms. The gate is labeled Hamilton House, and it was probably on this site, if not in this house, that Rachel Sarah Fawcett bore her illegitimate son, Alexander. From Nevis they traveled to St. Kitts, then to St. Croix; finally the brilliant young Alexander Hamilton, who overcame every possible disadvantage of birth and early environment, went to the United States to become one of the heroes of the new republic.

From Charlestown the narrow road leads down to Bath, half a mile away. A grand eighteenth-century hotel, unfortunately closed for many years, is located near the road. Some repairs have been made on it, and plans are continually being made to reopen it. The hot baths that run underneath the hotel are, like those of St. Lucia's Soufrière, still available to the public, but the process of finding the caretaker and arranging for towels and transportation to and from the baths makes their availability of doubtful value.

It is better to spend your time going in the opposite direction, for less than one mile north of Charlestown is a fine stretch of white sand. Pinneys Beach, entirely reef-protected, has a safe, gradual slope and wonderfully clear water for bathing, spear-fishing, and snorkeling. It is very private, too; in fact, you will probably be the only one using it.

Continuing north, the road goes through the village of Cotton Ground (Nevis's big cash crop is sea-island cotton) and on to Hurrican Hill, where there is a magnificent view (elevation 1,192 feet) of St. Kitts on the west and the small island of Barbuda fifty miles to the east.

Then comes the ruined village of Newcastle, looking as though it had been devastated by an earthquake and never rebuilt. High stone houses are still open to the sky, and splendid vistas of the sea, looking much like paintings by Salvador Dali, can be seen through great gaps in the walls. Along the waterfront, fishnets are drying and men are busy building fishing boats. A few of the large stone houses date back to the early eighteenth century. In this town a white face is so rarely seen that the natives stop to look in shocked surprise as you walk the streets.

On the way to Newcastle are a lovely palm-shaded lagoon and spring where Captain Horatio Nelson of H.M.S. *Boreas* found fresh water to supply his ships. It is an enchanting tropical scene, with small and large black boys running naked in the lagoon behind tiny ships they have made of bark with a twig for a mast and a leaf for a sail. Driving through this section during the rainy season (October, November, December) can be hazardous, as the road becomes almost impassable with the overflow from the lagoon.

It is not many miles from this point to Montpelier House, at which only the gate columns still stand. Here young Nelson found his first love, the pretty twenty-two-year-old widow Frances Hebert Nisbet. They were married on March 11, 1787, and no less a personage than the Duke of Clarence, later William IV of England, was on hand for the ceremony. The marriage register still reposes in the rectory at Fig Tree church; in it the names of Nelson and Nisbet may be seen today.

The windward side of Nevis has almost continuously good white sand beaches that back up to copra estates, with slender coconut palms framing the shore. The surf is too rough for good swimming except in some of the protected coves.

From the east-coast beaches and coconut groves the road cuts across the southern part of the island from Zion Hill village through Fig Tree and on to Charlestown. Magnificent vistas may be seen along the drive, and colorful semi-tropical foliage catches the eye all along the way. Occasionally a settlement is reached. Groups of children studying their lessons outdoors under a large banyan are a common sight. There are ten government primary schools supported by public funds, and one private school. Most of the sessions are held outdoors, partly because the buildings are too small, partly because it is cooler under the trees.

Fig Tree church, on the last lap of the way to Charlestown, should not be missed. It is a graceful structure of fieldstone set in the midst of eighteenth- and nineteenth-century tombstones.

Back in Charlestown there is a hotel that serves good drinks and unpretentious but appetizing food. Its biggest feature is a balcony overlooking the sea. It is even possible to have your dinner served on your own section of this gallery. Nevis has no organized night life, and not much unorganized except that engineered by United States or British sailors. A native bar or two and an occasional cocktail party given by the European residents are it.

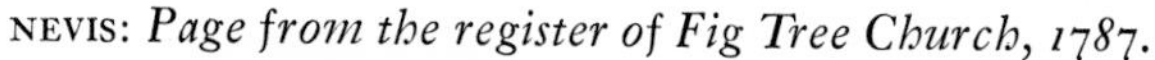

NEVIS: *Page from the register of Fig Tree Church, 1787.*

Thomas Erskine, Gentleman, to
1787
March 11. Horatio Nelson, Esquire, Captain of his Maj
Frances Herbert Nisbet, W
May 18. Andrew Hamilton, Esquire, to Ma
April 30. George Douglas, free Mulatto, to Mary
Herbert, free Mulatto.
1790
18. Charles Deming, Gentleman, to Amelia
Brodbelt, Spinster.
26. John Tobin, Coffee Planter, to Polly Burke,
Spinster.
Gentleman, to Mary
Spinster.

NEVIS: *The almost deserted village of Newcastle, once a center of British commerce.*

NEVIS: *Outdoor school in a tree-shaded classroom near Charlestown.*

NEVIS: *Here Horatio Nelson, who married Frances Nisbet on the island, came to obtain fresh water for his ships.*

REDONDA

Some islands are enchanting because of their appearance, others because of the people who live on them. Not so Redonda. This bare, rocky knoll one mile long by half a mile across lies between Nevis and Montserrat. Every inch of its one-thousand-foot elevation is barren and forbidding. As for people, there are none. Yet this is an enchanting island, for it has a living legend. As told by the Honorable Charlesworth Ross, Commissioner of the Island of Montserrat, the story began in 1865—almost four hundred years after Columbus passed it by and named it Santa Maria de Redonda—when a hardheaded Irishman named Matthew Dowdy Shiel, who was cruising between Montserrat and Nevis, saw the island and claimed it for his newborn son.

Shiel professed himself to be a descendant of early Irish kings. He had fathered eight daughters, and suddenly decided that his only son must inherit a kingdom, albeit a small one. He waited until young Matthew Phipps Shiel was fifteen years old. Then he sailed to Antigua, took a parson aboard, and set out for Redonda. Landing on the grim little island, he founded his dynasty, naming his son King Felipe the First. After one day of celebration they left the island to the goats and birds.

While the boy was growing up, old Matthew Shiel continued to barrage the Colonial Office in London with claims to the island of Redonda. Finally the Colonial Office tacitly admitted his claim. They awarded him a pension, which he received all his life.

King Felipe grew up in London to become the well-known writer M. P. Shiel. He discussed his kingdom lightly with many of his friends, and appointed several of them dukes of his realm. About a year before his death, in 1947, he requested passage back to Redonda, but the Colonial Office turned down his application.

Having no son to carry on his claim to the remote island kingdom, M. P. Shiel appointed his friend and favorite poet, John Gawsworth (Ian Fytton Armstrong), his legitimate successor. The succession was assured by the ancient rite of blood-brotherhood: they cut their wrists and mingled their blood. Then, when Shiel died in 1947, Gawsworth became King Juan the First. As Gawsworth's poetic career progressed, he established more and more dukedoms of Redonda. The list of dukes, past and present, is certainly imposing. It includes Dylan Thomas, Dorothy L. Sayers, Alfred A. Knopf, Eden Phillpotts, Henry Miller, and—as Grand Duke—Victor Gollancz.

The bleak little island of Redonda still stands deserted, of no importance to anyone except as a literary legend.

SAINT KITTS (SAINT CHRISTOPHER)

An island of grotesquely twisted volcanic lava; small, black-faced, gray monkeys; Shorty's international hotel; great sugar estates; the final resting-place of the first settler of the British West Indies (pioneer Sir Thomas Warner); site of the greatest fortress ever built in a new world; the mother colony of both the French and the British West Indies, with a history reaching back to 1623—all this is St. Kitts.

Columbus named it St. Christopher after the patron saint of travelers, or after himself, no one is quite sure. But the name did not stick, for the efficient British colonists soon began referring to it by the affectionate diminutive St. Kitts. Before the Admiral of the Ocean Seas arrived, the original Caribs had named it Liamugia, the "fertile land." Even today its deep-brown earth, adequate rainfall, broad valleys, and evergreen hills attest to their descriptive accuracy.

Travel from the United States to St. Kitts is convenient and relatively inexpensive. Golden Rock Aerodrome is only one mile from the leading city, Basseterre (population 8,000)—do not confuse with Guadeloupe's capital—and planes arrive daily from Puerto Rico, one hundred and eighty-five miles northwest, and Antigua, fifty miles southwest. Basseterre is busy with schooners from Nevis, ten miles away, Antigua, the Netherlands-French island of Sint Maarten, Montserrat, Barbuda, and St. Barts. Freighters from the United States, Canada, and Great Britain call regularly at this busy crossroads of the northern Caribee islands.

Viewed from the sea, verdant hills rise steeply back of the neat red, white, and green waterfront buildings and culminate in Mount Misery, the 4,314-foot peak that overlooks the entire island. Because St. Kitts gets more rain than many of her sister islands, the peak of Mount Misery is rarely visible, being mostly shrouded in dramatic clouds.

A small wooden pier juts out into the harbor, and passengers are sent ashore in lighters, rowed in by brawny black islanders. (St. Kitts is almost pure Negro. Less than one per cent of the population is white, but there are a number of mulattoes.) From the dock it is only a few steps to the colorful Treasury, Customs, and Health Building, cool and spacious inside, the outside blending British architectural solidity with French decoration to create a distinctive West Indian structure. Hundreds of feet of intricate iron grillwork make a romantic Gallic gallery, while continuous grillwork arches enclose another attractive porch that runs the entire length of the building. Back of the galleries, the structure is native stone painted black, with high white-brick-framed windows and white shutters, and is crowned with a red cupola of Oriental design. You enter this odd building through a center archway painted green and coral. Customs inspections here are likely to be more leisurely than at the airport, where everyone is rushed through. But here at the port much petty smuggling is attempted, and the Customs men work hard and slowly at their jobs.

From the Treasury building you step out into the very center of Basseterre. Four wide streets lead to the Circus, a central area with a high green Victorian clock-tower with a fountain at the base. The main streets meet at this point in the center of Basseterre. On one corner there is a vine-covered stone wall with a small gate and a stairway leading to a cool white balcony. This is the entrance to Shorty's, a hotel without luxuries, but, largely because of the personalities of the proprietor and his wife, blessed with considerable charm. It also has a great crossroads bar where the flow of conversation is as good and as continuous as the drinks. A local Planter's Punch, with the emphasis on the last word, is a specialty. It is a concoction of fresh lime (hours off the tree), homemade sugar (semi-refined), and a double portion of well-aged rum from Barbados (St. Kitts makes no rum because of a religious tradition). The sugar and lime are mixed first, rum is added, and then the entire drink is shaken thoroughly with lots of cracked ice. It is poured into a glass, bitters and nutmeg are floated on top, and the result is delicious.

The polished mahogany bar is arranged so that customers can sit along three sides, making conversation easy. On the wall back of the bar a large sign with a picture of a camel reads: "A camel can go eight days without a drink—but who wants to be a camel?" Other colorful signs promote KLM Airlines, Bols Gin, and Vat 19 Rum from Trinidad.

The lobby or lounge just off the bar is as cluttered as the bar is simple. Its heavy, locally made chairs and imported overstuffed sofa give an air of Gothic solidity. A blue ceiling with silver stars looks down, while from one wall a picture of George VI printed in bright colors gravely contemplates an ancient victrola. There is a cabinet full of old gilt-edged record albums bearing such names as Beniamino Gigli, Harry Lauder, John McCormack, Enrico Caruso, Amelita Galli-Curci, and Mary Garden. A large piano made by Heintzman of Toronto has an excellent tone, and next to it hangs a color print of a Dutch interior by P. de Hooch. The lobby is separated from the bar by a lattice screen.

A small dance could easily be held in any of the bedrooms in Shorty's Hotel. They give the general impression of an arena even after two large iron double beds, an old-fashioned armoire, and a rocking-chair have been added. Later in the evening, when the mosquito bars and netting have been put up, they begin to look a little less spacious. The dining-room is undistinguished, but tables line one side of the balcony to allow semi-outdoor dining.

Travelers to St. Kitts would do well to try a little restaurant not far from Shorty's Hotel: Restaurante de Consulo, where Chef Elada serves a fine meal if he knows you are coming. He is likely to tell you that "But for me and my food the United States Navy would be drunk all the time they are in St. Kitts." For further culinary exploration, try Kool Korner, a not so cool pension that serves good Creole dishes and has one ultra-modern front room with private bath. The other rooms in this little hotel are clean, but not so modern.

Basseterre has one other hostelry, called the New Royal. It lacks the personality of Shorty's and the cuisine of Kool Korner, but, being on the waterfront and overlooking the port, has a continuous breeze. Freshly painted rooms and more private baths are being added.

Before setting out to explore St. Kitts, one should understand that this is not a resort island. Beaches exist, but they are only fair—and Nevis has better ones. St. Kitts is exciting to explore, and no traveler to the Lesser Antilles should miss an expedition to Brimstone Hill Fortress, which rivals the Pyramids in Egypt in size and difficulty of construction by hand labor.

Once known by the British as the Gibraltar of the West, this sprawling giant of stone and mortar stands seven hundred and fifty feet high over waving fields of sugar cane. It is built on a steep plateau. The older natives say that their grandfathers said that this precipitous flat-topped mountain was once the top of Mount Misery, but was blown off by the volcano and deposited near the sea. The long view of Brimstone Hill and Fort George shows a huge mound of earth with a flat line of stone buildings across the top and a long flight of hand-hewn steps marching down the side of the mountain. Drive up the curving road that leads to these steps, then climb them to the top. The grade is not difficult, and exciting new vistas unfold as you go ever higher. It is an easy trip for all, including children and the elderly.

The fortress was built by the British with forced slave labor. (A certain number of slaves was taken from each plantation.) The feat of building anything so grandiose without any mechanical devices to aid them must have presented many obstacles. In this sense, Brimstone Hill can be compared to Henri-Christophe's Citadel in Haiti.

Arriving at the foot of the steps, you pay a small sum to the caretaker and proceed through the entrance arch. At the top of the steps, you cross the parade ground, where grass is beginning to grow between the large flagstones. Across the parade ground there is a magnificent view, a favorite with photographers, of the island of Sint Eustatius framed through a high stone arch, with the green shoreline of St. Kitts in the foreground. It merges into the ultramarine sea, with the gigantic cone of Sint Eustatius rising into the clouds in the distance. All around, cannon on carriages point through their ports toward the sea. One points directly at Sint Eustatius, others point toward the green hillocks shaped like the pointed breasts of young girls rising tier upon tier into the low-hanging clouds. All of the fortress is still here, and the steps of the men can almost be heard as you walk through the mess halls, the officers' quarters, and the soldiers' barracks.

In 1781, when the French landed to capture the island, they found at the base of Brimstone Hill many guns and much ammunition that the British had been unable to drag to the top. The French put these to good use, and the fortress capitulated when it was com pletely surrounded by French artillery fire. Only one British soldier was killed. Two years later St. Kitts was ceded back to England by France.

On the way from Basseterre to Brimstone Hill is the village of Old Road, where Thomas Warner and his band of settlers first landed. They set up their first permanent settlement northwest of this village at Sandy Point. But the French under the command of d'Esnambuc arrived almost simultaneously, and formed the first permanent French settlement in the Caribbean islands. Dividing the island, these first two early groups lived in peace for a number of years. They even joined to resist the Spanish, but by 1664 the French had taken over St. Kitts. In 1713 it became British. In 1781 it was regained by the French for two years, and since 1783 has been British. The name of the capital and many of the villages stem from the French occupation, as does the Creole cooking.

Also on the way to Brimstone Hill is the tomb of Sir Thomas Warner, who, in addition to forming the first settlements with his two sons, one by his English wife and one by his Carib mistress, was a great historical figure in the early days of West Indies colonization. The grave of Sir Thomas is located on a rise on the grounds of St. Thomas church in an overgrown and largely untended area. The tomb itself is covered with a slab of white marble broken across the center and chipped on one corner. His epitaph reads in part:

First Read then weepe when thou art hereby taught
That Warner lyes interr'd here, one that bought
With loss of noble bloud the Illustrious Name
Of a Commander Greate in Acts of Fame
Traynd from his youth in Armes his Courage bold
Attempted brave exploites, and Vncontrold
By fortunes fiercest frownes hee still gave forth
Large Narratiues of Military worth.

The white tomb is covered by a roof held up by arched wooden posts painted white, but the paint is beginning to flake and the posts are becoming rickety. This historically important gravestone is diffi- cult to photograph, for the canopy throws a shadow across the slab on which the epitaph is written. The near-by church of St. Thomas interests many visitors.

From Brimstone Hill the road follows the coastline around the island to the black rocks where the lava flow from an early eruption has cooled into fantastic shapes. The stones are damp and dangerously slippery with lichen. Camera lenses fog quickly with salt spray from the seething surf that boils up between the huge, forbidding rocky formations. The highest and most unusual formations are just off the shore, rising out of the surf. They can best be seen in the early morning when the sun outlines the shapes and throws reflections and highlights into the pools formed by the ebb and flow of the waves.

Mount Misery, near the Black Rocks, can be climbed in some three to four hours. It is a difficult climb through thick virgin forest, and although the view from the top is rewarding, it does not compare with the views from the Soufrières on Guadeloupe, Saba, and St. Vincent, or from Mont Pelée in Martinique.

The people of St. Kitts are friendly, dignified, and proud of their island. The Government is unusually efficient, and there has been a great deal of slum-clearance work since 1952. Many of the trash-roofed huts are disappearing, to be replaced by more comfortable wood and tar-paper houses. This does not add to the appearance of the island, but it is easy to see that the native population is bettering its condition. Throughout the school system, modern educational techniques, including the use of film strips, are being used, and the effect is reflected in the ability and intelligence of the natives.

Unlike most sugar islands (more is produced here than in any of the Lesser Antilles except Barbados and Trinidad), St. Kitts also has a high cotton yield; in addition, a considerable amount of subsistence farming is done in the fertile valleys. The sugar cane grows down into the sea and up into the hills. Just a mile out of Basseterre is the Central Sugar Factory, where, with ultra-modern equipment, cane is ground and refined on a co-operative basis. Visitors are welcome to the plant.

From this factory, Monkey Hill, a high green knoll (1,319 feet) is visible. It is named for the St. Kitts monkey, a small, black-faced, long-tailed marsupial with gray fur which lives in the depths of the forest. It is believed that these monkeys were originally brought in by early French settlers and set free when the French were dispossessed by the British. They found the semi-tropical climate and the natural food supply to their liking, and multiplied very rapidly. At one time the island was overrun with them and they were widely hunted for food and fur. An occasional one may now be seen in the woods. In Basseterre they are kept as pets by some families.

St. Kitts is not recommended to anyone looking for luxurious accommodations and good developed beaches. But it is a great place to sit in the bar and talk or to travel around seeing the historic sights for a day or two—and then to take off for Nevis across The Narrows.

SAINT KITTS: *Coconut palms and sugar cane grow down to the sea.*

SAINT KITTS: *The center of busy Basseterre; Shorty's Hotel is behind the clock.*

SAINT LUCIA

Many of the Caribbean islands have quiescent volcanoes, but this twenty-seven-by-fourteen-mile mountainous strip of land can claim the most distinctive Soufrière of all. It has a drive-in volcano where an automobile can come within one hundred feet of the steaming, sulphurous rocks and boiling springs. Reminiscent of the geysers and pools in Yellowstone Park in the United States, it has an even greater visual impact because the spectacle is confined to a single volcanic crater.

St. Lucia is twenty-one miles north of St. Vincent and about the same distance south of Martinique. It is part of the same volcanic chain. Its history has been tragic, for between 1498 and 1834 the island changed from French to British control and back fourteen times with considerable bloodshed. As a result, it suffers today from a split personality. The native mulattoes and Negroes who make up ninety-five per cent of the 84,812 population speak a French-English patois. The cooking has a French accent, but the British influence has been felt enough to make the food generally uninspired. The small hotels (none of them larger then a pension) serve what they hope British and American visitors will enjoy rather than what they themselves like.

St. Lucia is semi-tropical rather than tropical. The climate varies from warm to hot, the trade winds blow almost constantly, and mountains rise up as high as three thousand feet (Mount Gimie, 3,145). At the southwestern corner of St. Lucia are the most famous landmarks of the Lesser Antilles—Gros Piton (2,619 feet) and Petit Piton (2,461 feet). These twin cones rise steeply out of the quiet sea. They mark the location of the drowsy village of Soufrière, a little town nestled close to their base which is the second-largest community on the island. From this village, expeditions can be made to the volcano to view and photograph its wonders. It is only about two miles from the town, and cars are available for hire.

Although traveling to the volcano is easy, getting to the village of Soufrière is no simple matter. There is no direct road down the western shore of the island from Castries, the capital, and the only available road, running two thirds of the way around the island, is a long, rough journey. Travelers who arrive by plane come into Vigie Airport, the only Caribbean airport with a private beach, which is located quite close to Castries. Fortunately for visitors who want to go to Soufrière to see the unusual volcano, a daily mail launch sails along the coast. It takes about two hours from Castries to the little harbor nestled under the Pitons. It is possible to stay overnight in Soufrière, see the volcano and explore the town, and take the mail boat back the next day. Soufrière has two small but clean hotels.

The actual exploration of Soufrière should consist of more than a view from a car. Walk into the center of the gray, smoking, crater-like area, taking care not to burn your feet in one of the hot pools. To be on the inside of a volcano looking out is an amazing experience. Around you are hissing jets of steam, and beyond the steam stand the high red immortelle trees that cover the hills along the lip of the crater. The experience is like a sudden but safe descent into one of Dante's visions of the Inferno.

Picking up a guide at Soufrière is no problem: the guide is more likely to pick you up. He will lead you, after your inner view of the crater, to the once-famous hot baths located directly above the crater entrance. These baths were built by Louis XVI for the health and comfort of the French garrison on the island. Now the stone troughs are discolored by age and rarely used, but your guide will lead you through a thicket and then to an ancient wooden enclosure. Inside are tubs with hot water running through them. If you want a bath—and it is an exhilarating experience—the guide will clean out the tub, plug up the opening, and stand guard at the door while you luxuriate in one of the few natural hot baths now available in the entire Lesser Antilles.

The pleasures of visiting Soufrière do not end with the volcano and the baths. The tiny fishing village at the base of the Pitons is always an interesting sight, with children of all ages playing along the beach, fishing boats being repaired, and fishermen setting out for the day or coming home with their catch. The village is located along a lovely beach with coconut palms framing the two Pitons against the sky across the bay. The Pitons themselves offer a challenge to adventurous rock-climbers. Their sides are steep and heavy with brush. Thousands of birds nest on the rock ledges, which are said to be the habitat of the dreaded fer de lance, the poisonous snake found only in St. Lucia and Martinique. Any story of climbers being bitten by the fer de lance, however, is entirely untraceable.

Back in Soufrière, lunch at either the Home Hotel or the Phoenix can be very pleasant, with simple native cooking. It is important to let the hotel know whether you will be there for lunch, for otherwise there may not be enough food available. Soufrière has few visitors, but is eager to attract many more. There is no night life—indeed, no activity after dark. To any visitor who may elect to drive back around the east coast of the island to Castries, a word of warning. The distance is only sixty miles, but the trip can take all day. The road is good in spots, very bad in others. It is often steep and narrow, with extreme curves. The scenery is magnificent, ranging from clumps of flaming immortelle trees sheltering cocoa trees beneath them, to Vieux Fort, a quiet fishing village with a tiny harbor full of small boats. Below Dennery on the east coast the road forks. One branch goes over the mountains while the other follows the Grand Cul de Sac River flowing down from Mount Gimie to Grand Cul de Sac Bay near Castries. The road is also a very high one and finally leads to Morne Fortuné above the port of Castries.

Castries from this point looks like a much larger city than it is. There is a square look about the harbor caused by the docks being built out to deep water so that large ships can come directly into the town. In addition to the view, Morne Fortuné has Fort Charlotte, still in comparatively good condition and an excellent example of the type of fortifications built in the late eighteenth century. Islanders are proud that the Duke of Kent (father of Queen Victoria) hoisted the Union Jack over the fortress when he captured it in 1794. Today's visitors, however, are more likely to be interested in the magnificent cannonball trees at the top of Morne Fortuné. Their blossoms are unusual, and they bear round, heavy fruit that looks exactly like cannon balls. One reason Castries looks so large from above is that it has had a series of disastrous fires. Instead of rebuilding on top of the ruins, the city has built up alongside them. Modern buildings face completely gutted remains that give the city a highly distinctive look.

No distinguished architecture can be noted, but an indefinable, languid, tropical aura is generally felt. In spite of the shells of houses with flowers and green shrubs growing inside, a feeling of life going on pleasantly prevails.

The harbor is a particularly busy shipping center where sugar, copra, bananas, and cocoa go out, and foodstuffs and building materials come in. Because ships can come alongside the wharfs, occasional cruise ships and a number of scheduled freight vessels put in. Dominating the town itself is a large movie theater that always seems to do an excellent business. The natives of St. Lucia seem eager not only to see the picture, but to take part in it. This they do by shouting "*Egas*," which may roughly be translated as either "Look out!" or "Hit him again!" The shouting starts whenever the hero or heroine is in the slightest danger. It is an experience to hear from three to five hundred voices simultaneously shouting as loud as they possibly can, and in perfect unison. The authorities in the town have not been able to do anything about stopping this demonstration, though they have put up electric signs on either side of the screen. When the shouting becomes too continuous, red signs flash: "Observe order, please!"

There are few night clubs in St. Lucia, but night life is appreciated. Except for a very few staid Britishers, almost everyone can be found dancing at one of the clubs on Saturday nights and holidays. Biggest, coolest, and most attractive of the clubs where travelers are welcome is the Palm Beach. The club is particularly gay, and has a good-sized orchestra on Saturday nights and for pre-carnival dances in the winter season. The bar serves a good local rum, as well as famous rums from Martinique. The club is built high above the beach, with a stairway leading to the bar and large dance hall. Dancing and music follow a Trinidad style, but seem wilder and less patterned. The biggest dance of the winter season is held at the culmination of the Mardi Gras fete the night before carnival starts. Then St. Lucia's queen is selected in a full-dress beauty pageant. St. Lucians are modest, and the beauties appear in evening dress and sports clothes, but not in bathing suits. Dark colored girls are often chosen most beautiful in the St. Lucia celebration.

The carnival is an elaborate one that has been partly taken over by the children of the island. Costumes are interesting and imaginative. Each costumed group meets in the park on Mardi Gras day and is allowed a chance to act out a tableau. A light-skinned Raleigh is likely to spread his cloak for a dark-skinned Virgin Queen. A group representing the signs of the zodiac will move slowly around a member representing the moon, a white-garbed hospital group may wheel baby carriages, bear stretchers, and somewhat incongruously carry large signs reading "Drink Less Rum."

Almost as interesting as the carnival costumes are the traditional late-seventeenth-century garments worn by the older women of the island. To be seen every day, they would be prize-winners at any Mardi Gras celebration. Voluminous petticoats are worn beneath a bright-colored cotton or heavy silk dress. The skirt is gathered tightly at the waist, and an apron is worn over it. Around the neck goes a heavy silk neckerchief, a "foulard," that is draped over the shoulders, crossed over the breasts, and tied at the waist. The headdress is the traditional "madras," a brightly striped square cotton cloth fashioned into an intricate turban tied in front. Gold earrings and necklaces that are heirlooms complete the costume. This costume, originally French, is also worn by the older women of Martinique and Guadeloupe. It is rarely seen on a young girl except at carnival time. However the song "Adieu foulard, adieu madras" is still the most popular tango in the French islands, though it was written in 1786 by the Marquess de Bouillé, sentimental on leaving the islands.

In addition to being a gay island, St. Lucia has developed a considerable reputation as a tiny cultural oasis in the Lesser Antilles. The leader of this intellectual movement is a young schoolmaster named Derek Walcott, whose poems have been published widely throughout the Caribbean. His poem dealing with the great fire that destroyed Castries gives some idea of his work.

After that hot gospeller had levelled all but the
churched sky,
I wrote the tale by tallow of a city's death by fire.
Under a candle's eye that smoked in tears, I
Wanted to tell in more than wax of faiths that were
snapped like wires.

All day I walked abroad among the rubbled tales,
Shocked at each wall that stood on the street like a liar,
Loud was the bird-rocked sky, and all the clouds were bales
Torn open by looting and white in spite of the fire;

By the smoking sea, where Christ walked, I asked why
Should a man wax tears when his wooden world fails.

In town leaves were paper, but the hills were a flock of
faiths
To a boy who walked all day, each leaf was a green breath
Rebuilding a love I thought was dead as nails,
Blessing the death and baptism by fire.

From the sun-baked, half-burned city of Castries to the romantic beachcomber's paradise, Pigeon Island, is just eleven miles—ten of them by land, one by rowboat. The approach to the island is through the sultry little fishing village of Gros Islet, near the northernmost point of St. Lucia. Here an elderly gentleman named Tom Legh can arrange for a boat to take you to his sister's fabulous islet. If Mr. Legh is unavailable, it is usually possible for the taxi-driver to blow his horn and gesticulate until a tiny craft leaves the pier across the water and fetches the traveler. The island is very small, less than one mile long. It is named for Admiral Rodney's pigeons. Here Rodney made his headquarters and built the pigeon cote that still remains on top of one of the low hills. From an approaching boat the view is of a small knoll with a perfect beach at the base. In the center, facing St. Lucia, is a magnificent building constructed in a tropical style with a fantastically high, steep, heavily thatched roof, and with two green-shuttered windows to let the hot air out. The entire front and two sides are open to the trade winds. Nowhere in the West Indies is there a more comfortable bar, spacious dining-room, and lounge all in one. Food is good, and is usually only minutes out of the sea.

Mrs. Josette Legh Snowball, grande dame and sole proprietor of the island, meets the incoming boats often by wading out into the water and assisting them in tying up to the rickety little pier. In addition to doing the greeting and acting as host, Mrs. Snowball oversees the cooking and is a charming and relaxed hostess. No one dresses for any meal at Pigeon Island: shorts, bathing suits, or shirt sleeves are quite acceptable. Drinks flow quickly and easily and are plentiful. They are mostly rum or Scotch, but the wine cellar is well stocked.

Except in the tremendously large lounge and dining-room, space is limited, but there are a number of distinctive rooms in a comfortable, somewhat primitive style. One or two rooms even have a private bath. It is best to make reservations well in advance (Mrs. Josette Legh Snowball, Pigeon Island Club, St. Lucia, British West Indies). In addition to eating and drinking, there are, of course, swimming and sun-bathing, and the very ambitious sometimes hike up the hill to visit the almost nonexistent ruins of Admiral Rodney's old forts and pigeon cote. But the greatest asset that Pigeon Island has is its complete isolation. Everyone has plenty of time; there is nothing to do, nowhere to go, not a telephone to answer, and not an automobile to ride in.

SAINT LUCIA: *The beach-house restaurant on Pigeon Island.*

SAINT LUCIA: *Housewives in "foulard and madras" dating from the days when St. Lucia was a French island.*

SAINT LUCIA: *Young girl masquerades as a Japanese for the carnival.*

SAINT LUCIA: *A small boat anchors off Pigeon Island, with St. Lucia in the background.*

SAINT LUCIA: *It is possible to drive very close and then walk into the smoking crater of the Soufrière, only drive-in volcano in the world.*

SAINT VINCENT

The high, well-watered hills and fertile green valleys of this volcanic land suggest an island like Tahiti in the Pacific rather than one in the Caribbean. Its peaks go up to four thousand feet, and the foothills below sweep down gracefully in long undulations to the sea. The impression is one of a calm, peaceful island forgotten by the world. St. Vincent is just on the point of awakening to its possibilities as a winter and summer resort.

This off-the-tourist-track dot in the semi-tropical sea is mountainous throughout most of its eleven by eighteen miles. Its predominantly Negro population (there are only about five hundred whites) are farmers—and good ones. They have managed to cultivate nearly all of the island slopes by using contour plowing and terracing. Because the island is rich in arrowroot, from which the finest of starches are processed for use in baby foods, crackers, and canned soups, its economy has been relatively stable during the past twenty years. In addition to its arrowroot monopoly, St. Vincent also produces considerable amounts of sea-island cotton, coconuts, and bananas.

It is not easy for travelers to reach St. Vincent because at present there is no direct plane service. Passengers must go to Barbados, ninety-five miles east (a half-hour flight), or to Trinidad, one hundred and seventy-five miles due south. From either of these near-by islands a six-passenger Grumman Goose amphibian flies regularly. In addition, the *West Indian*, a comfortable steamer, passes twice a month, and many trips are made every week by native schooners with auxiliary motors. The latter are recommended only for highly seasoned travelers, and are difficult for women traveling alone or families with small children. Shortest of the schooner trips is via St. Lucia, which is only twenty-one miles north of St. Vincent. The sailing vessels hug the coast of St. Lucia from its capital, Castries, cross the short St. Vincent Passage, then sail along the St. Vincent coast to Kingstown harbor.

Kingstown looks much as it did when sailing ships from the United States, England, and Holland came to trade in the late eighteenth century. Well protected by towering cliffs, the harbor curves to a beach in the center of the town. Plenty of schooners and yachts sail in and out, but rarely does one see a large cruise boat anchored. It has been off the travelers' track for a long time.

A few students know St. Vincent as the island to which Captain Bligh first brought breadfruit from Tahiti. Fewer students know that it was St. Vincent's planters, looking for an inexpensive food staple, who petitioned the Crown to outfit a ship to bring the breadfruit plant to the island. Bligh set out in the *Bounty*, gathered the plants, and prepared to sail to St. Vincent. But Fletcher Christian and the crew had other plans. They seized command of the ship and Bligh was set adrift. He managed to reach England, and his second trip, in the *Providence*, was more successful. He finally landed in St. Vincent in 1792. The grateful citizens gave a huge party for Bligh and presented him with a piece of plate valued at one hundred guineas, the ship's crew with two fat bullocks. Then Bligh sailed to Jamaica, where more of the seedlings were planted. The breadfruit grew well in St. Vincent, as it did in all the islands. One of the original seedlings planted by Bligh still bears fruit in St. Vincent's ancient Botanical Gardens.

But this isle has more to recommend it to travelers than its breadfruit and the romantic story of Captain Bligh. Its beaches are safe; the water is pure, the climate delightful. Along the leeward coast at Chateaubelair a group of fishermen still goes out with whaling-gear after a whale they call the big black fish. Travelers may make arrangements to accompany them in their small craft and enjoy the excitement of old-time whaling in comparative safety.

St. Vincent's greatest attraction is its volcano, called, like so many West Indian volcanoes, Soufrière, a French word meaning "volcano." An ideal peak to climb, it can be scaled by anyone with fortitude, a sense of adventure, and a reasonable amount of expendible energy. Every year a number of children between the ages of ten and twelve climb it. The trip up to the base of the volcano should be made in the early morning. The road from Kingstown, misty in the early haze, winds along the wind-swept coast and finally through the sleepy little village of Georgetown, St. Vincent's second-largest town. Above Georgetown is Dry River, a fantastic bed of volcanic ash that in two or three minutes becomes a rushing torrent of white water when the rains pour down from the cloud-draped peaks above. Also in this area are large volcanic boulders formed by the eruption of the volcano in 1902. It has been inactive since.

You are met by either horses or jeep near the Orange Hill estate in the center of the largest coconut forest on the island. The jeep or horseback ride with your guide is short but exciting, through the brilliantly patterned, twisted coconut trees.

Then begins a walk up a gentle slope through a sugar-cane jungle. The sugar cane soon gives way to a thick bamboo forest as the road continues to wind upward. Then it takes a sharp downward path to the same dry river that was crossed earlier at the bottom of the mountain. This is a fine place to stop for a rest and picture-taking, but it is not a good plan to have lunch here. You will be much hungrier later on. The path is much steeper above Dry River. It winds in and out of giant fern trees with pretty little pink flowers, locally called bread and cheese, growing on thick bushes between them.

Then the vegetation becomes more sparse. Finally, near the top, there is little except huge blackened rocks with volcanic cinders lying among them. Over a steep rise on the rim of the crater, a magnificent vista is revealed. A sapphire-blue lake is set in the misty circle like a gem. It is cold here, and the slicker that has been a nuisance during the trip is very comfortable. Because there is a good chance of a sudden shower, it is essential to carry along a lightweight plastic raincoat and rainhat. If the weather is reasonably clear, lunch or rum punch will be welcome at the top of the mountain.

The trip down is easier, but still somewhat hazardous, for it is very easy to slip on the loose cinders of the eroded gullies. Don't go too fast. The slope does not look steep, but you will suddenly be running headlong, unable to stop except by falling. Other tips about climbing Soufrière: It is best to wear lightweight shoes that hug the feet to keep rocks out. Slacks are more practical than shorts even though they do get wet, because they protect the legs from scratches. Don't try to make the climb all at once! And don't feel that you are being too cautious if you stop every few hundred feet. It is the only enjoyable way to get up the mountain.

In contrast to the climbing expedition, St. Vincent offers a delightful sailing trip to the island of Bequia, largest of the near-by Grenadine Islands. It is a short sail (from two to four hours) over a smooth, incredibly clear green sea. Overnight accommodations are available in Bequia at a very pleasant though primitive little hotel called the Sunny Caribee.

Places to stay on St. Vincent are decidedly limited. There are two or three guesthouses, but the best food and lodging may be had at either the Blue Caribbean Hotel in Kingstown or the new Sugar Mill Inn a few miles out of town. The Blue Caribbean, primarily a commercial rather than a resort hotel, is located in the center of the city. It offers excellent cooking of the Creole French variety and specializes in native dishes. Food at the Sugar Mill Inn also has a delicious French flavor, and this is a resort-type hotel. Located two hundred feet up on a cliff overlooking the Grenadine Islands, it has a swimming pool and a dining-room that gives one of the finest views of the ocean and the islands in all the Caribbean. Owned jointly by Americans and St. Vincentians, the Sugar Mill is designed for travelers interested in a restful holiday.

A day at the Sugar Mill Inn goes something like this. At eight a.m. there is a soft knock on your bedroom door, and tea or coffee is brought to you by one of the soft-voiced English-speaking Negro maids. From seven thirty until nine thirty breakfast is served in the dining-room or by the swimming pool, and guests may bathe in the clear fresh water between courses.

After breakfast, visitors are taken by car down to the Aquatic Club or the Coronation Club on the beach below the hotel. Here guests laze, gossip, and swim, sometimes even going so far as to swim over to Youngs Island, about one-quarter mile across the bay. There are lots of small sailing boats around the Aquatic Club, and the spear-fishing off Youngs Island is fine. The waters are clear and safe.

Some visitors may want to go into Kingstown to shop or explore, and the car continues into the city, dropping them at about ten o'clock and making the return trip about noon, stopping to pick up the guests who have elected to stay on the beach. Lunch is from twelve thirty until two o'clock, and after lunch the entire hotel—guests and staff—goes to sleep until four thirty. At five o'clock guests go for another swim, have tea, or begin to appear in the cocktail lounge. Conversations and music begin. Citizens of St. Vincent come up to the hotel for cocktails and to see and mix with the guests. There is likely to be a yacht in the harbor, and its passengers join the group in the cocktail lounge. A dance is held once a week, usually on Saturday night, and a curry luncheon is served on Sunday afternoons. In the evening there is informal dancing to recordings. Visitors are invariably invited to parties throughout the island. Dinner is served late, between eight thirty and ten thirty p.m.

Visitors interested in exploration will find much to discover in the rural areas along the windward and leeward coasts. In the hills back of Kingstown lies the great Mesopotamia Valley, a fertile area, containing hundreds of individual farms etched neatly against the slopes. On the leeward side, five miles from Kingstown, is the picturesque fishing village of Layou, notable for a large black figure of Christ on the cross and for one of the largest Carib stones yet found in the islands. This huge boulder near a small, swift river is covered with animals and figures etched deep into the rock by the Carib Indians in pre-Columbian days.

The heritage of these Caribs may be somewhat responsible for the independence and character of the St. Vincent Negro today. The Caribs held the island of St. Vincent long after all the other Caribbean islands had been taken by the British, Spanish, Dutch, and French. It was here that the Black Caribs developed, a mixture of shipwrecked and escaped Negro slaves and the original Carib settlers of the island. The mixture blended so well that in the eighteenth century the Black Caribs successfully held the island against the French and later the British.

But not for long. There was a treaty giving the island to the Caribs in perpetuity. But settlers moved in, there were uprisings, and finally most of the Caribs—black, yellow, and mixed—were rounded up by the British and moved to Roatan island off British Honduras. Some tribes survive today on the mainland of British Honduras. But many escaped the evacuation by hiding in the thick woods and high mountains. A few relatively pure Caribs still may be found at the remote village of Sandy Bay on St. Vincent's windward coast, but most have mixed with the Negroes brought later from Africa. Today there is probably some Carib ancestry in most of the Negro population.

Back of the Sandy Bay area, where the Carib settlements still exist, is the home of the St. Vincent parrot. It is native only to this island, and is a great talker. It is becoming quite rare, but a few have been tamed and a wild one is occasionally seen.

The island has few birds and no native animals. It is also fortunate in having no malaria, for, according to the Public Health department, the anopheles mosquito is unknown on the island. There are lots of attractive small lizards and no snakes. To add to the assets for visitors, St. Vincent has a plentiful, pure water supply. It is piped all over the island and its purity constantly checked.

Except for the weekly dances at one of the clubs, cocktail parties or dinners and dances at the Sugar Mill Inn, there is little night life on the island. There are steel bands for the dances, though, and a few Calypso singers. It is not a place to go to be continuously entertained, but its beauty is rare. Although the traveler may find it difficult to reach, it is an unforgettable island—everything that a dream island should be.

SAINT VINCENT: *The great rock is Fort Duvernette, with historic gun emplacements. In the distance, Bequia in the Grenadine Islands.*

SAINT VINCENT: *The beach of Bequia in the Grenadines, just off St. Vincent.*

SAINT VINCENT: *An outdoor sorting area for sea-island cotton.*

TOBAGO

The citizens of this pleasant island, who call themselves Tobagonians, believe that Daniel Defoe had their homeland in mind when he wrote *The Life and Adventures of Robinson Crusoe.* They can back their opinion by expert reasoning. Although they admit that Defoe used the story of Alexander Selkirk, who was actually marooned on Más-a-Tierra Island in the Juan Fernández group in the Pacific, they insist that the descriptions of the island, including its location and its proximity to Trinidad, set it up as the actual locale of the Robinson Crusoe story.

Whether or not Defoe had Tobago in mind doesn't matter. His classic could easily have happened on this tropical island, because Tobago is located just eighteen miles north of Trinidad, which is mentioned by Defoe in the book. It has fertile valleys and plenty of vegetation and fish to support life. There is even a large cave corresponding to the one mentioned by Defoe. The island today has all of the natural beauty that Defoe described, plus the amenities that make for comfortable, civilized living.

Tobago is a long, narrow island shaped somewhat like a cigar. It is twenty-six miles long by seven and one-half miles wide. The southern portion, where most of the best beaches are located, is flat; in the north the land rises to eighteen hundred feet. Pigeon Hill, near the northeastern end of the island, is one of the highest scenic spots, while Pigeon Point, at sea level near the southwestern end, offers the finest beach and bathing facilities.

There are only two ways to go to Tobago. Cruise ships do not stop there, so one takes the daily plane operated by the British West Indian Airways from Piarco Airport in Trinidad or books passage on one of the two coastal steamers—the *Trinidad,* or the *Tobago*—that leave Trinidad every other day. The trip by boat is romantic, interesting, and inexpensive. But because it is a nine-hour overnight trip, it can be uncomfortable. Sleeping accommodations are located near the engine room, and are hot. The cargo may include cattle and pigs. Between the noise and the heat, sleep can become a difficult achievement. The quick, easy way to make the trip is to take the daily plane that leaves Piarco around noon and return to Trinidad on the coastal steamer (the boat trip back is shorter by an hour or more because of better wind and current). By arranging to stay up most of the night or by sleeping on deck (preferably under a tarpaulin, because a sudden squall often comes up before morning), one can make the journey a comfortable cool one. The air trip is fine, taking only thirty minutes between Piarco Airport and Crown Point Airport on Tobago.

Unlike many of the smaller islands, Tobago offers a variety of highly developed hotel accommodations. They fall into two categories: good and very good.

The tropical town of Scarborough reflects a great deal of the island's character. The streets are wide and clean. The market place is gay, busy, and full of local vegetables, for Tobago is the market basket for Trinidad. In spite of its modern aspect, however, Scarborough retains the charm of an early tropical village.

Along the docks either the *Trinidad* or the *Tobago* is likely to be tied up. Across from the docks is the office of the Tobago Tourist Board, where information about the island is intelligently organized and cheerfully supplied. The streets adjacent to the center of town are steep, and the little houses cling to the sheer cliffside, luxurious green foliage holding them in place. Tourists are considered quite a sight in Scarborough, and some of the natives, particularly small boys, come to town just to have a look at the fantastic costumes worn by some of the travelers. Noting the striped shorts, iridescent shirt, and the outlandish straw hat worn by one stout gentleman, one of the native boys is said to have run quickly home for his camera and recorded this colorful view on film.

Life in Scarborough moves slowly. There is little traffic, and it is pleasant to walk around during the early morning when the shops are open. Tobago does not offer buys of special interest to the tourist. Most of its straw work is similar to that of Trinidad and the near-by Windward Islands, and its British imports are, of course, exactly the same as those found in most of the British West Indies. The old Fort

George above the town is within walking distance. It is possible to look over the wall where an ingenious major, in the eighteenth century, found out about an impending massacre of whites, arrested thirty Negro leaders, took them to the fort, and then—to the amazement of the horrified onlookers outside the walls—hanged them all, one by one. Actually, he later received a ceremonial sword from the grateful slave-owners when they found that he had simply hanged the same man thirty times and had saved them a total of twenty-nine hundred pounds' worth of slaves. There is a small private museum containing the collection of Thomas Cambridge, former warden of the island. It is one of the best collections of Arawak relics in the entire Caribbean. Included are native stone axes with serrated edges and many decorative food vessels.

It is only a short drive from Scarborough or from any hotel in Tobago to its excellent beaches. These are at Store Bay, Milford Bay, and Pigeon Point. Any hotel can make arrangements for a visit to one of the great beaches. The long stretches of powder sand pack down hard as they slope gently into the clear green water. Outside the curve of the bay, the long line of Buccoo Reef protects the waters from large fish and rough currents.

It is a good plan to arrive early in the day, have a swim, and then take off for Buccoo Reef, which offers one of the finest coral sea gardens and spear-fishing grounds in the West Indies. Arrange for a boat and a guide to pick you up on the beach and transport you in some fifteen minutes to the reef. These guides supply snorkels and face-masks. Here an important word of warning: be certain to wear slacks or take a large bath towel to cover your legs, and wear a long-sleeved shirt over your arms and shoulders for the trip out to the reef and back. The reflected sun on the water is so intense that a serious burn can result from even a short exposure. Once out at the reef, follow the guides' instructions. They will suggest that you relax lazily on top of the water and let yourself float face down or swim very slowly and watch the sea life go by. It is important, however, when swimming around in this area to be careful of the coral, which, though beautiful, makes deep cuts that heal very slowly. If a small cut does occur on the foot or leg, the guides advise soaking it in salt water on the trip back. Everyone can enjoy the sights at Buccoo Reef. Children have a wonderful time and can wade in water up to their shoulders in complete safety. Elderly people will enjoy it as much as youngsters. Indeed, one of the guides, a tremendous hulk of a black man called Anthony, pointed out with pride that he had taken a number of clients over eighty out to see the reef. "Only had one mishap," he said. "One time I put a lady back in the boat too fast and cracked one of her ribs."

Give one entire day to the exploration of the Store Bay area and Buccoo Reef. If your stay is a long one, you will want to make many trips to the Aquatic Club. Another interesting day can be spent exploring the area around the old town of Plymouth, located on the same coast only a few miles north. Plymouth now is almost deserted, with its streets overgrown with grass and its street signs leaning at odd angles. Along the bluff overlooking Great Courland Bay are the ruins of Fort James, the oldest on the island. Near by is a tombstone with an unusual inscription. It has become traditional for every visitor to Tobago to go to this spot and read: "Within these walls are deposited the bodies of Betty Stivens and child. She was the beloved wife of Alex Stivens who deplored her death to the end of his days which happened on the twenty fifth day of November, seventeen eighty three in the twenty third year of her age. What was remarkable of her, she was a mother without knowing it, and a wife without letting her husband know it except by her kind indulgences to him."

There have been many interpretations of this inscription, the most accepted being that Betty Stivens was a slave who worked in the household of Alex Stivens. She bore him three children, but continued to work in his household as housekeeper–slave rather than wife and mother–while still making herself available to her master. There is another theory that she died shortly before her child was born.

In the food division is the Tobago version of creole gumbo, made with okra and native fish. Also, this island's Planter's Punch is an interesting and slightly different one. Here is a recipe of ex-bartender and under cook Loderick Adelabert Williams. Into a tall glass put one half ounce of sugar syrup, one ounce of lime juice or one half of a lime, three ounces of Vat 19 rum, five dashes of Angostura bitters, one half teaspoon of grated nutmeg. Fill glass with ice and add a sip of soda water.

Another sightseeing trip is highly recommended in Tobago. This is the drive along the coast between Scarborough and Charlotteville, located near the northernmost point of the island. The drive goes through cool cocoa plantations and along long stretches of virgin beach. Speyside is a particularly beautiful cove, with Pigeon Peak rising eighteen hundred feet on the left and Little Tobago—also known as Bird of Paradise Island—offshore on the right. The water comes right up to the highway, sometimes flooding it. At Speyside get a boat and go out past Goat Island to the only bird-of-paradise sanctuary in the New World. Little Tobago is an islet shaped like a cross. In 1909 Sir William Ingram, who owned it, imported twenty-six pairs of full-grown birds of paradise from New Guinea and set them free on the island. He had to supply the birds with food and water and install a caretaker for this purpose. The birds mated, and soon there was a considerable number of the golden-plumed beauties on the island. When Sir William died, his sons presented the island to the governments of Trinidad and Tobago under the condition that it be kept as a bird sanctuary. The terms have been kept. Food and water are taken regularly to the island. Guides are available at Speyside to go over to the island, but it is well to spend the night if the traveler wants to see the elusive birds, which are very shy and are rarely seen except in the early morning or late afternoon.

The road winding along the coast and then across the island toward Charlotteville is beautiful with the mountain immortelle trees that glow like red flames during the winter months. Earlier in the year the yellow poui is in bloom along this route, and a side trip along the trails may lead to a clump of silver-backed ferns. If this fern is laid on the arm and then taken away, it will leave its silver pattern stenciled against the skin. The road winds ever upward until from the summit Charlotteville, Tobago's second village, is seen nestled in a semicircle along Man of War Bay.

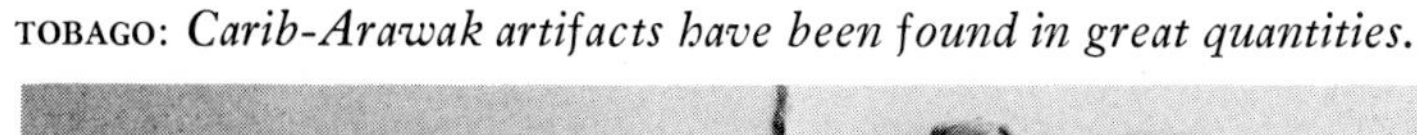

TOBAGO: *Carib-Arawak artifacts have been found in great quantities.*

TOBAGO: *Beach in the southeastern part of the island.*

TOBAGO: *Wind-swept Scarborough is located directly on the sea.*

TRINIDAD

Trinidad is the southernmost of the islands of the West Indies. It is a brilliant green island measuring thirty-seven by fifty fertile miles. When approached by sea, it is dominated by three mountain peaks that called to the mind of Columbus a vision of the Trinity: he named the island La Trinidad. It is shaped like a conquistador's boot with the toe pointed toward Venezuela and the heel toward the Atlantic.

Trinidad is separated from Venezuela by two narrow channels, each about fifteen miles wide. The northern one, known as the Dragon's Mouths, is the point of entry for cruise ships into the protected harbor of Trinidad's capital, Port of Spain. The southern channel, called the Serpent's Mouth, separates Trinidad from the delta of the muddy Orinoco River. Because of its proximity to the South American continent and because Trinidad was once geologically a part of the continent, from which it broke off millions of years ago, it has a greater variety of flora and fauna than any other island of the West Indies.

It is a large island and cannot be seen in a day, but from five to ten days will give a visitor an opportunity to see the greater part of it. Roads are good and lead to fascinating places, but some are also steep, narrow, winding, and dangerous. Most taxi-drivers realize this and drive at moderate speeds. The plane ride coming in to Piarco Airport, located sixteen miles southeast of Port of Spain, affords a fine preview of the countryside. Mountains covered with deep forest-green foliage rise to over three thousand feet. Sudden clearings reveal broad sugarcane fields, graceful coconut trees, neat citrus plantations. When the plane touches down on the airstrip (Trinidad has runways for large trans-oceanic planes), the doorway opens on a dazzlingly bright world of green, black, and white.

Piarco Airport is unique in the islands, having two comfortable, well-run hotels. These are especially useful for overnighting when island-hopping, but have the distinct disadvantage of being sixteen miles from Trinidad's largest city, called Puerto España during the Spanish occupation, which ended in 1798, and now called Port of Spain—certainly an odd name for a British capital.

Nearest to the airport is the Bel Air Hotel, reached by strolling across the roadway from the Customs Department, where your baggage is checked and released. Dapper, young East Indian boys in burgundy jackets meet all planes and carry luggage over to the outdoor lobby and registration desk. Rooms are mostly air-conditioned and usually much too cold, but if you can stand a considerable amount of noise (walls are paper thin, and windows must be left open in the non-air-conditioned rooms) you may find yourself comfortable in them. There is plenty of hot water. A clean, attractive, air-conditioned restaurant (also too cold) serves a tasty but limited menu. The Bel Air has an outdoor terrazzo dance floor and gives two dances a week, complete with steel band and Calypso singers. Guests of the hotel, even when traveling alone, have no difficulty joining in the festivities.

The equally well-run Pan-American Guest House is located about a half a mile from the airport. It too has air-conditioning and a good restaurant that concentrates on stateside cooking. Both hotels offer a refreshing no-tipping policy and operate on the European plan.

Except for stays of a day or two, the isolated position of these hotels makes them impractical for the average visitor. While the distance to town is only sixteen miles, the drive takes at least forty-five minutes, and it is impossible to leave the airport hotel in the morning, spend the day in Port of Spain, and go out the same evening without the long trek back. The heat of the town is too enervating, the pace too rapid, and places to stop during the day too infrequent to see the town all in one day. So visitors staying over and planning really to see the island should stay in Port of Spain. There are a number of comfortable small hotels and one large one, the venerable Queens Park hostelry. The Trinidad and Tobago Tourist Board operates a center on King's Wharf which supplies the names and addresses of recommended guesthouses and private homes. Plans are afoot for a sumptuous new hotel to be built and operated by the chain that runs the Caribe Hilton in Puerto Rico.

The sixteen miles from Piarco Airport to Port of Spain can seem like a very dull drive unless the passenger concentrates on details along the roadside as they flash by. Just a few miles from the airport on either side of the road the country begins to look like eastern India. Land has been cleared, and East Indians are at work in the flooded rice fields. A few miles farther along on the left are vegetables, again tended by East Indians, and whole families may be seen working in the cabbages, spinach, and beans. These East Indians, who now make up about one third of Trinidad's population of over 600,000 (the remaining two thirds are about equally divided between Whites and Negroes), arrived on the island between 1838 and 1845. Their importation as indentured labor was the result of the freeing of the Negro slaves by the British in 1834. Most of the Negroes took to the fertile hills of the island and set up their own small "yards," living on the fruits, roots, and herbs that they could gather without much effort. The East Indians adjusted to the climate and the farm life very quickly, finding them much like those of their native Bengal. Within a few years they were a solidly entrenched community, mostly Hindu but partly Moslem, keeping their distinctive customs.

On the right side of the car will be seen the outlines of the Mount St. Benedict monastery gleaming white, high up on the mountainside. The monastery, operated by the Benedictine monks, raises bees and bottles and sells the honey. It also operates a guesthouse, built in the Spanish style with large windows and rooms. There is an austere dining-room, where plain but well-prepared meals are served. The guesthouse is an excellent place for a traveler who wants to be alone, to enjoy simple food in pleasant surroundings—the atmosphere is quiet, and religious. Women are not permitted to wear shorts or slacks, and liquor is not served.

The taxi may stop at the railroad tracks to allow the passing of a stream of rattling brown cars with open windows crowded with Trinidadians on their way in or out of town. The total length of this railroad is a hundred and twenty-three miles. The engine is a very small one, and it takes considerable time for the little train to go by. Next, on the left is the Fernandez rum plant, consisting of a group of white stucco and red brick buildings. It is an interesting place to visit, and free samples of Trinidad's excellent rum are available.

Now the traffic begins to pile up. On the left is shanty town, a mile-long section with the most squalid habitations imaginable. They are made from tin cans or packing boxes, gunny sacks, and rotten pieces of timber. In these shacks live hundreds of the poorest families of Port of Spain. Beyond shanty town is a Government park with swings, seesaws, and modern play equipment. A few minutes farther along is Marine Square, the shopping and business center of Port of Spain. It is only a short drive from here to the busy docks where cruise ships enter the port and where the tourist center has an elaborate office equipped to change money and give information on any possible tour, accommodation, or shopping expedition.

Shopping in Trinidad is a slow but rewarding experience. The large stores are located on Marine Square and extend up Frederick Street for some ten blocks. The best buys are handmade silver ornaments and earrings. (Be sure to buy them from a reputable shop; much of the "silver" offered for sale on the streets has little or no silver in it.) Also British woolens, leather gloves, cashmere sweaters, and baskets of all shapes and sizes. While Trinidad also carries perfumes and imports from countries other than England, prices are not quite so low as in French and Dutch islands, the Virgin Islands (U.S.), or the free-port shops of Jamaica.

The downtown streets of Port of Spain are among the most picturesque in the world: Buddhist priests rub elbows with Sagaboys (flashy Negroes dressed in a style similar to zoot-suited teen-agers in the United States), sailors of almost every nationality, British officials in white duck or linen suits, and Moslems in red fezzes. For the traveler with a camera, Marine Square on a weekday morning or, even better, on Saturday offers a continually changing pattern for pictures.

More interesting even than the streets of Port of Spain is the architecture of the city. Within five miles of the center of the city are houses that, seen for the first time, are completely unbelievable: they look like castles built by hand. A house may have not just one peaked roof, but six, each rising higher than the other, without functional purpose, until they resemble a child's picture of a fairy palace or a monster's lair. In addition to the towers, an incredible amount of grille-like wood has been used to decorate balconies and roofs. Some of the houses show a distinctly East Indian influence, and the one at 25 Maraval Road looks as though it started out to be an Indian mosque, but stopped in the middle of construction and decided to be a residence instead.

While perhaps only eight or ten of Trinidad's town houses are as outlandish as the above description would indicate, literally hundreds of Trinidadians have utilized the wooden gingerbread motif to make their houses quaint, individualistic, and attractive. The most unusual of all is the fantastic town house at No. 9 St. Claire Avenue. The house at 31 Maraval Road looks like a feudal castle, and 2 Queens Park West is a house of the old estate type.

Within a few minutes of these architectural gems lie the Botanical Gardens, which were established almost a hundred and fifty years ago. No entrance fee is charged to a thrilling collection of tropical trees, flowers, and animals. The zoo is a small one, but contains specimens of a number of unusual and almost extinct animals: the lappe, a pig-sized member of the rodent family much prized for its flesh; its miniature cousin, the agouti, which resembles a rat-faced rabbit; the peccary, boa constrictor, red howler and white capuchin monkeys, and the small mongoose brought originally to rid the island of the deadly but extremely rare snake called fer de lance, but which has become a menace to the agriculture of the island.

The real glory of the Gardens is its majestic and colorful trees. Near the parking area a gigantic silk-cotton tree towers high above the giant trees around it. Ceylon willows; casuarina trees; the naked Indian tree with its flesh-like trunk; the cabbage palm, the heart of which makes an excellent salad; the silver box cedar; and the giant banyan from India also grow in the Gardens. Furniture is made from the locust and native mahogany trees, and interesting varieties of bamboo may be found. One of the curiosities of the Gardens is a tiny pink flower that grows wild in the grass: the guides call it the sweetheart flower because it opens and clings to your fingers when you touch it.

The near-by pavilion operated by the Tourist Board is an excellent place to have tea after exploring the Gardens. It is a short walk to Lookout Hill and the large octagonal resthouse on top. From this point the great panorama of Port of Spain and the Gulf of Paria sweeps away.

Even better than a trip through the Botanical Gardens is an excursion with picnic lunch and bathing suits over the steep highway to Maracas Bay on the north shore. On Sunday the water is likely to be full of splashing East Indians with women wearing saris, men the diaper-like dhoti, as well as of handsomely formed mulatto and Negro men and women in brief swim suits. There will also be a few British families digging in the sand, bathing, and sunning themselves. It is a pleasant family atmosphere. The water is warm and clear, but when there is high wind the surf can break with crashing impact. It is possible to buy a soft or a hard drink at the entrance to the beach. The ride back is over a different road that winds dizzily over a high point known as The Saddle. Excellent vistas may be seen on the way toward Port of Spain. It is an exciting full day's trip.

Other excursions are highly recommended. Most exciting is the one through the Arima Valley and on the Blanchisseuse Road to the sea. Giant ferns grow in great profusion. Cocoa trees, with their orange leaves, are shaded from above by flaming immortelle trees. This area teems with many of the two hundred varieties of tropical birds and myriad butterflies native to the island. On this road a few miles past Arima is Simla, the outpost of the Tropical Research Center of the New York Zoological Society, headed by Dr. William Beebe, where birds, butterflies, snakes, and other fauna that abound in the area are studied.

Once over the top of the mountain, it is a short trip down to the little village of Blanchisseuse. The coast is very wild, and the surf pounds the jagged shoreline incessantly. The local school has the most picturesque playground in the Caribbean. It is on a promontory jutting out into the ocean, and children play on the wind-swept plateau within a few feet of the sea.

The trip to Pitch Lake, which also includes a view of some of Trinidad's oilfields, is a distinct disappointment. Pitch Lake itself is a dismal expanse of gray, semi-solid asphalt. Uninteresting workmen cut blocks out of the lake and heave them to a moving conveyer belt that carries them up to waiting flatcars. Within a short time after the blocks are cut out, the area slowly fills up again with asphalt from the seemingly endless supply beneath the surface of the earth. The drive to and from the lake offers some spectacular views of the oilfields, third-largest in the British Empire.

It is good to be back in Port of Spain in time for tea, which in Trinidad is not taken lightly. There may be cheese and biscuits, hot scones, and occasionally kippers. After tea an hour's rest is usually taken before setting out to see the town in the evening. Trinidad dines late, usually between eight and nine, except on those nights when the most popular local attraction is available. This is a Calypso tent, a crude theater that springs up overnight in an empty lot or alleyway between brick buildings. A palm-leaf or corrugated tin roof is hastily thrown over the space, and backless wooden benches are crammed together on the dirt floor. At one end is an unpainted admission booth and at the other a raised platform, usually decorated with the Union Jack and a framed portrait of England's Queen.

These Calypso tents are operated by the singers themselves, but reservations for good seats can be made from the tourist center, hotels, or guesthouses. Tents spring up about the first of January and last through the carnival season. The two major Calypso groups are known as The Old Brigade and The Young Brigade. There are also many smaller groups. The whole aspect of the "tent" is unattractive and, to the uninitiated traveler, even frightening. But there is not the slightest danger except the possibility of having one's ego punctured or of being shocked at some of the ideas crudely expressed in the satire of the singers.

This is no strip-tease, no stateside or European dance music, no tired tap dancers, no scantily dressed brown-skin chorus line. This is strictly the home of the Calypsonian, a singer who is his own composer, and who is a direct cultural descendant of the early minstrels who told tales of the times with melody and wit.

These men—who call themselves Mighty Panther, Blind King Iere, Lord Melody, The Mighty Spoiler, Lord Superior, Lord Christo, and The Mighty Sparrow—have a real impact upon Trinidad's social, cultural, and political life, and, indeed, on that of the entire Lesser Antilles. Many a politician, after his personal foibles and political ineptitudes have been clearly outlined in song, has withdrawn from public life or been soundly defeated. Recently some political songs, and others attacking East Indians of Trinidad, have been banned by the radio broadcasting company. They are still lustily sung in the Calypso tents and soon penetrate into the smallest communities on the island. Mostly, the rough-and-ready composer-singers speak of love and sex and social customs. One recent song dealing with the selection of the annual carnival queen ended thus:

What will never be seen
is a black-skinned gal as carnival queen.

As the crude "tent" fills with people, a leading Calypso singer, a man of dignity though in shirt sleeves and straw hat, steps upon the platform and quiets the audience with a raised hand. Even the tourists who usually occupy the reserved-seat section stop chattering. In the simplest possible manner he announces the name of the singer and the title of the first Calypso. Then the Mighty Dictator, a young man with a diffident manner, comes to the platform. The five-piece Calypso band plays a rhythmic introduction, and he begins to sing in a unique but quite understandable accent.

I was reading the newspaper one Sunday morning
About how young people sex changing (REPEAT)
It said that some young women are turning to men
And some young men also are turning to women
Even after marriage some couples does change
So if it happen to you please don't think it strange

CHORUS: *At night while they sleeping if this change should happen*
Is captain turn to cook and cook turn to captain
Well in morning when they wake the east will be west
She go jump in he pants he drag on she dress.

For the next two hours some twelve different performers will sing their own compositions. A current favorite, The Mighty Panther, wrote the Calypso welcoming Princess Margaret Rose to the island.

At the end of the performance the most noted of the Calypsonians line up and engage in an ad-lib battle, insulting one another in verse. They refer in highly uncomplimentary terms to one another's appearance, future prospects, and present sex life.

Although the best place to see and hear Calypso singers is at one of their "tents," it is also possible to hear their songs any time of the year in Port of Spain at one of the large clubs. There are three of these to which visitors can secure cards through the Tourist Board or their hotel. The Trinidad Yacht Club has regular dances with Calypso singers and West Indian dancers as entertainers. The Country Club also has regular dances, and during the winter season the 400 Club has dancing and entertainment almost every night.

If none of these is open, there are some night clubs in Port of Spain. These are dark, evil-smelling caverns with a steel band, a Calypso band, a stripper (who does such a modest strip that by U.S. standards she would be considered overdressed), and prostitutes hanging around the bar. These clubs are perfectly safe for the traveler who goes with a group, drinks moderately, and stays with his friends. Calypso singers usually go from one club to another and expect to be tipped individually and collectively by each group they sing for. The singers are particularly good at sizing up the visitors and composing verses to fit the appearance of each member of the party. Occasionally, during the winter season, some good West Indian dancers can be seen at the night spots. These dancers are particularly adept at performing an acrobatic tribal dance called limbo. It is usually danced by four men, two of whom hold a long stick at chest level. The other two strut around the stage, then finally bend backward without touching the floor and glide under the stick. Each time the dancers pass under the stick it is lowered until at last it is held at knee height. The men act as though they cannot go under, one tries, then the other. . . . Incredibly they do it without touching either head or hands to stick or floor.

Another West Indian dance performed with sticks takes the shape of a battle between two athletic men, who fence as though they were using quarterstaffs of early England. This dance was performed on the streets of Port of Spain during carnival for many years, but led to so many broken heads that it is now banned.

One other important entertainment center in Port of Spain should be visited by every traveler whenever it is open. This is the Little Carib, a tiny theater devoted to the dances of the West Indies. It is a project started by Beryl McBurney, Trinidad's greatest dancer, singer, and choreographer. The theater itself seats only about two hundred and fifty. There is no orchestra pit, and the musicians who accompany the dancers are part of the audience. The early religious dances, such as the shango brought over from Africa, can be seen. The Little Carib group is well trained, the costumes are colorful and authentic, and prices are reasonable. Although there are many movie houses in Trinidad, this is the only "live" theater.

Everyone dances in Trinidad. The music has a basic beat and rhythm that are irresistible. Every traveler finds it easy to join in the fun, for the Trinidad step is a simple shuffle in time to the music. It is similar to the basic United States square-dance shuffle. Another aspect of the Trinidad dancing which should interest single travelers is the fact that a partner is not essential. It is entirely proper for a man or woman to shuffle about with intense concentration on the rhythm, eyes rapt, shoulders and elbows moving slightly to the beat. Even dancers who have partners travel along side by side, arms around waists, hips just touching. This does not mean that there is no conventional dancing. The Latin American influence has brought mambo, samba, rhumba, and tango.

But the usual Trinidad dance is called a "jump up." Except at carnival time and among the teen-age group, however, little actual jumping up is done. When it does happen, it is an unforgettable emotional experience. The phenomenon of jumping up is probably caused by the mass hypnosis induced by the repeated phrases of the steel-band rhythm. The beat is hammered into the dancer's consciousness until his movements become spasmodic. Suddenly a group of solo dancers will simultaneously begin to leap straight into the air, arms at sides, each bounce in time to the music. During carnival this "jump up" sometimes continues until the dancers or musicians are completely exhausted.

Most Trinidadians and a good many visitors confine their drinking to Trinidad rum, which is both good and inexpensive. Although it is not so light as most Cuban rum, it is considerably lighter than the Jamaica product. There is almost no United States whisky, bourbon, or rye, and practically no demand for it. Drinks in the order of their popularity are: rum and soda, water, or ginger; rum punch; Planter's Punch; Scotch and soda or water; and pink gin (made of gin and Angostura bitters, which is manufactured in Trinidad and distributed throughout the world).

While the quality of Trinidad's liquors is good, the same cannot always be said for its cuisine. The food is poor to average in the hotels, superlative in the homes, and good at the better restaurants. Topping the restaurant list is the Normandie, owned and operated by its French chef. Specialties include succulent native oysters, tiny spiced shrimps, broiled or stuffed lobster (which is not really a lobster at all, but a giant crayfish), turtle soup, native chicken and duck, filet mignon, or Chateaubriand. At the Normandie, dinner is always an event, and while a reservation is not essential, it is a good idea to make one a day ahead. Upon your arrival, a red-jacketed waiter seats you in a comfortable cocktail area, where he offers you a short but well-selected wine list and takes your food-and-drink order. When your table is ready you proceed into the dining-room. Desserts here include: crêpes Suzette, baked Alaska, and native fruits.

Other good restaurants are the Tavern on the Green, which has a large outdoor patio and terrazzo dance floor, and the Club Belvedere, located high above the city and affording a magnificent view of the harbor. Best of the Chinese restaurants are the Kimling, the Rainbow Terrace, and the Lotus.

The Trinidadian's love for good food and drink has led to the adoption of much of the best cuisine from France, Africa, Spain, India, and England. Trinidad's beef-and-kidney pie is excellent. The native cooks make a fine calaloo, a stew thicker than the soup of the same name served in Jamaica. This stew, which originated in the African bush, uses the leaves of the dasheen plant (called callia by the natives) for body and crab for its delicate flavor. It is a direct ancestor of the creole gumbo of New Orleans:

CALALOO:	3 *bunches dasheen leaves*	1 *bunch chives*
	2 *crabs*	1 *clove garlic*
	12 *okras*	2 *oz. fat pork*
SERVES 4	2 *onions*	2 *oz. salt beef*

Place in an earthenware "canaree" (pot): salt beef, fat pork, chives, garlic, and onions (all chopped fine), okra (cut in ½-inch pieces), dasheen leaves (having removed the veins), crabs (cleaned and broken in half). Put in two quarts of water, salt and pepper (to taste), and one whole green pepper. Cover and bring to boil. After half an hour remove pepper and stir vigorously. Continue to boil slowly for one hour, stirring every fifteen minutes. Serve with pounded green plantain or rice.

Among the other fine dishes are baked saltfish, roti (an East Indian concoction using mutton and rice), and a delicious thick soup called sans coche:

SANS COCHE:	SERVES 8	
2 *oz. fat pork*	½ *lb. split peas*	*sweet potato*
¼ *lb. salt beef*	2 *tbsps. butter*	*Irish potato*
½ *lb. pig tail*	*yam*	*green plantain*
2 *lbs. meat*	*dasheen*	*dumplings*
2 *onions*	*cush-cush*	*coconut*
1 *bunch chives*	*cassava*	*green pepper*

Brown fat pork, chives, onions (chopped fine). Add meat; simmer ten minutes, then add two quarts water and peas. When the peas are ready to burst, put in vegetables and milk squeezed from one grated coconut. Twenty minutes before serving add dumplings (cut small) and one green pepper (which must not be allowed to burst).

While the food is fine and the music even better, Trinidad's greatest attraction is the annual carnival, or Mardi Gras celebration, which precedes the Lenten season. On both Monday and Tuesday, bankers, housemaids, legislators, porters, street-cleaners, and indeed all of Trinidad's polyglot population join in two hysterical days of this non-commercial combination of creole fete, Spanish fiesta, and Roman bacchanal.

During the entire year, in tiny shacks and sumptuous town houses, costumes are planned and executed. Large social clubs called "carnival bands," some with more than one hundred members, plan elaborate pageants and tableaux. In 1955 a band of "Vultures" (known locally as John Crows) drove a donkey into the center of the black-clad, long-beaked group. Under cover of the costumes the donkey was spirited away. When the group opened ranks, there was only the donkey's skeleton. Other bands may dress as British and French Crusaders; a regiment of the United States Confederate soldiers (all black); a regiment of Union troops (Chinese). A cheerful, sweaty Alaskan Eskimo band may be followed by a Hindu group representing Knights of the Round Table. A great favorite is semi-nude, strikingly painted South American Indians.

The best way for a visitor to see the carnival is to plan to arrive in Port of Spain a few days before Mardi Gras. In this way he has an opportunity to meet the local people, attend the pre-carnival parties, and arrange for the carnival spectacle on the Savanna. There the queen of the carnival and the king of the Calypso singers are chosen, and on Tuesday the maskers parade in front of the grandstand and receive their awards.

Pre-carnival dances are gala affairs, with guests in elaborate costumes, in blue jeans and loud sagaboy shirts, or occasionally summer formals. Entertainment is by steel bands. The maskers who compete for awards put on acts in keeping with their costumes. Costumes are not so elaborate as those worn during the Mardi Gras celebration.

Now a word about steel bands, Trinidad's most recent contribution to music and the essence of the Mardi Gras. The instruments are homemade from empty oil drums. Since their creation during World War II, they have been developed to the point where classical and popular music can be beaten out by the rhythm-conscious Negro musicians. The musicians specialize in tunes written especially for them, and each year a new "road march" is added to the growing collection of compositions. To make these resonant instruments, oil drums are cut off at various depths. The largest drums are used for the bass, while medium-sized ones help to carry the melody along with the ping pong, a thin section from the bottom of the drum. To create a scale on these crude metal barrels, the bottom is heated and separate segments of different sizes and depths are painstakingly hammered out. They are played like a xylophone or marimba with the striking end of a stick covered with a strip of inner tube. To accentuate the beat, a piece of iron from an automobile brake lining is struck with an iron rod with ear-splitting impact. The final and only non-metal instrument is the shac-shac, a gourd with seeds inside.

Visitors should rise by five a.m. on Monday to celebrate the first day of carnival. The steel bands are tuning up, and the tinkle and throb of ping pong and bass spread rapidly over the island. On the cool, misty street shadowy figures of adults and children hurry to the centrally located Marine Square. Festivities are officially opened by the Mayor of Port of Spain at six a.m. This ceremony the creoles call "jourouvert," which has been loosely translated as "the day has dawned." To see these opening ceremonies one must reach the grandstand in Marine Square by 5:30. The Mayor's speech is short and to the point. He recommends that the people not drink too much water, that they make lots of noise, but obey all the instructions of the efficient, white-helmeted policemen. At about this time a character dressed as Charlie Chaplin, who has been crowned king of the carnival for many years, is likely to interrupt the Mayor, saying: "Let me borrow your face for a laugh." The Mayor crowns him, and the long-pent-up emotions of the crowd, which has waited a year for this moment, are released. The steel bands begin to play and to shuffle past; the maskers move gaily across the entire square; and the carnival breaks on the sleepy town like a jungle stampede.

By nine a.m. a crowd gathers at the ancient Hotel de Paris near by. Here Trinidadians have met for traditional toasts for many generations, and here many of the citizens have their "jourouvert" to celebrate the beginning of carnival.

What with watching the maskers go by and shuffling along with the steel bands, everyone is feeling the need for a drink and some food by eleven a.m. It is important to get into a restaurant or hotel early because all are crowded to the doors with hungry, thirsty, shouting celebrants. There is no need to worry about missing any of the carnival, for it follows right into the restaurants. The Calypso singers go from one restaurant to another, singing topical verses especially composed for the carnival. In the afternoon it is advisable to rest because, though there is a competition on the Savanna, there is an even better competition with more and better maskers on Tuesday, and some energy should be reserved for Monday night's Grand Charity

Ball. When the ball is over, the night spots, clubs, hotels, and private homes ring until the small hours with the sound of the steel drums and shake from the impact of the "jump up."

On Tuesday morning the streets begin to fill with steel bands by the hundreds and maskers by the thousands. The largest of the masked groups wait for the second day to show their incredibly ornate finery. Once again Marine Square is colorful with satin and velvet robes, dazzling headdresses—costumes ranging in cost from a few pence to hundreds of dollars are worn on this final day of the carnival.

The pattern of Monday is followed from Marine Square to the Savanna. On this afternoon every traveler with a camera should be ready to take pictures, for it is possible to leave the grandstand and roam the grounds, getting close-ups of the fantastically garbed maskers. By Tuesday night the bands are beginning to break up, and all Trinidad blends into one great rhythmic dancing island. Then at midnight the carnival is over and Lent begins.

TRINIDAD: *The island's drummers rank among the world's best.*

TRINIDAD: *School children's faces reflect Chinese, African, British, East Indian, and Spanish ancestry.*

TRINIDAD: *A fine example of the ornate island town house.*

TRINIDAD: *A carnival queen must be both attractive and talented.*

TRINIDAD: *Steel bands, playing on discarded oil drums, have become the most popular music-makers in the Lesser Antilles.*

Part Two

FRENCH WEST INDIES

MARTINIQUE: *Outdoor notion-stand in Fort de France.*

GUADELOUPE: *The magnificent rocks at Pointe des Châteaux look toward Désirade.*

GUADELOUPE

with Saint Barthélemy, Désirade, Marie Galante, Saint Martin, and the Iles des Saintes

An island of magnificent scenery, and by far the largest of the French West Indies, Guadeloupe is actually the twin islands of Grande Terre and Basse Terre separated by the narrow sea-water channel, the Rivière Salée. The shape on the map is like a pair of wings. The two islands are entirely different. Basse Terre has two hundred and fifty square miles of thickly wooded mountainous terrain (Soufrière is 4,869 feet high), and the capital of Guadeloupe, also called Basse Terre, is located on this island. The largest city, Pointe-à-Pitre (36,000), is located on Grande Terre, a low island of limestone formation and the center of the extensive sugar cultivation.

Guadeloupe is located thirty miles north of Dominica and sixty miles south of Antigua. It has almost always been French. In addition to the two central islands, it has five island dependencies: Marie Galante, a round, sparsely populated agricultural colony with no tourist facilities; Désirade, six miles east, a long, cigar-shaped island, the leper colony for the French Antilles; St. Barthélemy, far north of Guadeloupe, near the island of St. Martin; the French half of St. Martin (described in the chapter on Sint Maarten in the Netherlands West Indies section); and, finally, the Iles des Saintes, five tiny islands lying six miles to the south.

Travelers will find their time much more profitably spent outside the cities of Basse Terre and Pointe-à-Pitre than within them. Pointe-à-Pitre offers the large, rambling Grand Hotel, which advertises that every room has a bath. This is true, but on a number of occasions there has been no water in the bathrooms. The food, however, is good, as it is all over the island, and particularly good if meals are ordered in advance. Two blocks from the Grand Hotel is one of the city's street markets. It is a hot, dusty area with dozens of dark women squatting behind small assortments of fruits and vegetables. The entire city gives the impression of being poor.

The iron cathedral, considered a landmark, is composed entirely of pieces of iron crisscrossed and bolted together. It is said to be hurricane- and volcano-proof, and looks it. There are a few modern buildings, but something seems to be wrong with the cement in Guadeloupe, for most of them have cracks or discolorations running through them even though they are only a few years old. The most pleasant section of Pointe-à-Pitre is the little harbor full of sloops and schooners and the square called the Place de la Victoire adjoining it. Shopping along the streets of Pointe-à-Pitre can be profitable, but it is best for the purchaser to have some knowledge of French: very little English is spoken. Prices are about the same as in Martinique, which are among the lowest in the Caribbean, but the selection of goods is not nearly so varied.

If the traveler is fortunate, he may make the acquaintance of one of Pointe-à-Pitre's merchants and see how the more affluent citizens live. A town house on a dusty street will have a narrow stairway entrance between two heavy iron or wooden doors, usually bolted. At the top of the stairway is another world. The spacious living-room is decorated in good taste and furnished with imported sofas and chairs. It opens into an equally attractive dining-room with an outdoor terrace overlooking an interior garden surrounded by a balcony. On the third floor are large bedrooms complete with mosquito nets and a bath with bidet. The exteriors of Pointe-à-Pitre are largely unattractive and even forbidding.

Guadeloupe's second city, Basse Terre, is only twenty miles from Pointe-à-Pitre as the crow flies, but a half-day's trip by car. The road winds along the coast, and the distance is about the same whether one elects to go around the northern end, which is comparatively uninteresting, or around the southern end, where the road leads through Trois Rivières, a native trading center, the taking-off point for Iles des Saintes. Along a miniature dockside a schooner with an auxiliary motor is available almost every morning to make the rough six-mile trip to Terre de Haut ("high land"), largest and most populated of the five Saintes. Rugged seamen preparing for the two- to five-hour trip, depending upon waves and currents, look much like Chinese coolies in their round, flat-topped straw hats covered with white cotton cloth. The hats, intricately made from split bamboo and other straws, are extremely light and exceptionally well designed. The white cloth stretched around the slender frame reflects the hot sun and allows these unique headpieces to act as convenient tropical umbrellas. Only the men wear this headgear. It is said that a man who once managed to make his way to and from China returned with a hat from which this distinctive design was developed.

The trip to Les Saintes is likely to be wet, for Trois Rivières is on the same side of the island as Guadeloupe's Soufrière, and clouds release their moisture here almost every afternoon. As the schooner nears Terre de Haut, you will see two or three fishing boats bobbing up and down like corks half a mile or so offshore. They are likely to be after vierge, a deep-sea red fish, or the large vielle, which is sold in the markets of Trois Rivières.

As with all good expeditions in the islands, the best way to plan this one is with a picnic. A couple of fish can be purchased from the boats and prepared by one of the excellent cooks on the island. They flavor fish, incidentally, with an unusually hot pepper whose name is translated as "Madame Jackass."

The citizens of Les Saintes, who call themselves saintois, say they originally came from Brittany. There is no reason to doubt this, for the men have ruddy complexions, and blue eyes and often have blond hair. There is evidence of a great deal of inbreeding among them, and this is not surprising, for the white people of Les Saintes have seldom married Negroes. This also accounts for the fact that Terre de Bas, the second-largest island of Les Saintes, is inhabited primarily by Negroes.

The main street of Terre de Haut is lined with small white houses with colorful painted doorways of blue or red. A few houses have balconies, and at least one has a long gingerbread gallery that gives it a distinctly Victorian air. This large house faces the little center square near the quayside. There is little else to see except for one large house built out from a cliffside into the sea. It is a replica of an ocean-going cruiser. Only a bit more than half of it protrudes from the rock, making it appear as though it had run into the rock and partially disappeared. The most interesting sight, however, is the men in their extraordinary hats.

A cable office is open a few hours a day, and it is possible to make arrangements to spend the night with one of the residents. There is no hotel. All of the saintois are fishermen, and none of them likes having his picture taken. A traveler has only to reveal a camera to find every back turned and almost every doorway empty.

Back in Trois Rivières, it is a short trip to the city of Basse Terre. Cleaner and neater than Pointe-à-Pitre, it offers little sightseeing. The best restaurant is called Robertson's, a most unusual name for a restaurant on a French island. Basse Terre is a good place to arrange for cars and guides for a trip up Soufrière. The road from Basse Terre to St. Claude is a steep five miles. Then take a secondary dirt road a bit higher, almost to the foot of the volcano. This is a more difficult climb than the volcanoes of Saba or St. Vincent, and should not be attempted by any but healthy and adventurous travelers. Equipment should consist of plenty of lunch, a couple of bottles of rum (one for the guides at the top), a lightweight raincoat and hat, and close-fitting shoes to keep out stones. In the early stages the ascent is steep, but the terrain levels off for a mile after the first few hundred feet. This part of the climb is across a wide trail through a dense tropical jungle of mango, palm, and giant fern trees. Higher up is a resthouse where innumerable visitors have carved their initials over every available inch of surface, including ceiling and rafters. This resthouse is little more than a large room with rough tables, and, except when there is rain, it is more pleasant to take a breather and lunch outdoors. Near the resthouse stand gigantic acoma trees with trunks mossy from parasites and with long liana ropes swinging from the huge branches to bar the trail. But a path leads up and around them until the slate-gray volcanic rock appears. Here the going is treacherous. It is well to keep close to the guide, for near the top are many bogs—tricky soft spots that look firm. It is easy to sink into one and painfully burn foot or ankle in the steaming sod.

The trip should be made in the early morning—it is only then that the top is likely to be clear enough so that the magnificent view of Dominica to the south and Montserrat to the north can be seen. On the very top of the volcano stands a small stone hut useful only during rains and high winds: the ceiling is just five feet high and most climbers are unable to stand erect. In spite of its low ceiling, dank smell, and damp floor, it is a welcome retreat in heavy weather.

On the trip down, the guides will take climbers to a natural hot spring where a pool has been fashioned for bathing. The water is clear and warm. A dip is highly refreshing, and makes the trip down to the base seem much shorter.

Dozens of small white stretches of sand dot the southeast coastline of Grande Terre. Three of them are exceptional. Just five miles east of Pointe-à-Pitre and just beyond the little village of Gosier is a real find for travelers.

La Pergola du Gosier is an incredibly fine French restaurant with individual cottages (called Pergolettes) perched above a white sand beach shaded by almond trees. The terrace of the restaurant affords an unobstructed view over the sea to the peak of Soufrière. Handsome café-au-lait girls serve a cuisine hitherto found only in the restaurants of France. Every night the terrace is gay with Guadeloupe's senators, representatives, and local businessmen, with their wives and guests, as well as with visitors from France, Italy, the United States, and England. Talk is in two, three, and sometimes four languages. Champagne corks pop (La Pergola has an enviable wine cellar). Specialités de la maison such as Red Fish Courtbillion, Oysters en Brochette, Chicken Petroluzzi (named after the proprietor and chef, Mario Petroluzzi), delectable Stuffed Land Crabs, and Langouste au Vin are served. The air is soft and cool, waves lap softly on the beach, and the tiny Pergola glows brightly until the small hours of the morning. There are dressing-rooms with showers, and many residents of Pointe-à-Pitre come out for a swim and an always exceptional luncheon.

On the same road ten miles farther out is Ste. Anne, another fine beach. Here a small new hotel with a tiny restaurant and dance floor has opened. Ste. Anne has all the makings of a very fine resort.

Next in line, another ten miles along this coast, is the sleepy little town of St. François, which boasts one of the finest beaches in all the Caribbean. Unfortunately, like so many other fine beaches, it is still awaiting development. No one bathes here except an occasional village fisherman and his children. If this beach were located in the United States or Europe, it would be worth millions of dollars and crowded by thousands of bathers.

The most magnificent view in Guadeloupe is from Pointe des Châteaux on the southeast tip of the island. Here giant rocks reach out into the sea and the surf beats high. The island of Désirade, seemingly within swimming distance, is six miles away. On a steep hill back of the rocks is a giant cross overlooking the entire point of the island. But no other sign of civilization spoils the natural beauty.

North of Pointe des Châteaux there is one more beach worth a visit. This is Moule, sometimes referred to as the "beach of the skulls" or the "beach of bones." Many battles were fought here by the Caribs, French, and English, and many soldiers were buried in the hillocks back of the beach. During the past century the constant beat of the encroaching sea has unearthed many of these graves. Today, on a beach that is a perfect place for bathing, one is likely to stumble over a well-bleached thigh-bone or skull.

GUADELOUPE: *Pointe-à-Pitre's inner harbor.*

GUADELOUPE: *Coming down through the mist from the island's greatest adventure, the climb up the Soufrière.*

GUADELOUPE: *These natives of Les Saintes, descended from Africans and Bretons, wear hats unique to their islands.*

GUADELOUPE: *House in the shape of a ship on Terre de Haut (Les Saintes).*

SAINT BARTHÉLEMY

Far to the north, one hundred miles from Guadeloupe, lies this tiny island with magnificent beaches and unusual people. It is forty miles north of St. Kitts, fifteen miles south of St. Martin. The island is truly remote, for it can be reached only by occasional schooners or by chartering a yacht or plane. It is not a long trip from the Virgin Islands or Puerto Rico—one hundred and fifty miles from the former, less than two hundred from the latter. The thirty-six hundred people who inhabit St. Barthélemy are mostly white and of Swedish descent. Although the island is intensely loyal to France now, it still remembers vividly when it was Swedish. The capital is still known as Gustavia, and its harbor is so nearly perfect as to be almost indescribable. A narrow channel leads into a deep-water bay that lies in a perfect circle, with the little city nestled along the beach. High hills surround the harbor, leaving only the narrow entrance.

The islanders, mostly fishermen and traders, take their little schooners up and down the neighboring islands, selling chickens, eggs, and straw hats, and buying rum and other salable commodities. The seamen of St. Barts have a considerable reputation up and down the Caribbean for smuggling.

The hotel in Gustavia is perhaps the most unusual of any in the islands. Called the Paris-Stockholm, it has only three guest rooms, and is located directly above the only dry-goods and general store in the town. Rooms are small, beds lumpy, and the communal bath is at the end of the corridor across the bar. The manager's office is right next to one of the rooms, and he sleeps in it and snores. His snores are particularly noticeable because the walls extend up only a limited distance and every noise in every room can be heard throughout the hotel.

The dining-room is large and pleasant. A small lounge opens off it; here drinks are served. This room contains a large framed picture of the Swedish royal family, another of the yacht *Falkell*, which visited the island in 1953, a beer poster with a lovely Swedish girl in a golden evening dress, two maps, and a picture of Joan of Arc. The hotel is owned and operated by the Mayor of Gustavia, Mr. Alexander Magras, the best-known and most popular name on the island. In the dry-goods store under the hotel a considerable amount of shopping can be done. It carries a fine stock of madras cotton and perfumes. Unfortunately, the beach is a four-mile drive across the island. It is an entirely worth-while journey.

This beautiful beach compares in every way with any beach in Europe, Asia, or the United States. The three-mile stretch of curving white sand is backed by a high cliff that breaks the wind and keeps the surf from becoming too high. A reef, located about one sixth of a mile out, keeps large, dangerous fish from shore. The sand slopes gently, so that it is safe for children. Regrettably, there are no bathing facilities, although they are contemplated.

After Columbus, M. Remy de Haenen, Consul General, is the real discoverer and promoter of St. Barts. He lives on this beach, swims, spear-fishes, and operates two twin Cessna planes on charter to bring visitors to see his paradise. De Haenen has a tiny cottage overlooking the beach and an excellent St. Barts cook. He owns a piece of land on the beach and is particularly eager to build a hotel on this spot. He is ready now to fly visitors from St. Kitts, Guadeloupe, and St. Martin, and can make arrangements to fly them from Puerto Rico and the Virgin Islands.

St. Barts is an old-fashioned island in every way. People live much as they did in the nineteenth century. They speak some French-Swedish, but mostly English. Custom decrees that a young man woo a girl for a year and build a small house before he marries her. The girls are attractive, blue-eyed, tall, and well built. Older women wear stiffly starched white blouses and skirts and the frilled cap of Normandy. Although everything is spotlessly clean, the people are very poor. They are also very religious: holy pictures and statues of the Virgin are the only decoration in their immaculate homes. In the rural areas families gather together in communities having their own tiny stores. As many as thirty or forty members of a family are clustered together.

St. Barthélemy is now ready only for the most adventurous type of tourist. It has every natural facility to offer, and should be one of the great resorts of the future.

SAINT BARTHÉLEMY: *Wearing the headdress brought from Brittany by their ancestors, women weave fine hats from abundant grasses.*

SAINT BARTHÉLEMY: *This crescent of sand is one of the finest beaches in the Antilles.*

SAINT BARTHÉLEMY: *Girls gather around a shrine to the Virgin each Sunday afternoon to offer prayers and sing.*

MARTINIQUE

It is easy to see why the painter Paul Gauguin enjoyed painting in Martinique: it is even more lush and fecund than Tahiti, where he made his final home. The climate is warm or hot all year on this semi-tropical island, which is located twenty miles north of St. Lucia and twenty-five miles south of Dominica; the most comfortable period for visitors is from December to June. These are the dry months, but there is likely to be a sudden warm shower almost any afternoon. The winter months are also best because of Martinique's elaborate carnival and the unique festival of La Diablesse, which is in the nature of a wake and celebration for the dying carnival. It is held on Ash Wednesday. All the other pre-Lenten carnivals in the West Indies—indeed, in all the world—are over by the time La Diablesse starts.

This fete begins early in the morning of the first day of Lent, when over twenty-five thousand maskers (who call themselves diablesses) begin to appear in the capital city of Fort de France. They dress in grotesque black-and-white costumes and manage to achieve the most unusual effects by using wigs, masks, headdresses, and costumes in pure white and dead black. By ten in the morning the city looks like something out of the Middle Ages come alive, with witches, devils, and black magic. Much rum is consumed, and elaborate luncheons are given. As the day wears on, there are more and more shouts to "Bois-Bois," the king of the carnival, who must die that night.

All day the wake goes on. The black-and-white devils mourn and long corteges go by, with bands playing sometimes mournful, sometimes gay, music out in front. The diablesses insist to everyone who will listen that their hearts are breaking because the Mardi Gras is ending. At dusk the tempo becomes faster; the street dancing becomes wilder. Across the great savane, a huge pile of wood is laid for a gigantic bonfire. Darkness comes, the fire is lighted, and the celebrants, looking like participants in a great witches' sabbath, whirl and dance around it. As the fire rises to its peak, a figure representing Bois-Bois, the carnival deity, is thrown into the flames; the shouts become more shrill, the dancing more frenzied. As the fire dies down, the exhausted maskers wander off into the dark. But the celebration is not yet over. At the Lido, Martinique's largest hotel, as at other hotels and clubs, there will be dancing until midnight. Costumes will remain black and white, but are likely to be evening clothes instead of weird and fantastic costumes. On the Lido's terrazzo dance floor, Martiniquans will dance the beguine, as well as the waltz and fox trot. They will be very gay till midnight, when the mournful chants begin as a coffin with the effigy of Bois-Bois is brought in. Then, with the coffin leading the way, the dancers parade slowly to the spot where the spirit of carnival will finally be buried.

Next day in the savane the pure white marble statue of the Empress Josephine looks down on a sea of debris. Pieces of paper, cups, broken rum bottles, and the remains of the bonfire greet the marble eyes of this great heroine of the island. Josephine (Marie Joséphine Rose Tascher de la Pagerie) was born in the village of Trois Ilets in June 1763. She left Martinique for Paris, and when sixteen was married. By her first marriage, to Alexandre Beauharnais, she had two children who were later known as Prince Eugène and Hortense, Queen of Holland (she married Napoleon's brother Louis). They are as well known in Martinique as Hansel and Gretel in Germany. In the early days of the French Revolution, Josephine went back to her beloved Martinique and lived there for two years. When she returned to Paris she was promptly put in jail. Her thirty-four-year-old husband was killed in the Revolution. She was thirty-three years old when she married Napoleon; eight years later he crowned her Impératrice des français. Only five years later the Emperor divorced her. On Martinique, Josephine is still the Empress, and is revered almost as a saint. Outside the little town of Trois Ilets her childhood home has become a shrine. No part of the original house is standing, but from a section of one of the walls grows a pink-and-white flowering vine.

The mixed Negro and French peoples of Martinique—and they are in the great majority—have little color problem. Proud of their

African and French heritages, they have largely resolved the quarrel within themselves caused by their backgrounds as master and slave. Of the population of 260,000, almost all have some white ancestry, but less than five per cent of the population is pure white. The island is still poor, but is making a distinct effort to do more for its people. It has a good law school and a large technical school, and scholarships for study at the universities in France are given on a competitive basis.

Sugar is Martinique's biggest industry, and there are eighteen sugar factories. This is doubtless why there are a total of one hundred and seventy rum distilleries, more than on any other island. Among the best rums are Rhum Clément and a double-distilled rum called Couer Chaude, which is so light that ice will not float on it, but sinks to the bottom of the glass. Not much water is drunk because of the excellence of the French wines and rums, but water is a problem: unless boiled or bottled, it should not be drunk by travelers. Martinique has, however, a very fine bottled mineral water called Didier which gushes from the rock two miles from Fort de France. Almost everyone on the island drinks it, and all hotels serve it.

It is worth going to Martinique just to eat. Compared with fare on the British and the Dutch islands, the food is infinitely superior. This is true of the better hotels, most of the smaller cafés along the waterfront, and particularly of Le Manoir. This fine restaurant is located high on a hill outside the town of Fort de France. Always cool, it offers long vistas from its terrace over the southern end of the island. Food is prepared to order.

Because Martinique has a reputation for gaiety, it is assumed that there is a considerable amount of night life. This is untrue except for regular dances at the hotels, occasional dances at private clubs, and a wild middle-class dance hall known as the Select Tango. The dancing at the Select Tango is unrestrained, as is the drinking, but no more vulgar than the exhibition rumbas, sambas, and mambos seen in the night clubs in the United States or Europe. Customers of every shade from blond to black, the darker shades predominating, laugh and joke and drink at the small tables, rising from time to time to step into the tempo of an uninhibited beguine. The entrance to the Select Tango is on a narrow street in the business section of Fort de France. A wooden stairway leads to the spacious dance floor, and there is a balcony from which visitors can watch the proceedings without becoming a part of them. Late in the evening the room is cooled by the breeze from the sea blowing in through the tropical lattice-work and large front windows. The Ash Wednesday celebration is the beginning of Lent, which Catholic Martinique takes very seriously, and the Select Tango is likely to be closed during at least the early part of Lent.

Lent is a good time to visit the unfortunate city of St. Pierre, which was destroyed in 1902 by the most devastating volcanic eruption the West Indies has ever seen. The remains of the city, once the capital of the island, lie along the coast fifteen miles north of Fort de France. The road is fair, but narrow and steep in spots, dotted by a series of colorful little fishing villages with elaborate meshes of fishnets hung across tall poles and making interesting patterns against the sea. At Carbet a plaque along the white beach commemorates the spot where Columbus landed in Martinique. It is particularly easy to find, for there is always a long line of native women doing their washing near the memorial. The first view of St. Pierre nestled under Mount Pelée shows no devastation. The lush jungle has grown high and green through the shells of houses and public buildings. A considerable number of people have moved back during the past fifty years, and an attempt is being made to build a new town near the old one. It is upon close inspection that the traveler can see how thoroughly the town was destroyed. Marble statues lie tumbled about near the present small museum. Inside the museum are ancient photographs of the volcanic eruption. Who took them and how they were taken no one in Martinique knows. This little museum also contains a number of exhibits of volcanic rock and maps showing how the town originally was laid out. While nothing could be done to save the houses and buildings of St. Pierre when Mount Pelée erupted, an obstinate governor was directly responsible for the death of its people (just one man was saved—a condemned murderer who was incarcerated in a heavy-walled dungeon that can still be seen). The governor continuously urged the people to stay on even after clouds of smoke and rain of pebbles were descending on the town. He would not leave, and called out the militia to convince the population that there was no danger. He even brought his wife and children from Fort de France to prove that it was safe. Then, early in the morning, the mountain struck. Before anyone could grasp what was happening, a flood of fire swept over the city and out into the sea, pushing the water before it, gutting the entire city and killing all the residents including those in ships in the harbor.

Mount Pelée can be climbed, and it is a worth-while expedition.

Tall hardwood trees line the road at the base. It is possible to go halfway up by car and then make the summit on foot in about two hours. It makes a good all-day picnic. Plan to leave Fort de France early in the morning and go directly to the base of the mountain. It is a good idea to wear short boots and to eye the terrain carefully as you climb, for Martinique is the only island, with the exception of St. Lucia, inhabited by the rare but deadly fer-de-lance snake.

Good beaches are few on the northern end of Martinique, but there are excellent ones along the south coast. Many well-to-do families have bought property and are building homes along Diamant, a long white stretch of beach offering excellent swimming and surf bathing.

Just past this new private beach settlement is Diamond Rock, known to the British as *Her Majesty's Ship Diamond Rock.* Here a group of one hundred and twenty British sailors and one lieutenant held the French fleet at bay for seventeen months. They surrendered only when they were out of powder, and then to sixteen French ships. The total British loss during the period was two men killed and one wounded.

Near the southern tip of Martinique is the beach of Ste. Anne, a good place to swim and picnic. Farther down, on the tip is the Savane des Pétrifications, a clearing of petrified logs, which only those hardy travelers who have a particular interest in petrified logs will find worth visiting. In Fort de France there is a beach at the Lido Hotel, though the sand is not very white and the swimming only fair.

Shopping in Fort de France is very good. One particular shop, that of Roger Albert, carries more different gadgets than shops on any island with the possible exception of Curaçao. It also carries French perfumes at prices lower than those in France. Guarantees hold up well, for the merchants in Martinique have a long-standing reputation for honest dealing. The island is an excellent place to purchase Swiss watches, which can be bought at about forty per cent below stateside prices.

For travelers who like warm weather, French people, sightseeing, not much beach activity, little night life, good shopping, and fine food, Martinique is ideal.

MARTINIQUE: *In a typical cemetery, graves are decorated with hundreds of giant conch shells.*

MARTINIQUE: *Cell in which a condemned murderer escaped with his life when all other people of St. Pierre were exterminated by the eruption of Mt. Pelée.*

MARTINIQUE: *A carnival queen poses in traditional costume before the statue of the Empress Josephine.*

MARTINIQUE: *Almost melted, this bust lay among the ruins of St. Pierre after the eruption of Mt. Pelée.*

Part Three

INDEPENDENT ISLANDS

HAITI: *Women bring produce to market across long, steep trails.*

CUBA: *Surf fishing near Matanzas.*

CUBA

The largest of the Caribbean islands is a land of sunshine and sugar, beaches and baseball, cocktails and cockfights, fancy foods and fine fishing, rum and rumba.

Narrow and mountainous, Cuba stretches seven hundred and fifty miles across the entrance to the Gulf of Mexico. Ninety miles north across the Florida straits lies Key West. The eastern tip of Cuba points toward Haiti, visible forty-five miles away on a clear day. One hundred and twenty-five miles to the west across the Yucatán Channel is Mexico, and about one hundred miles south lies Jamaica.

The proximity of Cuba to Florida means that travelers may take their cars via the giant car ferry from Key West to Cárdenas, Cuba. Cubans commute to Florida to shop; United States visitors take off for Cuba every hour by plane for a flight that requires only thirty minutes. Comfortable overnight boats skim the calm waters from Miami to Havana. It is about a fourteen-hour trip.

Every visitor to Cuba is required to purchase a tourist card that costs $2.50. It may be bought before leaving the United States or upon arrival in Cuba. It is the best buy in all the West Indies, for in Cuba the Tourist Commission has done everything possible to make the traveler happy. Cars may be driven without an additional license for six months, and all United States driver's licenses are valid. A special group of tourist police who speak fluent English is at the service of the visitor. They are easily recognized by the "Police Department—Tourist Division" insignia on their sleeves. The island has even passed a special law that protects tourists from annoyances and abuses. Any cause for complaint is given immediate attention. In the event that court action is necessary, the complainant is not required to appear at the hearings. The visitor will be represented by a member of the tourist board.

Special taxis supervised by the Government are available for sightseeing trips. There is a continuous emphasis on transportation in the island. This is important, for it is impossible to see Cuba's resorts or even Havana's environs without covering considerable mileage. The island's long coastline, which includes golden beaches both primitive and developed, covers well over two thousand miles.

The fine beaches along the coast are largely patronized by winter visitors to the island. Cubans wait until summer to go near the sea. Although the water is warm enough for bathing all year, winter is winter to the Cuban and going to the beach during that season "No es costumbre."

This phrase is one that visitors will do well to heed, as Cuban customs are quite different from those in the United States. Women never wear slacks or shorts while traveling or when going into town to shop. Respectable Cuban women do not go to bars or night clubs unescorted. This does not mean that women traveling alone are unable to see Cuban night life. There are literally dozens of available tours that unaccompanied women may take.

Don't expect Cubans to move like most Latins. This is definitely not a mañana-land. Cubans move fast, work hard, and build well. This headlong pace leads to another custom that will be found in no other island. It is "Me dió una brava," which might be translated as "He gave me the brava" or "He put one over on me." A good example of this "giving the brava" occurs in the frantic scramble of Havana traffic. Two cars approach an intersection; it looks as though the one nearest the crossing will go first; at the last possible minute the car farther away speeds up and shoots across as the other is forced to slam on the brakes. This occurs often in Cuban business dealings, and is said to extend even to romance. When a girl who holds out great promise as a conquest is wined and dined and then gets herself home without even being kissed—she has given the young man the brava. This sometimes works out in reverse.

Cubans are friendly and hospitable people steeped in traditional Spanish reticence. You will meet them in clubs, restaurants, and hotels, drink with them, and be generally entertained, but it is quite unlikely that you will be invited to dinner at their homes. Social customs are more European than American.

While there is no official color pattern—Cubans are white, mulatto, and black—Negroes and Creoles do not generally intermarry. Travelers should know that "criollo" (Creole), a Spanish word meaning "descended from the early colonists," does not imply Negro blood. The Cuban Constitution guarantees freedom to all of its people in the following words: "Discrimination by reason of sex, race, color, or class is declared unlawful and punishable." But on the social level Creoles often say: "The races are together, but not mixed." Or: "A man has a right to choose his own friends." On the whole, the Cubans handle their color problems better than the United States and certainly better than any of the other Caribbean isles except Haiti.

Cubans love to gamble and do not consider it sinful. Every type of gambling is entirely legal. For the wealthy and the visitor there are a national casino and other plush clubs where craps, roulette, blackjack, chuck-a-luck, and many other games are available. The slambang, exciting basque game of jai-alai (hi-li) offers a chance to win or lose on every hard-fought game and every individual player. At jai-alai frontons in Havana, world-famous players can be seen in action every day of the year except for one month in midsummer.

Horse racing is another favorite method of gambling in Cuba, and Oriental Park at near-by Marianao has the finest track in the Caribbean. There are also gaming-rooms at both the grandstand and the Jockey Club. At night, dog racing takes over, and thousands of betters pack the Havana Greyhound Kennel Club.

Even the very poor gamble either on the national lottery or on the ever-present cockfights. A large part of the national lottery goes to the winners, a fixed percentage to charity and to the sellers for overhead; the rest goes to the government. The Cuban who loses is able to say that he has helped a worthy cause; if he wins, he can say that God has been good to him.

Cockfights may be seen every day of the year. There are more than eight hundred clubs; well over one thousand individual owners have fighting cocks. Vallas (cockpit arenas) are operated for the rich and for the poor. There are several vallas around Havana, the best known being Valla Havana and Valla Nacional. In Club Calisto in the Vedado section of Havana, reputed to be the most expensive in the world, members have their own cock-breeding establishment. Seats for tourists are available, and this unusual club even welcomes ladies. But here a word of warning—cockfighting is a duel to the death, and a fighting cock, blind, crippled, and bloody, can be a pitiful sight as he is slowly destroyed. Unless you have seen and enjoyed many bullfights and can stand the sight of lots of blood, stay away.

Cuba offers a combination of advantages to the traveler: excellent beaches, elegant cities remembering the past, fine hotels with reasonably good plumbing and the ever-present bidet, and the gayest night life in the western hemisphere.

First the beaches. The number-one beach, one of the finest in the world, is El Varadero, ninety miles east of Havana on the north coast. Varadero has its own airport, into which planes fly directly from the United States mainland or Havana. The drive to Varadero from Havana is an interesting one along a good highway, the only hazard being large buses that careen around the curves at high speeds. A stop for lunch is indicated at Matanzas, an easy half-day drive out of Havana. This sleepy town is a find for spelunkers, who will enjoy visiting the extensive Bellamar Caves, and for gourmets, who will enjoy tasting the boiled langustos (giant crayfish) taken fresh from the patio fountain at the Hotel Gran Paris. Lovers of beauty generally will be enchanted with the Hermitage Church of Mount Serrat high on a near-by hill. The top of the tower offers a remarkable view of the city, with the valley of the Yumuri River and Matanzas Bay in the distance. In the small chapel is an altar with a dark, almost black figure of the Virgin. Both altar and Virgin are copies of the originals in the chapel of Montserrat near Barcelona.

The last ten miles of beachside into Varadero are lined with the fine summer homes of wealthy Cubans. Then come five miles of the gently curving beach itself. Powdery white sand slopes gradually down to meet the green-blue-purple water.

The little village of Varadero has delightful native bars where old men sit at tiny outdoor tables, conversing and drinking and enjoying the breezes. On the main street there are a number of small shops. Along the beach barefoot boys sell shells and figures made from them. Architecturally interesting summer houses that overlook the beach have the wide verandas and gingerbread décor reminiscent of the beach boardinghouses of the twenties along the Atlantic seaboard.

Hotels of every kind are plentiful in Varadero, but are usually full; it is important to make reservations well in advance. Also note that a number of hotels operate on a restricted-club system in an effort to keep out what they consider undesirable patrons. Accommodations range from simple, inexpensive pensions to attractive boardinghouses; from small, reasonably priced hotels, such as the

Casa La Rosa, to the grandiose Internacional Hotel, with gambling casino, name bands from the states, and indoor and outdoor dining. A showplace with a watchtower and armed guard at the gate is Xanadu, the elaborate estate built by Irénée du Pont. Recreations at Varadero include fishing, yachting, riding, and tennis as well as the sun and surf.

The seacoast on both sides of Havana is rich in beaches. Eastward, out the Great White Way Highway, are Cojimar, Tarara, Santa María del Mar, Guanabo, Veneciana, and, finally, Jibacoa fifty miles from Havana. Some are public, some private. It is important to check before visiting one. West of Havana is Marianao, actually a suburb of the city, where La Playa, the coastal resort area, is located. The public beach here, with excellent dressing-rooms and restaurant, is known as La Concha. Just behind the beach is Cuba's Coney Island, replete with thrilling rides. The entire Marianao section is one long beach studded with resort hotels and yacht clubs.

Leaving Havana and continuing into Pinar del Río, westernmost of the six provinces, there is an interesting off-the-track beach at La Esperanza.

Almost directly across the island from Havana is the lobster-and-sponge-fishing town of Batabanó, best known as the take-off point for the Isle of Pines, Cuba's island within an island. The Isle of Pines, rising to almost fifteen hundred feet, has many peaks of pure marble. Boats big enough to carry cars make the overnight trip, arriving at Nueva Gerona, the Isle's largest town, at eight a.m. Daily flights from Havana take approximately thirty-five minutes and are more comfortable than the overnight boat trip.

For a quiet vacation with lots of fishing, sunning, and bathing in medicinal springs, Santa Fe, Isle of Pines, is a good choice. Although small in size and with its best beaches unapproachable except by boat, the island has much to recommend it. Hotels are old-fashioned and comfortable. The climate is slightly cooler than Havana's in summer and much the same in winter. The countryside is green, with acre after acre of large grapefruits that are shipped to Cuba and the United States. The two main towns are Nueva Gerona on the coast and Santa Fe in the cooler interior. Some of the finest fishing in all Cuba can be found off the coast of the Isle of Pines. Catches include swordfish, yellowtail, and snapper. Visitors get a thrill out of progging the langustos, crayfish as large as Maine lobsters. The two easily accessible beaches are somewhat disappointing. Columbo is an unattractive strip of sand, and the black sand of Bibijagua is not conducive to pleasant bathing. At present there are not enough roads on the Isle of Pines to justify transporting a car from the mainland, but plenty of taxis are available for sightseeing trips.

Sightseeing includes the Presidio Modelo (model prison); a house in which José Martí, Cuba's greatest hero, lived for a brief period; and caves and grottoes once frequented by buccaneers. Island legend says that Robert Louis Stevenson patterned *Treasure Island* after this locale, but Norman Island in the British Virgins also claims this distinction. Much treasure, however, is said to have been buried on the Isle of Pines. Some Spanish pieces of eight have been found.

It is difficult to separate Cuba's resorts from her picturesque, timeless cities. Even in the provinces the most venerable municipalities offer some resort facilities. This is true of Cienfuegos, Trinidad, and Santiago de Cuba. Cienfuego ("one hundred fires"), only two hundred miles from Havana, is easily reached by highway or plane. Because it was settled by Spaniards displaced when Florida was ceded to England in 1763, it has a personality distinctly different from any of Cuba's other old cities. The location is superb. It lies on a semicircular, almost landlocked bay, a magnificent harbor. The entire section is known throughout Cuba for wild-duck hunting, especially in the San Mateo and Guaranaca lagoons. It is also an outstanding fishing resort. Besides the usual red snapper and kingfish, there are good tarpon fishing grounds offshore. Available fishing boats range from small motorboats to yachts. Each of the fifty members of the Cienfuegos Fishing Association has his own yacht. A city of ornate, wealthy homes, it also has first-class accommodations and beach clubs, such as Punta Gorda, Pasacaballos, and Rancho Luna. Some have individual cabañas. The citizens of this city are hospitable and friendly, and a fair number speak some English. No traveler should miss a visit to Havanillo Falls fifteen miles from town. Wide, magnificent cascades of water fall over a great expanse of rock. The sides of the falls are covered with virgin forest growth. The drive is just long enough to make a picnic basket a good accessory.

At Soledad, in the immediate vicinity of Cienfuegos, is a most interesting Botanical Garden. This is the Atkins Institute, operated by Harvard University as a field station for postgraduate work in zoology, biology, and botany. It is well worth a visit.

About fifty miles farther down the south coast lies Trinidad, the Spanish-Cuban city that time forgot. Framed by high purple hills, founded in 1514 by Diego Velásquez, it was the wealthiest and mightiest of Cuba's cities. Today it looks like a city that has slept peacefully for three hundred years and has not yet quite awakened.

Narrow cobbled streets ring with the sharp footsteps of burros. Hand-carved paneled doorways open behind ironwork protective gates. Some homes have entrances shaped like iron cages; gracefully pointed at the top, these have entrance ways in the center. Intricate Moorish grillwork decorates the overhanging balconies. The city is rooted deeply in the past. The plazas, like green oases with statues, seem timeless. The great palaces of the Iznages, Borrells, and the Conde de Brunet, where the tourist commission has an office, are all open to the public through the Old World courtesy of their owners. These impressive palaces have been mellowed by time, but are still delightfully livable. In stone and marble and in every venerable detail of furniture and decoration they reflect their past elegance.

Twilight in Trinidad is the most beautiful time of day. The dusky purples, blues, and mauve tones of the time-worn buildings make it look like an enchanted city out of the romantic past. After dark, to complete the illusion, the parrandas, groups of violin-playing, guitar-strumming young men, stroll the streets singing.

One unusually interesting piece of evidence of the past is the unique coat of arms painted on the wall of the Mayor's office in the city hall. It is a shield with a leafy tree having a cross on the trunk. From the foliage an eye looks out; a bell hangs from one of the branches. In the foreground are two cannon, while above the tree is a revolutionary hat with a star on it. Then comes the great surprise: this shield is flanked by two British flags. Trinidad's unusual coat of arms goes back to 1762. A British man-of-war sent out a party of sailors to attack the city. Met in battle by the Trinidadians, they were defeated and their flags captured. This so pleased the king of Spain that the city was authorized to add the two British flags to its coat of arms.

Trinidad is one of the fortunate Cuban cities that have fine beaches and fishing. Interest in tourism in the city is increasing, and the Government, realizing its historic treasures, has declared it a national monument. New motels and resort projects are under way, for the Government hopes to make Trinidad's unusual attractions available to many more travelers.

The road from Trinidad leads back to the Carretera Central, the highway that winds like a snake across the entire length of the island. On its way to Camagüey it goes through Sancti Spíritus, a historic hamlet settled in 1514. Its oldest section reproduces the Moorish architecture of Toledo in Spain; its Honorato Square is patterned faithfully after the ancient plazas of Madrid.

South of Sancti Spíritus, in the center of the cattle country, lies Camagüey, a city of cowboys, dust, heat, and history. It boasts an adequate hotel, but lacks resort facilities. It has a good airstrip and a fine airport bar. Some travelers having a brief stopover will find time to taxi into town to see the church of La Soledad, the oldest in Cuba. The clock in the church was made in Barcelona in 1773. The hotel across from the railroad station is a good place to drop in for a cold beer and reflect on the history of the country.

Cuba's most popular beverage is a beer called Hatuey, named after an almost forgotten Indian who was Cuba's first revolutionist. Escaping from Hispaniola shortly after the Spanish took that island, Hatuey went to Cuba. In 1512 he led the Indians against the early Spanish settlers. At one great meeting of warriors he promised to reveal the god of the white man. When they were all assembled, he dramatically uncovered a large hamper filled with gold. Hatuey's resistance did not last long. Captured after being betrayed, he was sentenced to be burned at the stake. But the preaching of Bartolomé de Las Casas was beginning to be heard on the island, and the Spanish rulers had warned the settlers against useless cruelty to the Indians. So Hatuey was offered a chance to become a Christian and go to the Christian heaven instead of the hell of the pagans. "Will I find the Spaniards in heaven?" he inquired. "Yes, there are many," he was told. "Then let me burn! I do not want to go where there are Spaniards," he said.

Cuba has a way of writing its history in alcoholic drinks. Spain introduced sugar cane early in the seventeenth century, and the rum industry developed rapidly thereafter. The British got their first taste of Cuban rum in 1762, when they successfully attacked Havana and held it for one year. Then they traded the island back to Spain for the Florida territory. By the nineteenth century, Cuban rum was in great demand both in the United States and in England. Early rum was a strong, odoriferous liquor, strictly a man's drink. But in 1862 Don Facundo Bacardi, with a new refining and distilling process, took rum out of the tavern and into the drawing-room. Just as Bacardi was getting started, Cuba's unsuccessful ten-year war, which was to set the stage for her later independence, began. It effectively welded together the revolutionary leaders Máximo Gómez, Antonio Maceo, and Calixto García, giving then much of the experience that enabled them later, under the leadership and planning of José Martí, to gain independence for their country. When the final battle in Cuba's war for freedom started in 1895, her generals and army were ready.

Although the Cubans had the Spanish on the run, the United States entry into the war hastened its conclusion. When the battleship *Maine* was blown up in 1898, the United States declared war against Spain. It was during this year that the Daiquiri cocktail was created. It originated shortly after Teddy Roosevelt started up San Juan Hill (with most of his Rough Riders on foot, his horses not having arrived on time). A group of naval officers stationed at Daiquirí Beach was entertained at a luncheon by the manager of the Daiquirí copper mine. Before lunch he served a drink especially devised for the occasion. The officers, after consuming a great many, called for the recipe and the name. The manager of the mine explained the drink was light Bacardi rum, lime juice, granulated sugar, and ice (imported for the occasion) shaken well together and strained. Lime juice, incidentally, was then considered an antidote to yellow fever. After explaining the ingredients, the mine manager suggested they call the drink Daiquiri after both the beach and the copper mine.

One more important drink completes this brief outline of Cuban history. All through the bloody days of the ten-year war the battle cry was "Cuba libre!" Two years after the war's end, in 1898, the first shipment of Coca-Cola arrived at a small American bar on Neptune Street in Havana. Manuel Rodríguez, a Cuban who was there for the occasion, tells the story this way: "I was sixteen years old and a messenger for General Leonard Wood, commander of the United States troops. I liked to hang around the bar and listen to the americanos talk, and I used to help one of the officers home whenever he got too drunk. One hot afternoon the bartender decided to try mixing the rum with this new drink, Coca-Cola. The soldiers liked it very much, and one of them suddenly proposed a toast. 'Hey fellas,' he said, raising his glass, 'Cuba libre!' By the next day it had caught on, and everyone on Neptune Street was drinking Cuba libres."

The last battle for Cuba's liberation was fought not in Havana, but on the southernmost coast of the island, at Santiago de Cuba. The island's second city is a beautiful, busy port with its own Morro Castle, now in ruins, guarding the approach. Santiago is a bewildering assortment of architectural periods, with Moorish influence predominating. It is possible to sail across the channel where Lieutenant

Richmond Hobson sank the *Merrimac* in an effort to bottle up the Spanish fleet. Across the deep blue-green harbor is Smith Cay, with red-roofed, pastel-colored summer homes. Near the eastern tip of the island is Baracoa, where Diego Velásquez started the first settlement. The capital was later moved to Santiago de Cuba, and then to the port that was to become Cuba's greatest city, Havana.

Havana is three distinct cities: the ancient city of the Spaniards; the modern metropolis of the Cubans; and the exciting city of the night.

In the old city every structure is a historical landmark. Statues of Spanish and early Cuban heroes mingle with opulent palaces of the Spanish rulers. On the Plaza de Armas, center of the old city, is the palace occupied by the early governors, which is now the city hall. Also on this plaza is La Fuerza, a fortress built forty-six years after Columbus discovered the island. Another old and even more famous fortress, Morro Castle, still guards the approach to Havana. In addition to the view of the dungeons, cannon, and early relics, the visitor to Morro Castle can also get the best view (and take good pictures) of the skyline and waterfront.

Modern Havana is a beehive of building activity where buildings seem to spring up overnight. While many of them resemble square beehives, a great number of the new skyscrapers are designed for both beauty and utility. Broad new avenues are planted with tropical flowers and decorated with towering monuments to the heroes of the island's struggle for independence. In the downtown section some streets are wide and clean, others incredibly narrow and dirty. All bustle with continuous activity.

More than either the old or the new, it is the after-dark city that offers most to the visitor. Historic buildings are scattered throughout the island and modern buildings can be seen all over the world. Havana, however, offers the gayest, most varied night life of any city in the western hemisphere.

In preparation for the pleasures of the evening, Cuban businesses close early. By four thirty in the afternoon most of the streets of the capital are deserted. By seven, when most United States restaurants are filled, Cuban dining-rooms are empty. In their suburban homes habaneros are dressing for the evening. Slowly the famous bars begin to fill; the Floridita, Sloppy Joe's, and Tally Ho are noisy with staccato conversation and the continuous whirring of electric shakers mixing daiquiris to a creamy, icy consistency. Although a great deal of Scotch is consumed, rum is the national drink—be it golden (Carta de Oro), silver (La Plata), transparent white (Blanca), or Anejo, a fine old rum liqueur.

The Floridita (actually the Florida, but called Floridita by aficionados) serves three versions of the popular Daiquiri. One old-time favorite calls for two ounces of Carta de Oro rum, one spoonful of granulated sugar, one teaspoonful of Maraschino liqueur (not the artificial cherry juice), and one-half fresh lime. This is shaken well with finely shaved ice either by hand or electric mixer. Strain into cocktail glasses and drink gratefully while very cold. The classic number-one Daiquiri is even simpler; use Carta Blanca rum and leave out the Maraschino. There is a new version of this called the mulatto —just use amber rum instead of white.

By nine o'clock most habaneros are thinking about dinner, but the drinks and conversation are so good that nothing is done about it before ten. Almost every good restaurant in Havana is crowded between ten and twelve.

It is possible to dine in almost any language in this cosmopolitan city. Some restaurants specialize in French cuisine. The Chinese section offers superlative Cantonese food. The Cubans themselves have a few dishes that should be translated into every tongue: congrejos moros (giant crabs), whose long black claws contain succulent pink-coral meat, are delicious either stuffed or boiled; the langosto (large crayfish), with a tail like that of a Maine lobster, is tender and tasty. One soup, a simple one, is served in all Cuban restaurants and should not be skipped. It is caldo gallego, made of ham, cabbage, and diced potatoes. Cuban fish and poultry courses are varied and uniformly excellent. Almost all restaurants serve a good arroz con pollo (chicken and rice), and the better ones serve a delicious paella a la valenciana, a dish of chicken and shrimp, peas, sausages, and saffron rice. Cooked to order, it takes thirty minutes, but when it does arrive—mmm!

Many travelers are shocked at the bitterness, blackness, and strength of Cuban coffee. It is strong enough to stain the inside of the cup, and is served very hot. After the visitor learns that Cubans use lots of sugar and milk, it becomes more palatable. Unlike most Caribbean islands, Cuba has lots of good restaurants outside hotels. In addition to such fine dining establishments as La Zaragozana, Monseigneur, and El Palacio de Cristal, there are literally dozens of more than adequate indoor and outdoor restaurants. One of the great pleasures of the Cuban twilight is to sit with a drink at a sidewalk cafe and watch the habaneros go by.

Cuban night life has more to offer than food and drink. The Grand Nacional Casino supplies gambling-rooms, entertainment, and dancing as well as dinner. Night clubs, many with gaming-rooms, exist at every economic level, but the most beautiful of all is the Tropicana.

Imagine a spacious garden with a high wall of flowering shrubs and towering trees. Into this garden introduce a gleaming dance floor, tables and chairs, concealed spotlights, and a large, well-designed, effectively lighted stage. This is only the beginning, for next to this open-air terrace the Tropicana has a magnificent crystal-arch room with a movable ceiling that opens to reveal the treetops and the heavens. The food at the Tropicana is reasonably good, the entertainment is exciting and rarely vulgar, and the two orchestras are exceptional. Service is sometimes slow, as it is in most Cuban night clubs, but the entertainment, décor, and music more than make up for delays. Stage shows at the Tropicana include both domestic and imported entertainers, and the local artists are usually superior. There is always at least one rumba-dancing team that carries this barnyard routine to heights never dreamed of by the country Negroes who first developed it. If there is any criticism of the entertainment, it is that it is too elaborate and there is a tendency for entertainment values to get lost in the too-long production numbers. It is nevertheless the best night club in the Caribbean and one of the most beautiful in the world.

Also in the suburbs of Havana, in the Vedado section, is the San Souci, another excellent open-air night club in a garden. In décor, music, and entertainment it is similar to, though not quite so spectacular as, the Tropicana. For entertainment without spectacular scenery the Montmartre, just a few blocks from Havana's Hotel Nacional, is unparalleled. Full Spanish orchestras have been imported to entertain here, as have the finest entertainers from South America, Spain, and the United States. Its two shows are long, but every exciting minute is packed with pleasure. Like the San Souci and the Tropicana, it has gambling-rooms. The best place to see the native rumba (it is never danced by Cubans on the dance floor) is in the small clubs out at La Playa, in the Marianao sector. In the area of smaller clubs, dance halls, and bars the "real rumba" can be seen.

Cuban dancing in the various dance halls or night clubs has none of the wild abandon seen in the United States rumba. While there is no objection to Americans throwing themselves about, Cubans prefer to dance the són, which has a rhythm based on the march, and the danzón, a simple one-step that has a very unusual feature. At the end of each sixteen bars of music, more or less, the dancers pause, talk, and rest for a moment while the music continues. At just the right beat they pick up exactly where they left off. Every visitor will find it difficult to figure out how the Cubans know when to stop and start. The cha-cha-cha, mambo, and merengue are also popular.

Cuban music is played on the usual instruments except for the addition of three indigenous instruments: the güiro, a rough-surfaced gourd played by scraping a stick along the side; the claves, two round sticks of polished rosewood that give a sharp clack when struck; and the now familiar maracas, gourds filled with seeds or shot.

Cuban culture, though new, has deep roots in the island. Cuban composers produce serious music as well as dance rhythms. There are many rumba dancers in the clubs; there is also a national ballet company. The architects who design the night clubs and casinos are also responsible for the skyscraper office buildings and the modern hospitals.

CUBA: *Havana's skyline changes constantly. The pool of the Hotel Nacional in the foreground.*

CUBA: *A typical outdoor bar along the Central Highway.*

CUBA: *Jacal (family dwelling) in Las Villas Province.*

CUBA: *Beach at Varadero—Cuban resort in summer, American resort in winter.*

DOMINICAN REPUBLIC

Never did one island contain two countries so different in character as those on Hispaniola. The Dominican Republic, with a passion for modernity and progress patterned after that of the United States, occupies the eastern two thirds of the island; Haiti, with a culture distinctly her own, occupies the other third. There is plenty of room for both, as Hispaniola is the second-largest of the West Indies, only Cuba being greater in area.

The Dominican Republic covers almost twenty thousand square miles. Larger than any of the New England states except Maine, its terrain varies from the highest peak in the Caribbean, Pico Trujillo (10,200 feet), through fertile valleys down to fine beaches.

Inside the Dominican Republic there are again two countries, and both are of interest to the visitor. One is the land of Columbus, strewn with great historical monuments and relics; the other affords air-conditioned hotels with Hollywood-type swimming pools, gay-nineties night-club tours, television, and native markets antiseptically clean.

When Columbus landed in 1492, he called the island La Española, the Latin form of which is the island's present name, Hispaniola. With Puerto Rico located sixty-five miles to the east and Cuba approximately the same distance to the west, Columbus had a choice of countries. He preferred Hispaniola, and there left his first settlement. When it was wiped out by the Taino Indians, the Admiral returned with his brother Bartholomew to set up a new and more permanent colony, the first in the New World. He referred to it in his journals as "the fairest land under heaven."

It is still a beautiful country, though the ancient ceiba tree where the first ships were tied is now a concrete-covered relic, and the walls of Columbus's son Diego's palace are moss-grown and time-worn. The country has seen many historic changes and been host to most of the great figures of the Caribbean. Diego Velásquez stopped here on his way to Cuba; Hernán Cortés was another visitor. Other famous Spanish and Portuguese explorers who became part of the web of history of Hispaniola are Ponce de León, Alonso de Ojeda, Balboa, Pizarro, and Hernando de Soto.

The Spanish did not always have everything their own way, however. First the colony was all Spanish, then half French, later all French. Great importations of slaves then changed the bulk of the population to Negro, and as these slaves became independent, the Haitians took over. The region became independent of Haiti and joined Spain. After freeing itself from Spain, the Dominican Republic was occupied for eight years by the United States, but since 1924 it has remained a completely independent country.

It is a shock to land at an airport called General Andrews, named for a United States general who did much to set up the original air service in and out of the island. Other American names that visitors will notice are George Washington Avenue and a street named for the late Cordell Hull.

Ciudad Trujillo, once called Santo Domingo, looks clean, prosperous, and modern. Buildings of gleaming white are spotless, but by far the most interesting sections of the town are the ancient buildings of the old Spanish colonists. The city was founded not by Columbus, but by his brother Bartholomew, and it was the discoverer's son, Diego, who became the first viceroy and built the Columbus castle. The walls of this remarkable building still stand, though the roofs have long since caved in. From the window through the thick wall one can look out as Doña María, Diego's wife, did, onto the Ozama River and Colón Street, once a main artery of commerce. The formal gardens of the patio are brilliant with tropical flowers contrasting with the deep-green, well-shaped hedges and shrubs. A walkway through the garden leads to the San Diego gate and looks out on the waterfront beyond.

But the Santo Domingo of Columbus's day contains many places of historic interest in addition to the palace of his son. The arches and towers of the Monastery of St. Francis still stand, and magnificent flowers grow in the well-kept gardens lining the ancient stone walls. The Primate Cathedral, first in the New World, rises like a Gothic palace. Its thick stone walls are a weathered brown now, and two Moorish minarets rise above the double arch to decorate the façade. Started in 1514, the cathedral was constructed during the years when Don Diego lived in his near-by palace and the grandchildren of Columbus played along the waterfront. The heavy unhinged mahogany doors of the cathedral are so carefully fashioned and balanced with pins in the floor and ceiling that they swing open at fingertip pressure. Inside the church rest the remains of Diego and, in all probability, the bones of the great Admiral himself.

A well-authenticated story tells that Don Diego's widow, Doña María de Toledo, brought the remains of her husband and her illustrious father-in-law to the cathedral from Spain. They were placed in separate crypts near the altar. The markings outside the crypts were removed during the years of the buccaneer raids on the island. When the island was ceded to France, the Spanish priests, thinking to preserve the Admiral's bones on Spanish ground, opened what they thought was the crypt of Columbus, but in error removed the casket of Don Diego to the cathedral in Havana. Why they did not take both caskets has never been satisfactorily explained. But much later, in 1877, while the church was being repaired, workmen stumbled upon the other crypt. Opened before representatives of Spain and other countries, it was found to contain bones, a lead bullet, and a plate reading: "Última parte de los restos del primer almirante don Christoval Colón escrubidor." These words were translated to mean that the last fragments of the remains of Admiral Christopher Columbus, discoverer, rest here. These remains are now enclosed in an elaborate tomb of onyx and marble just inside the arched entrance.

The treasures of the first cathedral do not stop with the tomb of Columbus. There is a painting of Nuestra Señora de la Antigua (after whom Columbus named the island of Antigua) which was presented to him by Ferdinand and Isabella. The one-handed statue of Bishop Rodrigo de Bastidas stands in mute evidence of the ferocity of Drake's pirates, who mutilated the statue by cutting off the right hand. The English pirates held the city of Santo Domingo for seven days, destroying a public building each day until their ransom was paid. Also in the cathedral are a silver carillon made by Benvenuto Cellini, and some of the court jewelry of Queen Isabella.

Not far from the cathedral is the Church of the Rosary, the first small stone church built in the Americas. Here Friar Bartolomé de Las Casas, the first priest ordained in the Americas, started his attack on the rape, torture, enslavement, and murder of the Indians. This church might be said to represent the early conscience of Spain, and even of Columbus himself, who, though he was willing to enslave the Indians, made every effort to have them treated humanely. But neither Las Casas nor the Admiral was successful, and there is no trace in the Dominican Republic of the Tainos, who were part of the Arawak cultural group. At least two hundred and fifty thousand of them were wiped out by the Spanish colonists within less than one hundred years after the island's discovery. Because slaves from Africa took the place of the slaughtered Indians and finally greatly outnumbered the Spanish, sixty-seven per cent of the Dominican Republic's citizens today are café-au-lait-colored, their blood lines a mixture of Spanish, Negro, and French. Of the others, some thirteen per cent are white, and twenty per cent pure Negro.

The old city is surrounded by the ruins of forts built as a defense chain against waves of English, French, and Dutch. Now in various stages of decay, these forts and gates still lend historic color to the new city built up around the old one. They kept off Admirals Penn and Venables, who hurled the sea and land might of England against Santo Domingo in 1655. The English left defeated, but sailed to Jamaica, where they easily took that almost completely undefended island and added it to the British empire.

The change from Santo Domingo to Ciudad Trujillo was much more than the swapping of names. In 1930 a tropical hurricane devastated the city, killing six thousand people and injuring over twenty-five thousand others. Modern building began at this time. The leader of the island and its present hero is Generalissimo Rafael Leonidas Trujillo, who started the big push toward modernization and held the presidency for a total of eighteen years. Today his brother Hector Trujillo is President, but "the Old Man," as he is often called, is still the great power in the country. Two names dominate the entire country: Columbus and Trujillo. Monuments, ancient buildings, and mountains are named for the discoverer, but the highest mountain is Pico Trujillo; the Dominican Party palace is located on Trujillo Street; Ciudad Trujillo is located in Trujillo Province, and the entrance to the Ozama River is Puerto Trujillo.

This port is an unusually busy one. Freight and passenger ships of the United States, Britain, France, and Canada, together with the considerable fleet of the Dominican Republic, move in and out of the well-protected deep harbor. Facilities for loading and unloading are extensive, and an ever-increasing amount of goods is handled for import and export.

The new city, which surrounds and mingles with the ancient one, is dazzlingly white in contrast to the dark-gray stone of the older buildings. Broad, tree-shaded avenues are sprinkled with monuments and fountains. The architectural tendency is toward simple, boxlike buildings more distinguished for efficiency and cleanliness than for architectural excellence. The Capitol, built in 1947, is patterned after that of the United States; a long line of stone steps approaches a Greek façade with eight columns and surmounted by a high dome. Other notable buildings are the ultra-modern University of Santo Domingo, which has become a small city in its own right, and is the oldest university founded (1538) in the western hemisphere; the model market; the cantilevered firehouse; and the luxurious Hotel Jaragua.

Constructed with travelers in mind, the Jaragua was the first of a group of vacation resorts designed especially to please vacation visitors to the fast-growing country. This elaborate hotel, located only a few miles from General Andrews Airport, has a magnificent swimming pool, air-conditioned rooms, and a gilded gambling casino. It is managed by a group of Florida resort experts who know and provide what most United States travelers seem to want. The recent trend in the country has been toward resorts located in the cool mountain areas or along the ideal beaches.

Most distinctive of the beach resorts is Boca Chica, nineteen miles from Ciudad Trujillo via a new four-lane highway. On the beach at Boca Chica the Hotel Hamaca is a slim, two-storied, pink-and-blue dream of a hotel on a perfect beach. In addition to fishing, swimming, and sunning, Boca Chica offers a tropical fish and bird aquarium, zoo, and sanctuary on the tiny island of La Matica across the clear blue lagoon. Fish pens are stocked with sharks, barracudas, and giant rays, which visitors to the West Indies rarely see. Other pens show tropical fish, and there are even a few crocodiles and iguanas. An aviary is vivid with flamingos, ibises, cranes, toucans, and parrots. Across another miniature bridge is a second little island, where small capparos and Capuchin monkeys frolic and chatter in the trees. Children will also like the dwarf deer from Costa Rica and a variegated collection of shells and coral.

It was not of the shore, but of the green countryside in the mountains that Columbus wrote when he mentioned the beauties of the country. Still sparsely settled, the great Vega Real (Royal Plain) looks much as it did to the early explorers. Now good highways, started during the eight-year United States occupation, crisscross the fertile valley, where huge fields of sugar cane wave like verdant banners. This great plain is rich in bananas, plantains, coconuts, tamarinds, and mangoes. North of the Vega Real the great Yaque del Norte River has its source high in the mountains; it flows two hundred and fifty miles into the Atlantic Ocean. Columbus explored part of this river, and his men found here much of the first gold they sent to Spain. Even today natives occasionally find tiny pebbles of the precious metal in the mountain streams. Other great rivers keep the land fertile, and the country has adequate rainfall throughout the year. Flowing from the mountain range south of the Vega Real is the Río Yaque del Sur, which winds its way down through the mountain peaks and empties into the Caribbean. The mountains are rich in mahogany, pine, and cedar. Flowering trees include the spathodea campanulata, the African tulip tree, and the mountain immortelle. Another of the most fertile sections is the Cibao Valley, which Columbus thought might be Japan, whose name he knew as Cipango from the tales of Marco Polo. The city of Santiago is in this area. North from Santiago the roads lead to Puerto Plata, the largest port on the Atlantic side of the island.

Near Puerto Plata is the scene of an extremely interesting experiment. This is the town of Sosúa, where hundreds of displaced Jews were invited to settle after World War II. Some went into the manufacture and distribution of cheese, which has become an important, though small, local industry. Others left the colony, migrating to the United States and other countries. Besides being an interesting social experiment, Sosúa has a fine natural beach and is an interesting area to visit. There is an excellent restaurant serving Viennese-Dominican cuisine, perhaps the most unusual food combination in the entire West Indies.

The country people of the Dominican Republic differ greatly from those of the city. Small huts with thatched roofs are scattered over hills, mountains, and valleys. Life in the most remote areas is primitive and living-standards are low. Goats graze alongside the tiny houses, and small patches of land are cultivated. But because the cities are growing rapidly, with roads, hotels, and public buildings under construction, and sugar centrals are expanding, there is a distinct labor shortage, and the rural population is moving toward the cities.

The countryside cannot be explored in a day or a week. There are many cars for hire, and some good drivers who speak English. Taxi rates within Ciudad Trujillo are low and are controlled by the government. Buses are clean and reasonably efficient; the double-deckers provide good sightseeing. For travelers in a hurry, and even for those who are not, the Dominican Republic operates an internal airline that brings the cities of the north and east only minutes away from the airport near Ciudad Trujillo. There is a two-way service between Ciudad Trujillo and Port au Prince, Haiti, so that visitors may go back and forth on a frequent schedule. It is said that many Haitians prefer to fly to the Dominican Republic and then directly from Ciudad Trujillo to New York rather than go through the embarrassment Negroes are subjected to when they travel through Florida and the southern states.

Guided tours are particularly well organized in the Dominican Republic; red tape is cut to a minimum, customs delays are few, and visitors may use their cameras freely. Tours are relatively expensive, but still cheaper than resort tours in the United States. Every possible type of trip can be arranged, from a half-day in Ciudad Trujillo to a week in the country. Many make three- to seven-day trips into the remote mountains to comfortable resort hotels that have sprung up on the cool, wooded peaks.

The Dominican Republic is weak in the shopping department, but every visitor should walk down El Conde Avenue in Ciudad Trujillo and also visit the Artes Dominicanas Shop. Not much creative imagination is shown in the handwork, but there are some handsome carved pieces of green ebony. Beautiful mahogany and oak pieces are offered, as are tortoise-shell ornaments, some needlework, lots of straw baskets, and many small grotesque figures made from black and red tree seeds. The Mercado Modelo (a version of the supermarket) offers sisal and mahogany articles, handbags, mats, and straw work, but does not have the romantic flavor or the pungent smell that one expects of a native market in the Caribbean.

Sports include tennis; a limited amount of golf (it is possible to get a guest card to the Golfito, a private eighteen-hole course); deep-sea fishing for sailfish, marlin, tuna, bonito, kingfish, and mackerel; and spear-fishing at Boca Chica, where the lagoon is protected and very clear. There is a well-kept race track with regular meets, and the island is baseball crazy. The Dominican League takes its cue from the big-league teams that go into winter training here, and games are highly popular and well attended. Horseback riding is pleasant over the country trails and in the mountains. But cockfighting still remains the national sport, and it is possible to see a fight any day of the week not too far from wherever you may happen to be.

Keeping account of your money is easy, for the peso and dollar have the same value. It will be found, however, that prices are somewhat high, though they are a shade lower than in Cuba or Puerto Rico, and definitely lower than in the United States. Much of the money spent in this country goes for gambling, for, like Cuba and Puerto Rico, the Dominican Republic has plush, smoothly operating gambling casinos. Night life consists of more than a visit to the dice or roulette tables, however, for the Hotel Jaragua offers a Spanish patio and a roof garden for dancing, and La Voz Dominicana, which is a kind of miniature "Radio City," has a big night club, good music, good food, interesting shows, and the television center of the country.

By far the most popular dance in the island is the merengue, an active dance claimed by Cuba, Haiti, Martinique, and Guadeloupe as well as the Dominican Republic. The merengue has been danced in most of these countries for hundreds of years, and some authorities insist that the typical limp or dip made after three steps, and always on the right leg, originated when the slaves could make just that number of steps before having to stop to drag the ball and chain attached to their leg. Whether this has anything to do with the origin or not, it is certainly true that the limp, or swerve to one side with bended knee, is an essential part of the merengue. Drums are featured, with the soprano or the tenor sax wailing the high notes above the thump of the drums and the delicate cadences of the guitar. Two types of merengues are popular. The formal, restrained one is somewhat like the fast march of a paso doble, with the limp added. To see the other type of merengue properly, it is necessary to go to the small outlying native clubs, where it is danced with a gay abandon that is often more humorous than sexy.

One of the pleasantest surprises in the country is the abundance of good restaurants that are open all night. In Ciudad Trujillo it is possible to find native Dominican food at the Trianon, Chinese food at Mario's, or steaks at El Acordeón even at five or six in the morning. Native Dominican food has a Spanish accent, and some of the dishes are similar to those in Puerto Rico and Cuba. This is true of arroz con pollo (chicken and rice) and pastelitos (tiny pastries filled with meat or fish). Roast pig is very popular, and there is a distinctive dessert called piñonate (a confection of coconut and milk). Salcocho is a native dish somewhat like the African calaloo, a stew with a variety of meats and whatever local vegetables are available. Rum in the Dominican Republic is good, beer fair, and water drinkable.

DOMINICAN REPUBLIC: *In Trujillo City's Primate Cathedral, the remains of Christopher Columbus hang surrounded by an elaborate shrine. The silver lamp is kept permanently lighted with oil from Genoa.*

DOMINICAN REPUBLIC: *During a romería (pilgrimage), devout Dominicans often carry shrines on their heads for thirty miles.*

DOMINICAN REPUBLIC: *Petronila Valdez, entertainer on Dominican television and at hotels and night clubs.*

DOMINICAN REPUBLIC: *Afro-Dominican dancers often do unrehearsed primitive routines in the early morning hours at the Club Taino.*

DOMINICAN REPUBLIC: *Entrance to the ruined Monastery of San Francisco, begun in 1512.*

HAITI

The second-largest island in the Caribbean is Hispaniola (Española). Its mountainous terrain measures three hundred miles by one hundred and seventy-five miles. Its eastern two thirds are occupied by the Dominican Republic; the western third is the republic of Haiti (pronounced *Hay*-tee), an independent Negro nation shaped like an extended thumb and forefinger. The thumb points across the Windward Passage toward Cuba, fifty miles northwest, the forefinger points southwest toward Jamaica, one hundred and thirty miles away. In the center is the Golfe de la Gonave, with Ile de la Gonave between two long pincers. North are the Caicos Islands in the Atlantic, and south across the Caribbean Sea is the coast of Colombia and Venezuela.

Steep, lime-green mountains dominate Haiti's ten thousand square miles. The ranges run along both peninsulas and across the back of the island, separating it from the Dominican Republic. Fertile plains where sugar cane and sisal grow lie in the northern, eastern, and central valleys.

Upon arrival in Haiti it is wise for visitors, especially white ones, to remember that they are guests in a black nation. Not that the Haitian people resent white visitors–indeed, they welcome them and do everything possible to make their stay pleasant–but that they take great pride in their independent country and recognize no inequality between black and white. Unlike the upper classes in the British, French, Dutch, and United States Virgin Islands, the social, cultural, and political aristocracy in Haiti is Negro.

It is easy, exciting, and inexpensive to be a visitor in Haiti. The unit of currency, the gourde, is worth exactly twenty cents

U.S. There is no problem with exchange. Any hotel, bank, or merchant will gladly exchange gourdes for dollars, or U.S. currency may be used. Taxi rates are low, but should be arranged in advance. All rates are legally doubled after dark.

Language problems exist because French is the official and Creole the unofficial language of most of the people, but these problems are easily overcome by the visitor. All hotels have some English-speaking employees. Some taxi-drivers speak a little English, and everyone talks with gestures, French fashion, so that even French-Creole patois becomes partly understandable. The Creole language is not simply a corruption of French, though it uses many basic and ancient French words. It is rather a fresh new language formed from French, Indian, Spanish, and English, expressing thoughts in colorful, lusty words. Haitians do not like to have their pictures taken, especially without permission. Some will acquiesce for money, but many will refuse even though offered money. It is best, therefore, to concentrate on buildings, scenery, and people some distance from the camera.

The capital of Haiti, Port au Prince (pronounced Port au Prance), is a city of continuous contrasts; its dazzling Government buildings are only a few hundred feet from antiquated wooden structures; unpaved streets run into modern paved avenues; beautifully kept lawns compete with cluttered alleyways.

Port au Prince is also a city of beautiful suburbs, fine hotels, and delicious French cuisine. It is a rural city where quiet, sun-splashed forest glades are just off the busy streets. Brilliant bursts of flowers grow everywhere, even between cracks in old buildings. Within a few blocks in almost any direction camellias, oleanders, hibiscus, bougainvillaea, jasmine, poinsettias, and crape myrtle grow in profusion. But, in spite of its flowers and occasional rural aspects, the central streets of Port au Prince are dusty, hot, and architecturally unrewarding. Beneath the ancient arcades that shade cobblestone sidewalks are street vendors and beggars. There is nothing shy or humble about the Haitian mendicants, who beg only from foreigners. They look you in the eye and ask for money; nor are they particularly surprised when they are refused. Just one word of advice about giving to beggars: don't!

More noticeable than the beggars on the streets are the dogs, for Port au Prince has the most fantastic collection of mongrels to be seen in the islands. Some look as though they had been crossed with rabbits and ant-eaters. Others resemble wolves, pigs, agoutis, and foxes. Inbreeding among these anemic dogs has completely hidden any resemblance to a known breed.

In the shopping center is Port au Prince's busiest, noisiest enterprise, the smelly, clamorous Iron Market. It has an entrance composed of two tall minarets looking for all the world as though they had been imported from Arabia. The market itself is exactly what its name implies; a large, ugly, open-sided iron building painted red and green. Inside it explodes with movement and the noise of hundreds of native women intent on selling their produce. Nothing is said in a normal tone. Vendors scream their wares and prices in high-pitched voices, and conversations sound like furious arguments. It is a difficult but not impossible place for tourists to shop. In addition to tobacco, maize, rice, cocoa, cassava, bananas, mangoes, breadfruits, coconuts, yams, sugar, guava, coffee, and strong-smelling fish, there are also decorated gourds, drums of every size, shape, and color, carved mahogany vessels, and straw hats. It is much easier to buy most of these articles, as well as French perfume, sisal handbags, mahogany bowls, salad forks, trays, and coffee tables in the dark, cool shops along the Grand Rue, Port au Prince's main thoroughfare.

There is much to see in this black metropolis. It is only a few blocks from the Iron Market to the great historic and cultural centers located on the Champ de Mars or along the waterfront. Three distinctive churches are near the center of town. The new Catholic church, with two towers looking like giant beehives, is an architectural landmark in pink and white. Next to it is the cathedral that dates back to the French occupation. The Cathedral Ste.-Trinité, a near-by Episcopal church, contains important murals painted by Haiti's great primitive artists. They depict a series of Biblical scenes as imagined by the painters Bazille, Obin, Levèque, Bigaud, and Benoit, who painted the scenes as though they had happened in Haiti in their time. The work required two years to complete, was supervised by the American poet and critic Selden Rodman, and is ranked among the great religious murals of the world.

The Champ de Mars, a spacious expanse of lawn and palm trees, is the park around which the gleaming public buildings cluster. The national palace, called the White House, where the president traditionally lives, is a dazzling two-story edifice surmounted by three domes with a cupola on the center one.

Dominating the Champ de Mars are statues of the heroes of the republic. Within the near-by government buildings are impressive busts of all the presidents and grandiose oil paintings of "Les Quatre Grandes," the four great liberators of the country. The first of these was Toussaint L'Ouverture, an intelligent pure-blooded Negro.

In 1791 two important events set the stage for Haiti's ultimate independence and the subsequent action of these patriots. One was the French Revolution, which led the mulattoes of Haiti to believe that they could become free by legislation. The other was a violent uprising of slaves in the north, led by a voodoo priest named Boukman, in which thousands of colonists were massacred.

For the next three years war raged, but by 1801 Toussaint L'Ouverture had emerged as the strong man of the island. His capture of Santo Domingo from the Spanish made the entire island free under one leader for the first time. He was a wise administrator, doing much to improve the economy of the country and to show the world that a Negro state could earn the respect of other free countries. Unfortunately, Toussaint was not destined to rule long. Napoleon dispatched a force of twenty thousand men to reclaim the island. Toussaint was defeated in battle, then kidnapped and shipped to France. He died ten months later after penning a series of futile letters to Napoleon. But even in defeat Toussaint L'Ouverture had laid the groundwork for Haiti's final independence.

With the aid of yellow fever (Haiti has none now), Jean-Jacques Dessalines, one of Toussaint's most important generals, drove the French from the island and became the first president of Haiti. On January 1, 1804, in the village of Gonaïves, Dessalines established the independence of the country and renamed it Haiti, the ancient Arawak Indian name for the island, meaning high or mountainous land. At a meeting six months earlier Dessalines and Alexandre Pétion had discussed the future and final liberation of the country. During this meeting the Haitian flag was born. By tearing the white band, which represented the hated white colonists, from the French flag of red, white, and blue, the red and blue were brought together as a symbol of the union of the Negroes and mulattoes of the island.

Dessalines, who had risen from slave to president, was assassinated by a military clique less than two years from the day he proclaimed Haiti's independence. He is now revered as Haiti's greatest hero.

Henri-Christophe has been the most publicized of all Haitians, but he was by no means their greatest leader. He took his name from the British island of St. Christopher (St. Kitts) and joined the army under Toussaint L'Ouverture. Because of his courage and natural leadership he soon became a general, and, upon Dessalines's death, was elected president of the country. A year later he isolated himself in the northern province and had a new constitution voted naming him president for life. This undemocratic procedure and his insistence upon choosing his successor from among his generals caused the Senate to impeach him and elect General Alexandre Pétion president.

This divided the country into two factions. Christophe reigned as emperor in the north, Pétion as president of the south. Christophe governed his portion of the country like an extremely efficient dictator. He built schools and roads, outlawed voodoo, and forced education upon the people. He built the palace of Sans Souci, perhaps the most beautiful structure ever conceived and executed in the West Indies. Then, at the cost of thousands of lives, he forced the completion of a giant fortress, the Citadelle, on top of a cliff near Cap Haïtien. He ruled as King Henry I for thirteen years, then in 1820 suffered a paralytic stroke and shot himself.

Meanwhile, Pétion in the south governed in a different manner. Democratic by inclination, he distributed national lands to officers and soldiers of the army of independence, thus creating the small holdings of the land-owning class which are spread over Haiti's mountains today. He established schools, including a secondary school for girls and a lycée for boys. He also gave important financial and military aid to Simón Bolívar, the Venezuelan patriot, asking in return that Bolívar free the slaves in that country. Because of Pétion, two thirds of the Haitians live in the country and cultivate small land-holdings. Alexandre Pétion earned the respect and regard of all Haitians for his intelligent and democratic administration of the country. He was the first of the early leaders to die a natural death.

Also facing the Champ de Mars is the National Museum, where the eight-foot-high anchor, said to be from the *Santa María*, Columbus's ship that was wrecked off Haiti, may be examined. When Columbus arrived in 1492, he set up his first colony not far from the present village of Cap Haïtien, and it was near there that this ancient anchor was found. Also close by is the point where

Columbus wrote in his journal that three mermaids were sighted holding themselves high above the surface of the sea. He added that they were not so beautiful as they had been previously represented. It is almost certain now that the "mermaids" Columbus described were actually manatees, ocean mammals that have been called sea cows. They rise high out of the water holding their young to breathe and nurse. Because they have two distinct breasts and arm-like flippers, they do give the impression from a distance of figures half female and half fish. An embossed cannon from Christophe's Citadelle is one of the exhibits here; hundreds of cannon can be seen in the positions where they were originally placed in this grim fortress.

Also on the Champ de Mars is the United States Embassy. Visitors sometimes find it helpful to check in at the Embassy for information or advice. The staff is courteous and helpful.

The exposition grounds, built to celebrate one hundred and fifty years of Haitian freedom, is the newest section of Port au Prince. Well designed and landscaped, a series of attractive modern buildings lies along the coastline. The main thoroughfare, Harry Truman Boulevard, is the site of the Théâtre de Verdure, where travelers may see authentic native Haitian dancers and hear drummers perform regularly. It is a delightful outdoor theater; the benches are hard and uncomfortable and the stage lighting is inadequate, but these are small matters. It is spacious, has a good stage, and serves outstanding performers. Also along Truman Boulevard is the Casino Internationale, Haiti's gambling casino and the most popular night club in Port au Prince. Dancing is to rumbas, tangos, sambas, and the Haitian meringue. The food is French or Italian, the service slow, the drinks excellent. It is said that the gambler gets as good a break as the house. Also in this section is the cockfight arena, where first-class fights are put on every Saturday and Sunday.

Hotels in Haiti fall into three important classifications: the "in town" hotels; the hostelries in the near-by foothills, which combine holiday facilities with a great deal of delightful Haitian atmosphere; and the luxury hotels located high in the hills of Pétion-Ville, a suburb of the city. The cooking, predominantly French-Creole, is invariably excellent in all of them.

The visitor enters Haiti either by boat at the Rue de Quaie in Port au Prince harbor or by air at Bowen Field, a short distance north of the city. An interesting monument near the runway marks the exact spot where Dessalines was brutally assassinated. The drive into town from the airport is straight down the Grand Rue past the Iron Market and into the center of the city.

Port au Prince is more than one town; it is a series of layers like a wedding cake. The shopping center, with cathedrals, art centers, and the Casino, forms the base. On the next tier are some marvelous examples of Victorian architecture and such popular hotels as the Sans Souci, Splendide, and Olaffson. The last has been described as having more island atmosphere than a Somerset Maugham short story. Other buildings on this level are the Kurt Fisher Museum and the Haitian-American Institute.

The road to Pétion-Ville, the residential section above the city, is steep and full of sudden dangerous curves. On either side of the road, native women walk leisurely up and down in contrast to the busy taxis. Houses here are modern, and such hotels as the Ibo Lélé and El Rancho are comfortable and lavish. Most of Haiti's well-to-do "elite" group lives in this area. Parisian French is spoken fluently and all are well educated.

Pétion-Ville is also the home of a night club unique in the West Indies, the Cabane Choucoune, a building of bamboo shaped like an inverted ice-cream cone. Its high-peaked roof has a small thatched cupola on top. From a distance it looks like the chief's hut in an African village. But the inside is in great contrast to the rough exterior. It has a large, smooth dance floor and a good orchestra. Here a visitor can see and learn to dance the meringue.

On the fourth tier of the cake is the village of Boutelliers, where a fine restaurant called the Perchoir offers a superlative view of Pétion-Ville and colorful Port au Prince harbor. The food here can be highly recommended, and the rum punch, a specialty of the house, is made with four-star Barbancourt rum, wild honey, lime juice, and grated nutmeg.

From Boutelliers the road continues upward, and at five thousand feet reaches the village of Kenscoff. A thousand feet above this the highway ends at Furcy. Because of the cooling breezes, these windswept heights are fast becoming summer resorts for wealthy Haitians. The mountain town of Kenscoff has an outdoor market place of amazing beauty, a broad, open area surrounded by poinsettias, varicolored bougainvillaea, oak, and flaming immortelle trees. The deep green of the grass is broken only by the orange-yellow of the earth. On Saturday morning it looks like a gay country fair in a verdant tropical setting. Blue smoke from charcoal fires seeps through the brilliant sunshine. Hundreds of women in faded, much-washed blue or white dresses squat, stand, walk, and gossip among their wares.

For this is the province of the "marchande," the Haitian peasant woman, backbone of the island. It is the marchande in her colorful kerchief and wide-brimmed straw hat who climbs Haiti's miles of steep mountains, lugging heavy cans of water, cooking over a wood or charcoal brazier, bearing and caring for numerous children, raising chickens and pigs, and sometimes cultivating a tiny garden. She is seen everywhere in Haiti, most often strolling gracefully down the long mountain trails, her bare feet slapping firmly against the hard-packed earth. On her erect head she carries the sustenance of the country: baskets, huge or tiny, containing live chickens, coffee, oranges, small yellow bananas or large green plantains, coconuts, cotton, corn, Congo peas, yams, avocados, guinea hens. Occasionally a woman will go by carrying long bamboo poles or lumber for building, while another may carry one small piece of soap carefully balanced on her head.

The peasant woman is a person of great dignity and the actual head of the family. She is seldom married in the legal sense, for there is much "placage" in the island. This means that a man "places" a common-law wife in charge of a piece of ground and then goes off to work elsewhere. He often places another "keeper" in another spot on the island, and sometimes has as many as four part-time wives, each one taking care of a home. The Haitian male builds his own "caille" (hut) and works the land, and while the women go to market, he attends a cockfight in the same neighborhood.

At the market place, sucking on her short pipe or bargaining in argumentative tones, the marchande is a woman of importance. Market day is an occasion the Haitian woman looks forward to as an important weekly social and economic event. Although there is little for visitors to buy at these outdoor markets, there is a great deal to see. On one side bleating goats are tethered. On the other, tiny burros carrying beautifully carved wooden or high straw-work saddles stand stoically by while the marchandes arrange and rearrange their fruits, vegetables, charcoal, and calabashes.

The gourd or calabash is Haiti's most useful plant. It is used as a vessel for carrying water, as a bowl, as a drinking-cup, and as an ornament. At one time, according to legend, Henri-Christophe made the gourd a unit of monetary value. In voodoo ("vaudou" in Creole) services, a gourd wound with colored beads and snake vertebræ becomes the symbol (assan) of office of the Houngan (high priest) or Mambo (priestess) of this African-West Indian religion.

For voodoo is a religion to most of Haiti's four million peasants. It is a cult that takes into its own ritual whatever is offered from other religions. Most peasants are simple and sincere in their belief in voodoo, but find it difficult to tell you exactly what it is. They can, however, tell you how it is practiced. Haitian voodoo came from Africa, where it was the religion of the Dahomey Negroes. From this beginning Rada, the form of voodoo most prevalent in Haiti, developed. In it are the drums (maman, the biggest; seconde, the medium-sized one; and boula, the smallest one) that set the pace of the ceremony and guide the Houngan and his followers through the ritual. Then come symbolic drawings in the earth, hypnotic chants, and the dances that invite the spirits (Loas) themselves. These spirits have human strengths and weaknesses and control all the elements in which the Haitian peasant lives. Wind, water, fire, air, trees, jungle, old age, death—all are spirits who release their subjects into a different world through possession. In addition to the Rada form of voodoo there are also the Congo and the Petro forms. The last is indigenous to Haiti, and its gods are violent, seemingly emulating the grim and chaotic history of the island.

Voodoo spirits are generally used for good, and most Houngans or Mambos will not practice Wanga, the black magic of spells, poison potions, and evil charms. They will, however, through simple psychology or the use of a paquet (a good charm), take away or erase the evil ones. There are, of course, many disreputable Houngans and Mambos in the religion only for what they can get out of it.

Catholic ritual, saints, and symbols have been absorbed into the voodoo religion. The peasant can see no reason why Erzulie Freda Dahomin, who started out as a goddess of love in Africa, and whose symbol is the heart, should not also be worshipped as the Virgin Mary. The cross, a very ancient symbol, is used by Guedé Nimbo, a Petro Loa who is also Baron Samedi, the god of death. He wears a black bowler or a top hat, a black frock coat, and dark glasses, smokes a huge cigar, and drinks rum during the services invoking him.

A typical voodoo service in the foothills of Port au Prince, where more voodoo is practiced than anywhere else on the island, is held in a tonelle, an open-sided palm- or tin-roofed shed with a decorated pole in the center to serve as an entry and exit for the spirits. A door usually leads off this into the houmfor (chapel), where there are an altar to the spirits and jars and calabashes decorated with voodoo symbols. The service opens with an invocation to the Loas. Then the drums begin to talk, and ancient chants are sung by houncis (assistants). Papa Legba, a spirit in the form of an old man who later brings in other spirits, is invariably invoked first. If the meeting is successful, one of the participants will suddenly stiffen, lose control of arms and legs, and thrash about the tonelle or fall to the floor. After being "mounted" or possessed by the spirit, he will begin to limp about in the manner of a very old man and speak in the unknown tongue of Papa Legba.

After this manifestation, the ceremony moves on to an appeal to the next Loa. This may be Damballa, perhaps the most important single Loa in all Haitian voodoo. The Houngan will draw a vever, an intricate symbolic design identified with this spirit. Important in the design is a snake climbing a pole in the center of the picture. This design looks much like the medical caduceus with one snake instead of two. These vevers are often well-executed artistic efforts. The Houngan makes the design by moving his hand rapidly about while allowing cornmeal to slip through his fingers. The light lines of the meal form patterns on the dark dirt floor. As the spirit enters the enclosure, the design is rapidly danced away by the shuffling feet of the worshippers.

There are many gods and many kinds of voodoo services. Chickens are often sacrificed, pigs occasionally, goats rarely. Trial by fire is practiced in a voodoo ceremony called Brulé-zin. Believers walk on glowing coals and pass their hands through flames without being burned.

As the ceremony proceeds, the drumming and dancing become increasingly hypnotic. Often many believers are possessed at the same time. All participants become highly excited. The drums talk, whisper, and even seem to shout their directions to the dancers. Dancers move their heads, shoulders, and hips until the Loa has departed and everyone is thoroughly exhausted.

Nothing in voodoo dancing is sexy in the European meaning of the word. Dancers shuffle and shake and are "possessed" singly, never with partners. Motions often look vulgar to the eyes of foreigners who associate them with erotic positions, but to the peasant voodoo dancer the movements are instinctive and impersonal.

It can be hazardous for visitors to try to seek out voodoo ceremonies and attend them without a competent guide or a Haitian friend. This is especially true for travelers with a camera. Photographs of real rituals are rare. Many cameras have been smashed and photographers injured trying to take pictures of the forbidden rites. Even if pictures could be taken they would be uninteresting, for the sound of the drums and the movements of the dancers are what makes the rites stimulating.

Because all visitors to Haiti want to see a voodoo ceremony, a number of semi-professional groups have sprung up which perform for tourists each Saturday night for a fee. The drumming is excellent, as is all drumming in Haiti, and to the uninitiated the performance is as effective as a real service. Possession occasionally occurs at these arranged rituals. Recommended also for visitors is attendance at a Saturday-night bambouche, a non-religious peasant party, fiesta, or dance.

While Port au Prince certainly offers more of interest to tourists than other sections of the island, two tours should be made by every visitor to Haiti. One is across the southern peninsula to the delightful village of Jacmel. This is only from four to five hours away by car or a half-hour by plane. The drive may be a damp one, for a considerable portion of the road lies along a shallow river bed. It is no trip to take during the rainy season. Jacmel has lovely narrow streets and old houses decorated with intricate iron grillwork. A famous pension called the Excelsior is known throughout Haiti as a fine place for food and for lodging for the night. About ten miles from Jacmel is an excellent white sand beach called Carrefour Raymonde.

The second trip, even more exciting than the journey to Jacmel, is the pilgrimage to Cap Haïtien, located on the north central coast. There are daily flights, taking forty minutes, to the airport in Cap Haïtien. The planes are modern and the pilots well trained. It is possible to make the trip by road through rough but historically interesting country. There are two routes from Port au Prince to Cap Haïtien (called Le Cap), and it is well to consult the local tourist board before starting out on either of them.

The city of Cap Haïtien, two hundred miles from Port au Prince, is still unspoiled, with a considerable number of buildings dating back to French colonial days. Founded in the seventeenth century, it is Haiti's oldest and most historic spot. Many old buildings were destroyed when Henri-Christophe fired the town to keep it from being used by the French. There are at least three adequate hotels; one of them, the Mont Jolie, offers not only fine cuisine, but an excellent view. Every traveler should plan to spend from three to five days in the Cap Haïtien area. It takes at least one day to get settled and another to see the old fountains and churches. Arrangements should be made to travel to Minot, where the ruins of Christophe's fabulous palace, Sans Souci, lie. If time is limited, however, the visitor may fly to Cap Haïtien to see the palace and the Citadelle on one day and return to Port au Prince the next.

Upon arrival at the village of Minot, the visitor will pick up a horse and guide to accompany him from Sans Souci up the trail to the Citadelle. Here there are likely to be continuous discussions as to which guide and which horse shall be selected. Although the matter of a guide is not critical, the selection of a horse certainly is. At best, the trip from Sans Souci to the Citadelle is a rough one. The magnificent palace can still be seen through the ruins that remain. The grand staircase, built in perfect proportion to the total building, has steps rising to the second floor. The shell of the palace is pink, gray, and white, for tropical rains have washed away much of the stucco that covered the handmade bricks. Thick walls, roofless, rise to the sky above the second floor's colonnade. The impression is one of beauty and grandeur, with the lush jungle on either side and the steep mountains in the background.

Although the spacious beauty of Sans Souci is impressive, nothing in any of the West Indies islands prepares the visitor for the fabulous sight of the Citadelle located high on the mountainside behind the palace. The path is narrow and matted with jungle vegetation. The trip is not for the elderly or infirm. Even comparatively young travelers have occasionally fallen off their horses. Banana, orange, and mango trees grow alongside the road as it rises higher and higher on the cool, misty mountain. Suddenly the great structure bursts out of the jungle, its knife-edge wall looming incredibly high like the prow of a giant ocean liner cast in stone. This amazing fortress was built by forced, if not slave, labor as a sanctuary from the forces of Napoleon. It was designed to allow the garrison and the Emperor to hold out for months or even years. Henri-Christophe built a network of cisterns to provide water, and huge storerooms for foodstuffs. More than three hundred cannon—some marked with H for Henri I, others marked with the crests of the original English, French, or Spanish owners—bristle from the impregnable twenty-foot-thick walls. The spacious parade ground covers much of the top of the building. It is said that, in order to impress a visiting foreign delegation, Christophe once ordered and watched a squad of his select soldiers march off the parade ground to drop almost three thousand feet into the sea. Of the hundreds of rooms, some were royal apartments, other hospitals and dormitories.

Across the ten-mile-wide channel near Cap Haïtien is the Ile de la Tortue, once the headquarters of the buccaneers who infested the Caribbean, now a peaceful fishing center. It is an easy and pleasant sail over in the morning, but there are no overnight accommodations, and visits to the island must be brief. It is an excellent place to search for Arawak Indian relics. The Haitian villages on this tiny island are as primitive as any in the West Indies.

HAITI: *A voodoo ceremony in the mountains outside Port au Prince.*

HAITI: *A vever, design drawn by the priestess for each voodoo ceremony.*

HAITI: *Painting by St. Brice gives impression of Haitian mother and child.*

HAITI: *Lunch in an outdoor market place is the hour for gossip.*

HAITI: *During a voodoo ceremony, a woman is "possessed" by a god.*

Part Four

NETHERLANDS WEST INDIES

SABA: *Sabamen are excellent seamen. Here they launch a boat to row out to the bimonthly steamer.*

ARUBA: *Unusual rock formation serves as a picnic ground.*

ARUBA

Lying west of Curaçao, the nineteen-by-six-mile island of Aruba is true desert country broken only by an area of giant rocks, clumps of cactus, and golden-yellow kibra-hacha ("breaks ax") trees. But in spite of the dryness caused by its annual average of only seventeen inches of rainfall, Aruba offers attractive beaches and excellent vacation facilities for the traveler who is strictly interested in the outdoors.

Palm Beach is a curved, four-mile stretch of white sand equal to any in the West Indies. There is no coral to lacerate the feet of swimmers, and there are no sea nettles. A line of tall coconut trees shades the shoreline, and convenient dressing-rooms are clustered under the trees. The beach has a clubhouse, complete with bar, outdoor dining and dancing terrace, and billiard room. Visitors can make arrangements to use the club through the Tourist Board. A group of new cottages is being built along the beach front to afford accommodations for travelers who want to spend some time fishing and swimming in the area. The water at this point is so calm that water-skiing is developing as an important sport. It is only a short drive to one of Aruba's two golf courses.

The city of Oranjestad has nothing in common with its sister city of Willemstad in Curaçao except its red roofs. Many of the houses here, dazzlingly white instead of pastel, are hard on the eyes. The tempo is rather that of a quiet suburb than that of a bustling metropolis. Neat houses are surrounded by bursts of a colorful creeper called mannenkarakter, a pink-and-white vine that climbs along the porches. Another pink-and-white flower in most Oranjestad gardens is bruidstranen—"bride's tears."

Shopping is good, but not quite so good as in Willemstad because the selection is not nearly as large nor is there as much competition among merchants. Oranjestad has one excellent hotel, the Strand, which is air-conditioned and on Saturday nights even supplies a night club with local singers, dancers, and steel-band music. There are two good restaurants on the island, the Scala and the Trocadero. Menus incline toward Spanish cuisine, and the arroz con pollo is excellent.

On the southern tip of the island is Lago Colony, a company town, built and supported by the Standard Oil Company of New Jersey, which operates near-by Lago Oil Refinery, largest in the world. The oil town of Sint Nicolaas is Aruba's second-largest city. Standard Oil directly or indirectly supplies work for seventy-five per cent of the population of Aruba. Most (about thirty-five thousand) of these people are descendants of the Carib Indians, early Spanish, and later Dutch settlers. There is little African blood in Aruba because the Carib Indians were neither killed nor enslaved, but absorbed by the early settlers. The remainder of the population is made up primarily of men and women from Holland and the other Netherlands islands in the Caribbean, plus two thousand Americans, many of whom are two-year bachelors who sign up to work in the oil refineries.

The Sint Nicolaas area has some good beaches, a yacht club, the Esso Club, which supplies entertainment for the oil workers, and the Aruba Golf Club.

Fishing in Aruba for red snapper and barracuda is quite good, and small boats are available by the day. Surf-fishing from the rocks on the north shore draws a considerable number of local fishermen. Along with the development of Palm Beach there are plans afoot for a large boat club and more deep-sea fishing facilities.

The big native celebration in Aruba comes at New Year's with an imaginary character known as "Dandee." The celebrants proceed from house to house, singing, playing drums, maracas, and the wiri (weary), a unique homemade instrument fashioned from a ribbed piece of steel. When scraped with a long nail, it produces a repetitive bell-like sound.

Biggest attraction for visitors other than Palm Beach is Ayo, Indian name for the great rocks located near the center of the island. This is no small pile of rocks built up into a tourist attraction, but an unbelievably huge mass of individual rocks balanced one on top of another to a height of over three hundred feet. The rocks are flat enough and jagged enough to make fine climbing for amateur rock-climbers, and it is possible to crawl through the cave-like openings between the rocks into the cool, shady depths. This is a good place to take along a lunch and picnic. Even the cactus here, some of which rises to twenty feet, offers shade.

Aruba's second great sight is the ghost town of Balashi near the central south coast, where gold was once mined. The ruins of the town and the mines lie dusty and deserted. Travelers who are willing to wait for an occasional rainfall can still pan some gold dust in the river bed.

The most sensational sight on Aruba is the feeding of the sharks, which occurs in the late afternoon on a desolate strip along the coast where the ruins of a pirates' castle built in 1499 still stand. Trucks carrying offal from the stockyards and fish market drive up the cliffside to this built-in garbage-disposal plant, and the refuse is shoveled into the sea. The sharks cut through the water, devouring the garbage almost as it hits the surf. It is a terrifying and intensely interesting performance.

Little is known of the early occupants of the castle on the cliff, but it was occupied by pirates for many years, and the 1499 date, although doubtful, is guaranteed by a number of Aruba's citizens. Certainly the castle could have been built at that time; it looks, in every great stone and small dungeon-like room, exactly as a pirates' castle should look.

ARUBA: *A "pirate's castle," this ancient structure is on the island's windward side.*

BONAIRE

Native schooners ply between this little-known island and Curaçao every day, and KLM (Royal Dutch Airlines) wings from airport to airport daily in just twenty-five minutes. Like the island of Curaçao, it is dry. Unlike Curaçao, it has many more women than men (of its 5,500 population, 3,500 are women). Also unlike Curaçao, it is poor financially, but rich in beaches and potential tourist attractions.

Bonaire exists in another world from the commerce and bustle of Curaçao. It is an island for escapists who can stand tropical heat, unadulterated natural surroundings, and a considerable amount of solitude. Spear-fishing in the quiet bay near the equally quiet town of Kralendijk or at the incredibly beautiful Lac Lagoon is unsurpassed. This is an outstanding spear-fishing ground—a landlocked bay affording a good beach with shade trees. Fantastically large piles of pink conch shells dot the shoreline, and native fishermen may be seen preparing conch or drying small fish in the sun. The waters are so clear off Lac Lagoon that it is possible to see coral on the bottom at a depth of thirty feet. It is reef-protected, safe for swimming.

The miniature resort hotel Zeebad has its own beach. It was created by converting a wartime internment camp into a series of tourist cabañas; each includes living-room, bedroom, and bath, and is well furnished and screened. Meals are included in a low daily rate, and there is plenty of food, which, except for the local fish dishes, is uninspired.

In the lobby of the Zeebad is a seventeenth-century ship's figurehead of a beautiful woman. Her tender blue eyes look up imploringly, her raven-black hair falls over her bare shoulders. She has expressively arched eyebrows and provocatively full red lips. She is fastened to the bar, which is shaped like the prow of a ship. The island's other hotel, the unpronounceable Pasanggrahan, has no beach, but does offer private baths. Near this hotel is a red-and-white Greek temple that is the local fish market. It is a fascinating but somewhat gruesome sight to watch men stripped to the waist bringing in and cleaning the fish on the beach below the market till the clear blue waters become a vivid blood red.

Besides Bonaire's good beaches, the island offers fine sailing, though there is a shortage of available vessels. The fishing is so good that wahoo and blue marlin, some more than nine feet long, are regularly shipped by air to Curaçao.

But Bonaire should become famous even without its beaches for two truly unique attractions. Great flocks of flamingos, bright pink and easy to observe, breed in the great salt lake in the spring. Their large round nests with the young can be seen close up, usually in May and June. The huge scarlet-headed adult birds inhabit the island most of the year. They feed on tiny shrimp found in the hot salt lagoons. Visitors with cameras, if they are careful to move slowly and use a telephoto lens, can get strikingly beautiful pictures of these unusual birds.

Explorer types will also want to see the grotto at Boca Onima. Its walls, carved by the early Indians, tell of their occupancy of the island in the twelfth or thirteenth century.

At the southern end of the island is an almost equally colorful and interesting sight. These are the thirty-foot-high red, white, and blue obelisks built to guide the early salt ships to their moorings, when the salt industry was of prime importance to the island. Near by are long lines of stone slave huts so low that no man or woman can stand erect in them. The slaves are gone, and so is the economy based on salt. Today there is a small work-clothes industry employing about sixty women. A thousand sheep and goats are raised for export, and seem to run wild all over the island. But the greatest income comes back to families in the form of checks from their men working in the oil industry of Curaçao.

BONAIRE: *One of the longest beach shorelines in the Caribbean.*

BONAIRE: *A single morning's catch.*

CURAÇAO

Wealthiest and largest of the six Netherlands Antilles islands, Curaçao is located in the southern Caribbean just thirty-eight miles north of Venezuela. A narrow thirty-seven-mile strip of arid land seven miles at its widest point and only two and one-half at its narrowest, it is clean, cosmopolitan, and frankly commercial. Its riches come from a highly successful international shopping center, excellent port facilities, and its position as one of the great oil-refining centers of the world. The island's acquisition of wealth has been so sudden that there is a saying in Curaçao that the native population has fallen out of the coconut trees into the convertible.

The capital and only city, Willemstad, is distinctively European in character and equally fascinating whether approached by land or sea. As the cruise ships enter a narrow channel called St. Anna Bay, the gay, gabled houses of seventeenth-century Holland seem within touching distance. It is a fairytale town with houses like well-frosted wedding cakes and fanciful palaces. In addition to the older houses, there is modern architecture that utilizes the best of the earlier designs. Willemstad is in no danger of losing its Old World charm.

The color of the city is overwhelming. Every possible pastel shade is represented in the gabled houses: purple, violet, indigo, cerulean, aquamarine, apricot, plum, lilac, emerald, magenta, and soft chocolate and terra cotta. There is just one white house, and thereby hangs a story. The house belongs to Dr. Charles J. H. Engels, a distinguished physician, poet, and painter. The doctor and his wife, Lucilla, contribute much to the artistic life of the island,

and their unique, newly restored eighteenth-century house is a center of cultural activity. But to build his house he first had to get special permission from the Governor, for white houses have not been allowed by ordinance in Curaçao for many, many years—since, the story goes, one of the island's early governors began to have violent headaches. His doctors advised that the dazzling glare from the white houses of the capital contributed to his discomfort, and that his eyes would be rested if they looked on soft colors—so the Governor promptly passed an ordinance prohibiting white houses in Curaçao.

The city has two major sections: the Punda and the Otrabanda ("other side"). They are separated by the deep channel of St. Anna Bay and joined again by the most famous bridge in all the Caribbean. This is the Queen Emma, which floats on twelve great pontoons and swings silently aside when a ship noses through the channel.

The best place to get oriented in Willemstad is from the high, cool veranda of the Hotel Americano. While not the best hotel, for its meals are ordinary and its rooms bare and badly equipped, it offers the finest balcony in Curaçao from which to sip a drink and watch the Queen Emma in full swing. Because the bridge is the only way a car can get from one part of Willemstad to the other, an almost constant line of automobiles and pedestrians impatiently waits to cross. A few hundred feet beyond the bridge a ferryboat takes passengers across when the bridge is open. Sometimes even this is not possible when a large ship goes through. Both bridge and ferry are free now, but this has not always been true. In the early days a fee of two cents was charged to pedestrians wearing shoes, one cent to those without shoes. Older residents claim that early visitors removed their shoes.

All life in Curaçao revolves around the bridge, which is cordially hated by almost all citizens. Many a crisis has occurred as a result of the hospital being on one side and the doctor on the other waiting for a big ship to pass by. Curaçao's expectant mothers are continually hopeful that their doctor will not happen to be on the wrong side of the bridge at the right time. But it supplies a fine excuse for Curaçaoans whenever they are late. With all this in mind, order a Curaçao punch and sit at dusk watching the bridge slowly swing open as the huge, silent shape of a ship slides by on the quiet waters, then watch the lights on the span make a slow arch as the bridge swings back and pedestrians and cars hurry across.

From the veranda of the Americano one looks across to the

Punda side, the best shopping center in the Caribbean. This is not a shopping center with limited selections. Shops like El Globo carry lenses, cameras, and binoculars by the hundreds. The jewelry firm of Spritzer and Fuhrmann has a world-wide reputation for the manufacture and sale of jewelry, and keeps an incredibly large stock of watches, precious stones, and European silver. These are just two of the dozens of fine shops that line the narrow streets of the Punda. Prices are unbelievably low. The merchants of Curaçao can keep them down because the three-and-three-tenths-per-cent duty on goods imported to the island makes it practically a free port. Other contributing factors are intense competition, huge stocks, and the fact that the dealers are responsible merchants who have been in business for many years and expect to continue for many more.

In Curaçao it is not necessary, as it is in most Caribbean islands, to dine at the hotel of your choice. You may arrange to pay for room and breakfast only, and there are good restaurants that serve interesting, if sometimes heavy, cuisine. The menu is frightening at first glance, but the food is good. One great specialty of the island is Java Dog's Dish, listed on the menu as Java honde portie. Its relationship with the canine world stops with the name. The dish is made up of filet mignon completely surrounded by rice, onions, french-fried potatoes, and two fried eggs. The eggs are placed temporarily on the steak, while curry, paprika, hot peppers, coconut, shrimp, and fish flakes are added to the rice. The egg is then transferred and mixed with rice and condiments, and the steak is eaten on the side. Another favorite is nasi goreng, a succulent dish of Javanese ancestry, consisting of fried rice, pork loin, shrimp, and chicken in a tasty casserole. Either of these dishes is well prepared at the colorful Old Dutch Tavern or the equally famous Washington Tavern. The big before-dinner drink is Scotch whisky, but a considerable amount of Holland gin with or without bitters is consumed, and some Curaçao ladies like this mixture with sugar added.

There is another important mixture in Curaçao. A new—perhaps the first new—language in hundreds of years has emerged. Called Papiamento, it has its roots in Dutch, Spanish, French, Portuguese, and African. The natives describe it as a cocktail—three ounces of Spanish, one ounce of Dutch, one-half ounce each of English, French, and African, and a dash of Portuguese. Spoken by everyone, it is fast becoming a written language as well. The Dutch- and Spanish-speaking people understand it easily and quickly, as many key words are from their languages, and even the British and Americans can make out an occasional sentence.

There is a distinct shortage of good beaches throughout Curaçao, and there is none in Willemstad. Closest to town is a man-made stretch of sand on the waterfront at the Piscadera Beach Club. It is not particularly inviting, for there is a net enclosing the natural swimming area to keep out barracuda and shark, making it safe enough, but definitely detracting from its appearance. The club itself was originally built for the use of the Royal Dutch Shell employees, and, while they still get priority, other guests are accepted. Reservations should be made well in advance. It has an attractive clubhouse with air-conditioned rooms, and this main building also contains a cocktail lounge with twenty-five-cent (¼ guilder) slot machines. Best accommodations are the modern detached cottages, complete with private baths.

Willemstad has a place to swim overlooking the Caribbean. This is a small pool located at the Hotel Avila on the edge of town. The Avila has one particular distinction: outdoor showers and washbasins just outside the double doors of many of the rooms. It is a delightful feeling to step outside in the cool of the morning in complete privacy for a not-too-cold shower.

The best beaches are on the northeast tip of the island at Knip Bay and West Point. While beach facilities at both of these spots are primitive, the stretches of fine powder sand and gradual slope make them pleasant places for a swim. It is a thirty-mile drive to the beaches over roads that vary from fair to good. Compensation for the long drive comes at West Point, where at Janchi's the proprietor himself makes a marvelous fish soup by bringing onions, tomatoes, pimento, garlic, and potatoes to a boil. Then he adds an entire fish, head and all, split down the middle. Finally parsley, red peppers, and salt go in and the fish is boiled for five to ten minutes, depending on its size. The result is delicious.

The countryside to and from West Point is barren, almost desert, spotted only by tall cactus and a few scrawny divi-divi trees so wind-blown that they grow sideways rather than vertically. An occasional tiny village with clean adobe houses, some with thatched roofs, looks sleepy and dusty along the roadside.

This desert-like quality gives Curaçao its greatest problem: the island has been short of water throughout its history. There is very little rainfall (twenty-two inches per year), and there is a distinct shortage of water to be pumped from subterranean reservoirs. These two sources yield only about twenty per cent of the total water needed. The other eighty per cent is distilled from sea water by the island government. This makes water a fairly expensive item, even though the government sells it at a loss. The oil companies import most of their water in tankers, and this water has a definite tendency to smell of kerosene. In a standard local joke one man says to another: "You didn't have a bath tonight—you don't smell like kerosene."

Drinking-water is safe and readily available to visitors, but there are a number of other interesting things to drink in Curaçao, including Heinekens beer on draught at many of the good hotels and restaurants. The curaçao liqueur, a specialty of the island, is both cheap and popular. It comes with two different labels denoting different degrees of sweetness: orange label meaning very sweet and white label slightly sweet. It is flavored with the bitter Curaçao orange peel. The oil of the peel is extracted: two gallons of curaçao liqueur can be flavored with a single orange. A too-sweet, ladylike drink offered by some of the hotels and clubs is a curaçao punch. It is made in a tall glass using lemon or lime peel, canned peaches, rum, green curaçao, and ice, and is topped by a maraschino cherry.

Some of the early history of the island can be imagined while sightseeing in Willemstad. There are three interesting statues in the city. The first is of Peter Stuyvesant, the governor, who lost his leg while leading an attack on Sint Maarten in 1644, one hundred and forty-five years after the island's discovery by the Spanish navigator Alonso de Ojeda. In 1646 Stuyvesant became governor of New Netherlands and its capital, Nieuw Amsterdam, now New York City. Another important statue is that of Simón Bolívar, who for many years lived in Curaçao and did much to cement relations between that island and its neighbor Venezuela. This has proved particularly important in view of the development of the oil-refining industry in Curaçao and the migration of many Venezuelans to the oil fields. But the third and most impressive statue is of Queen Wilhelmina, under whose rule the island became wealthy through oil and shipping.

Sightseeing in the city includes two other monuments dedicated to the liberal spirit of the residents of Curaçao. The best view of the city is from the Franklin D. Roosevelt house, built by the people of the island and presented to the United States Government. It is the official residence of the Consul General of the United States. Also of interest is the Mikve Israel Synagogue, a quiet building of great age where fresh sand is sprinkled over the floor daily and where the orthodox Jewish congregation has met for over three hundred years. Near the synagogue is the floating market, a long line of tiny schooners anchored almost on the sidewalk and loaded with produce and fish from various sections of the island. This is a particularly fine spot for color photographers. Women visitors will enjoy walking along the market and visiting the large department stores just across the street.

Willemstad does not retire early, and visitors will find its two night clubs intriguing. The Chobolobo Club is a twenty-minute ride from the center of town; the Afro is in the middle of the city. Most young Curaçaoans go to the Club Chobolobo to have a few drinks, dance in the outdoor patio to stateside and Spanish tunes, and flirt with the Dutch girls. Most nice girls who are seen in night clubs in Curaçao are chaperoned by their mothers in the old Latin-American tradition. It is possible to dine well at Chobolobo, but the younger crowd goes late and orders saté—hot tidbits of pork flavored with ginger, salt, and garlic sautéd in deep fat. These go very well with gin, Scotch, or beer.

The Club Afro is an entirely different type of operation. It jumps only on Saturday night or when a cruise ship stays over. A small, dark room, none too well ventilated, offers some twelve tables. The trumpet-playing is ear-splitting, and the drums rattle the windows. Although the music is technically terrible, it is highly successful emotionally. Even non-dancers find themselves giving it a whirl after sitting out a few inflammatory choruses. Prices are reasonable, but the choice of food and drink is strictly limited. On week nights the music is likely to be on records.

It is difficult to find native entertainment in Curaçao. There are some practitioners of such early African dances as the tambu left. This folk dance has, however, long been frowned on by the authorities, and it is forbidden by law for the participants, inflamed by the tambu drums, to touch one another during the dance. However, on Christmas, New Year's, Carnival, and especially April 30, the Queen's birthday, the police are likely to look the other way, and it is sometimes possible for a visitor to witness one of these passionate routines.

There are frequent Negro weddings in Curaçao, and festive

singing and dancing goes on throughout the night. Visitors rarely get to see them, but sometimes, now that the music is amplified by loudspeakers from the houses, it is possible to hear one from a distance and perhaps even observe the goings-on from a near-by vantage point. Don't worry about wandering around Curaçao alone. There is almost no major crime, and there has not been an execution on the island since 1870. Crime is limited primarily to the pilfering of small objects.

Curaçao, is not yet ready for the long-staying vacationist. It is, however, a fine island for a stopover of from one to five days—and a great place to shop. Fortunately, there are two other Netherlands Antilles islands that specialize in the attractions Curaçao lacks. These are Bonaire, thirty miles east, and Aruba, fifty miles west.

CURACAO: *The famous floating market.*

CURAÇAO: *Giant oil refineries cover a large section of the island.*

CURAÇAO: *Near Noord Punt, a native village built of palm fibers in the traditional mud-and-wattles construction.*

CURAÇAO: *The Queen Emma floating bridge at Willemstad.*

SABA

Saba is a jagged, rocky cone rising twenty-nine hundred feet from the sea. Cumulus clouds hang above the volcano top, their dark edges dipping down to the brown-green slopes. The blue-purple sea shades into green as it approaches the shoreline. There is no harbor in Saba. There are two landing-places, Fort Bay and Ladder Bay.

Fort Bay is a strip of black volcanic beach with rocks on either side. A narrow road rises from the shore, and a small, square, gleaming white building serves as observation and customs house thirty feet above the water. Vessels arriving at Fort Bay must anchor offshore in the open sea and wait for the lighters to swing alongside to take off passengers. The trip from ship to shore is exciting, adventurous, and likely to be damp—but the sailors of Saba have never lost a tourist overboard.

The little craft rides lightly on the high waves. The sailors maneuver the long oars until the tiny boat is riding high on a breaker, then ride it in, their weight carefully distributed on either side. As the craft touches the beach, they leap out quickly to drag the boat up on the shore before the next breaker wets down the passengers.

There is no area on Saba level enough for an airplane runway. Ladder Bay, a rocky ledge once used for landing ship's passengers, is little used since the road up the mountain from Fort Bay has been completed.

Since 1640 the stubborn Dutch settlers have clung to this semi-barren rock located one hundred and seventy-five statute miles east of Puerto Rico and thirty-five miles northwest of St. Kitts.

The early Saba settlers cut stone steps in the rocky cliff from the landing at Fort Bay to the only flat spot on the island, called The Bottom, where they founded their main village. Timber, tiles, chairs, tables, beds, and even pianos were carried up those steep steps. The steps can still be traversed.

The Hollanders colonized extraordinarily well. The little town of Bottom is a transplanted European village, complete with carefully tended gardens around neat white houses with red-tiled roofs. The few narrow streets are spotlessly clean. The village is so quiet that the sound of one person calling to another comes as a shock.

Government Guest House is the only place in The Bottom with accommodations for visitors at present. It is a two-story white frame building with gingerbread trim and an incongruous royal palm in the front yard. It is further enhanced by a flagpole flying the red, blue, and white colors of the Netherlands. Downstairs there is a large living-room with a well-worn guest registry. The book dates back twenty years, but contains comparatively few names: few visitors land on Saba. On the left of the hall is an attractive, though very plain, dining-room. Stairs lead to four large bedrooms. At the end of the hall is the bathroom, with a cold shower. The rooms are plain, but the beds are good, and everything wears a scrubbed look reminiscent of Dutch kitchens.

Each visitor who stays at the Guest House is called on by neat, middle-aged women and rosy-cheeked children who sell handmade lace. Their lace is excellent, and by United States or European standards the prices are reasonable. It is simple in design and well executed. Although the patterns lack originality, they make pleasant mementos and perfect gifts for a stay-at-home aunt.

Much lace is exported to the larger Netherlands islands of Curaçao and Aruba. The women spend a great deal of time in lace-making because the men leave very young to go to sea or to work in the oil fields of Curaçao. There are five women for every three men on the island, and they are supported largely by checks sent back from Curaçao. These checks make up the greatest source of revenue for the island.

The tiny area of Saba, only five square miles, is brought home to the traveler with continuing impact. There are few houses in The Bottom, and it takes but a short time to meet all of the ambulatory citizens.

There is almost no crime. The major crimes on the books are listed as gossiping, loud talking, screaming in the streets, and occasionally the ill-treatment of a man by his wife. Most arrests are made for being in a state of visible drunkenness. In Saba there are two official degrees of drunkenness. Simple drunkenness requires not that the inebriate be arrested, but merely that he be helped along his way. In the case of visible drunkenness, the police officer must answer three questions affirmatively before making the arrest. Is the defendant staggering so badly that he is unable to continue under his own power? Is his speech so impaired as to be incomprehensible? Is there a strong smell of liquor about his person? If the answer to all of these is yes, he may be taken to jail and locked up overnight on the charge of visible drunkenness. The fine is from two to five guilders.

When citizens of Saba do get drunk, it is on Geneva gin, Dutch whisky, or an unusual homemade concoction known as "spice." This last is made by taking a liter of boiling water, adding fennel seed, four or five cinnamon sticks, a pound of brown sugar, and three or four cloves. When this has boiled to a syrupy consistency, a bottle of Barbados rum is added. It is then taken off the fire and strained. After a week or ten days the brew settles down to an excellent, highly spiced rum liqueur. "Spice" is recommended for chills and fever and is usually drunk in small quantities in the afternoon or after dinner.

For lovers of American cleanliness a great deal can be said for the manner in which food is served on Saba. Certainly there is no question about all foodstuff being sterile: it all comes from familiar cans imported from the United States. Lunch at the Guest House is likely to start with Campbell's tomato soup, continue with Spam and canned green peas, and end with tinned peaches and evaporated milk. Dinners and breakfasts are similar. Food is ample, but, though filling, is typical of a certain type of can-opener cookery well known in all regions of the United States.

There is little farming on Saba. On occasional small plots scratched out of the flinty rock a few vegetables are grown. Most of these are at The Bottom, but a thousand feet above, at Windwardside, and four hundred feet higher, at Hellsgate, a few tiny, neat Dutch gardens and farm plots attest to the perseverance of the people.

The road from The Bottom to Windwardside is the most spectacular and dangerous single-track road ever engineered. It hugs the rocky edge of the mountain, going up at such a steep grade that few cars other than the jeep, for which it was specifically built, could negotiate it. It is still possible to walk up the road to Windwardside, but because a jeep, whizzing dizzily around a curve on the incline, may cause, at the least embarrassment, or at the worst annihilation, it is more practical to spend a guilder or two to ride up.

The village of Windwardside has perhaps two dozen houses, a tiny Government Guest House with two bedrooms, and a general store. The Guest House is only for the rugged traveler. Beds sag, the dining-room is bare, with a single table and four chairs, the living-room has a deserted, unlived-in look. No bath, no hot water, and the w.c. is rudimentary.

Stone walls frame the quiet streets on both sides. All day children play along them—blond, blue-eyed youngsters, the girls usually in overalls, the boys in short pants, white shirts, and green, red, or back berets.

The general store, inside and out, is the gathering-place for the townsmen. There is likely to be a boy with a guitar sitting on the floor. A group of men who may have purchased a bottle of Dutch whisky or Barbados rum take an occasional drink and discuss world politics.

The town of Windwardside has one great distinction: here lives the schoolteacher who imported the first passenger car to the island. Until then no one had thought about traffic laws because there had been no traffic. But the excitement of having a car come down the one-car road when a jeep might be starting up from The Bottom has caused the Administrator to worry.

Most of the population was on hand when the teacher's car was unloaded from the freighter. Two rowboats were lashed together, a few planks laid across them to form a raft. They were rowed to the freighter and the car was carefully lowered over the side, while gasps of tension rose from the crowd on shore. Sinewy arms managed to balance it on the little platform. Slowly, riding high on the rough sea, sometimes disappearing entirely behind a rising wave, the boat came closer. Hand over hand it was pulled to shore by a long rope, until a breaker caught it and brought it rapidly up onto the rough beach. One of the young men of Saba was already seated inside the car. He released the brake and stomped on the gas pedal, trying to jump the foot or two of water between raft and shore. He did not make it. Wheels hit wet gravel, spinning madly, as another breaker started toward shore. For a moment it looked like the end of the first passenger car of Saba. But fifty men, all of whom had been watching, rushed down to lift the car onto firm ground. The young man inside the car poked his head out, waved a triumphant welcome to the crowd, and again pushed down on the gas. The wheels spun, this time in the sand, and a cloud of smoke came from under the hood. Immediately as many heads as possible were under the hood. Someone thought of water. There was no water in the radiator. This was taken care of, and that same evening the car rested quietly in front of the schoolteacher's house in Windwardside. For days the people of Saba stopped by to look at the beautiful new metal object that might bring far-reaching changes to the island. There is an equally good chance that it will bring no changes at all because the road cannot be widened to support two cars, and it is impossible to drive through many of the narrow streets of Windwardside or The Bottom.

Hellsgate is the northernmost village on Saba. It consists of a few houses clinging precariously to a rough, wind-swept slope. This tiny village is made up of even greater individualists than those who pushed their way up to Windwardside. They have gone about as far as human beings can to get away from it all, living in almost complete isolation, occasionally going down to Windwardside for supplies, less frequently down to The Bottom. In spite of their voluntary isolation, they are friendly and, although shy, happy to see visitors.

Most of the way from Windwardside to Hellsgate stone steps have been cut in the rocks. It is an impressive climb, with a sheer drop to the ocean on the right and the steep slope of the volcano on the left. The trip down is even more exciting, for new vistas to the sea open up around every turn, and at one point, Windwardside, its tiny houses clinging to the bare mountainside, is dramatically revealed.

A climb to the crater of the volcano is a rewarding and exciting experience. It is also the only tourist attraction on the island. Begin the ascent near the centrally located church in Windwardside. Here it is easy to pick up a guide who will precede you on the climb, his swinging machete cutting a trail through the brush.

The climb is easy at first, but becomes more rugged and steep. An unusual sight along the way is the tombstones that dot the yards of tiny white houses, marking burial places of the early citizens of Saba. Although there is a law in the Netherlands islands that burial must be in a cemetery, a special dispensation was passed for Saba. Because the rocky earth is almost impenetrable and the distance from one place to another is measured in perpendicular ascents, in Saba only can you be buried in your own back yard. The effect is more pleasant than gruesome, probably because the housewives of Saba have planted little gardens around the graves of departed parents, grandparents, and even great-grandparents.

Going higher and higher, the trail leads through giant ferns, which form a lush tropical jungle. Vines become trees, and exotic parasitic plants grow high on their trunks. Up, still higher, across the jungle, is the most breathtaking sight on the island. A banana plantation with hundreds of trees, deep green and graceful, grows inside the volcanic crater. This hard-to-reach peak is the last fertile land, and many of its citizens are finding that their economic salvation lies in the raising of bananas on this strange savanna. High up on the edge of the crater is a large boulder from which, lying flat to avoid being blown off by the wind, one can see the village of The Bottom. Below it runs the silver ribbon of road down to the white breakers at the base of the mountain, a mountain that got lost on the edge of the Atlantic.

SABA: *Landing is still hazardous in the rough surf among the rocks.*

SABA: *The pleasant, clean little guesthouse in The Bottom.*

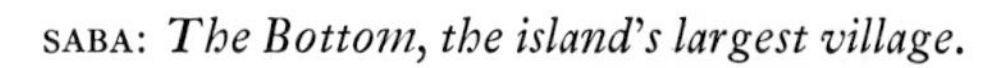

SABA: *The Bottom, the island's largest village.*

SABA: *Steps leading from Windwardside to Hell's Gate.*

SINT (SAINT) EUSTATIUS

Between Saba and St. Kitts is an island within sight of both and in the path of most of the yachts going through this section of the Caribbean. It is, however, seldom visited. Once Statia, as it is now generally known, was the most important transshipping point in the Leeward Islands. As many as seven hundred ships have checked into the deep roadstead in a single week. Today this blue-green harbor is deserted.

The United States of America is in a measure responsible for the present poverty and isolation of this once important Caribbean port. For Statia was the first possession of a foreign country to recognize the United States as a nation when the Colonies revolted against the British in 1776. At Fort Oranje the small guns, at that time considered big guns, were the first to salute the newborn republic. This salute was the beginning of the end for the island; Holland, too, was at war with England. Four years later the British fleet under Admiral Rodney attacked Sint Eustatius and looted and burned the capital. The tiny island never recovered. Its population has been reduced from twenty thousand in 1780 to less than one thousand in 1956.

It is a wonderful island to visit if the traveler is interested in history, ruins, and memories. Color photographers will spend a pleasant and profitable day finding interesting compositions in the deep yellows of the brick ruins of the ancient Jewish synagogue. But it is not the place to spend more than a day or so. After that time the eleven square miles become too small. Everything can be explored so quickly and there is so little variety in the scenery that claustrophobia is likely to set in.

The clean and very quiet Government guesthouse is in the capital, Oranjestad. It has four small comfortable bedrooms and two (no hot water) bathrooms. There is a good chance, particularly during the winter season, that these will be filled, so reservations should be made in advance by writing to the Government house on the island.

Shopping is strictly limited: a little lace and a few baskets. Transportation to the island is also difficult. The *Antilia*, the Netherlands Government motor ship, serves Saba, Sint Maarten, and Sint Eustatius once a month. Of course, it is occasionally possible to find a schooner sailing north from St. Kitts.

Many Americans sailing or flying into this section of the Caribbean will want to visit Fort Oranje to view the little fortress that greeted the birth of their nation.

SINT MAARTEN (AND SAINT MARTIN)

The best example of two countries living at peace with each other can be found in the small (thirty-seven square miles) island of St. Martin, which the French and Dutch have shared since 1648. There is a preponderance of French on the island—about five thousand to sixteen hundred Dutch. Possibly two hundred and fifty of these citizens are white, the rest are mulatto or Negro. But the Dutch don't mind the fact that the French side has the greater population because it also has higher taxes; besides, the Dutch have the airport in their area.

Near the center of the island is a simple plaque and a wooden sign reading: PARTIE FRANÇAISE. There are no guards, no fences, and no arguments. The Netherlands capital is Philipsburg, a quiet, almost deserted town. The main street is a simple row of neat cottages with an occasional large, gabled, Holland-type house. Near the center of town is the harbor, where small fishing craft may be rented.

The capital of the French section is Marigot, a town completely dissimilar to Philipsburg. Houses are smaller and not nearly so neat, and show lots of gingerbread decoration on porches and eaves. Also, Marigot's harbor is somewhat busier with fishermen than Philipsburg's, because there is a greater market for fish. In both harbors the traditional old fishing gear is used and the catch is seldom large enough to properly supply the demand. Visiting fishermen, however, with good equipment and patience can pull large catches of yellowtails, snapper, and kingfish from either the French or Netherlands shores. There is a little pleasure sailing, but comparatively few citizens have either the time or the inclination to sail strictly for fun.

There is excellent horseback riding throughout the island. Horses are raised for export by both the French and the Dutch, and a fair income results from their sale to the French islands of Guadeloupe and Martinique. Mules are also an export item. During the First World War mule-selling became a big business, but mechanization has cut off that source of income.

All the waters surrounding the island and the roads across it are used jointly by the French and Netherlands citizens. Both groups celebrate Bastille Day, though the French make a bit more of it, and both celebrate April 30, the Netherlands Queen's birthday. These are all-out festivals, with foot racing, horse racing, donkey racing, bicycle racing, and boat racing, as well as fireworks and public dancing. An even bigger celebration occurs on July 21 to commemorate the end of slavery on the island. This day is feted with primitive music played on the bongo drums, slavery songs are chanted throughout the night, and dimly remembered African dances are performed. This festival ends in a great feast of fish.

No restrictions exist regarding ownership of land. If a Frenchman wants to buy a piece of property on the Dutch side, he is very welcome, and vice versa. A child becomes a citizen depending upon his paternity. A most unusual feature of life is the religious situation. There are only two denominations, Catholic and Methodist, almost equally divided with perhaps ten per cent more Catholics (the Dutch say that the priests are more active). Both groups attend each other's churches as though there were no differences at all. Citizens of both nations insist that they could not have better neighbors.

St. Martin has a number of good beaches, but only one has been developed. At Little Bay on the Dutch side a modern, comfortable thirty-four-room resort-type hotel lies along the fine white sand beach. A high, densely wooded bluff behind the building gives it privacy.

On the Great Salt Bay peninsula stand the ruins of the once great Fort Amsterdam. The gun emplacements are still here, a grim and desolate sight over the now-deserted salt beds.

Netherlands Sint Maarten is on the way to being a new, though tiny, resort center. It has the advantage of being a completely free port, and already some of the merchants of Curaçao have opened branch shops. At the new hotel, arrangements may be made for deep-sea fishing, spear-fishing, and snorkeling.

French St. Martin also has plans for tourist facilities, and both sides of this ambivalent island are splendid working examples of peaceful coexistence.

SINT MAARTEN (SAINT MARTIN): *From the air.*

Note the lovely white beaches and the roads across the island.

SINT MAARTEN (SAINT MARTIN): *On the French side, fishing is popular as both work and recreation.*

Part Five

UNITED STATES WEST INDIES

VIRGIN ISLANDS: *Saint John's Caneel Bay has an excellent harbor and a fine beach.*

PUERTO RICO: *In the best Spanish style, the town square at Mayagüez has church, Columbus statue, stone benches.*

PUERTO RICO

There is a Spanish phrase "¿Qué pasa?" which, translated freely, means "What's new?" In the boisterous one-hundred-by thirty-five-mile rectangular island of Puerto Rico the answer is—plenty. No island in the Caribbean is changing and growing so rapidly.

Change is not new to Puerto Rico. Even the names of the island and its leading city have been reversed since early Spanish occupation days. The original name for the entire island was San Juan Bautista (St. John the Baptist). Ponce de León, the first governor, named the city located on an island in the harbor Puerto Rico, meaning rich port. San Juan is now the city, Puerto Rico the entire island.

Its location in the Caribbean is fortunate. It lies at the crossroads of the Greater and Lesser Antilles and on an air route between North and South America, making it an ideal air and sea terminal. West, seventy-five miles away, is Hispaniola; east are the Virgin Islands; north, sixteen hundred miles away, is New York; Miami is a thousand miles northwest.

The old-new city of San Juan, on the north coast, consists of two distinct geographical sections. First is the island city, which includes the old Spanish town, a small modern business and shopping section, most governmental buildings, the Caribe Hilton Hotel, and the beginning of the gold-coast strip of resort hotels and clubs. This glittering line-up of beaches, swimming pools, cabañas, and tennis courts clustered around modern hotels continues across the Dos Hermanas (two sisters) Bridge, along Ashford Avenue, into the Condado suburb of Santurce (pronounced san *ter*-say), San Juan's second-largest section. Santurce, with its suburban areas—Miramar,

Condado, Hato Rey, and Río Piedras—and the old city constitute greater San Juan, with a population of over four hundred thousand.

San Juan is not Puerto Rico. Even the busy residents say that to get the feel of the country one must go out on the island. There beauty is encountered in many forms; multicolored fields of calla lilies grow in the valleys near San Germán in the southwest; and magnificent vistas of fertile, rich brown soil and leafy green vegetation are revealed from the central mountain range, which rises to thirty-five hundred feet and sprawls lengthwise across the center of the island. To see the island as the Puerto Ricans do, take a público, or jitney. This is a converted station wagon or sedan identified by *P* or *BA* on the license plates. Crowd in with the friendly Puerto Ricans to make a leisurely but rough trip around the island. The driver of the público may not speak English, but someone in the vehicle is almost certain to. If the spine is weak and the pocketbook stronger, rent a drive-yourself car, get some maps, and start out to explore the rural countryside. Driving is easy, as traffic stays on the right and driver's licenses take only a few moments to secure. Car rental rates and arrangements are similar to those in the States.

Puerto Rico has a great advantage over other islands in the Caribbean in its fine new network of highways extending all around the island and crossing it. Roads are excellent, many of them four-lane. In the north-central section south of San Juan on the road to Ponce is the pineapple country, where acre after acre is devoted to the culture of giant succulent fruit sometimes weighing as much as fifteen pounds each. Farther south is the tobacco area. Here gently waving purple-green leaves dominate the plains. Then comes Puerto Rico's second-largest city, Ponce.

Ponce is not a resort city, but an old Spanish town with a heavy overlay of modern businesses and new ways. Its major claim to fame is an almost unbelievably garish architectural structure located on its otherwise beautiful plaza. This is the Parque de Bombas (Fire House), with a cupola, a lookout tower, and fanlike decorations of Moorish extraction over doors and windows, all painted like a wild checkerboard in red, white, and black squares.

Ponce and the area around it are good places to shop for santos, the primitive carved wooden figures that were made by the early religious settlers of Puerto Rico. Santos range in height from two inches to two feet, and some are important art treasures. In personality and execution they are very different from those of Mexico or New Mexico. Occasionally a santero carves an entire scene rather than a saint alone.

Puerto Rico being a Catholic country, saints are important in all sections, and fiestas are held almost every day in their honor. Attending a festival on the outskirts of Ponce is an experience not to be missed. Most fiestas have a little carnival with rides and donkeys, candy, and an impromptu dance hall. Visitors are welcome, and dancing and singing often go on all night. Everyone in the family has a marvelous time. The Puerto Rican family is a very fine thing to observe; watch them celebrating the birthday of a ninety-year-old grandfather, toasting him in beer or local wine, and singing sentimental or military songs accompanied on the guitar, mandolin, and accordion. When a member of a Puerto Rican family leaves or returns, the entire family, and occasionally the whole neighborhood, gathers to welcome him home or see him off.

Following the well-marked highways is no problem, and the western roadway leads through the coffee country and the island's third city, Mayagüez—center of the needlework and embroidery industries. Mayagüez has a fine harbor and, for an old Spanish city, unusually wide and shady streets. It, too, is not a resort city, but it has an interesting atmosphere and adequate hotels. Among other things, it is an important fishing center. Southeast of Mayagüez is San Germán, second settlement founded in Puerto Rico and perhaps the most unspoiled and picturesque today. Its ancient church was built by and for Indian slaves whom the Spaniards were determined to Christianize or annihilate. Ten miles from San Germán is the important small fishing resort of Parguera. It offers a pleasant place to stay overnight and an exciting view of the phosphorescent bay at night which makes the entire harbor look like a brilliantly lighted festival. Puerto Rico has an abundance of the better-known game fish. Off the coast are barracuda, bonito, bonefish, white marlin, sailfish, tarpon, and tuna. They come in all sizes and colors. Other excellent fishing towns are San Juan, Aguadilla, Guánica, Ponce, and Fajardo.

The weather is always good for fishing, for seasons do not change in Puerto Rico, and the temperature remains in the 70–85 range all year. In the spring the leaves of the almond trees turn orange-red, giving some coastal areas the appearance of autumn in New England. High in the mountain rain forests at Luquillo, the hardwood trees never change except to put down deeper roots and extend upward. West Indian satinwood (tabonuco), Spanish cedar (aceitillo), and laurel grow profusely in the high, damp forest. The Luquillo, part of the Caribbean National Forest, together with the majestic mountain El Yunque (The Anvil) constitutes an extraordinary resort a short distance from San Juan. Here is the longest improved beach on the island—five miles of sand, with tall coconut palms, dressing rooms, parking areas, and all the necessities for beach living. Higher on the near-by mountain are two swimming pools that are fine for Americans, but seem too cold for Puerto Ricans. Hiking trails through the rain forest reveal a wonderland of wild begonias, fragile orchids, air plants, and a jungle of giant tree ferns. Not expensive, and certainly convenient, Luquillo is an ideal playground for many Puerto Ricans and visitors.

Before a visitor returns to San Juan, there are a few more facts of life in Puerto Rico to consider. Spanish is the language of the island, though English is taught in every grade in school. Most people speak Spanish, and a few words of Spanish in your own vocabulary, while not essential, will certainly help, especially with taxi-drivers. Shops in Puerto Rico close at noon and open again at 2:30. The siesta is still a pleasant custom and a good idea for travelers to adopt. Because Puerto Rico is a part of the United States, there are many conveniences. Currency is the same, time is just one hour later than Eastern Standard (the same as Eastern Daylight Saving). Telephones work every time, and all operators speak both English and Spanish, making communication far simpler than on most Caribbean islands. Stores, including Sears Roebuck, carry the same brands of merchandise; drugstores are on every corner; and the New York *Times* and *Herald Tribune* may be purchased the day they are published. Drinking-water is good in San Juan, fairly good throughout the island. Milk in San Juan is pasteurized.

There are some drawbacks, too. Being a United States island, Puerto Rico has a tendency to be too United States for some travelers. Radios blare noisily all over the cities. Neon lights cast lurid reflections on the timeless Spanish buildings. Everyone seems to be rushing from someplace and hurrying elsewhere, especially the citizens of San Juan. Shop carefully. Although such items as mahogany and embroidered garments are cheaper, you can wind up making purchases that were imported from the United States and paying a higher price for them than you would at home.

Being part of the United States has meant a great deal to Puerto Rico. As its population rapidly increased, because of a low death rate and high birth rate, the economy of the island had to change from primarily agricultural. Its population of 643 persons to the square mile is more than twice that of Haiti and thirteen times that of the United States. Puerto Rico is therefore engaged in an ambitious "Operation Bootstrap" to lift its economic level by promoting industrialization; developing electric power, highways, and other public works to support this increased industrialization; and increasing agricultural efficiency and diversification.

Because goods manufactured in Puerto Rico can be brought into the United States duty free, and because of a series of important concessions to manufacturers, Puerto Rico is an excellent place for industry to settle. Over the past decade many United States businesses have been established there. The island devotes a large percentage of its income to education, and is producing more and better-trained workers continuously. Because of the population growth, there is an almost endless labor supply. No Federal taxes apply to a new industry, nor is there any Puerto Rican tax for the first few years. Municipal and excise taxes also take a holiday, and property taxes are eliminated for between five and ten years. During the first seven years there is no tax on dividends paid to established residents of Puerto Rico.

In addition to being all out for industry, Puerto Rico is all out for culture. Its art center shows important local artists, as well as artists from other islands. It has made an effort to develop a writers' colony, and has passed special legislation allowing writers and other creative workers to live on government land and buy it at an extremely low cost.

Let us take a quick look at the history and sightseeing possibilities of the old city of San Juan. In 1511, eighteen years after its discovery by Columbus, San Juan received its great seal from Spain. Much of the early history of the island is reflected in the pictures and symbols on that unusual coat of arms. Against a field of light green that may symbolize the fertility of the new land a silver lamb of peace sits upon a red book representing the Bible and the Church. Among the first buildings was the church of San José, which can be seen today in the old city just as it was when Ponce de León worshipped there in the early sixteenth century. In the near-by plaza stands a statue of this Spanish explorer. The lamb on the seal carries the white banner and insignia of San Juan Bautista; the motto across the bottom reads "John is his name," dedicating the island in effect to St. John the Baptist. On the other side of the shield the initials *F* and

I stand for Their Catholic Majesties Ferdinand and Isabella. The letters are crowned and joined by a yoke. A sheaf of arrows represents strength and power, and two famous fortresses still stand in San Juan to attest to their efficacy. On the tip of the island is El Morro, one of the great fortresses of all time. It was never bested from the sea, and fell only once—when attacked by land by the British. Even when United States ships fired on El Morro in 1898, none of the shells got through the sturdy walls. Today the fortress is a historic shrine, although it has a most unusual golf course inside its ancient walls. The nine-hole Fort Brook course is actually constructed in and around the fortress. On one hole the approach is over a thirty-foot wall. Non-golfers will want to visit the underground rooms and look out over the towers to the sea. Incongruously enough, there are modern residences near by; one next door has Venetian blinds, and the week's wash may often be seen hanging out on the line to dry.

Other important sights in the old city are San Cristobal (St. Christopher's Fortress); the Cathedral of San Juan Bautista, with the tomb of Ponce de León; San Juan Gate, the only one remaining of the original four; and La Fortaleza, the traditional and venerable home of the governors of the city, still in use for that purpose. The building is partly palace, partly citadel. Its gardens are magnificent all year and can be visited by special permission.

This old section of San Juan can be seen on foot. Indeed, many of the streets and alleys are too narrow for automobiles. It is a short walk from one historic spot to another, with occasional shade trees, camera shops, and Coca-Cola stands on almost every corner. It is a good plan to stop at the tourist bureau located in the center of the city for information about all of Puerto Rico. United States uniforms on the soldiers stationed in the old city are a reminder of its occupation by the United States in 1898. Many citizens of the United States do not realize that the Spanish-American War was fought here as well as in Cuba. Puerto Rico gave up with little resistance, and less than five hundred men were lost in its capture. Occupied for two years, it became a part of the United States by the Treaty of Paris in 1898. All Puerto Ricans became United States citizens by action of Congress in 1917 (Jones Act). Until 1946, when Truman selected a native-born Puerto Rican—Luis Muñoz Marín—as governor, the governors appointed by the President of the United States had been from the mainland. In 1949 the island for the first time elected its own governor, and in 1950 drew up its own Constitution.

Let us get back to the food, resorts, and night life for which San Juan is famous. Breakfast is always a delight. Fruit is plentiful, French bread good, and coffee strong and hot. Add to this the cheery sunshine, clear blue skies, and a little bird known as the honey-creeper which flies right into the dining-rooms (dozens live in the dining-room of the Kasablanca Hotel) and even comes to the table for bits of sugar.

The beaches in San Juan proper are not so good for swimming as are the large modernistic swimming pools that are part of each gold-coast hotel. One innovation at the Isla Verde Club is cabañas backing on the beach and facing toward the magnificent king-size swimming pool. Food in San Juan is varied and, while not unique, generally good. Occasionally, as in the case of the old-fashioned, mirrored La Mallorquina Restaurant, it is superb. Besides being able to eat in a Swiss chalet, a Hungarian restaurant, or at a smörgåsbord, the visitor can find Puerto Rican dishes served both in San Juan and in the countryside. Such are lechón asado (roast suckling pig cooked outdoors on a spit over a wood fire) and asopao (a thick gumbo or soupy rice made with fish, chicken, or crab). Of course, the steaks, chops, and vegetables familiar to United States palates are available.

During the Christmas season and especially between Christmas Day and Twelfth Night (January 6), known as the Day of the Three Kings, all Puerto Rico celebrates. Gifts are given on both days, the latter ones in remembrance of the gifts given the Christ Child by the three kings. On January 5, Puerto Rican children put containers of corn and grass under their beds to refresh the camels of the wise men. In the morning their offering has been replaced by gifts.

At this season come the parrandas, strolling musicians who play and sing and are invited into each house they serenade. They are traditionally served morcillas (three kinds of sausages), arroz con dulce (rice pudding), pasteles, and lechón asado.

San Juan does not celebrate just once a year. There are cockfights somewhere in the town almost daily. A weekly lottery (the only legal one on United States soil) is extremely popular. Baseball games during the season are held in the Sixto Escobar Stadium. There is plenty of music and dancing every evening for the many visitors and pleasure-loving natives, as well as floor shows in night clubs in every price range. Some of the clubs have gambling casinos.

But perhaps the most revealing experience in all of Puerto Rico is a walk through the old city late at night. Then modern encroachments blend into the shadows, and the city can be imagined as it once was. Down on the docks, where the grandees of Spain landed, take the little ferry and sail across the bay to Cataño. The round trip takes half an hour, but in that space of time, while the moonlight shines on the Old World's palaces and fortresses, it is easy to push time back four hundred years and see San Juan as Ponce de León saw it.

PUERTO RICO: *Ancient church at San Germán, said by Puerto Ricans to be the oldest still standing in the Western Hemisphere.*

PUERTO RICO: *Ponce's colorful Parque de Bombas (firehouse).*

PUERTO RICO: *Entrance to the University of Puerto Rico.*

PUERTO RICO: *A fiesta in the plaza of Mayagüez.*

SAINT CROIX

Almost three times as large as St. Thomas, this wedge-shaped, eighty-four-square-mile island concentrates on the rural rather than the urban life. Its economy has always been based on sugar and rum. But the tourist business is booming, and all St. Croix is busy building and enlarging its facilities for visitors.

The personality of the island has not been affected by all this bustle. It can be described as distinctly placid and reserved. Physically, the island consists of rolling hills rising to 1,165 feet at Mount Eagle near the north coast and gradually sloping to pleasant plateaus in the south. The center is covered with sugar cane; it is grown and ground by the Virgin Islands Corporation, a company subsidized by the United States.

There are a number of beaches around the shoreline, but few good public ones: many are restricted to private use by their owners. Near-by Buck Island, less than one mile off the north shore, is popular, as is the beach on the little cay in Christiansted harbor, site of the Hotel-on-the-Cay. Best of the public beaches is at Cramer Park on the eastern tip of the island, which is also the easternmost point of land owned by the United States. On the exact opposite end of the island, near Frederiksted, is a good beach that has gained something of a reputation because swimmers there have occasionally been known to dispense with bathing suits; this, however, has been the exception rather than the rule.

The capital of St. Croix is Christiansted, and a more beautiful West Indian harbor cannot be imagined. It is deep enough to take vessels drawing up to eighteen feet of water, and the water is amazingly clear. The city itself is a complete eighteenth-century

Caribbean port that could be called a living restoration. For the ancient buildings are still in use, and their soft pastel pinks, powder blues, and yellows look like a perfect stage setting. The area around the dockside has been designated a national historic site, and the old fort, museum, library, and church are perfectly preserved, as well kept as they were two hundred years ago. From the hills back of the city, the red, steeply pitched roofs look down on the long coastal schooners reminiscent of the early clipper ships. The spacious harbor area is uncluttered with modern buildings or modern signs. Next to it lies an attractive shopping center, which, like that of Charlotte Amalie, St. Thomas, enjoys practically free-port status, meaning that the prices on many items are considerably lower than stateside prices. This is particularly true of perfume, Danish and Swedish silver, and glass. Some items, however, are almost as expensive as in New York; but there are many bargains for those travelers who do not plan an extensive trip through several foreign islands. Avocado Alley, with its little shops and patio, and the International Shop on King Street offer a wide variety of valuable and interesting things to buy.

St. Croix's variety of inns, old plantation manor houses complete with swimming pools, modern luxury hotels of stucco and terrazzo with private beaches, and small pensions is unequaled on any other small island of the Caribbean. The plantation houses take from eight to twelve guests; the tiny pensions both in and out of town take from two to six. The newest development is the group of private cottages called St. Croix-by-the-sea, which is built somewhat in motel style for individual comfort. It has a huge salt-water pool, partly natural and partly man-made, with a net to keep barracuda out, and is a particularly good place for travelers with children (who are welcomed at all of St. Croix's resorts). There is even a private school, The Island School, for youngsters from kindergarten through eighth grade.

St. Croix's hotels still are operated on the American plan (meals included), but there has recently been an important break in this pattern. Many guests want to take lunch or dinner outside their hotel, and a new inn, The Henge, has been opened in downtown Christiansted. This is a tropical branch of Stonehenge, a New England inn located near Ridgefield, Connecticut. Much of the food served at The Henge is imported from the States. The delightful patio and fine cuisine make a welcome addition to the social and corporeal life of St. Croix. Another restaurant worthy of note is The Rubaiyat, primarily a waterfront café serving good short orders and sandwiches; it has a bar excellent not only for drinking, but also for long, happy conversational hours.

On the west coast is the much smaller (two thousand people to Christiansted's four thousand) but very lovely city of Frederiksted; it lies fifteen miles across the island from Christiansted by roads that are partly good, partly rough. Frederiksted's greatest charm is its gingerbread and curlicued architectural decorations, which came into being when the city was rebuilt after a disastrous fire in 1878. The old stone fort, built in 1760, is a formidable and forbidding-looking structure of two stories with arches and pediments. Its four-foot-thick stone walls back up the spacious stone courtyard where the proclamation freeing the island slaves was read in 1848.

Between the two cities, the countryside is completely devoted to agriculture. The native Negroes who work the land lead a simple, monotonous existence. Almost all of them express desire to work in the United States. There are many sugar estates across the island. Some of their manor houses are in ruins, but others are in excellent repair. The names of some of them excite curious travelers. It is only a few miles to such fascinating places as Blessing, Envy, Jealous, Upper and Lower Love, and Judith's Fancy, the last a particularly lovely ruin of a French-style plantation house. One of the most interesting private estates is Annaly, in northwestern St. Croix. Here a sugar mill has been transformed into a modern dream house. It is round, of course, and rugged on the outside, but is a miniature castle within. The lounge, dining-room, and kitchen are combined on the ground floor. The whole second floor is a round bedroom, exquisitely furnished, with small but adequate windows for ventilation. This room is reached by a circular iron stairway that comes up through the floor and extends through the ceiling to a roof garden, from which the view of rolling hills and waving sugar cane is magnificent. Like many of the other old estates (and town houses as well), Annaly can be seen by applying to the St. Croix Landmarks League, a civic group that arranges tours through the island's beautiful homes.

The white residents of St. Croix mean to be friendly, and they say that they are eager for new businesses and more people to come to their island, but their attitude is ambivalent. They do advertise for new businesses and other enterprises, but they show a tendency to discourage the new businessman when he investigates possibilities on the island. This seemingly snobbish attitude stems from the fact that the residents of St. Croix are realistically afraid that their quiet little island will develop some of the Coney Island characteristics of St. Thomas or Bermuda. Now it is quiet and pleasant and has little night life. They would like to keep it this way. For this reason, new businesses are difficult to start, and land is particularly hard to acquire. Residents tell you that this is because you have to be one of them, the kind of person they want on the island. It is also necessary to have a considerable amount of ready money.

Real estate on St. Croix brings higher prices each year. Naturally, the local people are eager to see this trend continue. Many older residents will tell you that no land is available—that there is no possible place for a new business. This is untrue. There is considerable land in St. Croix for those who wish to pay the price. Nor is there any question that land values should be high. The climate of St. Croix is slightly warmer than that of islands with higher elevation, such as Dominica. At times there is a definite shortage of water, meaning that much of the drinking-water must be boiled. But, in spite of these minor drawbacks, St. Croix is such a beautiful island and so close to Puerto Rico and the United States by air that it must ultimately become one of the great resorts of the West Indies.

At present, St. Croix has no golf club, but plenty of tennis, and the St. Croix Tennis Club gladly extends temporary playing privileges to tourists. Fishing is as good as off St. Thomas, as are sailing and pleasure travel from island to island, though not nearly so many boats are available and there is less variety of size and price.

Exploring the back country of St. Croix by road is rewarding. Good riding horses can be rented. Manning's Bay has a good racecourse, and many horses are raised and trained to race during the meet in February and March. Bicycles are plentiful and popular, and can be used to cover a lot of miles. The roads are so steep in many sections, however, that sightseeing by taxi is preferable. Taxis are rarely new vehicles, but the drivers are courteous and know the island scenery and customs. There are at least a hundred and fifty miles of good road, most of it hard-top or gravel; the roads in the lowlands are much better than those in the mountains.

Wherever one travels on St. Croix, the name of Alexander Hamilton is prominent. The airport is named for him; the store in which he worked when he was thirteen—still known as the Alexander Hamilton Store—is located across from the Government building near the center of Christiansted. It is also pointed out that he lived on the estate where the Buccaneer Hotel is located, and a monument to his mother, Rachel Sarah Fawcett Levine, stands at The Grange, a mile or so from Christiansted. Hamilton lived in St. Croix from 1765, when he was ten, until 1772, when he set out for New York.

Travelers have a choice of ways to reach this delightful island. Freight ships that call at St. Thomas, forty miles to the north, bring visitors to St. Croix as deck passengers. Interisland boats, mostly schooners with auxiliary motors, and yachts are available out of St. Thomas. It is only a few minutes' flight from the Harry S. Truman Aerodrome in St. Thomas to the Alexander Hamilton Aerodrome in St. Croix.

SAINT CROIX: *La Grange House.*

SAINT CROIX: *Christianstad Harbor.*

SAINT CROIX: *Ancient cannon guard the approaches to a Danish fort in Frederiksted.*

SAINT JOHN

Some islands seem to try to please everyone, but not St. John, smallest of the populated United States Virgin Islands. It is the most primitive, and yet the most luxurious, of them all. Located three miles west of St. Thomas, this hideout from civilization can be reached in half an hour by boat. It is about as different from St. Thomas as Glacier National Park is from New York or London. In fact, St. John is so beautiful and so unspoiled that the Secretary of the Interior has recommended that the Congress set aside a large part of it as a National Park. The land for this park was offered to the United States by St. John's heaviest investor and greatest developer, Laurance S. Rockefeller. Although Mr. Rockefeller has developed a fine resort in his Caneel Bay Plantation (at present operated as a private commercial enterprise), St. John is more than a park or a single resort.

From the moment when the Caneel Bay launch leaves Red Point Landing in St. Thomas, there is an almost continuous aura of excitement about this trip to an island with few motor roads and a few jeeps, but depending almost entirely upon horses and mules. When a white sand beach with twisted coconut trees comes into view and you look down deep into the clear, clean waters, it is easy to tell that you are in for a pleasant day, week, or month. This is a well-heeled beachcomber's haven, for the countryside is just as the Caribs left it when they were forced out by the colonists who followed Christopher Columbus.

Today St. John has comforts, even luxuries, that the Caribs would never have understood. At Cruz Bay, on the west side of the island, the traditional big white house of the Administrator sits high on a hill. Below, near the quiet beach, a few wooden buildings lie almost in the shadows of the ruins of a great plantation. Cruz Bay, though the capital of St. John, is a very small town indeed.

The flowering trees and giant bushes of the jungle have taken over many early plantations, for St. John was a rich and densely cultivated island early in the nineteenth century. Sugar cane almost covered the island, making great fortunes for the men who owned the slaves who worked it. But the natives tell a hair-raising story, suggesting that you can hear it from the ghosts of departed slaves if you listen to their groans and protests at Murray's Point. These are the voices of the past, telling how extreme cruelty and starvation at the hands of their Danish masters led the slaves to massacre the whites in 1733. Then, the story goes, French soldiers were imported to fight the slaves. The Negroes were driven back to the cliff at Murray's Point, where they threw themselves over the rocks into the sea rather than be captured. Their ghosts still haunt Fungi Passage at the base of the promontory. This story may be entirely true—but the natives of Grenada, a British island, tell almost the same story about the Caribs who leaped into the sea from the cliffs of Sauteurs.

The native Negroes of St. John, about seven hundred and fifty of them, live mostly in the hills back from the shore. There they still pick bay leaves in the bay forest and send them to St. Thomas, where bay rum, a pungent men's toilet water, is manufactured much as it was a century ago. They farm, fish, make baskets and mix little with the white newcomers except as maids, gardeners, and guides.

Because almost no automobiles and few jeeps are available (they do not negotiate the trails as well as horses), guides are essential for sightseeing. Trails through the mountains are well marked, but if you really want to see the Carib stones on the Root Bay trail, a guide will make the trip more comfortable and more interesting. These rocks have markings somewhat similar to those in Grenada, Dominica, and St. Vincent, but not so large or so distinct. This trail trip and another across the northern route from Cruz Bay to Coral Bay can be made easily in one day.

Coral Bay lies only seven miles from Cruz Bay, and the Government boat stops there, too, so the trip does not have to be made by horse. The Coral Bay harbor is magnificent, much larger than those of Christiansted (St. Croix) or Charlotte Amalie (St. Thomas). It is guarded by an old fort on a high cliff from which the Danes once controlled the harbor entrance.

The prize package for beach-hungry Americans is the perfect resort at Caneel Bay—not one but ten perfect beaches. It offers a choice of hotel rooms or independent cottages with a cook and a maid. There are a dining-terrace, bars, and a large commissary supplying a wide choice of food and liquors. Sailing and fishing boats are available, and spear-fishing expeditions enlist expert guides and teachers. The tennis courts could not be better. At Caneel Bay the emphasis is on complete privacy and a carefree, happy life. It is expensive by comparison with hotels in the other islands of the Caribbean, but it is also more comfortable than most of them.

Because of the cookie-cutter pattern of St. John's shoreline, many other fine beaches and coves may someday be developed. Not so luxurious as Caneel Bay is the Trunk Bay Guest House, where prices are lower. The swimming, fishing, and snorkeling are just as good. Other small guesthouses are inexpensive and very pleasant.

So don't skip St. John if you go to St. Thomas or St. Croix. Here is a good life, with no night clubs and no movies, but with some of the finest beaches and best fishing in the Caribbean.

SAINT THOMAS

Facilities for travelers are more highly developed in St. Thomas than in any other small Caribbean island. Although only thirty-two square miles in area, St. Thomas boasts a large yacht center and lots of fishing and pleasure boats for hire. It has at least twenty-five hotels of various types and a modern shopping center that even includes a Food-o-Mat. It is a stay-out-late island with gay night life. Some of these facts point to the obvious conclusion that St. Thomas is a part of the United States. But it has both a distinctive character and a highly romantic history.

St. Thomas was settled by Denmark in 1647 while its sister island, St. Croix, was being battled over by England, France, and Spain. Denmark quietly moved into St. Thomas without any fighting; forty-four years later it took over St. Croix as well. It was the Danes who originally made St. Thomas a free port, and this undoubtedly resulted in its becoming a haven for pirates. It has also resulted in considerable benefits for modern visitors: imported liquors are extraordinarily cheap, and such items as Danish silver and French porcelain are inexpensive. Columbus had discovered the islands before the Danes, and, noting the great number of them (over forty islands and cays), had named them after St. Ursula and her ill-fated 10,999 virgins.

From the air St. Thomas does not look small, and it is actually the second-largest of the Virgin Islands, only St. Croix being larger. The streets of Charlotte Amalie, its capital, are lined with shops effectively occupying ancient warehouse buildings. The walls bloom with red and purple hibiscus and bougainvillæa, though signs over the store entrances may say Sears Roebuck or Berettas Center. Plenty of rum and other liquor is for sale, as are perfumes, Swedish glassware, French and Austrian jewelry, and handbags. The shops also carry tropical clothing, baskets, and hats made in the Virgin Islands. There is a busy art center in the downtown section.

Rising behind the shopping street is a series of small streets lined with interesting buildings. The Government House is a colonial structure with a lovely iron grillwork balcony. Almost directly next door to it are ninety-nine weathered stone steps with an interesting early Danish building at their base.

The hotels in this section of Charlotte Amalie are showplaces in themselves. "1829," a thick-walled ancient building with an unusual patio, was built in that year and is furnished with antiques of the period. Farther up the hill is Smith's Fancy, a good place to live in St. Thomas, and an excellent place to visit at cocktail time, when it glows with flowers and paintings of the island.

St. Thomas has two groups of native Negroes. One is descended from African slaves brought in during the Danish occupation; the other, the Cha Chas, migrated from the near-by French island of St. Barthélemy. The Cha Chas have retained their odd French patois, and make a point of keeping separate from the other island Negroes. It is important for the visitor to remember that this island belongs to its people, most of whom are Negroes and mulattoes. Almost all Government offices are staffed by intelligent, well-educated Negro men and women, as are many of the stores, shops, and hotels. The taxi-drivers are men of considerable dignity who have a great deal of knowledge about places to go and ways of getting there. They have been somewhat spoiled, however, by high rates and excessive tipping by American visitors. Actually, they did not expect tips until very recently. Many of the taxi-drivers are trained by the Government as guides, and a few will refuse to accept more remuneration than is due them for the time they are hired. Although it is fairly easy to rent a drive-yourself car in St. Thomas, it is not worth while unless one expects to spend a considerable time there. In addition to getting a license, it is necessary to take a road test after learning the local road rules.

St. Thomas takes its driving seriously; the drivers are skillful and careful. They have to be, for the roads are steep and narrow. A drive around the island can be made in three or four hours, but if the entire day is available, it is a good plan to prepare a picnic and set out for an all-day tour. The narrow roads lead through highly scenic vistas over the hills, through the valleys, and out to the sea. The road past the Hotel Flamboyant hugs the coastline and leads to Red Point, where the boats take off for Caneel Bay on the near-by island of St. John. The road finally leads past a high point known as Drake's Seat, where Sir Francis Drake is said to have sat and charted the islands. Next comes Magens Bay, with a beautiful beach, one of the great picnic spots of the Caribbean. The swimming is good, the water calm and clear. Unfortunately, it is so far from the major hotels that the trip takes almost too long for anything but a half-day expedition.

St. Thomas has other beaches, such as Morningstar, not nearly so far from the hotels, but they are not comparable to Magens Bay and can be considered only fairly good at best. After spending a day or so on land, it is a great idea to enjoy St. Thomas by boat, the island at its best. There is fishing all around the island—for as many as a hundred and eight different kinds of fish, including such familiar ones as sailfish, bonefish, dolphin, and king, as well as native-named mulatto curvalley, bastard angel (also Swedish and ordinary angel-fish), blue doctor, and wenchman. Because the fishing is so good, plenty of gear is available for hire, as are lots of boats. It is actually cheaper to live on some of the boats than in the hotels. All types are to be rented, from small ketches to large yachts taking from two to eight people. It is easy and pleasant to arrange a three- to five-day trip, pack the kind of food most enjoyed by all, and sail away for St. Croix, St. John, and the near-by British Virgin Islands.

Prices depend upon the equipment and size of the boat, but are higher than in the British, French, Netherlands, or even independent islands. But if plenty of night life, a considerable social whirl, cocktails, swimming, and sailing are your dish, you will like St. Thomas by land and by sea. Remember that it has been described as the night club of the Virgin Islands: if your interest is in a quiet, altogether restful holiday, try the quieter islands of St. John and St. Croix—or divide your time among the three.

VIRGIN ISLANDS: *The pool of the Virgin Isle Hotel overlooks the clear harbor of Charlotte Amalie, Saint Thomas.*

VIRGIN ISLANDS:
*Waiting at the airport,
Saint Thomas.*

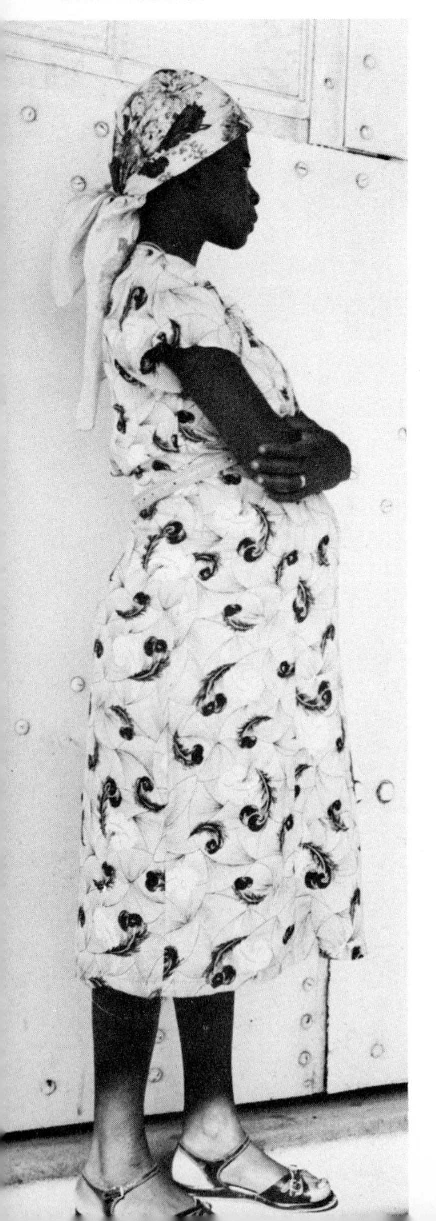

VIRGIN ISLANDS:
*A favorite late-hour hangout,
especially for sailors,
in Charlotte Amalie, Saint Thomas.*

VIRGIN ISLANDS: *Said to have been Bluebeard's Castle, this is now a fine hostelry in Charlotte Amalie, Saint Thomas.*

VIRGIN ISLANDS: *Harbor of Charlotte Amalie, Saint Thomas.*

NAVASSA

The loneliest island in the Caribbean is a two-mile-long strip of rocky cliff located almost midway between Haiti and Cuba, where a giant light warns shipping of the dangerous reefs in the channel. The men who once occupied the island and cared for the light are no longer there, for the light was electrically equipped several years ago. It will come as a surprise to most Americans to know that this remote island, Navassa, belongs to the United States.

Barren and uninhabited except for a few goats and cats, it is an extraordinarily dangerous island for exploration. Seemingly bottomless depths dot the jagged, deep-pitted limestone plateau. Its only water is the rain that collects for short periods in some of the shallow pools. Navassa has no harbor, and it is said that the deeper holes seem to have no bottom at all.

This is an island that men wrested from the elements (it is in the hurricane belt), the land crabs, and the sea. Why did anyone want this sterile rock? In spite of its grotesque appearance and terrain, Navassa is important to United States and South American shipping because it is in the middle of the important route taken by ships between New York, the Eastern seaboard, and the Panama Canal. Before the United States put up Navassa Light, numberless ships piled up on the dangerous reefs surrounding the island or smashed against the rocky promontory itself.

If ever a country acquired an island by sheer accident, it happened with Navassa. In 1856 a young man named Peter Duncan accidentally sailed to this uninviting sea-girt cliff. He negotiated the tricky landing at a little cove now called Lu Lu Bay, which is little more than a shelter from the open sea between high rocky walls. (A supply ship that tried to put in at Lu Lu Bay in 1918 was battered to bits.)

Exploring the island, Duncan found no signs of habitation or evidence of ownership. He planted the United States flag, and on July 1, 1857, officially notified the United States State Department "that he had discovered a deposit of guano [bird manure rich in phosphates] on an island or cay in the Caribbean Sea not occupied by citizens of any other country and that he did take peaceable possession and occupy said island or cay of Navassa in the name of the United States."

When his claim was accepted by the United States, Duncan worked the phosphate deposit, and even today the ruins of a processing plant remain on the island. But in 1889 a major disaster struck the project. Some one hundred and fifty lonely men who had been imported to work in the plant were cooped up on this two miles of barren rock. The weather was hot, supplies became dangerously low, and tempers were short. One day a riot broke out; the project superintendent was killed. It took some time for word to reach the United States and have a ship dispatched to remove the innocent men and the murderers. The trial was held in Baltimore, and for a time it looked as though the killers might be set free. The defense argued that Navassa was not a bona-fide possession of the United States, that it had never been properly annexed, and that Haiti also claimed the island. The case dragged on, but the Supreme Court, referring to the gift and memorandum of Peter Duncan of twenty years before, held that Navassa was a United States possession by right of discovery and occupancy. This decision resulted in the prompt execution of the murderers.

What neither the Supreme Court nor Peter Duncan knew was that Navassa had been discovered and explored as early as 1503. It happened when Columbus, on his last voyage, was wrecked off St. Ann's Bay, Jamaica. Marooned there, and with a mutiny on his hands, he sent his most trusted captain, daring Diego Méndez, to Hispaniola for aid. The only craft available for the trip was a frail dugout canoe, making it a perilous voyage. The Indian oarsman drank the entire supply of water the first day out. Other Indians in the crew refused to paddle, and high seas battered the tiny, ill-equipped craft. Then they sighted Navassa. On the island Méndez found rainwater standing in the pits. The men replenished their food supply with birds. Strengthened, the expedition rowed on to Hispaniola and finally arranged to rescue the Admiral.

For years after the trial in Baltimore the island was deserted. It began to develop a reputation among seafarers as one of the danger spots of the Caribbean. Then, with the opening of the Panama Canal in 1913, the United States realized that there must be a light on Navassa. Today mariners within a distance of twenty-five miles can see the seven-thousand-candlepower beam that shines from the one-hundred-and-sixty-two-foot gray cylindrical tower located on the highest spot on the island, bringing the light three hundred and ninety-five feet above sea level. Giving aid and comfort to seamen throughout the eastern Caribbean, this light exists only because of Peter Duncan's gift and its confirmation by riot and murder.

Part Six

VENEZUELAN ISLAND

MARGARITA: *An ancient citizen sells sweets at one of the frequent fiestas.*

MARGARITA: *Hotel and restaurant with adjoining beach near the airport, Porlamar.*

MARGARITA

For an island as easy to reach as this one, Margarita has fewer visitors than any major island in the Caribbean. It is fairly large, forty-one by twenty miles in size—much bigger than most of the Lesser Antilles—and just twenty-three miles off the coast of Venezuela, within clear view.

Surprisingly enough—for it is unknown to most travel agents and airline guides—Margarita has excellent air service and a fine airport, called Porlamar. From two to four planes fly in and out of Margarita every day, via Maiquetía Airport at Caracas. Planes also fly in from Trinidad, making stops through northeast Venezuela. Some freighters stop at Porlamar every week. But, in spite of all this transportation, a visitor from the United States or Europe is a rare occurrence.

Several reasons account for this situation. One very important one is that Venezuela requires a visa and a passport for tourists traveling through Caracas and on to Margarita. This can become quite complicated, for many travelers prefer to decide where they will go next after their trip is well started. A second reason for the dearth of tourists is the fact that very little English is spoken on the island and in Venezuela. While it is possible to find a few English-speaking officials on the mainland, almost no one on Margarita speaks English at all, and a traveler without some knowledge of Spanish cannot communicate with the local citizens.

Until recently, Margarita has had very few facilities to attract travelers, but now its magnificent beaches are beginning to be developed and a luxurious little hotel, the Bahía, is open for business with its own private beach. This gleaming white two-storied modern resort is so new that it is almost unknown even in Venezuela. It offers large, comfortable rooms, good beds, and both indoor and outdoor dining, with Spanish-French cuisine prepared by a French chef. Because it is located near Porlamar, there are lots of fishing vessels close by, and it is easy to arrange a fishing trip into the bay. The beach at Porlamar is only one of the beaches, and not the best, of an island surrounded by them.

Visitors planning to go to Margarita should write for reservations to the Hotel Bahía, Porlamar, Isla de Margarita, Venezuela, as far in advance as possible, as officials of the Venezuelan Government and the Venezuelan army sometimes reserve the entire hotel for meetings or week-end parties.

Margarita and two tiny near-by rocky islets—Coche and Cubagua—make up the Venezuelan state of Nueva Esparta. Other uninhabited exposed rocks are also part of Venezuela's island empire, but few of them have any water or fertile soil. Margarita is different; there are plenty of people (some seventy-six thousand); they are attractive, Spanish-speaking, and of Spanish and Indian descent, with very few Negroes. In addition to its beaches, Margarita has magnificent scenery, including barren red hills looking much like the Arizona desert, where only the windswept divi-divi trees grow. The islanders make use of the juice of the fruit of the divi-divi to produce a tanning liquid for leather.

The high hills rise, rocky and sharply etched against the sky, but the valleys are fertile and have been cultivated with sugar cane, corn, and yucca. The island is divided into two major sections, and it is remarkable that the eastern section does not sink into the sea, for there all except two thousand of the inhabitants make their homes. The eastern and western sections of the island are almost entirely separated, being joined only by a narrow isthmus that creates the Lagoon of Arestinga, a quiet, lovely body of water with mangrove swamps around the edge and oysters growing on the mangrove roots. The mountains of the mainland can be seen back of the lagoon and look almost close enough to swim to. The little village of Boca del Río sprawling on the edge of the lagoon is composed of tiny straw and adobe buildings with occasional substantial wooden houses having thatched or tin roofs. The drive to Aristinga is pleasant, but it is advisable to warn the driver to be careful not to get stuck on the sand along the broad expanses of open beach.

The scenery in this area gets monotonous, for there is almost no foliage and the land is dry and baked: Margarita gets very little rainfall. Yet, in spite of this, perhaps because of the surrounding sea and the trade winds, it stays reasonably cool. One unusual climatic feature distinguishes it from other Caribbean islands: its rainy months are December, January, and February. Even these months, however, are not very wet, for the afternoon rain usually lasts only a few minutes, and most of the rain falls during the night—so these are still excellent months for visitors. The weather is never really unpleasant except in midsummer, when the temperature begins to rise above ninety.

There is a noticeable lack of water throughout the island, which is one of the few places left in the Caribbean where water is sold by vendors. The Venezuelan Government is trying to produce enough water to take care of all the needs of the island: in addition to four new deep wells, a new dam has recently been put into operation. Water is a real problem, for if it were possible to irrigate some of the land, much badly needed food could be produced.

Because it is difficult to grow things, the sea is the home of the margariteño. From the sea comes most of his food, a large part of his travel, and much of his education and entertainment. The natives are fine seamen and great fishermen; deep-sea fishing has become one of the two most important businesses of the island. Over eight million pounds of fish are caught—much of it to be exported—every year. The waters abound in red snapper, Spanish mackerel, bonefish, dolphin, and all the fish of the southern Caribbean. A favorite dish on Margarita is escabeche, a succulent mackerel sautéd in olive oil and stuffed with chopped onion and pimento.

Margariteños have another great gift from the sea, their pearl-fishing grounds. Even before the days of the early Spanish conquerors four hundred years ago, the people of this island had been great pearl-divers. Today the pearl-fishing grounds are not so rich as they once were, and the Government sets aside alternate years for pearl-fishing. But the influence of the pearls touches the island all year round. Margarita is the only island in the West Indies where the visitor can see whole baskets and tubs of pearls for sale. Diving methods are interesting and very old-fashioned.

One man's treasure is a venerable navy diving-suit with the type of helmet worn twenty-five years ago. A man who owns such a suit is an important citizen. The usual arrangement for pearl-diving is to take out a boat, crew, and diver and stay in the waters for a number of days. A diver is considered a very good man if he can hold his water all day and not have to get out of his rubber suit. Of the final loot, one third goes to the diver, one third to the boat-owner, the final third to the crew. Many of the poorer divers have no diving-suits; no aqua-lungs are used on the island so far, and a number of men dive without equipment, managing to stay underwater for three or four minutes at a time.

In the dark little shops of the towns there are hundreds of pearl items for sale, running mostly to earrings, brooches, rings, and crucifixes made of pearls of all sizes mounted in silver and gold. The shopkeepers enjoy bargaining, and do not expect to be paid the price mentioned or marked on the object. Margarita is a good place to buy pearls and pearl jewelry, for prices are much lower than on the Venezuelan mainland or on any other Caribbean island.

Margarita has a number of pleasant small towns, but its leading city, La Asunción, very old and very Spanish, is the most beautiful. The ornate cathedral faces a square around which the life of the town moves. Brilliantly painted houses surrounding the square make it look like one of the small towns in Spain. Streets are quiet, with an occasional bicycle passing by, and the whole town has the appearance of having been asleep for generations. The small hotel, looking like a large boardinghouse, has a green front, a lovely patio, and good food, but not a single word of English is spoken. La Asunción and other towns of Margarita have at least one drugstore each. It also has a motion-picture house and vaudeville, including the Margarita version of the striptease and the exhibition mambo at special Saturday-night shows.

The island is full of contradictions. The people are all highly religious, but only a few ever bother to get married. The social pattern is largely matriarchal, and most children take the names of their mothers, with whom they live until they are fifteen or sixteen. Many women have a series of husbands, for the men of Margarita have a tendency to move on after a few years. When they can, they help to support their children, but most of this burden falls on the island's women, who are fiercely possessive. They love their children deeply, and will make any sacrifices for them. They work very hard to hold their families together, but do not seem to expect a great deal from their men. Physically, the women range from swarthy to reasonably fair. When they are young they are very attractive. They mature very early, and many girls of thirteen, fourteen, or fifteen have children. The church has tried, and continues to try, to control its people, and has put much emphasis on the importance of marriage and the family, but the margariteños are stubborn and learn very slowly.

They are a friendly, gay, and gentle people among whom crime is almost nonexistent. The jail, having been empty for fourteen years, has been made into a small museum.

Most of the excitement and entertainment come from fiestas, and there is a fiesta going on somewhere on the island all the time. It is estimated that there are some forty a year. The only time the island quiets down is during Lent. There are grand outdoor affairs, with drinking and dancing (men are often seen dancing together). Music is a mixture of Venezuelan, Cuban, and Spanish. Plenty of edible delicacies are sold by white-garbed, wrinkled old women. Ices, bottled drinks, and dried fish are all popular. A fiesta is usually held in an area near a church. One of the most exciting ones occurs in February at the Plaza de Paraguachi. Here well-scrubbed children will be going to Communion in their white suits and dresses while the grounds around them are a riot of color and noise. Babies are being photographed in their mothers' arms by the tintype photographic process of twenty-five years ago. Swarthy teen-age boys and colorfully dressed black-eyed girls ride on the donkeys or on the modern carrousel that features models of sports cars and motor bikes rather than the conventional horses. While some children and teen-agers get a chance at this modern ride, most of the riders are adults, who wave and have a hilarious time going round and round in the little car or motorcycle attached to the whirling platform. These rides move from one fiesta to another all over the island and are busy every week-end.

A major festival of the year is given in honor of the miraculous Virgen del Valle, the patron saint of the island. The margariteño tells a wonderful story of how the image of the Virgin arrived. He says that a wandering priest came across the sea to Venezuela carrying with him a beautifully carved image of the Virgin. He planned to take this image to the city of Cumaná on the mainland coast between Caracas and Barcelona. But though he set out by boat for Cumaná many times, the wind would not take him there, but blew him toward Margarita. Finally the priest realized that this was where he and his precious cargo were destined to go. He was royally welcomed by the margariteños, who built a great cathedral near the port of Porlamar. This image of the Virgin may be seen today in the Cathedral de la Virgen del Valle.

There is another image on the edge of the busy port of Porlamar, a large and unusual figure of a mermaid carved of stone. She is a lusty wench, deep-breasted and broad-shouldered, holding a horn of plenty. From the waist down her legs become not one, but two fishtails. This statue is little noticed by the islanders, most of whom pass by without seeing it. It has been there for many years, and there is no identifying placard on it, but certainly it symbolizes the strength of the women of Margarita and the bounty of the Caribbean Sea.

Behind this statue is a busy port with schooners and freighters anchored in the roadstead, lighters coming almost to shore, and lines of men pushing their way through the clear water to the hard-packed sandy beach as they unload foodstuffs from the lighters. Although a good deal of food still comes in by sea, much of it is flown in. The port is well worth visiting. There is no rising ground behind it, but it has a fine beach, where children work alongside their parents or play at the water's edge. It is a pleasant sight to watch the mothers bring their babies down to the municipal water supply to bathe them in the morning. Porlamar has a fish-canning plant, and many women, wives or mistresses of the fishermen, can be seen making nets along the shoreline. Small fishing boats are built here, and there is a shark-processing plant. The tempo is slow, and, while visitors are something of a curiosity, they are smilingly welcomed.

Evidence of the women's work on the island can be seen in the hills as well as along the shores. They make hammocks and straw hats and bags, and are particularly adept at making two types of sandals. The cheapest ones, made from old inner tubes, are important items of trade in the island. Thousands of them are for local use, and some are exported to the mainland. One of the centers of this odd business is the town of Negro Gato. Here, women with their children around them can be seen sitting in the doorways at almost any time of day with piles of finished and unfinished sandals beside them.

Northwest of Porlamar in the interior is the tiny historic town of Santa Ana, which has become a shrine. Here the liberator of Venezuela, Simón Bolívar, came to worship in the cathedral. Farther in the interior is the pleasant village of San Juan Bautista, with a forest of date-bearing palms and with adobe buildings giving the impression of a village in Palestine. Deeper in the interior of the island, where the hills are higher and there is a bit more rain, the high green stalks of sugar cane wave in the wind and there are a few small rum distilleries.

The northern end of the island has the fine beach of Puerto Fermín.

Taxis are good, and roads fair but steep and narrow. One taxi has inside it a complete shrine to the Virgin with a small altar and pictures. Rates are perhaps a little lower than those in Venezuela, but not so low as in many other Caribbean islands.

MARGARITA: *On a back street near Porlamar.*

MARGARITA: *A lusty mermaid holds a horn of plenty while a housewife takes home her morning purchases.*

APPENDIX

Tabular Information for Tourists, Travelers, and Prospective Settlers

ANTIGUA

(ăn-tē′-gwä or ăn-tē′-gȧ) British West Indies

LATITUDE: *17 deg. 6 min. N.* LONGITUDE: *61 deg. 45 min. W.*

POPULATION: *49,692 (1953)* AREA: *108 sq. mi.*

CAPITAL: *St. John's*

Location Antigua is part of the Leeward Islands group. It is ringed by Barbuda, 40 miles north; Nevis, 49 miles west; Montserrat, 37 miles southwest; and Guadeloupe, 40 miles south.

Of Special Interest to Tourists (Electricity: 115V AC)

The best tourist buys are English tweeds and linen, French perfumes, and liquor.

Cars and taxis may be hired by the hour or day.

Boats for fishing may be hired.

The Antigua Beach Hotel keeps horses on its estate.

Visitors can enjoy tennis, golf, shooting, fishing, swimming, yachting, spear-fishing, boating, and hiking.

The Antigua Turf Club holds two race meetings a year at Cassada Gardens.

On near-by Barbuda, a small island dependency of Antigua, there are wild fallow deer, wild guinea birds, ducks, and pigeons to shoot.

The best beaches are Fort James, Dry Hill, Corbison Point, Morris Bay, and Half Moon Bay.

Some spots of interest are: the Anglican Cathedral, Court House, and old Georgian buildings in St. John's; Fort James; the Antigua Sugar Factory at Gunthorpes; the Central Agricultural Station and the Cotton Research Station at Friars Hill (those interested in agriculture and cotton-growing will find this trip rewarding, but arrangements must be made with the authorities concerned); the Agricultural Department's Nursery and Fruit Farm at Bendals; Parham Church, built in the Italian style in 1840, with a remarkable roof; Nelsons Dockyard at English Harbour; Shirley Heights and the Ridge overlooking English Harbour, with beautiful views; the road from English Harbour to Shirley Heights, passing Clarence House, the country home of the Governor of the Leeward Islands, built in 1787 for Prince William Henry, Duke of Clarence, afterward William IV; Fig Tree Hill drive along a 20-mile stretch over the main mountain range and back along the coast; Half Moon Bay, with its fine bathing beach and scenes of the coast and sugar-cane lands along the route.

Physical Characteristics The northern part of Antigua is of coral formation, while the mountainous southern part consists of the eroded remnants of extinct volcanoes. It is ringed by beaches.

Antigua has a drier climate than most of the West Indies. The annual average rainfall is from 43 to 45 inches. (The average annual rainfall over a 44-year period was 44.99 inches.) It is subject to periods of drought. The rainy season is from August to January.

The annual average temperature is 80 degrees, the warm season from May to October.

The highest elevation is Boggy Peak, 1,319 feet.

Antigua has no true rivers, but Bendal's Stream is dammed to catch and conserve rainwater for drinking because of the scarcity of water. Pools, ponds, and wells are also used to catch water.

St. John's is the chief port. Its harbor can accommodate vessels drawing only up to 6 feet.

Principal City St. John's, the capital and principal city, has a population of approximately 12,000. The Coolidge Field airport, which can handle all sizes of international planes, is about 6 miles from the city. The ships' landing is at the lower end of the city.

How to Get to Antigua

Sea: Alcoa Steamship Company, Compagnie Générale Transatlantique, Canadian National Steamships.

Air: Pan American World Airways, British West Indian Airways.

Entry Requirements Passports are not required of citizens of the United Kingdom, Canada, or the United States who are visiting Antigua for a period not exceeding 6 months and who possess a valid ticket for their return. It is advisable, however, that travelers should have in their possession some evidence of citizenship such as birth or naturalization certificates, especially for return to the United States.

A smallpox-vaccination certificate is necessary.

Business Opportunities The principal industries are sugar and hotels. A sugar factory, rum distillery, and two cotton gins are in operation. There is an opportunity to develop lands for residential and resort building. Native handwork and crafts could be further developed. In 1950 Antigua passed an ordinance to encourage the establishment and development of new industries and to make provision for the granting of certain relief from customs duty and income tax to persons establishing factories in connection with such industries. There are not many jobs available, and many people are unemployed. Individuals or corporations wishing to invest money in Antigua should make application to the Administrator of Antigua.

Government Antigua is a British colony, with a Governor appointed by the Crown and a Legislative Council and an Administrative Council, some of whose members are nominated by His Excellency the Governor and some of whom are elected by open franchise.

Language and Nationalities English is the only language spoken.

The population is made up of British citizens of African descent, Portuguese, and Syrians. There are few Europeans or Americans.

Banks, Currency Branches of the Royal Bank of Canada and Barclays Bank are operated in St. John's. The monetary unit is the British West Indian dollar (approximately 60 cents U. S.).

Exports and Imports

Principal exports: cotton, cottonseed, molasses, rum, sugar, tamarinds, tomatoes.

Principal imports: wearing apparel, fertilizers, medicine, metals, railway rolling stock, rice, sugar machinery, wood and timber, and tobacco.

Agriculture Sugar and cotton are the principal agricultural crops. Ninety per cent of the population is directly or indirectly dependent on the sugar industry.

Flora and Fauna

Flora: banana, bay tree, cacao, castor-oil plant, coffee, corn, cotton, ginger, limes, logwood, sisal, sugar, tamarind, tobacco, vanilla, begonia, bougainvillæa, poinsettia, verbena.

Fauna: agouti, bat, toad, turtle, mongoose, lizard. Fish—bonito, shark, grouper, tarpon, jack, kingfish, barracuda, porpoise, eel, snapper, garfish, sprat, whiting, balahoo, mullet, butterfish, dolphin, Spanish mackerel, grunt, whale.

Churches Anglican, Methodist, Moravian, Pilgrim Holiness, Roman Catholic, Salvation Army, Seventh Day Adventist.

Schools Twenty-seven free Government schools provide primary education. The Antigua Grammar School for boys and the Convent and High School for girls provide secondary education.

Hospitals and Health Holberton Hospital is 1.5 miles from St. John's. Private and Government-service doctors practice. Two dentists have offices in St. John's.

Drink only boiled water and boiled milk in rural areas.

Architecture The predominant type of architecture is colonial; there are some Victorian and modern buildings.

Arts and Crafts

Tailoring, dressmaking, painting, basketwork, and pottery.

Hotels

Name	*Rooms*	*Baths*	*Classification*	*Additional Information*
White Sands Hotel (Hodges Bay)	All Double	All	M*	Private beach, picnics
Kensington House (St. John's)	10	Some	I*	Swimming, fishing, and golf arranged
Antigua Beach Hotel	23	23	M*	Private beach, tennis small golf course, station wagon for sightseeing.
Mill Reef Club	20 suites	20	E*	Tennis courts, excellent private beach, 3 fishing boats

(application for accommodations must be made to Manager, Mill Reef Club)

*American Plan E–expensive M–moderately expensive I–inexpensive

Restaurants No restaurants. Meals only at hotels.

ARUBA

(ä-rōō'-bä) Netherlands West Indies

LATITUDE: *12 deg. 30 min. N.* LONGITUDE: *70 deg. W.*

POPULATION: *57,303* AREA: *69 sq. mi.*

CAPITAL: *Oranjestad (11,670)*

Location Aruba is the most western of the "ABC" islands of the Netherlands Antilles (Aruba, Bonaire, Curaçao). Curaçao lies 71 miles east, Bonaire about 100 miles northeast. Cape San Román, Venezuela, is 18 miles to the south. Miami is 1,030, and New York 1,709 miles from the island.

Of Special Interest to Tourists Best buys are cameras, French perfumes, liquors, liqueurs, Delft china, porcelain, Swiss watches, jewelry, old Dutch silverware, ivory from the Orient, Chinese curiosities, lacework, embroidered linen, silks, and native articles from Mexico, Jamaica, Peru, Guatemala, and many other countries. Because Oranjestad is practically a free port, many bargains may be obtained.

The giant monoliths at Ayo (a group of solid diorite boulders weighing several thousand tons) are an unusual and interesting sight. This is a good spot for taking pictures. Caves may be explored at Quaridikiri and at Fontein, where Indian symbols in red (pigment supposedly taken from campeche wood) date back to pre-Columbian days. Visits may be made to the ruins of the so-called "Pirates' Castle" and the ghost town at Balashi, with the remains of Aruba's first industry—gold-smelting.

Many activities may be engaged in as well as watched: game-fishing, surf-casting, sailing, water skiing, tennis, golf (course at Bubali), soccer, baseball, and basketball.

Cars may be rented (a temporary license may be obtained from the local police upon presentation of your own driver's license). Taxis may be hired, and buses service the island.

The Palm Beach Club and the Pova Club are private beach clubs. Tourists, however, may apply for guest cards. Palm Beach, on the northwest coast, is Aruba's finest. Others along this coast are Eagle Beach, Pova, Malmok, and Arashi. On the opposite side of the island, in the Lago Concession, is Rodger Beach.

The public library is in a spacious building in Wilhelminastraat,

Oranjestad. It is open each day from 9 to 5:30 (closed from 12 to 2:30). On Tuesday and Friday evenings it is open from 7 to 8:45.

Physical Characteristics The island is 19.6 miles long by 6 miles wide and covers an area of 69 square miles. The terrain is mostly flat, with the exception of Mount Hooiberg, which rises to 630 feet and dominates the landscape. It is a warm, arid land with an average annual temperature of 83 degrees—December, January, and February are the coolest months—and an average annual rainfall of 17 inches. Most of the rain falls from November through January. The constant trade winds cool the island.

Aruba has no rivers, only a fresh-water spring at Fontein in the northeastern section. The island uses distilled sea water as its main water supply. Small quantities of gold, phosphate, and crystal are found.

Principal City Oranjestad, the capital and principal city, is located in the center of the southwest coast. It is also the principal port, and its harbor, 36 feet deep, can accommodate large passenger ships with a draft of 35 feet. The population is 11,670. The Dakota Airport is one mile from town. The ship's landing is less than half a mile from the center of the city.

How to Get to Aruba

Sea: Grace Line, Alcoa Steamship Company, Hapag, KNSM (Royal Netherlands Steamship Company).

Air: KLM (Royal Dutch Airlines).

Entry Requirements A vaccination and health certificate not more than 3 years old must be presented.

Tourists from the United States need not have passports or passport pictures, but must present proof of citizenship and a return ticket.

Business Opportunities The principal types of business operating on the island are oil-refining; general trade in articles imported for re-sale; hotels; restaurants; shipping and airline agencies; factories making soft drinks, ice, ice cream, concrete blocks, floor tiles, woodwork, and furniture; and building.

In order to encourage tourism, the Government will greatly lessen the tax burden on any new business related to the tourist industry. Nationals are given preference over foreigners with regard to available jobs. Skilled or professional employees may be imported when the local labor market is not adequate.

Government Aruba is part of the Kingdom of the Netherlands, and its people have the same rights of citizenship as the inhabitants of the mother country. Aruba is administered by a Lieutenant Govenor appointed by the Queen of the Netherlands. The local Legislative Council has 21 elected members. All men and women of Netherlands nationality who have reached the age of 23 have the right to vote. Women may be elected to office.

Language and Nationalities The principal language is Dutch. All lessons in school are conducted in Dutch. Arubans, however, speak their own language, known as Papiamento, a mixture of Dutch, French, Spanish, Portuguese, English, and some African. The majority of the population speaks English and Spanish as well.

About 72 per cent of the population is native-born. The other 28 per cent is made up of people from Holland, Curaçao, the Netherlands, the Leeward Islands, Surinam, Venezuela, the United States, France, Colombia, and Portugal.

Banks, Currency

Banks: Hollandse Bank Unie, Aruba Bank, Aruba Commercial Bank.

The local currency is the Netherlands guilder or florin (fl.), worth about 53 cents U.S.

Exports and Imports The principal exports are 42 different blends of refined oil. Also many of the imported articles are resold to tourists.

As Aruba's economy is mainly based on oil-refining and the soil is not conducive to extensive farming, all commodities are imported, including building materials and raw materials for the industries.

Agriculture Aruba's main agricultural product is mais, which is not corn, but sorghum. The other important crop is aloe, used for medicinal purposes. The barren, dry soil does not produce good crops. Some vegetables, peanuts, and tropical fruits are grown.

Flora and Fauna Cacti, mangoes, sapodillas, cashews, dates, bananas, tamarinds, citrus trees, coconuts, kibra-hacha trees, divi-divis, dyewoods, aloes, papayas, bougainvillæa, orchids.

Donkeys, sheep, goats, cows, pigs, lizards, iguanas, rabbits, parakeets, trupials, chuchubis, yellowbellies, blue doves, partridges.

Several varieties of snakes, including a few rattlesnakes.

Insects: cockroaches, mosquitoes (not many and no anopheles), flies, ants, spiders, beetles, moths, butterflies, centipedes, scorpions.

Fish: swordfish, marlin, sailfish, dolphin, kingfish, barracuda, wahoo, bonito, tuna, tarpon, red and gray snapper, grouper, sea bass, pompano, yellowtail, devilfish, amberjack, sardine.

Crayfish, turtles, and clams are found in moderate quantities.

Churches The majority of the people in Aruba are Roman Catholics, and there are 6 Catholic churches. There is a Protestant church in Oranjestad.

Schools Forty-three schools located all over the island accommodate

12,318 pupils. The Dutch school system is followed. Schools are free up to the seventh grade. Government scholarships are available for those students who wish to continue their studies in Holland.

Hospitals and Health San Pedro Hospital in Oranjestad. Lago Hospital in Sint Nicolaas, operated by the Lago Oil and Transport Co. for its employees. The island has 24 doctors, among whom there are 4 specialists, 2 surgeons, and a psychiatrist. The Lago Oil and Transport Co. employs a staff of 22 doctors. Eleven dentists, graduates of Holland universities, are in practice.

Architecture The most interesting buildings, because of their colorful façades and roof decorations, are the native Indian homes. In the cities and villages, eighteenth-century Dutch houses are scattered among Spanish and modern structures.

Arts and Crafts Because of the prosperity that the oil company brought to the island, there is not much home industry. Some needlework and ceramics may be purchased. Records of Aruba's own characteristic music, danzas and tumbas, are available.

Food Specialties Most fruits and vegetables are imported. The best home-grown fruit is the papaya. Fresh fish is a staple item in the diet.

Giambo cu funchi is a soup made of gumbos and funchi (millet).

Ayaca, a blend of white corn millet, chicken, olives, prunes, capers, cashew nuts, and red pepper, is wrapped in banana leaves and cooked.

Hotels

Name	*Rooms*	*Baths*	*Classification*
Strand (Oranjestad)	30	16	I*
(Rooms include 11 suites with bath)			
(Some air-conditioned)			
Scala (Oranjestad)	11	11	I* & **
(All air-conditioned)			
Marchena (Sint Nicolaas)	24	12	I* & ***

* American plan — I—inexpensive

** Modified American plan

*** European plan

Restaurants Bali (Oranjestad), a floating restaurant featuring Javanese food, Strand Hotel (Oranjestad), Trocadero (Oranjestad), Scala Hotel (Oranjestad), Rio (Oranjestad), Prinses (Oranjestad), Astoria (Sint Nicolaas), Chesterfield (Sint Nicolaas), Marchena (Sint Nicolaas), Lido (Sint Nicolaas), Permier (Sint Nicolaas).

BARBADOS

(bär-bā́-dōz) British West Indies

LATITUDE: *13 deg. 4 min. N.* LONGITUDE: *59 deg. 37 min. W.*

POPULATION: *222,942 (1953)* AREA: *166 sq. mi.*

CAPITAL: *Bridgetown (15,000)*

Location Barbados is the most easterly of the Caribbean islands. It is 95 miles east of St. Vincent, and 115 miles east-southeast of St. Lucia.

Of Special Interest to Tourists (Electricity: 110V AC)

The best tourist buys are cashmere sweaters, topcoats and sports jackets, doeskin, English tropicals and tweed by the yard, sea-island cotton fabrics, shirts and underwear, Irish linen goods, basketwork, tobacco, English bone and Wedgwood china, Scotch whisky, Barbados rum, and native handicraft.

There are many places of interest to visit in Barbados: Bathsheba, a seaside resort with sweeping views of the windward coast; Tent Bay, where the flying-fish fleet arrives daily; Chalky Mount, with its pottery industry; Hackleton's Cliff, which is 1,000 feet high and commands a wonderful view of the Bathsheba coast; St. John's Church, with the tomb of Ferdinando Paleologus, one of the last descendants of the Christian emperors of Greece; Codrington College at St. John; Sam Lord's Castle, dating from about 1820; Gun Hill; Christ Church; Cherry Tree Hill and its avenue of old mahogany trees overlooking Scotland Valley; Holetown, with its monument commemorating the first landing of the British; Freshwater Bay, which derives its name from the fresh-water springs on the beach.

Barbados is almost surrounded by beaches; among the best are The Leeward Coast, Rockley, Worthing, St. Lawrence, Maxwell Coast, Crane, Bathsheba.

The Barbados Museum and Historical Society is open weekdays from 10 to 6 and Sundays from 2:30 to 6.

The public library at White Park, St. Michael, is open every day except Sunday and Wednesday from 9 to 5: Wednesday 9 to 12:30. Tourists may borrow books by making a deposit.

Conducted tours may be arranged with travel agents.

Cars may be hired, but a Barbados driving license is necessary. Application may be made to the Police Commissioner.

Sailboats, including guide and tackle, may be rented.

Fishing-party boats may be chartered by the day or half-day, and cost includes guide and tackle.

Horses and bicycles are also for rent. Visitors can enjoy tennis, golf, bathing, and yachting. Cricket, football, basketball, hockey, polo, and water polo are played in season. Dances are held at the hotels and at various clubs, and motion-picture theaters are available.

Physical Characteristics Barbados is hilly, but not mountainous. The land rises in terraces to a ridge near the center of the island. Near Bathsheba and Horse Hill in the northeastern section, the hills run near the coast and the seascapes with jagged rocks and cliffs are very impressive.

Barbados has a moderate temperature, with an annual average of 78.9 degrees. The highest recorded temperature in 1953 was 89 degrees, the lowest was 65.5 degrees.

The average annual rainfall is 66.18 inches.

The waters surrounding the island remain at a temperature between 76 and 82 degrees all year, and the average temperature of the water is 77 degrees.

The harbor at Bridgetown, the chief port, is an open roadstead about 4 fathoms deep. Schooners and small vessels can come alongside the quay. Passengers on larger ships are brought ashore in launches, and cargo is unloaded into lighters towed ashore by launches.

There are no important rivers in Barbados and only a few small springs.

Drinking-water is obtained from subterranean reservoirs and streams beneath the island's coral cap.

Principal City Bridgetown, the capital and principal city, has a population of approximately 15,000. Seawell Airport is 11 miles from Bridgetown.

How to Get to Barbados

Sea: Alcoa, Canadian National, French, Fyffes, Harrison, Moore-McCormack, Nourse, Royal Netherlands, and Saguenay Terminal lines.

Air: Trans-Canada Air Lines—direct service from Montreal; British Overseas Airways Corporation and British West Indian Airlines Viscount Service—from New York via Bermuda and San Juan; British West Indian Airways—an island-hopping service and flights from British Guiana and Venezuela; Línea Aero-postal Venezolana—scheduled service twice weekly between Maiquetía, Maturín, and Barbados; St. Vincent Government Air Charter Service—twice weekly service from St. Vincent and Dominica. Air France from Martinique and Guadeloupe.

Entry Requirements All travelers should have smallpox-vaccination certificate not more than 3 years old.

Persons entering the island must be in possession of a valid passport *or* birth certificate *or* naturalization papers satisfactorily establishing their nationality and identity.

Travelers should have in their possession their through transportation, or security may be required.

No entry permit is necessary. Permission may be given to remain for 3 months, at the end of which time a visitor may request an extension for another 3 months.

Persons who wish to settle in Barbados must provide tangible proof that they are not likely to become a charge of the Colony.

A non-British citizen who desires to work in Barbados must obtain written permission from the Commissioner of Police.

Business Opportunities The principal types of business operating in Barbados are: (a) local produce dealers (sugar, molasses, rum); (b) retail and wholesale businesses of all classes; (c) commission agencies of all classes.

The best types of business for investment purposes would be the retail, wholesale, and resort development. Unlimited foreign capital may be invested.

The few available jobs are given to qualified nationals by preference. A non-British citizen may sometimes be given a specialized job that the local labor market cannot fill.

Government Barbados is a British Crown Colony with an appointed Governor. There are an Executive Council, an Executive Committee, a Legislative Council, and a House of Assembly. Local government is administered through bodies called Vestries, one for each of the 11 parishes, elected annually.

Language and Nationalities English is spoken generally throughout the island. A few people also speak French, Italian, Spanish, and Portuguese. About 10 nationalities are represented in Barbados. The great majority are British subjects of African descent, but there are a considerable number of white citizens of British descent and a small number of Canadians, United States citizens, Indians, and various Europeans.

Banks, Currency Barclays Bank (Bridgetown), Canadian Bank of Commerce (Bridgetown), Royal Bank of Canada (Bridgetown, Hastings), Government Savings Bank, Peasant's Loan Bank, Sugar Industry Agricultural Bank, Bank of Nova Scotia.

The British West Indies dollar is the monetary unit (approximately 60 cents U.S.).

Exports and Imports

Principal exports: sugar, spirits (rum), cotton lint, molasses.

Principal imports: merchandise of all kinds, foodstuffs, textiles, boots, shoes, wearing apparel, motor cars and trucks, electrical supplies, medicines, metals, oil, paints, soap, tea, wood and timber.

Agriculture Sugar cane is the principal agricultural crop; other important crops are cotton and foods. Good annual sugar crops are essential to the island's continued prosperity. Food crops, grown chiefly for local consumption, consist of yams, sweet potatoes, cassava, eddoes, maize, pigeon peas, and green vegetables.

Flora and Fauna

Trees—casuarina, palm, cannon-ball, cherry—ferns, tropical shrubs, flowers.

Animals: mongooses, monkeys, rats, mice, bats, raccoons, lizards, toads, whistling frogs.

Insects: centipedes, cockroaches, spiders, ants, beetles, moths, flies.

Fish—flying, snapper, bream, mackerel, dolphin, bonito, wahoo—turtles, crayfish, crabs, sea urchins.

Birds: 16 species of resident birds including sparrows, blackbirds, and doves; and a number of migratory birds.

Churches Church of England, Roman Catholic, Methodist, Seventh Day Adventist, Moravian, Salvation Army.

Hospital and Health The General Hospital, the Clinic, and Dr. Scott's Nursing Home are located in St. Michael. A few small private nursing homes are available. Qualified doctors, surgeons, and dentists practice on the island. Water safe. Hotels serve boiled milk on request.

Schools Education is free at the elementary level only. For girls, the secondary schools are Codrington High School, the Ursuline Convent, and Queens College; for boys, the Lodge School, Harrison College, and Codrington College (theological). A General Certificate of Education, at the scholarship level of the Oxford and Cambridge School Examination Boards, is awarded. Students wishing to continue their education go abroad.

Architecture Mainly Georgian and traditional West Indian, some modern.

Arts and Crafts Native basketwork, pottery, shellwork, tortoise-shell work, woodwork, paintings. Bags, baskets, carpets, jars, dishes, ash trays, figurines, jewelry, platters, boxes, book ends. Some furniture made locally from mahogany. Also dolls and toys.

Foods

Fruits: mango, avocado, banana, papaw, golden apple, melon.
Vegetables: squash, eggplant, yam, eddo, sweet potato, cassava.
Pig, chicken, fish.

Hotels

Name	*Rooms*	*Baths*	*Classification*	*Additional Information*
Coral Reef Club (St. James)	25	25	E*	Swimming.
Colony Club (St. James)	25	25	E*	Tennis, boating, dancing.
Miramar (St. James)	11	11	E*	Good beach, fine cuisine.
Sunset Gardens (St. James)	6	3	E*	Also operates Le Bistro restaurant.
Four Winds Club (St. James)	6	4	E*	Small, exclusive, on beach.
Barbados Country Club (St. James)	10	10	E*	Beachside.
Marine Hotel (Hastings)	120	100	M*	Dancing, shops.
Ocean View Hotel (St. Lawrence)	47	42	M*	Locally popular.
Windsor Hotel (St. Lawrence)	40	40	M*	Windward coast.
Hastings Hotel (Hastings)	40	24	M*	Swimming, fine view.
Hotel Royal on Sea (Hastings)	39	39	M*	Music, swimming, outdoor dining.
Crane Hotel (Hastings)	26	11	M*	On sea.
Cacrabank Hotel	22	20	M*	Excellent food.
Barbados Aquatic Club (near Bridgetown)	21	21	M*	Water-polo tournaments.
Rockley Beach Club (Hastings)	24	20	M*	Recently redecorated.
Accras Beach Club (Hastings)	16	14	M*	Recently redecorated.
Paradise Beach Club (Black Rock)	39 (furnished bungalows, hotel plan)	28	E*	Beach, dancing.
Sam Lord's Castle (St. Philip)	11	11	E*	Furnished with Georgian antiques.
St. Lawrence Hotel (St. Lawrence)	11	8	M*	On sea.

*American plan E—expensive M—moderately expensive I—inexpensive

Name	*Rooms*	*Baths*	*Classification*	*Additional Information*
Super Mare Guest House (Hastings)	7	4	I*	On sea, good food.
Bagshot House (Hastings)	17	12	I*	New, excellent food and service.

Restaurants Goddard's (Bridgetown). Cockade Bar & Lounge (Bridgetown). Flying Fish Club (Bridgetown)—snacks. Club Poinciana (Hastings, Christ Church)—snacks. Bird & Bottle (Marine Hotel)—steaks, etc.

Night Clubs Morgan's. Coconut Creek. Chez Jean-Pierre. Beau Brummel.

*American plan E—expensive M—moderately expensive I—inexpensive

BONAIRE

(*bô-nâr'*) *Netherlands West Indies*

LATITUDE: *12 deg. 5 min. N.* LONGITUDE: *68 deg. 18 min. W.*

POPULATION: *5,500* AREA: *111.9 sq. mi.*

CAPITAL: *Kralendijk (1,500)*

Location Bonaire is the most easterly of the three Netherlands "ABC" Leeward Islands (Aruba, Bonaire, Curaçao) located in the southern Caribbean close to the coast of Venezuela. It is about 30 miles east of Curaçao.

Of Special Interest to Tourists (Electricity: 120V AC)

Best buys are articles made of tortoise shell.

Bonaire is a quiet, restful, untouched little island with no night clubs or restaurants. It has some good beaches. Arrangements for goggle- and spear-fishing, deep-sea fishing, and exploring the Lac (a landlocked lagoon) can be made with hotels.

A trip to the southern saltpan district with the waist-high slave huts and tall obelisks of blue, red, and white which were used as guides by the captains of the salt ships is interesting.

A thrilling sight is thousands of flamingos in flight over Great Salt Lake.

Fontein Plantation appears like an oasis in the arid country around it.

In a grotto at Boca Onima, ancient Indian inscriptions and drawings may be seen.

The Lac, in southeast Bonaire, is a good spot for swimming, picnicking, and fishing. Great piles of conch shells are an unusual sight. The shells are eventually made into souvenirs.

A glass-bottomed boat, rowboats, fishing boats, and motor boats may be rented from the Hotel Zeebad. Tennis courts are available.

Physical Characteristics Bonaire is hilly in the northern section. Its highest peak, Brandaris, rises to 800 feet. The southern portion is flat, with desert-like vegetation.

The average temperature is 82 degrees. Coolest months are January and February, when the temperature averages 79 degrees. Trade winds blow constantly. The climate is arid. The rainfall averages only about

22 inches a year, and November and December are the rainiest months.

Principal City Bonaire's capital and principal city, Kralendijk (called Playa by the natives), has a population of approximately 1,500.

How to Get to Bonaire

Sea: Once a month the Government motor ship *Antilia* sails from Curaçao.

Air: KLM (Royal Dutch Airlines) from Curaçao.

Entry Requirements All temporary travelers must be in possession of a return or through ticket to a destination outside the territory.

Travelers from the United States do not need a passport, but should have proof of citizenship in the form of a birth certificate. A vaccination certificate is necessary.

Business Opportunities Goat- and sheep-breeding, fishing, growing divi-divi and aloe. The southern part of the island produces salt, which was once a most important industry. Not many jobs are available, and most natives work in the oil refineries of Curaçao and Aruba.

Government Bonaire is part of the Kingdom of the Netherlands, its citizens having the same rights as the inhabitants of Holland. The island is administered by a Lieutenant Governor, 2 deputies, and an elected Island Council of 7 members.

Language and Nationalities The official language, Dutch, is taught in the schools, but English and Spanish are also spoken. Natives speak their own language, called Papiamento, a mixture of Dutch, French, English, Spanish, and Portuguese. The majority of the people are native born.

Banks, Currency The guilder or florin (fl.) is the national currency, equal to about 53 cents U.S.

Exports and Imports All necessities are imported.

Salt, goats and hides, work clothing, aloes, and tannin are exported.

Agriculture Aloe and divi-divi are raised. Tannin from divi-divi is used in processing leather.

Flora and Fauna Divi-divi, brazil tree, kibra-hacha.

Hummingbird, parrot, sandpiper, flamingo, parakeet, blue and white heron, snipe, seagull.

Iguana, goat, sheep, lizard, turtle, sea bass, kingfish, sailfish, bonito, barracuda, snapper, perch, grouper, pompano.

Sea crayfish can be speared in shallow water along the coast.

Churches St. Bernard's Church (Roman Catholic) and Protestant churches.

Schools Bonaire has 5 schools.

Hospitals and Health Kralendijk has a hospital. Government water supply is safe. Drink boiled water in rural areas. Drink boiled or canned milk.

Architecture The houses are Dutch Colonial style, very neat, and painted in various colors.

Arts and Crafts Native-made tortoise-shell combs and cigarette cases, coral and conch-shell ornaments may be bought.

Hotels

Name	*Rooms*	*Baths*	*Classification*	*Additional Information*
Hotel Pasanggrahan (Kralendijk) (formerly Government Guest House)	8	4	I*	Restaurant.
Hotel Zeebad (south of Kralendijk)	9 cottages	9	M*	Each cottage has sitting-room, single or double bedroom, and bath. Meals in central dining-room. Fishing, sailing, and a glass-bottomed boat for rent.

*American plan I—inexpensive M—moderately expensive

BRITISH VIRGIN ISLANDS

(Tortola, Virgin Gorda, Anegada, Jost Van Dyke, Norman Island, 'Guana Island, Sombrero, Salt Island, Peter Island, Thatch Islands)

LATITUDE: *18 deg. 27 min. N.* LONGITUDE: *64 deg. 39 min. W.*

POPULATION: *7,300* AREA: *67 sq. mi.*

CAPITAL: *Road Town, Tortola (1,000)*

Location These islands are 60 miles east of Puerto Rico, 140 miles north of St. Kitts, and a few miles across the narrows from St. John (U.S.).

Of Special Interest to Tourists Yachting, swimming, fishing, hunting, and exploring these untouched islands hold the greatest appeal for travelers. Horseback is the chief mode of transportation in Tortola, and there are trails along the coast and over the hills.

Small sloops are available for a day's outing. Launches are available on the days when they are not engaged in passenger traffic between Tortola and St. Thomas.

Physical Characteristics Tortola (6,200) has a hilly and rugged terrain. Mount Sage rises to 1,780 feet. The island is 10 miles long and 3.5 miles wide.

Virgin Gorda (450) is almost square in shape. One half is flat and the other is mountainous, rising to 1,370 feet at Gorda Peak.

Anegada (400) has an area of 13 square miles.

Jost Van Dyke (400) is a rugged, mountainous island.

Sombrero (5) has been known to generations of sailors as Spanish Hat because of its peculiar shape. It is a bare rock rising 40 feet from the sea. A lighthouse has been erected on it because it has caused many wrecks.

Salt Island (50) has salt ponds that visitors might enjoy seeing. Peter Island has a population of 50, and Great Thatch and Little Thatch islands have 20 inhabitants.

'Guana Island was bought by a group of Americans as a private club devoted to hunting, riding, swimming, and big-game fishing.

The annual average temperature is about 76 degrees, and the annual average rainfall is 55 inches.

Principal City Road Town on Tortola is the capital of the British Virgin Islands. It contains a school, public library, Government offices, a few shops, a small hotel, and two boardinghouses. The Commissioner resides in Road Town.

How to Get to the British Virgin Islands

Sea: By launch, yacht, or schooner. It is a 3-hour trip from St. Thomas. Road Town is the point of entry.

Air: Chartered or private amphibian planes. There are no airfields.

(Anegada is the most difficult to reach. The shallow waters surrounding it make it impossible for ships to anchor closer than 3 or 4 miles offshore. Passengers are transferred to ship's boats for about 2 miles and then to a shallower boat for another mile. Then they must wade or be carried for the last 100 yards.)

Entry Requirements There are no visa or passport requirements for visitors of British, Canadian, or American nationality. They are admitted without formality for a stay of up to six months if they have return-trip tickets. Persons of other nationalities must possess valid passports. All visitors to any of the British Virgins must get clearance from the officials at Road Town harbor, the port of entry for all these islands.

Business Opportunities There is little paid labor in the British Virgin Islands. Many natives find employment in the American Virgin Islands. The British Virgin Islanders are mostly fishermen or peasant farmers engaged in stock-raising and gardening.

Government The islands are governed by a resident Commissioner and are one of the four units—referred to as "Presidencies"—of the Federal Colony of the Leeward Islands. A Legislative and an Executive Council assist the Commissioner.

Language and Nationalities The language is English, and the population is almost entirely Negro of African descent.

Banks, Currency Road Town has a Government savings bank, but there are no commercial banks in the Presidency. The nearest banking facilities are at St. Thomas.

The British West Indian dollar is the legal tender, but United States dollars are in everyday use.

Exports and Imports

Principal exports: vegetables, livestock, fish, charcoal, fruits.

Principal imports: timber, butter, meat, fish, oils, boots, clothing.

Agriculture Sugar cane and food crops are raised for local use.

Flora and Fauna

Fruits: avocado, banana, cashew, coconut, guava, lime, mango, melon, orange, pear, plum, sapodilla, soursop.

Vegetables: breadfruit, cassava, eddo, maize, okra, papaw, pigeon peas, plantain, potato, yam.

Plants: bay tree, cacao, castor-oil, sugar, vanilla.

Creepers: mignonias, honeysuckle, morning glory, jasmine, solanum, stephanotis, begonia, bougainvillæa, hisbiscus, poinsettia, verbena.

Shellfish: conch, crab, oyster.

Sea fish: bonito, shark, grouper, tarpon, jack, kingfish, barracuda, porpoise, snapper, garfish, sprat, whiting, mullet, butterfish, dolphin, Spanish mackerel, grunt.

Avifauna: wren, grosbeak, sparrow, hummer, kingfisher, hawk, dove, pigeon, pelican, tern, shawck owl.

Churches Anglican, Roman Catholic, Wesleyan, Moravian.

Schools Twelve elementary schools: 8 in Tortola; 2 in Virgin Gorda; 1 in Anegada; 1 in Jost Van Dyke. Attendance is compulsory for children who live within a 2-mile radius. One coeducational secondary school in Road Town is voluntary.

Hospitals and Health Tortola Cottage has one doctor and limited facilities. Water and milk should be boiled.

Architecture Houses are mainly wooden, with galvanized tin roofs.

Hotels Fort Burt Hotel in Road Town has modest accommodations for from 6 to 8 guests. Bedrooms have baths with showers and toilet. Rates are inexpensive.

Five cottages located near Road Town may be rented. Direct inquiries to Mrs. W. C. Roy or Mr. H. R. Penn at Road Town.

Many visitors who charter launches visit the islands by day and sleep on their boats at night.

CAYMAN ISLANDS

British West Indies

LATITUDE: *19 deg. 20 min. N.* LONGITUDE: *79 deg. 83 min. to 81 deg. 30 min. W.*

POPULATION: *7,500* AREA: *93 sq. mi.*

CAPITAL: *Georgetown, Grand Cayman*

Location The Cayman Islands consist of Grand Cayman, Cayman Brac, and Little Cayman. Grand Cayman, the largest, is 180 miles northwest of the westernmost point of Jamaica, and 200 miles south of Cuba. Cayman Brac is 69 miles northeast of Grand Cayman. Little Cayman is 5 miles west of Cayman Brac.

Of Special Interest to Tourists Best buys are tortoise-shell combs, wristwatch bands, and pins.

Swimming at West Bay Beach (Grand Cayman), yachting, deep-sea fishing, skin-diving, sailing, and lawn tennis are the principal forms of entertainment.

Duck-hunting, shuffleboard, bicycling, picnicking, horseback riding, shooting in winter, dancing, lobster-progging, and hunting for rare shells may be enjoyed.

A glass-bottomed boat can be rented in Georgetown.

Physical Characteristics All three islands are low-lying and are formed of calcareous rock. Grand Cayman is about 22 miles long and 8 miles wide, with an area of about 76 square miles. Its highest elevation is 60 feet. Cayman Brac is 12 miles long and a little over a mile wide, with an area of approximately 14 square miles. Its highest elevation is 140 feet. Little Cayman is 10 miles long with a maximum width of 2 miles and an area of about 10 square miles. Its highest elevation is 60 feet.

Because of the porous limestone formation, all the islands are entirely devoid of streams; even dry valleys are absent.

The average annual rainfall is 60 inches. Rain is particularly heavy between May and October, when temperatures range from 70 degrees to 85 degrees. The prevailing winds are from east to south. During the cool or dry season the temperature ranges between 60 and 75 degrees; the prevailing winds are from northeast to southwest. The pleasantest period is from mid-November to mid-March, when the weather is warm.

Almost dividing the island of Grand Cayman in half is a shallow, reef-protected harbor at North Sound, 7.5 miles long and 6 miles wide.

Georgetown, Grand Cayman, is the principal port for the Cayman Islands. The anchorage area is deep enough for ocean-going vessels, but the port facilities are poor, and there is only one small concrete wharf.

Principal City Georgetown, Grand Cayman, the principal city, is located on the western side of the island. It is about 8 miles from the airfield.

How to Get to the Cayman Islands

Sea: A steam vessel, the M. V. *Merco,* a turtle freighter carrying 12 passengers, operates 3 weekly passenger, mail, and cargo services between Jamaica, the Cayman Islands, and Tampa, Florida. The S.S. *Caymania* operates a similar service between Jamaica, the Cayman Islands, and British Honduras. Schooners and other small vessels carry supplies and occasional passengers between the islands.

Air: British West Indian Airways has flights from Miami and Jamaica. LACSA has flights from Miami and Panama.

Entry Requirements British, Canadian, and United States tourists do not need passports and may stay for 6 months if they show return tickets when they arrive in the Colony or produce other evidence that they do not intend to reside there permanently.

No health certificates are required, but it is advisable to have a certificate of vaccination against smallpox.

Business Opportunities To encourage the erection and equipment of hotels and the setting up of pioneer industries, legislation is in force exempting from customs duty and tonnage tax all materials imported for these purposes.

The occupations employing the greatest number of inhabitants are transportation, communication, manufacturing, and agriculture. Because such a high percentage of the male population between 20 and 50 years of age is engaged in seafaring, male labor is scarce and there is virtually no unemployment.

Deep-sea fishing for turtle and shark is one of the main industries of the dependency. In the straw-rope industry, women supply the greater part of the labor.

Government The Cayman Islands, a dependency of Jamaica, are governed by a Commissioner who resides in Georgetown, Grand Cayman. He is appointed by the Governor of Jamaica. The Legislative Assembly of

Justices and Vestry consists of the Commissioner as President, 2 commissioned Justices, and 27 Vestrymen elected each 2 years.

Language and Nationalities The principal language spoken is English. The population of Grand Cayman is one-third white, two-thirds Negro and mulatto.

Banks, Currency Barclays Bank (Georgetown, Grand Cayman); Government Savings Bank (Georgetown, Grand Cayman, and Stake Bay, Cayman Brac).

British silver and copper coins and Jamaican coins are in circulation.

Exports and Imports

Principal exports: turtles, turtle soup, turtleskin, rope, sharkskin.

Principal imports: flour, cornmeal, rice, sugar, textiles, oil, canned foods.

Flora and Fauna Orchids, guinea grass, mahogany, thatch palm. Wild canaries, parrots. Horses, donkeys, cattle, goats, poultry, pigs. Turtles, sharks, lobsters.

Churches Presbyterian, Seventh Day Adventist, Church of God.

Schools Primary education is free and compulsory for all children between the ages of 7 and 14. Four private secondary schools—three in Grand Cayman and one in Cayman Brac—are run by religious denominations.

Hospitals and Health A new hospital was completed in Georgetown in 1955. The health service consists of one medical officer, one dental officer, one dispenser, one health officer, two general and maternity nurses, one general nurse, two practical nurses, and one dispenser-nurse.

Precautions should be taken against malaria; water should be boiled in country districts, and unpasteurized milk should be scalded.

Architecture On Grand Cayman, wooden dwellings predominate, though new construction is of concrete. The wooden houses are built on hardwood piles that raise them about 2 feet above ground level. They are roofed with either shingles or corrugated iron, the roof serving as a catchment for rainwater, which is stored in concrete cisterns or galvanized drums. The roofs of the kitchens and latrines, which are usually a short distance from the main building, are sometimes of palm thatch. In the West Bay district many of the houses are on a plot laid out with fruit trees and flowering shrubs. In the Eastern district the traditional local style of house walled with lime mortar and wattles set between hardwood frames is occasionally seen.

Arts and Crafts Turtle-shell work (combs, boxes, cigarette-holders, and wristwatch bands), basket-weaving, sharkskin items.

Food Specialties The basic diet is rice and beans, flour and corn-meal, supplemented by locally grown vegetables, fresh and salt meat and fish, and turtle.

Hotels

Name	*Rooms*	*Baths*	*Classification*	*Additional Information*
Galleon Beach Hotel (Grand Cayman)	35	35	E*	Next to Galleon Beach Club. Continental cuisine.
Galleon Beach Club (Grand Cayman)	14	All	M*	Private club on beach.
Seaview Lodge (Grand Cayman)	20	Some	M*	Pool.
Bay View Hotel (Grand Cayman)	8	Some	I*	Pool.
Pageant Beach Hotel (Grand Cayman)	20	20	M*	Pool.

*American Plan E—Expensive M—Moderately expensive I—Inexpensive

CUBA

(kōō'bä; English: kū'ba)

LATITUDE: *between 19 deg. 48 min. and 23 deg. 13 min. N.*

LONGITUDE: *between 74 deg. 7 min. and 84 deg. 57 min. W.*

POPULATION: *5,824,691* AREA: *44,164 sq. mi.*

CAPITAL: *Havana (789,431)*

Location Cuba, the largest of the Greater Antilles, is situated in the Atlantic Ocean at the entrance to the Gulf of Mexico. It is 200 miles south of Miami. Jamaica is 100 miles south of Cuba's eastern end. Hispaniola (Haiti and the Dominican Republic) is 45 miles away in a southeasterly direction. The Isle of Pines, one of Cuba's provinces, is 60 miles south of Havana.

Of Special Interest to Tourists Best buys are French and Cuban perfume, jewelry, Spanish table linens, lingerie, lace, shawls, Panama hats, alligator and leather goods, cigars and rum.

Official guides are registered and authorized by the Cuban Tourist Commission.

Cars, taxis, and horses may be rented.

Visitors to Cuba may bring their own cars, boats, or private planes in accord with existing regulations. Information as to the procedure may be obtained from your travel agent, the Cuban Consulate, or the Cuban Tourist Commission at Carcel 109, Havana.

Fishing boats and yachts may be rented at Havana, Caibarién, Cienfuegos, and Varadero Beach; the last also has a glass-bottomed boat for hire.

Cuba has many fine beaches; the most famous is Varadero.

Some fifteen theaters show motion pictures in and around Havana. A few are air-conditioned. Most show American and English pictures, but a few show only Spanish films. The Auditorium Pro-Arte is a musical center where the Philharmonic Orchestra of Havana gives concerts each winter season, and where famous artists from other countries appear in concerts. The National Theater shows musical and dramatic plays in addition to motion pictures. The Amphitheater, an open-air theater on Port Avenue, is the scene of special festivals and free concerts.

Cuba's calendar of events for the year includes jai-alai matches, horse races, dog races, cockfights, boxing, concerts, carnival, professional baseball, regattas, and an annual Miami-Havana air cruise.

Tourists who enjoy hunting may bring shotguns and hire guides. A license is necessary and can be obtained from the Cuban Tourist Commission for a fee of $7.20. Big-game hunting is confined to wild boar and deer. There are many wild pigeons, doves, snipes, ducks, tree ducks, and quail.

Many guided tours, ranging from night clubs to beach picnics, are organized for the enjoyment of visitors.

Physical Characteristics Cuba has 2,000 miles of coastline. The north coast is steep and rocky, and its central section is bordered by many sparsely populated islands and reefs of coral formation. The northeastern coast, with the exception of the eastern end, is low and swampy. On the southwest coast lies the immense Zapata Swamp, about 100 miles long and 35 miles across at the widest part.

Surrounding the fertile valleys are the three principal mountain ranges, with the Pico de Turquino (6,560 feet) the highest point.

The temperature is moderate in winter, hot in summer. The average temperature is 77 degrees. The average annual rainfall is 54.9 inches.

Cuba's principal harbor is Havana. Close to the docks it is deep enough to accommodate all but the largest cruise ships, which anchor offshore and transfer passengers to lighters to be brought ashore.

The island has many rivers, the three principal ones being the Cauto, which is 155 miles long and navigable for a distance of 56 miles; the Zaza, 93 miles long; and the Sagua la Grande, 93 miles long and navigable for a distance of 19 miles.

The following minerals are found: manganese, copper, chromite, iron, limonite (iron oxide), petroleum, and asphalt.

The island's water is supplied by rivers and springs, which include many mineral-water spas.

Principal City Havana, the capital and principal city, has a population of 789,431. The José Martí International Airport is 30 minutes from the center of the city, and Columbia Airport is 20 minutes away. The docks are from 10 to 15 minutes' drive from the center of town.

How to Get to Cuba

Sea: American President Lines; Atlantic, Gulf and West Indies S.S. Lines; Bee Line: C. A. Venezolana de Navegación; Canada-Mexico Line; Canadian National Steamships; Cia. Transatlántica Española; Empresa Naviera de Cuba; Flota Mercante Grancolumbiana; Hamburg-American Line; Holland-America Line; Lykes Bros. Steamship Co.; Norgulf Lines; Nourse Line; Pacific Steam Navigation Company; Peninsular & Occidental Steamship Co.; Pickford & Black; Royal Mail Lines; Royal Netherlands Steamship Company; Saguenay Terminals; Standard Fruit & Steamship Company; Swedish American Line; United Fruit Company; Ward Line.

Air: Aerovías de América; Aerovías Q.; Braniff International Airways; British Overseas Airways; Cía. Cubana de Aviación; Mexicana de Aviación; Cuba Aeropostal; Delta C. & S.; KLM (Royal Dutch Airlines); Línea Aeropostal Venezolana; National Airlines; Pan American World Airways; Peruvian International Airways; Aerolíneas Argentinas; Aerovías Internacionales; Aerovías Cubanas Internacionales; Air France; Líneas Aéreas Nacionales.

Entry Requirements United States and Canadian citizens do not need passports to enter Cuba as tourists, but they must have bona-fide documentary evidence that will prove to the transportation companies that they are citizens of these countries. Visitors from other countries must comply with passport regulations. French and Swiss citizens are exempt from the visa requirement, and British subjects holding United Kingdom and Northern Ireland passports may also enter Cuba without visa.

Visitors to Cuba receive a Tourist Card valid for 2 years. The fee is $2.50.

Tourists may bring their own automobiles, motorcycles, scooters, or trailers. These are permitted to enter free of customs duties and are allowed to circulate with their own license plates for a period of 180 days.

Visitors who wish to establish permanent residence in Cuba must make application directly to the Minister of the Interior, under whose jurisdiction is the Department of Immigration.

Business Opportunities Agriculture is Cuba's most important industry, engaging about half of the employed population. The production of sugar and its by-products is the most important factor in the economy of the island. Tobacco is the second agricultural crop, followed by coffee, fruits, cocoa, and rice.

There are about 30 distilleries in operation, producing alcohol, brandy, and rum. Fishing is an important industry; both fresh and canned fish are exported, as are valuable fish oils. The mining and shoe industries have increased in recent years. There are petroleum-refineries, textile factories, and chemical and pharmaceutical plants.

Foreign concerns may operate in the Republic of Cuba by (a) establishing a branch in Cuba, or (b) organizing a subsidiary Cuban corporation. Information with regard to foreign investments in Cuban industry or the establishment of a business there may be obtained from the various Cuban Consuls or the Government of Cuba.

According to Cuba's labor laws, non-citizen help can be employed in a technical capacity only when help is not available among skilled or professional Cubans. A non-citizen may be granted permission to work in Cuba when his services are requested in a technical capacity by any of the established firms, and the firm complies with the regulations of immigration and of the Ministry of Labor.

Government Cuba is an independent republic, with a semi-parliamentary government. There are three branches: Legislative, Executive, and Judicial. Legislative power is represented by the Congress of the Republic, consisting of Senate and House of Representatives. In the provinces and cities also, the government is divided into executive and legislative branches, each of the 6 provinces having a Governor and Assembly, and each city a Mayor and City Council. The President of Cuba is elected by universal suffrage every 4 years.

Language and Nationalities The official language is Spanish, and domestic business correspondence is conducted in this language, but English is spoken by many in the larger centers.

There are approximately 12,000 North American residents in Cuba, 28,000 British subjects (the majority from Jamaica), and 154,000 Spaniards and members of minority groups.

Banks, Currency Banco Nacional de Cuba, Banco Agricola e Industrial, Banco Continental Cubano, The First National City Bank of New York, Chase Manhattan Bank, First National Bank of Boston, Royal Bank of Canada, Bank of Nova Scotia.

The monetary unit is the peso. One peso equals one dollar U.S.

Exports and Imports Principal exports: sugar and cane derivatives, leaf and manufactured tobacco, food products, stones, earth and mineral products, animals and animal products, forest products, metals and manufactures thereof, chemicals and pharmaceuticals, perfumery.

Principal imports: food products and beverages, machinery and apparatus, substances used in pharmacy and chemical industries, stones, earth, ores, glass and clay products, metals and alloys, vegetables, fibers including rayon, paper and paper products, animals and animal products, tobacco and products, silk and products.

Agriculture Cuba's principal agricultural crop is sugar. Tobacco, cacao, coffee, fruit, and rice are also very important.

The raising and production of sugar and its by-products is the most important factor in the country's economy. About half of the gainfully employed population works in the sugar industry, which accounts for over 90 per cent of the country's total exports.

Flora and Fauna Cuba's flora and fauna are rich and varied. Trees include the mangrove, palm, mahogany, pine, coconut, and hardwood. Fruits include pineapple, coconut, avocado, mamey, banana, mango, papaw, soursop, and grapefruit. In addition, there are all sorts of vegetables and garden flowers.

Animals include the deer, wild boar, wild pigeon, dove, snipe, duck, quail, and parrot.

An abundance of fish, covering 750 species, ranges in size from the tiny sardine, anchovy, and mullet to the large game fish such as barracuda, bonefish, sailfish, marlin, bonito, amberjack, wahoo, shark, and tarpon. Crabs and lobsters (langusto) are found in profusion.

Churches The predominant religion of Cuba is the Roman Catholic, but the Constitution guarantees complete religious freedom. Many churches of various denominations hold services in English for the convenience of visitors.

Schools Education is compulsory and free. In each province the Government maintains a number of institutes or high schools for advanced learning. These are free except for a small registration fee. Four provinces have normal schools for teachers, and there are three official universities. There are 9 English-language schools.

Hospitals and Health Cuba has many Government hospitals, in addition to private clinics. In Havana a private clinic called the Anglo-American Hospital has an English-speaking staff.

The Medical Association of Havana will furnish information on physicians and surgeons who practice in Havana.

The Dentists' Association of Havana will furnish information on dentists who practice in Havana.

Tap water is safe to drink in Havana and the large cities, and pasteurized milk is obtainable. Drink only boiled water and milk in the rural areas.

Architecture The Spanish style of architecture predominates. The houses have patios and courtyards with fountains. The rooms have high ceilings; balconies overhang the courtyards.

Ruins of monuments, forts, and palaces date back to Cuba's earliest settlers.

Arts and Crafts A new National Palace of Fine Arts has recently opened. It is showing an interesting collection of classic and modern Cuban paintings and a rich collection of objects relating to the Cuban wars for independence.

A local ballet company is under the direction of the internationally known ballerina Alicia Alonso. The Philharmonic Orchestra of Havana gives concerts during the winter season. Havana is the home of the conga and the rumba, but they may be seen throughout Cuba.

Food Specialties Visitors can enjoy French, Spanish, American, and Cuban cooking. Some typical Cuban dishes are:

Rice and chicken (arroz con pollo), a combination of chicken and rice which is a favorite Latin American dish;

Moorish crabs (cangrejos moros), the Moorish crab being the leading crustacean of all the Seven Seas—its enormous black-tipped claws are more succulent than lobster claws;

Filet of pargo, a filet of this fish, peculiar to Cuban waters, blanched with almond crumbs and accompanied by a sauce;

Picadillo, the Cuban version of beef hash, served with rice and fried eggs;

Congri, rice with black beans or red navy-beans;

Pot tamale, grated fresh corn, seasoned with a tomato sauce, combined with chicken or pork;

Deserts—guava jelly or grated-coconut preserve served with cream cheese are favorites.

Hotels (These are some of the best hotels in various provinces. Others are as good, and many are more moderately priced.)

Name	*Rooms*	*Baths*	*Classification*	*Additional Information*
Nacional de Cuba (Havana)	549	549	E***	Pool, tennis, dancing.
Sevilla Biltmore (Havana)	350	350	E* & ***	Pool, dancing.
Plaza (Havana)	300	300	E* & ***	
Presidente (Vedado)	154	154	E* & ***	Pool.
The Lincoln (Havana)	126	126	M* & ***	
Gran Hotel (Camagüey)	150	150	I***	
Comodoro (Miramar)	100	100	E***	Swimming, dancing, tennis.
Pasacaballos Club (Cienfuegos)	16	12	M*	
Santa Fe (Isle of Pines)	28	Some	M***	Pool, mineral spring.
Casa La Rosa (Varadero)	19	19	M*	On beach.
Varadero Internacional (Varadero)	161	161	E* & ***	Casino, golf course, riding, swimming, boating.
Casa Granda (Santiago de Cuba)	60	53	I***	

*American

***European

E—expensive

M—moderately expensive

I—inexpensive

Restaurants and Night Clubs Among the many excellent restaurants in or near Havana are:

Carmelo (Havana).
Floridita (Havana). Famous for its daiquiris.
Frascati (Havana). Italian food.
Monseigneur (21st & O. Sts., Vedado). Excellent food.
La Zaragozana (355 Bélgica Avenue, Havana). Good sea food.
La Estrella Oriental (Galiano & Barcelona Sts., Havana). Chinese.
La Concha (Marianao Beach). Good Cuban food.

The following night clubs are in or near Havana:

Tropicana. Open-air night club. Two dance floors—one air-conditioned indoors, one outdoors surrounded by palm trees. Good music and entertainment.

San Souci. Supper club and cabaret beyond Havana limits in Country Club Park. Good music and entertainment.

Montmarte. Luxurious night club on 23rd Street, Vedado. Good shows and orchestras.

Bambu Club. Ranco Boueros Road. Typical Cuban music and shows. There are many other night clubs in and near Havana.

CURAÇAO

(kōō'-rä-sä"-ō) Netherlands West Indies

LATITUDE: *12 deg. 6 min. N.* LONGITUDE: *68 deg. 56 min. W.*

POPULATION: *114,683* AREA: *173 sq. mi.*

CAPITAL: *Willemstad (45,099)*

Location Curaçao, largest of the Netherlands West Indies, is located in the southern part of the Caribbean 38 miles off the coast of Venezuela. Bonaire is 42 miles to the east, Aruba 71 miles to the northwest.

Of Special Interest to Tourists (Electricity: 120 V AC)

Best buys are Swiss watches, clocks, sterling silver, china, handbags (beaded, petit-point, and alligator), French perfumes, cashmere sweaters, linens, Panama hats, cameras, binoculars, and Oriental curios.

Taxis and drive-yourself cars are available. A driving permit may be obtained upon presentation of a driver's license. Fishing boats may be rented at St. Michiel and West Point villages. The fishing fleet goes out very early in the morning.

Beaches are located at Piscadera Bay Club, Boca, Knip Bay, West Point, and Jan Tiel, where there are dressing-rooms.

Soccer is the most popular local sport, and many night games are played in an illuminated stadium. Basketball, baseball, and tennis are also played.

The St. Christoffel Hill is good climbing for those who enjoy hiking. Wild orchids grow on its slopes.

The Government Experimental Garden at Cas Cora, a suburb of Willemstad, the public library, and the Curaçao Museum are very interesting. The museum is housed in an ancient Dutch building decorated in the old Curaçao style with antique dark wood furniture and some early paintings. Various exhibitions of local art, modern Dutch painters, and visiting artists take place here. Part of the building is devoted to recent industrial and economic history. In its garden are examples of nearly all the trees and plants found on the island.

A local travel bureau, Taber Tours, has organized sightseeing trips with English-speaking and Spanish-speaking guides. There are five tours from which to choose.

Queen Juliana's birthday, April 30, is a public holiday and everyone celebrates. Just before Lent there is an annual carnival.

Physical Characteristics Curaçao's volcanic base is overlaid in part with sandstone and in part with coral that has hardened into limestone. Its elevation ranges from sea level to 1,230 feet at St. Christoffel Hill.

The average temperature is 82 degrees. The rainfall is light, the rainy season short: the yearly average over a period of 20 years was 23 inches. There are no rivers or springs. To add to the water supply, the Government pumps many gallons of water each year from deep wells. This water is softened and chlorinated. There are also Government-operated plants for distilling sea water. In the country districts the Government maintains reservoirs from which the population may tap water free of charge. In the cities, however, piped water is a relatively big item in the household budget.

Principal City The capital and most important city is Willemstad, with a population of 45,099. It is located on a harbor that is 47 feet deep. The city is divided into two sections connected by the Queen Emma pontoon bridge. The Dr. Plesman Airport is about 9 miles from the city.

How to Get to Curaçao

Sea: Grace Line, Royal Netherlands Steamship Company, Alcoa Steamship Company, Italian Line, Johnson Line, Pope and Talbot Lines, and interisland coastal and steamer services. There is frequent schooner service between Curaçao, Aruba, and Bonaire.

Air: Pan American World Airways, KLM (Royal Dutch Airlines), and Línea Aeropostal Venezolana.

Entry Requirements United States tourists require a smallpox-vaccination certificate not older than 3 years, a return or through ticket, proof of citizenship, and sufficient means to support themselves during their stay.

Visitors who intend to leave within 24 hours need only to be able to identify themselves.

Business Opportunities The most important businesses are the oil-refineries. In addition there are shipping and airline agencies, commercial business, and manufacturing of ice, ice cream, soft drinks, oil drums, earthenware, concrete blocks, floor tiles, furniture, and woodwork.

A tax-exemption ordinance issued in 1953 provides that the corporation building a modern hotel in the island costing at least $260,000 can obtain tax exemptions. The Government, in order to encourage tourism, will greatly lessen the tax burden on any new business started in this connection.

Nationals are given preference over foreigners with regard to available jobs.

Government Curaçao is part of the Kingdom of the Netherlands. Its people are citizens of Holland. The Netherlands West Indies is administered by a Governor representing the Queen. He is assisted by an appointed Advisory Council consisting of 9 members, an Executive Council, and the Legislative branch of the Government (the Staten), whose 22 members are elected by the people. All citizens above the age of 23 have the right to vote. Women may be elected to office.

Language and Nationalities The official language is Dutch, and all lessons in schools are conducted in Dutch. The Curaçaoans also speak Papiamento (a mixture of Dutch, French, Spanish, English, and Portuguese). Most people also speak English and Spanish.

Seventy-five per cent of the population is native born. A few thousand are from Holland, the British West Indies, Portugal, Syria, China, Cuba, Haiti, the Dominican Republic, Venezuela, Colombia, and some 25 other countries.

Banks, Currency Edwards, Henriquez & Co.'s Bank; Maduro & Curiel's Bank; Hollandsche Bank Unie, Inc.; Curacaosche Bank.

The monetary unit is the guilder or florin, equal to 53 cents U.S.

Exports and Imports The most important exports are refined oil products, rock phosphate, hides, orange peels (for making the famous curaçao liqueur), and salt. As a trade center, Curaçao imports many articles that are re-exported.

Almost every necessity of life must be imported, the principal ones being machinery, foodstuffs, textiles, and consumer goods.

Agriculture Because of the dry climate, agriculture is not successful on the island. Most produce is imported. A few estates grow fruits and coconuts. Dried cornstalks are used as fodder for cows. Fresh milk is an expensive commodity. Canned milk (dried and evaporated) is imported. There are few farm animals. Cattle for slaughter are imported from South America.

Flora and Fauna Cacti range from the small melon type to the 15-foot-high candelabrum. Trees are mahogany, divi-divi, wabi, and dyewood.

Goats, lizards, iguanas (much sought after because of their delicious white meat), rabbits, deer (which are protected), pigeons, and parakeets are some of the fauna.

The usual insects, including centipedes and scorpions, are to be found, but no anopheles mosquitoes.

Fish include wahoo, sea bass, pompano, devilfish, corbino, sardine, and marsbango.

Churches Nearly 87 per cent of the population is Roman Catholic. There are about 20 Catholic churches on the island. The United Protestant Church in Fort Amsterdam was erected in 1769. There is an old Jewish synagogue, Mikve Israel, dating back to 1732. Other denominations are the Seventh Day Adventists, Methodists, Evangelists, and Anglicans.

Schools The school system in Curaçao conforms to that of Holland. There are 92 schools—18 public, the rest denominational. There are several technical schools. Students who pass the final Government examination are entitled to enter universities in Holland. Students who receive Government scholarships may be obliged to work for the Government for at least 5 years after graduation.

Hospitals and Health There are 2 fully equipped hospitals in Willemstad. Doctors must possess a diploma from a Holland university and specialists a Specialist Certificate from Holland.

Many dentists are available.

Water from the tap is safe to drink.

Architecture The predominant type of architecture in Willemstad is Dutch, and the narrow gabled houses are in the style of seventeenth-century Holland, but several buildings also show Spanish influence. The old plantation houses of Curaçao resemble the landhouses in South Africa.

Arts and Crafts Straw hats are woven by a few families for export. Some basket-weaving, embroidery, and primitive pottery may be purchased from the Home Industry shop. Records of Curaçao's characteristic music are available. Curaçao has a small painting colony working in water colors and oils.

Food Specialties Awi di playa ("beach water")—a thick soup of fresh-caught fish, vermicelli or macaroni, tomatoes, onions, and garlic.

Sopita—a fish soup made of pressed dry coconut cooked with fresh fish and salted meat.

Keshi llena ("filled cheese")—scoop the cheese out of a ball of Edam, fill the shell with meat or fish and other ingredients of your own choice, and bake in the oven.

Pastelitos—a pastry filled with meat or fish, raisins, onions.

Nasi goreng (Javanese dish)—fried rice mixed with fine-cut pork, shrimps, ham and vegetables (soybean sprouts).

Java honde portie (Javanese dish)—filet mignon surrounded by rice, covered with two fried eggs, asparagus, tomatoes, fried onion, and french-fried potatoes. Condiments with this include soy sauce, pepper, curry, coconut, chutney, paprika, and an East Indian pimento sauce that is very hot.

The main native food is white or yellow cornmeal cooked as a porridge. It is called funchi, and is eaten with soup, fish, or meat.

Hotels

Name	*Rooms*	*Baths*	*Classification*	*Additional Information*
Americano (Willemstad)	45	45	M*	Air-conditioned rooms available. Overlooks harbor.
Avila (Willemstad)	28	Some	M* & **	Pool. Seaside terrace. Air-conditioned rooms available.
San Marco (Willemstad)	15	15	M* & **	Air-conditioned rooms available. Telephone in each room.
Bellevue (Willemstad)	42	Some	I* & **	Air-conditioned rooms available.
KLM Hotel (At airport)	20	20	M**	Air-conditioned rooms available.
Piscadera Bay Club (Piscadera Bay)	68	Some	E*	Air-conditioned rooms available.
Park (Otrabanda)	28	Some	I* & **	Air-conditioned rooms available.

A large new hotel is under construction on the waterfront in Willemstad on the Punda side. It will have a pool, gambling casino, restaurant, and dancing.

*American Plan

**Modified American Plan (with breakfast)

E—Expensive

M—Moderately expensive

I—Inexpensive

Restaurants and Night Clubs Americano Hotel Restaurant specializes in lobster dishes.

Avila Hotel—French cuisine. Meals under coconut palms.

Bellevue Hotel—Dutch cuisine.

Chobolobo—Dutch cuisine. Night club, dancing.

Chunking—Chinese cuisine.

Hato Restaurant in terminal building at airport. Glass-enclosed lounge overlooking airport.

Old Dutch Tavern—Dutch beefsteaks. Old Dutch setting.

San Marco—Italian food.

Washington Tavern—Fine Dutch food.

DOMINICA

(dŏm′-ĭ-nē″-kȧ or dō-mĭn′-ĭ-kȧ) British West Indies

LATITUDE: *15 deg. 20 min. to 15 deg. 45 min. N.*

LONGITUDE: *61 deg. 15 min. W.*

POPULATION: *57,022* AREA: *308 sq. mi.*

CAPITAL: *Roseau (10,000)*

Location Dominica is 27 miles southeast of Guadeloupe; 25 miles north of Martinique.

Of Special Interest to Tourists Best buys are Carib baskets and fiber rugs.

Morne Diablotin, Morne Trois Pitons, the Boiling Lake, and the falls at Layou and Pagoua are spots of special scenic beauty. Guides (who are woodsmen) take tourists through the dense growth on the mountainsides, or on fishing, hunting, and camping trips.

The 40-acre Botanical Station contains specimens of almost every known variety of tropical plant.

The reservation of the few remaining Carib Indians is in the forested mountains.

Roseau has a public library, small museum, and Government House.

Cars may be rented for sightseeing. Dugout canoes may be rented anywhere along the coast, sailboats at Portsmouth and Roseau, and motor launches in Roseau.

Best beaches are at Cachacrou, Indian River, Malalié, Woodford Hill, and Hattan Gardens.

The Dominica Club, offering tennis and billiards, and the Union Club are open to visitors.

A few horses are available for riding. Between Christmas and Lent, dances are given, and the village fetes are picturesque.

Physical Characteristics Dominica is a volcanic island, very mountainous, with many rivers (about 365). It is 14 miles wide, 4,747 feet high at Morne Diablotin, and 29 miles long.

Average temperature along the seaboard is about 80 degrees and in the mountains 70 degrees. The average annual rainfall varies considerably from

70 inches along the coast to 250 inches in the interior. Rainy season is from June to October.

Principal City Roseau, population 10,000, is the capital. It is 20 miles by motor launch from Portsmouth. There is no land route to Roseau from Portsmouth. Passengers and cargo are rowed ashore in small boats.

How to Get to Dominica

Sea: Alcoa Steamship Company; Canadian National Steamships from Montreal and Nova Scotia; Harrison Line from England; French Line from Le Havre and Plymouth. Interisland schooner weekly from Martinique.

Air: St. Vincent Government Air Service (amphibian) flies in twice a week from St. Vincent, Barbados, and Martinique.

Entry Requirements English and American citizens are admitted on proof of identity and nationality, such as birth certificates. Other nationals require passports.

Business Opportunities Principal businesses are agriculture, construction, and transportation. There are some small business agencies and garages. There are not enough jobs available for the natives.

Government Dominica is a United Kingdom Crown Colony of the Windward Islands group. It is governed by an appointed Administrator, who acts as a representative of the Government of the Windward Islands. He is assisted by an Executive Council. Municipal affairs are handled by a Town Council.

Language and Nationalities Dominica is bilingual. French Creole is spoken extensively. English is spoken, especially in Roseau.

The population is Negro, white (less than 1 per cent), Carib, English, American, Polish, and Lebanese.

Banks, Currency Royal Bank of Canada, Barclays Bank.

The B.W.I. dollar is the monetary unit. It equals about 60 cents U.S.

Exports and Imports Dominica exports citrus fruits, citrus juice (raw and concentrated), oil, and bananas.

Imports include wheat flour, canned food, textiles, autos and parts, and gasoline.

Agriculture Economy is based on agriculture. Most important crops are limes, bananas, grapefruit, oranges, lemons, copra, cocoa, and vanilla. These crops pay for imports. Other crops are grown for local use.

Flora and Fauna There are many varieties of tropical flora.

Parrots, wild doves, pigeons, hummingbirds, opossums, agoutis, and other animals abound.

Unusual are the Hercules beetle, which is over 6 inches in length, a giant frog, and the boa.

River and sea fish include flying fish, a few turtles, river and sea crayfish, and a few clams and oysters.

Churches Roman Catholic, Anglican, Methodist.

Schools Elementary schools are free. High schools charge tuition.

Hospitals and Health At Roseau there are Government doctors and dentists.

Architecture The houses are mostly wooden. Some buildings in the towns are stone on the first floor, wood on the second.

Arts and Crafts The natives make Carib baskets, dugout canoes, and fiber squares used in rug-making.

Food Specialties Unusual and tasty native dishes are mountain chicken (frog), stuffed land crab, heart-of-palm salad, and a fish fry of titiri (a very tiny fish).

Hotels

Name	*Rooms*	*Baths*	*Classification*	*Additional Information*
Hotel de Paz	6	Some	I*	Shop, snack bar.
Cherry Lodge	10	Some	I*	
Kingsland House	(small pension type)	Some	I*	
Sutton House	(small pension type)	Some	I*	

*American plan I—inexpensive

Restaurants Hit Parade, Maple Leaf, Royal Saloon (all in Roseau, all very small).

DOMINICAN REPUBLIC

(República Dominicana)

LATITUDE: *between 19 deg. 58 min. and 17 deg. 38 min. N.*

LONGITUDE: *between 68 deg. 18 min. and 74 deg. 30 min. W.*

POPULATION: *2,121,083* AREA: *19,129 sq. mi.*

CAPITAL: *Ciudad Trujillo (241,228)*

Location The Dominican Republic occupies the eastern part of the island of Hispaniola (the western part is occupied by Haiti), which lies 50 miles southeast of Cuba and about 65 miles west of Puerto Rico.

Of Special Interest to Tourists (Electricity: 110V AC)

The best buys for tourists are mahogany-ware, sisal-ware, tortoise shell, and embroidered articles.

There are 7 guided tours from which to choose: sightseeing tour of Ciudad Trujillo (3 hours); Boca Chica Beach tour (3.5 hours); San Cristóbal tour (3 hours); Tour of underground caves, tropical gardens, and Haina Sugar Mill (3 hours); Boca Chica Beach overnight tour (2 days, 1 night); La Montaña mountain tour (2 days, 1 night); Night-club tour (9 p.m. to 1 a.m.).

Sightseeing trips are made in 5-passenger sedans with English-speaking chauffeurs. For parties of 10 or more, official English-speaking guide-lecturers are supplied without extra charge. On large parties, one guide is assigned to each group of 25 persons. The Dirección General de Fomento y Turismo (Tourist Commission) makes no charges and accepts no commissions for services.

There are no cars for rent, but tourists may arrange to bring in their own cars.

Fishing and sailing boats may be rented at Boca Chica and Samaná.

Taxis are available in all cities. The regular rate for transportation from steamship piers and airports to hotels is $1 per person, including handbags. Regular taxi rate within city limits of Ciudad Trujillo is 50 cents between any two points, for a car with up to 4 passengers. An additional 50 cents is charged for each stop. The hourly city rate is $3.

Horse-drawn carriages are available at an hourly rate of $2.

Double-decker buses for sightseeing are operated at a 5-cent fare. There is bus service between the capital and the principal cities of the island. Fares according to distance.

Air service between the capital and Santiago, Jarabacoa, and Montecristi is available through Cía. Dominicana de Aviación.

Horses may be rented in most cities at a charge of approximately $1 an hour.

Hunting is permitted during the official season: February 1—November 30. Certain birds may be hunted only after March 1 or April 1. Tourists are permitted to enter the island with their own guns.

There is a golf course at the Santo Domingo Country Club; tennis courts are found at the Hotel Jaragua in Ciudad Trujillo and other spots. Deep-sea fishing, swimming, and sailing can be arranged through the Tourist Commission or hotel. Spectator sports are also available: horse racing at the Pearl of Antilles track in Ciudad Trujillo near the airport, cockfights in the larger cities, and baseball everywhere. There are gambling casinos at the Hotel Jaragua and at La Voz Dominicana.

The Jaragua and the Voz also have night clubs, as does the Casino de Guibia overlooking the Caribbean, where there is dancing and entertainment.

Boca Chica, 20 miles east of Ciudad Trujillo, and Sosúa on the north coast are among the best beaches. Beaches are open, and free except for a bathhouse charge. At Boca Chica the facilities of the private beach clubs are available to tourists on application.

Several hotels maintain private beaches for their guests; a few have swimming pools.

Physical Characteristics The Dominican Republic is a mountainous country with elevations ranging from 47 feet below sea level to 10,200 feet at Pico Trujillo, the highest elevation in the West Indies. Four mountain ranges run from east to west, the principal one being the Cordillera Central. The ocean floor at the harbor at Ciudad Trujillo is 30 feet deep. Temperatures vary according to the location. The seacoast areas average about 79 degrees, whereas the mountainous regions average 68.8, but temperatures as low as 32 degrees have been recorded in January on the peaks. The average annual rainfall is 13 inches. The rainy season comes between May and December.

Four major rivers start in the mountains and flow to the sea, supplying the country's water. There are also many springs and some mountain lakes.

Principal City The principal city, capital, and chief port is Cuidad Trujillo, which was founded in August 1496. It has a population of 241,228. Just outside this city is the General Andrews Airport.

How to Get to the Dominican Republic

Sea: Bull Insular Line, Dominican Republic Steamship Company, Royal

Netherlands Steamship Company, Alcoa Steamship Company, Cía. Trans-atlántica Española.

Air: KLM (Royal Dutch Airlines), Cía. Dominicana de Aviación, Caribbean Atlantic Airlines, Delta C. and S. Air Lines; Varig Brazilian Airlines flies direct from New York to Ciudad Trujillo; Pan American World Airways runs three flights a week from New York to Ciudad Trujillo.

Entry Requirements Citizens of the United States, Cuba, Canada, Haiti, and Venezuela do not require passports, but must have some form of identification such as a birth certificate or military papers. Citizens from other countries are subject to the passport regulations of those countries and require a Dominican visa. A vaccination certificate for smallpox, not over 3 years old, must be carried.

A tourist card, costing $1 and good for 15 days, is required of all visitors. This card may be renewed for another 15 days at no additional cost.

In the event that a visitor desires to become a permanent resident of the island he may enter on a 6-month visa. At the end of that time, if he has been a law-abiding citizen, he may apply for permanent residence.

Business Opportunities The principal types of business are farming, agricultural industries, and commerce. Some stock-raising and forestry are carried on. Distilleries and peanut-oil refineries are in operation.

The best type of business for investment would be industry based on natural resources or produce. There is no limit to the amount of foreign capital that can be invested, nor is there a limit upon the amount in dollars that can be taken out of the country.

To encourage the investment of new capital and hasten the full economic development of the country, the Government has enacted an Agricultural and Industrial Franchise Law exampting investors in new industries utilizing Dominican natural resources or crops from 20 years' taxation. Other industries of foreign origin seeking to operate in the Dominican Republic must apply for incorporation through the Secretaría de Economía and and obtain a license, which is taxable commensurate with capital invested.

Seventy per cent of those employed in any business enterprise on the island must by law be Dominicans. The remaining 30 per cent may be foreigners.

A foreigner who desires to obtain a permit to work on the island must go to the Immigration Department for a temporary permit valid until his 6-month visa lapses. At that time, with the permission of the Immigration Department, he can be given a permanent work permit.

Government There is a Senate composed of a senator from each district, and a House (Camera de Diputados) with a representative for every 60,000 persons. The president is elected by popular vote every 5 years.

Language and Nationalities Spanish is the principal language. English is taught in schools, where 8 years' study is required. Many hotel employees speak English.

Spanish, English, Austrian, Hungarian, Russian, Czechoslovakian, and Chinese minorities live on the island.

It is estimated that the population consists of 13 per cent white people, largely of Spanish descent; 20 per cent Negroes; and 67 per cent of mixed blood. The foreign group includes Haitians, Puerto Ricans, Spaniards, Englishmen, several colonies of European and Chinese refugees, North Americans, and various Orientals.

Banks, Currency

Banks: Dominican Republic Reserve Bank
The Royal Bank of Canada
Bank of Nova Scotia
Central Bank
} Branches in Cuidad Trujillo and throughout the Dominican Republic.

Agricultural and Industrial Bank of Dominican Republic

The peso is used as currency. One peso equals one dollar U.S.

Exports and Imports

Principal exports: sugar, cacao, coffee, tobacco, cigarettes, rice, corn, gold, tapioca, hides, fine woods, cattle, plantains, bananas, citrus fruits, meat, eggs, poultry, gypsum.

Principal imports: cotton, cotton textiles, paper products, gasoline, chemicals, building materials, cement, rubber, machinery, automobiles, pharmaceuticals, jute bags, paper.

Minerals Gold, salt, iron, cobalt, bauxite, gypsum, and some other minerals in small quantities may be found.

Agriculture The Dominican Republic is an agricultural exporting nation. Sugar accounts for approximately half the Dominican revenues. Industries based on agriculture have become increasingly important. Investment in such industry has increased greatly since 1936. The principal agricultural crops are sugar, tapioca, cacao, coffee, tobacco, bananas, rice, sisal, corn, plantains, and citrus fruit.

Flora and Fauna The major flora are palm, cava, and coconut trees, grass, amapola, bougainvillæa, and hibiscus.

The major fauna of the island are cattle, horses, burros, goats, pigs, chickens, doves, ducks, and deer.

There are small non-poisonous snakes, mosquitoes, spiders, and crocodiles.

In near-by waters there are tarpon, wahoo, mero, savord, sailfish, dolphin, king, bonito, bonefish, amberjacks, snook, groupers. In inland rivers are large- and small-mouth bass and trout. There are also some turtles and clams.

Churches The Primate Cathedral of Santa María in Ciudad Trujillo is the oldest in the western hemisphere. It was begun in 1514, and claims the tomb of Christopher Columbus. The predominant and state religion is Roman Catholic.

Schools Primary education is free and nominally obligatory for children between the ages of 7 and 14. The study of English is required in the last 4 years of elementary school and in the 4 years of high school. There are a number of vocational schools, a National Conservatory of Music and Declamation, a National School of Fine Arts, a University of Santo Domingo, and other specialized schools.

Hospitals and Health Ciudad Trujillo has 9 hospitals, and 32 others are scattered throughout the country. Medical service is available through hospitals, private physicians, and clinics. Resort hotels have resident doctors.

Dental service is available through private dentists and dental clinics.

Architecture The architecture of the country is predominantly modern. The historic buildings are of Spanish Colonial design.

Arts and Crafts Tourists may buy paintings, pottery, mahogany ware, embroidered items, and tortoise-shell objects made by Dominicans.

Foods The best fruits grown on the island are limes, pineapples, papayas, bananas, plantains, mangoes, oranges, avocados.

The best vegetables are yucca, beans, corn, peas, sweet potatoes, cabbage, and rice.

The native meats are chicken, pork, and beef.

Hotels

Name	*Rooms*	*Baths*	*Classification*	*Additional Information*
Embajador (Ciudad Trujillo)	310	310	E***	Newest resort hotel.
Jaragua (Ciudad Trujillo)	139 (also six 4-room bungalows—2 baths)	139	E***	Casino, tennis, swimming, dancing, entertainment.
La Paz (Ciudad Trujillo)	200	200	E***	Large sea-view suites, swimming pool.
Comercial (Ciudad Trujillo)	75	75	E*	In town; air-conditioned.

*American plan E—expensive M—moderately expensive I—inexpensive
***European plan

Name	*Rooms*	*Baths*	*Classifi-cation*	*Additional Information*
Fausto (Ciudad Trujillo)	42	42	I*	
Europa (Ciudad Trujillo)	36	Some	I*	
Victoria (Ciudad Trujillo)	28	28	I*	
Nueva Suiza Hotel (Constanza)	56	56	I* & ***	New hotel, 4,000 feet above sea level in scenic surroundings.
Hotel Matún (Santiago de los Caballeros)	40	40	M* & ***	New hotel.
Hotel Montaña (Jarabacoa)	40	40	M*	Pool, dancing, entertainment on weekends.
Hotel Hamaca (Boca Chica)	28	28 (Suites available)	E*	Private beach, water sports, spear-fishing, deep-sea fishing.

*American plan E—expensive M—moderately expensive I—inexpensive
***European plan

Restaurants (all Ciudad Trujillo)
Adamanay.
Cremita. American food—curb service.
Agua Luz. Merengue restaurant at the fair grounds.
La Bonbonera. Sandwiches, sodas, etc. Open all night.
Vesuvio. Sidewalk café—Italian food.
Vieja Roma.
Mario. Chinese food—open all night.

Night Clubs
Agua Luz. Elaborate floor shows, water display.
Voz Dominicana. Good food, floor shows.
Embassy Club. Good orchestra, strolling violinist.
Taino. Late spot, uninhibited native shows.
Yumuri. Dancing, hot music.

GRENADA

(grė-nā-dȧ) *British West Indies*

LATITUDE: *12 deg. 3 min. N.* LONGITUDE: *61 deg. 20 min. W.*

POPULATION: *80,056 (12/31/51)* AREA: *120 sq. mi.*

CAPITAL: *St. George's (5,774)*

Location Grenada, the most southerly of the Windward Islands, is 75 miles south southwest of St. Vincent and 85 miles north of Trinidad. Between St. Vincent and Grenada stretches a chain of small islands—the Grenadines—the southernmost of which, including Carriacou, Little Martinique, and Islet Ronde, are included in the Colony of Grenada. Carriacou is 13 square miles.

Grenada is 55 minutes by air from St. Lucia and 50 from Trinidad, where air connections to the United States, Canada, and Europe can be made.

Of Special Interest to Tourists (Electricity: 230V AC)

There is little night life in Grenada. The pace is slow and relaxing.

Before Lent begins, Grenada has an annual carnival.

Five annual racing meets are sponsored by the Grenada Turf Club at Queen's Park Race Track.

Small craft may be hired for fishing: trolling, drop line, and deep sea. Fresh-water fish may be caught in the rivers.

Golf, tennis, horseback riding, yachting, and swimming are the favorite tourist sports. Grand Anse Beach is very popular.

Cricket matches are played regularly.

Tours of St. George's and the entire island may be arranged. Visitors may hire cars and tour independently if they wish. Taxi and bus service are available.

Interesting sights include: Fort George, built in 1705 at the southern end of the capital; Hospital Hill Forts, 400 feet high, where the British defended themselves against the French in July 1779; Richmond Hill (750 feet), with forts and parks; Morne Fedon or Fedon's Camp (2,000 feet), commanding an excellent view of both sides of the island. The Grand Etang (1,800 feet), about 7 miles from St. George's, is a small lake in the center of a volcanic crater; there is a resthouse here where refreshments may be obtained and visitors can make arrangements to stay. The Botanic Station, with its interesting tropical vegetation, is a rewarding trip.

Physical Characteristics Grenada, 21 miles long and 12 miles wide, somewhat mountainous in structure, is a moderately eroded volcanic pile. The principal peak, Mount St. Catherine (2,749 feet), rises in the northern half of the island and is surrounded by lesser peaks and ridges. South of St. Catherine the land rises again into a long system of ridges running to the south, then bending east and northeast, with four peaks over 2,000 feet. There are several old crater basins, one of which is still occupied by the lake known as the Grand Etang. From the central mountains the land descends to the sea and, though there is no coastal plain, the slopes are gentle enough throughout the country to permit extensive agricultural development.

The distribution of rain in Grenada, as in the other islands in the Lesser Antilles, follows a uniform pattern, being low in the coastal areas and high in the mountains of the interior. The climate along the coast and lowlands is almost arid. On the coast, rainfall is about 60 inches a year; it ranges from 150 to 200 inches in the interior. The rainy season is from June to December, with November the wettest month.

The average yearly temperature is 74 degrees.

The principal harbor, at St. George's, is a landlocked bay known as the Careenage, with its entrance opening to the southwest. It covers an area of about 120 acres and can accommodate ships drawing up to 30 feet.

Grenada has numerous rivers, mountain streams, and springs. The water supply is obtained both from many small catchments piped from springs and by damming mountain streams.

Principal City St. George's, the chief town, was originally built in 1732 and named Port Louis. In 1763, when the island was ceded to Great Britain, the name was changed to St. George's, and it became the island's capital. It is located on a promontory near the southwest end of the island. It has a population of about 5,800. Pearls Airport is 13 miles from the city.

How to Get to Grenada

Sea: Alcoa Steamship Company, Canadian National Steamships. Inter-island motor vessels are available.

Air: British West Indian Airways, St. Vincent Government Air Service.

Entry Requirements Generally speaking, any person in possession of a valid passport bearing a British visa may enter. British subjects traveling within the West Indies, and United Kingdom, United States, and Canadian citizens on a visit for a period up to 6 months are required to carry passports or birth certificates, or other valid identification. They must produce a return ticket and are given special tourist cards, which they will hand back to the immigration authorities on their departure. Under a system of landing-cards, bona-fide cruise passengers of any nationality will be granted permission to land and remain on the island for the duration of the stay of the vessel on which they are traveling, and it will not be necessary for such passengers to be in possession of passports.

Business Opportunities Grenada's principal business is agriculture: cocoa, nutmeg, and mace. On the flat, arid lands at Point Saline some stock-raising is carried on. Banana production is small, but efforts are being made to encourage its expansion.

Government Grenada is a British Colony with a Governor appointed by the Crown; he also governs St. Vincent, St. Lucia, Dominica, and the Grenadines. He is assisted by an Executive and a Legislative Council in each island. These councils are partially elected and partially appointed. Municipal affairs are largely in the hands of district boards in each parish, composed of an equal number of nominated and elected members.

Language and Nationalities The principal language is English. Ninety per cent of the population are descendants of African slaves. The other 10 per cent includes English, French, Scotch, and East Indians.

Banks, Currency

Banks: Barclays Bank, Royal Bank of Canada, Grenada Co-operative Bank Ltd.

The monetary unit is the British West Indies dollar, equal to 60 cents U.S.

Exports and Imports

Principal exports: cocoa, nutmegs, mace, fruits, and sea-island cotton from the island of Carriacou. Most of the exports go to Great Britain and to other British colonies.

Principal imports: foodstuffs, apparel, cloth, household goods, gasoline, bags and sacks, cement, oils, medicine, soap.

Flora and Fauna

Trees: white cedar, tamarind, mahogany, samn, locust, casuarina, cashew, fruit trees.

Shrubs and bushes: ginger, vanilla, cacao, castor-oil plant, bayberry, pomegranate, arrowroot, cassava, indigo, clove, bamboo.

Animals: manicou (large opossum), armadillo, hare, agouti, mouse, rat, mongoose, bat, Mona monkey.

Reptiles: snakes (7 species, all non-poisonous), lizards (7 species, non-poisonous).

Amphibians: toad and 3 species of frogs.

Birds: included in the 106 varieties of birds to be found in Grenada are man of war, red-billed tropic bird, tern, yellowleg, spotted sandpiper, turnstone, gree-gree, ground dove, bluebird, cowbird, blackbird, green hummingbird, mocking bird, and thrush.

Fish: Salt-water—kingfish, eel, sprat, tarpon, small whale (in winter), barracuda, bonito, dolphin, flying fish, bonefish.

Shellfish—turtle, oyster, crab.

Fresh-water—mullet, mudfish, snapper, borchet, eel, crayfish.

Churches Anglican, Roman Catholic, Methodist, Church of Scotland, Indian Mission Stations, Glad Tidings Pentecostal Church, Salvation Army.

Schools

Primary: 13 Government schools, 12 Anglican, 24 Roman Catholic, 4 Methodist, 2 Church of Scotland.

Secondary: Grenada Boys' Secondary School, Church of England High School for Girls, St. Joseph's Convent High School, The Model School (girls).

Hospitals The Colony Hospital, St. George's. A district hospital in St. Andrews Parish, about a mile from Grenville. In addition, 18 medical visiting stations are located in rural districts. A trained nurse is in attendance at all times, and they are regularly visited by the District Medical Officer.

Architecture The town of St. George's was totally destroyed by fire in 1771 and again in 1775. As a result, an act was passed prohibiting wooden dwellings, and St. George's today is almost entirely built of brick and stone; roofs are tiled. Other towns are similar—Grenville, Gouyave, and Victoria. In the interior districts, wooden houses are usual; roofs are of shingle or galvanized tin. There are some peasant houses built of wood and wattling, roofed with palm leaves.

Arts and Crafts Curios, baskets, needlework, and preserves are made by natives and sold at the store in St. George's maintained by the Home Industries and Self-Help Association.

Food Specialties "Pepperpot" (cassava boiled with peppers and meat).

Best fruits are bananas, avocados, plums, apples, breadfruit, lemons, limes, and oranges. Best vegetables are beans, cassava, corn, cucumbers, yams. Fresh fish, turtles, and beef are used in many dishes.

Hotels

Name	*Rooms*	*Baths*	*Classification*	*Additional Information*
St. James (St. George's)	21	Private, share	M*	Good food.

*American plan M—moderately expensive I—inexpensive

Name	*Rooms*	*Baths*	*Classification*	*Additional Information*
Santa Maria (St. George's)	35	35	M*	Overlooks sea. Near beach.
Antilles (St. George's)	19	Some private	I*	
Green Gables Guest House (St. George's)	13	Some	I*	Good food.

*American plan M—moderately expensive I—inexpensive

(Two-, three-, and four-bedroom houses may be rented at Point Saline, Grand Anse Beach, and the Quarantine Station. The Tourist Board has full information.)

GUADELOUPE

with St. Barthélemy—Marie Galante—St. Martin—

Désirade—Iles des Saintes

(gwä'-dĕ-lōōp") French West Indies

LATITUDE: *between 15 deg. 59 min. and 18 deg. 5 min. N.*

LONGITUDE: *between 61 and 63 deg. 22 min. W.*

POPULATION: *278,864 (including dependencies)*

AREA: *680 sq. mi. (including dependencies)*

CAPITAL: *Basse-Terre (12,500)*

Location Guadeloupe and its 5 dependencies—St. Barthélemy, Marie Galante, St. Martin, Désirade, and the Saintes—lies between Montserrat and Antigua to the north and Dominica to the south.

Of Interest to Tourists Best buys are perfume, madras, dolls in local costume, rum, French wines, shells, baskets, woodwork, and an unusual hat peculiar to the fishermen of the Iles des Saintes.

Taxis and cars with or without chauffeurs are for hire.

Schooners may be chartered for fishing, and a glass-bottomed boat is available.

Active sports include swimming, fishing, climbing, and camping.

The best beaches are La Pergola (small fee) at Gosier, Ste. Anne, Moule, La Grande Anse, St. François, Rocroy, and Malendure.

Football and bicycle races may be seen.

Sightseeing spots include the pre-Columbian Carib rocks at Trois Rivières; Ste. Marie, the landing-place of Columbus; and, in Baillif, the tower of Père Labat, the French priest who was a famous explorer.

Touring Grande Terre around the coast to the beaches takes about half a day; the harbor of Moule, where the battle between Admiral Rodney and De Grasse took place, may be seen.

Boats leave almost every day for Marie Galante and the Iles des Saintes; visitors may picnic, swim, and explore these little islands.

Basse Terre offers two volcanoes to climb: the Soufrière, with a rain forest on its slopes, and Grand Etang, near Capesterre. The climb up the Soufrière must be made on foot; a guide is required. It takes about four hours. Other mountain-climbing expeditions necessitating overnight stays may be arranged with hotels or the Tourist Bureau.

Physical Characteristics Guadeloupe is two separate islands joined by a bridge. It has an area of 532 square miles. Its northeastern section, Grande Terre, is a low-lying island of chalky formation rising to a height of 330 feet. The other section, Basse Terre, is high and has many volcanic mountains, the highest peaks being La Soufrière (4,869) and Sans Toucher (4,856). Seventy rivers flow from the mountains.

Basse Terre has an annual average temperature of 68 degrees. Grande Terre's annual temperature averages between 75 and 88 degrees.

Principal Towns Basse Terre (12,500), the capital and governmental center, has no harbor, but offers a protected anchorage.

Pointe-à-Pitre (42,000), the commercial center, near Le Raizet Airport, has a harbor that is from 36 to 45 feet deep.

How to Get to Guadeloupe

Sea: Alcoa, Canadian National, and French lines stop monthly and semi-monthly.

Air: Pan American World Airways, British West Indian Airways, KLM (Royal Dutch Airlines), Air France, Air Antilles (a new service to some smaller islands).

Entry Requirements A smallpox-vaccination certificate is required. No passports are required of Americans, Canadians, or British travelers staying less than 7 days. Proof of citizenship will be accepted.

Visitors who do not have onward passage must make a deposit equal to the amount of such passage.

No entry permit is required of Americans, Canadians, or British travelers staying less than 3 months.

Business Opportunities The main industries are rum, sugar, and banana-raising. Foreign capital may be invested in hotels, tourist businesses, or the fiber industry subject to French regulations; the majority of stock must be French. Profits in dollars may be taken out in accord with existing regulations.

Government Guadeloupe is a Department of France, and governs its 5 dependencies. Guadeloupe is administered by a Prefect appointed by the French Minister of the Interior. It has a 36-member General Council elected by popular vote. This Council assists the Prefect.

Language and Nationalities The official language is French. Creole patois is spoken by most natives. Very little English is spoken.

Foreigners include Italians, Syrians, Lebanese, and British West Indians.

Banks, Currency Banque de la Guadeloupe, Banque Nationale pour le Commerce et l'Industrie, Crédit Guadeloupéen.

The monetary unit is the franc. 350 francs equal one dollar U.S.

Exports and Imports

Exports: sugar, bananas, rum, coffee, vanilla.

Imports: foodstuffs, oils, textiles, automobiles, clothing, construction material, fuel.

Agriculture The island's economy is mainly based on agriculture. Sugar and bananas are the main crops. Others include coffee, cocoa, pineapple, vanilla, and spices.

Flora and Fauna Coconut palms, arborescent ferns, wild orchids, lauriers, and other lush tropical plants.

Mongooses, agoutis, raccoons, iguanas, lizards, wood pigeons, turtle doves.

Most abundant varieties of fish are snook, barracuda, Jack Crevalle, rayfish, shark, kingfish, snapper, marlin, tarpon, and tuna. Also tortoises, turtles, lobsters, clams.

Churches Roman Catholic is the predominant religion. Seventh Day Adventist and West Indies Mission have congregations.

Schools Free elementary education is provided. Some private primary and secondary schools are operating.

Hospitals and Health Five public hospitals, 5 private clinics (2 newly equipped), 66 doctors, and 54 dentists attend to the public health.

Mosquitoes are plentiful; an anti-malaria campaign is being carried on. Water and milk should be boiled.

Architecture New construction is modern and of concrete. Older buildings are Colonial in style, with verandas. Native houses are wooden shacks with corrugated tin roofs.

Food Specialties Cuisine is French and Creole and includes chatron (octopus stew), matété (land crabs and rice), calalou (soup of native vegetables), and colombo (curry).

Hotels

Name	*Rooms*	*Baths*	*Classification*	*Additional Information*
Grand Hotel (Pointe-à-Pitre)	65	Most	M* & ***	

*American Plan M—moderately expensive I—inexpensive
***European Plan

Name	*Rooms*	*Baths*	*Classifi-cation*	*Additional Information*
La Pergola du Gosier (Gosier)	Two cottages.	All	M* & ***	On beach.
Hotel Royal (Basse Terre)	15	Some	I* & ***	
Le Cottage (Ste. Anne)	3	Some	I*	On beach.

*American Plan M—moderately expensive I—inexpensive
***European Plan

Restaurants

Robertsons (Basse Terre): good food.
La Pergola du Gosier (Gosier): excellent food.
Grand Hotel (Pointe-à-Pitre): good dinners.
In all instances meals should be ordered in advance.

SAINT BARTHÉLEMY

St. Barthélemy is a small, rocky island whose 2,231 inhabitants raise cattle for export. It has little except beaches to offer tourists. There are a very modest hotel, a restaurant, and a movie.

A free port, St. Bart offers good buys in perfume, liquors, and madras cotton goods.

Straw and shell souvenirs are sold by the natives.

An unusual sight is the older women's Norman hair-style and headdress.

MARIE GALANTE

This island, just southeast of Guadeloupe, is a short trip by sea. Its 30,213 natives raise sugar cane, rum, stock, and a very high grade of cotton.

SAINT MARTIN

The island of St. Martin is occupied by both the French and the Dutch (see Sint Maarten). The French section is in the northern part; Marigot is its principal town. It lies northwest of Guadeloupe and is served regularly by Air France and KLM (Royal Dutch Airlines). The plane trip from Guadeloupe takes about one hour.

It is a free port, and its best buys are perfume and liquor.

The border between the French and Dutch sides is open, and visitors travel back and forth freely.

Stock-raising, fishing, and farming are the principal occupations of the 6,786 natives.

French, Dutch, and some English are spoken.

There is a tiny guesthouse with 4 bedrooms and 2 baths.

Visitors may explore, climb Sentry Hill (1,360 feet), fish, sail, ride, and watch cockfights.

DÉSIRADE

Some cotton-raising and fishing occupy the natives of this small island, who speak a Creole patois. No foreigners live here.

Travelers who enjoy seeing remote islands can get to Désirade by sloop from Guadeloupe. It is only a few miles.

There are no accommodations for tourists.

ILES DES SAINTES

The fishermen of these islands wear a very picturesque hat, which travelers enjoy photographing. The 2,358 natives speak a Creole patois and fish for a living. There is a small guesthouse at Terre de Haut. Tourists may buy souvenirs, shells, and stuffed tortoises.

HAITI

(ă′-ē′-tē″; English: hā′-tĭ)

LATITUDE: *between 18 and 20 deg. N.*

LONGITUDE: *between 72 and 73 deg. W.*

POPULATION: *3,111,973* AREA: *10,714 sq. mi.*

CAPITAL: *Port au Prince (142,800)*

Location Haiti occupies the western third of the island of Hispaniola, which lies between Cuba and Puerto Rico (the eastern two thirds are the Dominican Republic).

Of Special Interest to Tourists (Electricity: 110V AC)

Best buys are French perfume, Swiss watches, liquor, sisal-ware, dolls, embroidered goods, jewelry, and ceramics, Haitian paintings, hand-woven cottons, rugs, and mahogany items.

Active sports include swimming at hotel pools; fishing; hunting from July through January for wild boar, goats, and crocodiles; golf; tennis; horseback riding; and spear-fishing. Glass-bottomed boats make daily trips to the coral reefs.

Regular exhibition voodoo ceremonies are performed for tourists. Haitian dancers may be seen at the Théâtre de Verdure.

Gambling is legal. Soccer matches, basketball games, and cockfights can be seen at various towns around the island.

Taxis, cars, and horses may be rented. In addition, Haitian Air Corps planes may be chartered for private use.

There are museums, art centers, and buildings that travelers will want to see, and guided tours to all parts of the island may be arranged.

Physical Characteristics Haiti is heavily wooded and mountainous and shaped somewhat like a horseshoe. Its highest elevation, La Selle, rises to 8,793 feet. There are four large, fertile plains.

The average temperature at Port au Prince is 80 degrees. The annual average rainfall is 54 inches at Port au Prince. The heaviest rains occur in May and September.

There are a number of rivers, the longest being the Artibonite, navigable for 100 miles.

Principal City Port au Prince, with a population of 142,800, is Haiti's capital and largest city. It is located on the large Gulf of Gonaïves, and has a fine harbor. Bowen Field Airport is one mile from the center of the city.

How to Get to Haiti

Sea: Alcoa, Cunard, French, Furness Bermuda, Lykes Bros., Panama, Pickford & Black, Royal Mail, Royal Netherlands, Saguenay Terminals lines. Also schooners from Cuba and Puerto Rico.

Air: Pan American World Airways, KLM (Royal Dutch Airlines), Air France, Delta C. and S., Cubana de Aviación, and Haitian Air Corps Passenger Service.

Entry Requirements American citizens and Canadians coming directly from Canada do not need passports or visas for a visit of 30 days or less.

Proof of citizenship, a smallpox-vaccination certificate less than 3 years old, a general health certificate, and a through ticket are required.

A tourist card—cost $1—is given each traveler; this card must be returned upon departure.

Business Opportunities The principal business is agriculture.

Mineral resources are few, bauxite and lignite being the principal ones. An American mining company received a concession to exploit bauxite deposits and has begun preliminary work. Efforts toward industrialization have resulted in the operation of new sugar-refineries, textile mills, an iron foundry, and other factories.

Tourism has increased 70 per cent since 1949, and many new hotels and extensions to old ones have been built. Certain tax exemptions are granted to encourage new industries.

Government Haiti is a republic. The President is elected by the men (women do not have the franchise). The President names 5 or more Secretaries of State. The Congress consists of 37 Deputies and 21 Senators.

The judicial power is vested in a Supreme Court, a Court of Appeals, a Civil Court, and a Court of Peace.

Language and Nationalities French is the official language, but a Creole patois is spoken by everyone. Very little English is spoken.

The population consists of Negroes, mulattoes (descendants of early French settlers), and about 5,000 foreigners, of whom approximately 10 per cent are white.

Banks, Currency The National Bank of Haiti, Royal Bank of Canada. The monetary unit is the gourde. Five gourdes equal one dollar U.S.

Exports and Imports

Principal exports: coffee, sisal, cacao, handicrafts, raw sugar, primitive paintings, cotton, essential oils.

Principal imports: wheat flour, cloth, agricultural machinery and tools, cars and other vehicles, medicines, foodstuffs, footwear, iron and steel manufacturers, paper, soap, wood.

Agriculture Agriculture is a vital element in the economy of the country. Coffee, bananas, sugar, sisal, cotton, and cacao are the principal crops.

Flora Frangipani, mimosa, pine, cedar, mahogany, oak trees, and tropical flowers.

Churches The Roman Catholic religion is predominant. There are Episcopalian, Presbyterian, and Wesleyan congregations.

The Episcopal cathedral in Port au Prince has interesting murals depicting scenes from the Bible in the primitive style of the Haitian artist.

Schools The school system, modeled after that of France, is free and compulsory. English is taught. There are 2 teachers' normal schools, a military school for training army officers, and a central school for agriculture. The University of Haiti was established in 1944.

Hospitals and Health General Hospital, St. Francis Hospital, and Asile Français, all in Port au Prince, are the largest. Hotels generally have a resident doctor.

Drink only boiled milk. Use bottled water outside Port au Prince. (Most hotels use boiled water.)

Architecture Hotel construction is modern. Large stone buildings and small wooden ones with balconies stand side by side in Port au Prince. Residential sections are made up mainly of modern homes. The Citadelle near Cap Haïtien is one of the most amazing architectural structures extant.

Arts and Crafts Haitian painting and sculpture have become very famous and are widely exhibited. Craftsmen make jewelry of metal or shell, mahogany carvings, woven carpets, and hats of sisal and straw.

Food Specialties Langouste flambée (flaming lobster), tassot de dinde (dried turkey), griot (fried pork), riz djon djon (rice and black mushrooms), riz et pois (rice and beans), pain patate (sweet potato pudding).

Hotels

Name	*Rooms*	*Baths*	*Classification*	*Additional Information*
(Port au Prince)				
Beau Rivage	50	50	M*	Air-conditioned, pool, tennis, yachts on bay.

*American Plan *** European Plan
E—Expensive M—Moderately expensive I—Inexpensive

Name	*Rooms*	*Baths*	*Classification*	*Additional Information*
Oloffson	30	30	M*	Pool. Hunting and fishing parties.
Riviera	75	75	M*	Pool, night club.
Splendide	40	40	M* & ***	Pool, library. Some rooms air-conditioned.
Sans Souci	18	18	M*	Pool, badminton, ping pong.
International Club	19	19	M*	Cottage colony. Pool, horses, tennis.
(Pétion-Ville)				
Beau Site	30	30	E* & ***	Pool.
Choucoune	30	30	E*	Pool, gift shop, terrace overlooking pool. Dinner dancing Mon. and Wed. evenings. Night club. 25 rooms air-conditioned.
Damballa	15	15	E*	Pool, tennis.
El Rancho	32	32	E*	Pool. Masseur. Dancing Mon. and Fri. nights.
Ibo Lélé	37	37	E*	Pool, ping pong. Dancing Tues. and Fri. nights.
(Kenscoff)				
Berg Hotel	10	10	I*	French and German cuisine.

*American Plan *** European Plan

E—Expensive M—Moderately expensive I—Inexpensive

For further hotel information, consult your travel agent.

Restaurants In addition to the hotel restaurants, the following are recommended:

Casino (Port au Prince)—French and Italian cuisine, dancing, bar, gambling casino.

Pigalle (Port au Prince)—Creole, French cuisine, bar.

Bar Italia (Port au Prince)—Italian cuisine, bar.

Nobbe & Bondel (Port au Prince)—bar.

Aux Cosaques (Port au Prince)—Haitian food; air-conditioned.

Savoy (Port au Prince)—bar.

New Canton (Port au Prince)—Chinese cuisine, bar.

Le Perchoir (Boutelliers)—bar, situated on mountaintop.

Picardi (Pétion-Ville)—bar.

JAMAICA

(jȧ-mā'-kȧ) British West Indies

LATITUDE: *between 17 deg. 42 min. N. and 18 deg. 32 min. N.*

LONGITUDE: *between 76 deg. 11 min. W. and 78 deg. 23 min. W.*

POPULATION: *1,429,800 (1951)* AREA: *4,411 sq. mi.*

CAPITAL: *Kingston (307,600)*

Location Jamaica lies 90 miles south of eastern Cuba, 100 miles west of Haiti, and 170 miles southeast of Grand Cayman. It is about 500 miles south-southeast of Miami.

Of Special Interest to Tourists (Electricity: 110V AC)

Best buys are such duty-free items as Swiss watches, cameras, Danish silver, French perfumes, china, liquor, English woolens, linens, silks, doeskins, tweeds, and sweaters. Other good buys are sports apparel, local perfume, straw hats and baskets, embroideries, rums, liqueurs, ginger wines, linens, and Jamaica dolls.

Guided tours may be arranged through local agencies.

Drive-yourself cars are available. Chauffeur-driven cars may be hired. Taxis are available in Kingston and its environs. Visitors may bring cars; check with American Automobile Association.

Motor boats and sailing craft can be rented—including a captain, mate, gas, oil, bait, ice, and tackle.

Horses may be rented. On a large plantation near Falmouth, Good Hope ranch provides excellent riding along trails.

The visitor can enjoy both spectator and active sports: swimming, tennis, golf, big-game fishing, spear-fishing, yachting, shooting (crocodiles; game birds from August to November), horse racing (6 tracks), polo, cricket, and football. Rafting on the Rio Grande near Port Antonio on bamboo rafts with native pilots is a favorite and unusual sport.

Some spots of interest are—inland near Kingston—the Institute of Jamaica with its library, museum, and art gallery, Hope Botanical Gardens with tropical plants, orchids, and trees, Knutsford Park race track, the ruins of Port Royal; and—farther from Kingston—the Windsor Great Cave in Trelawny, Peru Cave in St. Elizabeth, and scenic drives into and across the Blue Mountains.

Best beaches are Doctor's Cave at Montego Bay, Port Antonio, Ocho Rios, Negril. There are private beach clubs to which tourists may apply for temporary membership.

Physical Characteristics Jamaica is the largest of the British West Indies, being 146 miles long and 51 miles wide. It is very mountainous, the main east-west range having numerous subsidiary ranges. The island's summit, Blue Mountain Peak, rises to 7,402 feet.

The most important of its many rivers are the Black River in the southwest and the Rio Grande in the northeast.

The average annual rainfall is about 77 inches, but there is great variety throughout the island. In Kingston the annual average is from 30 to 35 inches, while in other regions it varies from 40 to 100 inches. The rainy season is short, and even then the sun usually shines for part of the day. The months of May, October, and November are the rainiest.

The average temperature over a 36-year period was 78.7 degrees, with variations from a low of 56.7 to a high of 97.8. The temperature along the coast is much higher than in the mountains.

The waters surrounding the island remain at a temperature between 79 and 84 degrees all year.

Kingston Harbour, the principal port, is from 7 to 10 fathoms deep and can accommodate ships drawing up to 30 feet.

Principal City Kingston, the capital and principal city, has a population of 307,600. It is situated in the southeastern section of the island, on Kingston Harbour. Palisadoes Airport is directly across the harbor from Kingston. The Chatham Airstrip at Montego Bay is about 115 miles away.

How to Get to Jamaica

Sea: Alcoa, American Pioneer, Canadian National, Flota Mercante Dominica, Fyffes, French, Harrison, Jamaica Banana Prod., M.A.N.Z., Moore-McCormack, Nourse, Pacific Steam Navigation, Pickford and Black, Royal Mail, Royal Netherlands, Saguenay Terminals, United Fruit, Horn lines.

Air: British Overseas Airways, British West Indian Airways, Caribbean International, Trans-Canada Air Lines, Pan American World Airways, Delta C. and S., KLM (Royal Dutch Airlines), Avianca.

Entry Requirements No passenger may land without the permission of an Immigration Officer. The landing-fee is $1.40.

Passports are required of all passengers arriving in the island except (a) cruise passengers who intend to remain only during stay of vessel in port and to leave by the same vessel; (b) citizens of the United States who arrive from the United States, Puerto Rico, or the U. S. Virgin Islands on a tourist visit for not more than 6 months; (c) British subjects who arrive from British territory on a tourist visit for not more than 6 months. Those coming under provisions (b) and (c) must hold a return ticket showing place of origin, and must return to place of origin.

Those requiring passports must have valid British visas except those in transit up to 14 days; citizens of the United States on a visit not exceeding 6 months; and nationals of countries with which the United Kingdom has a reciprocal agreement for the abolition of visas.

Business Opportunities The Government encourages the development of existing local industries and the setting up of new ones. An Industrial Development Law, passed in 1952, formed a corporation to assist in the financing of new industries and the improvement of existing ones. A Pioneer Industries Law passed in 1949 makes concessions to starting industries manufacturing certain products. In 1944 a Hotel Aid Law was passed to encourage investment and building of hotels.

The major industrial activity of Jamaica comes under the following categories: bauxite, canning, cement, citrus, coconut products, cornmeal, leather, logwood extracts, matches, milk, sugar and rum, tobacco, and miscellaneous manufacturing.

There are not many available jobs. Many Jamaican workers, particularly agricultural, are recruited for work in the United States.

Government Jamaica is a British Crown Colony governed by an appointed Governor, a Privy Council, an Executive Council, a Legislative Council, and a House of Representatives. Local government is administered by Parochial Boards, one in each of the 14 parishes.

Language and Nationalities The principal language is English.

The population consists of Negroes, Canadians, British, Portuguese, East Indians, Chinese, Syrians, Americans, and natives of other West Indies islands.

Banks, Currency Bank of Nova Scotia, Barclays Bank, Canadian Bank of Commerce, Royal Bank of Canada.

British, United States, or Canadian currency may be brought into and used in Jamaica. The monetary unit is the Jamaica pound, equivalent to one pound sterling.

Exports and Imports

Principal exports: sugar, rum, bananas, fruits, syrups, tobacco, cigars, wood and timber, cocoa, coffee, coconuts, spices, pimento, bauxite.

Principal imports: clothing, foods, cars, butter, rubber, machinery, medicines, furniture.

Flora and Fauna Mango, sapodilla, cherimoya, papaya, cashew, oleander, hibiscus, bougainvillæa, air plants, cactus, night-blooming cereus, palm, fern, bamboo, orchid.

Fifty-seven varieties of resident birds include the owl, grackle, dove, pigeon, Jamaican tody, heron, gull, swift, parrot, Jamaican petrel.

Pigs, poultry, rabbits, goats, and sheep form the largest part of the domestic animal life. Manatees, agoutis, and bats may be found.

Insects: ants, cockroaches, mosquitoes (some anopheles are found in lowlands), crickets, flies, ticks, butterflies, scorpions, centipedes.

Fresh-water fish: bass, snook, hognose mullet, mountain mullet, calipoeva. Salt-water fish: marlin, sailfish, tarpon, barracuda, pompano, cabio, rayfish, kingfish, snapper, Spanish mackerel, yellowtail, dolphin.

Churches Church of England, African Methodist Episcopal, Church of Scotland, Congregational Union, Baptist, Presbyterian, Roman Catholic, Jewish, Salvation Army, Seventh Day Adventist, Society of Friends, Pocomania.

Schools Elementary schools are grant-aided; there are 688 of them, attended by 209,000 children. Of the secondary schools, 27 receive Government aid. A school of agriculture and the University College of the West Indies make it possible for students to go on to specialized higher education. The entrance requirements for the university are those of the University of London.

Hospitals Jamaica has 26 Government, general, and other hospitals. In addition, there are clinics and 46 medical districts with 106 dispensaries. Competent doctors and dentists are readily available.

Architecture Some old Spanish buildings remain, but the architecture is mainly fairly modern and Georgian.

Arts and Crafts Inlaid boxes and trays of ornamental native woods; wood carvings of lignum vitæ; raffia bags; and baskets of palmetto leaves, jipijapa palm, banana bark, wire grass, and raffia are made by native artisans.

Food Specialties "Pepperpot" is a famous native dish. It consists of pork (cut small and browned), chicken (partially roasted and cut up), onion, shallots, dried chiles, and a sauce made of two tablespoons of sugar, 1½ teaspoons of salt, 1 teaspoon of cayenne pepper, and from 7 to 10 teaspoons of cassareep (concentrated juice of cassava). This is simmered for several hours before being served.

Hotels (These are some of the best hotels in various sections. There are others as good and many more moderately priced.)

Name	*Rooms*	*Baths*	*Classifi-cation*	*Additional Information*
Melrose (Kingston)	36 guests	Most	I*	In town, pool.
Myrtle Bank (Kingston)	205 "	"	E*	Pool, dancing.
South Camp (Kingston)	50 "	"	I*	Pool.
Manor House (Constant Spring)	38 "	"	M*	Pool, golf course.
Courtleigh Manor (St. Andrew)	23 "	"	M*	Pool, tennis.
Mona (Liguanea)	41 "	"	M*	Pool, adjoins Hope Botanical Gardens.
Shaw Park (Ocho Rios)	75 "	"	E*	Private river, pool, beach (10 minutes).
Tower Isle (Ocho Rios)	175 "	"	E*	Pool, cabaña club, riding, tennis, fishing.
Titchfield (Port Antonio)	60 "	"	M*	Pools, rafting, beach, tennis, fishing.
Sunset Lodge (Montego Bay)	90 "	"	E*	Private beach.
Montego Beach (Montego Bay)	74 "	"	E*	Beach, glass-bottomed boat.
Gloucester House (Montego Bay)	105 "	"	M*	Near sea front.
Round Hill (Montego Bay)	164 "	"	E*	Cottages available, beach, horses, dancing.
Ethelhart (Montego Bay)	48 "	"	I*	Overlooks sea and town.
Casa Blanca (Montego Bay)	88 "	"	M*	Adjoins Doctor's Cave Beach.
Good Hope Ranch (Falmouth)	46 "	"	E*	18th-century house, large estate, riding, beach.
Silver Sands (Duncans P.O.)	20 "	"	M*	Swimming, riding, tennis.

*American Plan

E—expensive M—moderately expensive I—inexpensive

Restaurants and Night Clubs

Esquire (Kingston)—American and Chinese food.

Glass Bucket and Rainbow night clubs (Kingston)—native floor shows, dancing, food served.

Sugar Hill night club (Kingston)—native and foreign floor shows.

Montego Bay area has the Jolly Roger and Coconut Grove night clubs.

MARGARITA

(mär′-gä-rē′-tä) Venezuela

LATITUDE: *11 deg. N.* LONGITUDE: *64 deg. W.*

POPULATION: *78,899* AREA: *630 sq. mi.*

CAPITAL: *La Asunción*

Location Isla de Margarita lies 23 miles off the northern coast of Venezuela and about 175 miles east-northeast of Caracas.

Of Special Interest to Tourists Best buys are raw pearls, and native-made pearl earrings and bracelets, straw hats, bags, slippers, and embroidered goods.

Margarita has magnificent scenery, beautiful beaches, and lakes.

Best beaches are Juangriego and Tirano.

Physical Characteristics Margarita and the tiny islands of Cubagua and Coche form the State of Nueva Esparta.

Margarita's western sector is almost uninhabited; the eastern side contains nearly the entire population. The two sections are joined by a sandy isthmus.

The very low annual rainfall averages 27.56 inches. The average temperature is about 80 degrees. It is very hot in summer.

Principal City La Asunción is the capital. Porlamar is the commercial, industrial, and tourist center as well as chief port.

How to Get to Margarita By boat or plane from Trinidad via Barcelona, Venezuela.

By plane from Caracas (175 miles).

Entry Requirements Visitors must go to Margarita from the Venezuelan mainland. A visaed passport, smallpox-vaccination certificate, through ticket, and 4 front-view photographs are necessary. Travelers staying less than 48 hours do not require passports, but the transportation company must assume responsibility for them and see that they leave within the time limit.

Business Opportunities Although Margarita's pearl-fishing industry is valued at $500,000 annually, deep-sea fishing is probably the most important single occupation. A canning plant processes fish. Women make fishnets. Porlamar makes small fishing boats.

Tourism is being encouraged; several hotels are under construction.

Government Margarita is part of Venezuela.

Language Spanish is spoken exclusively.

Currency The monetary unit is the bolívar. 3.35 bolívars equal one dollar U.S.

Agriculture Agriculture is limited because of the semi-arid conditions.

Flora and Fauna Divi-divi tree, cactus, yucca, mangrove, sugar cane.

Spanish mackerel, bluefish, shrimp, lobster, oyster, red snapper, and many other fish.

Churches Religion is Roman Catholic. At Porlamar there is the Church of the Virgen del Valle, patroness of all Margarita fishermen.

Arts and Crafts Islanders make pottery, hammocks, straw hats, bags, slippers (alpargatas), embroidery, and pearl earrings and bracelets.

Food Sugar cane, fruits, corn, yucca, and vegetables are produced for home consumption. Fish is a diet staple. A favorite dish is fish stew. Another is escabeche, consisting of red snapper or Spanish mackerel fried in olive oil with onion and pimento.

Hotels

Name	*Rooms*	*Baths*	*Classification*	*Additional Information*
Bahía (Porlamar)	10	Some	I*	Private beach, French chef, good dining-room, outdoor patio.

*American plan I—inexpensive

Hotel de Turismo in Porlamar is under construction; others are contemplated.

MARTINIQUE

(*mär′-tē′-nēk′*) *French West Indies*

LATITUDE: *14 deg. 40 min. N.* LONGITUDE: *61 deg. W.*

POPULATION: *280,000* AREA: *385 sq. mi.*

CAPITAL: *Fort de France (66,000)*

Location Martinique is in the Windward Islands, between the British islands of Dominica to the north and St. Lucia to the south.

Of Special Interest to Tourists Best buys: French perfume, Limoges miniatures, Swiss watches, dolls in native dress, straw hats, and baskets.

Cars may be rented for touring the island, and taxis are available in Fort de France.

Beaches: Les Salines, at the extreme southern end of the island; Ste. Anne, L'Anse à l'Ane and Grande Anse on the coast opposite Fort de France; L'Anse Mitan, the most popular holiday resort; and a small, only fair one at the Lido Hotel in Fort de France. The beaches are undeveloped.

Mountain-climbing is very popular, with Mount Pelée the favorite climb. Starting from the village of Morne Rouge at the base of the mountain, a trip to the crater and back takes 6 hours. The ruins of St. Pierre, destroyed by the eruption of 1902, may be seen. There are warm springs on the way, and traces of lava are visible. The Pitons du Carbet, extinct volcanoes, are exciting to climb. Experienced guides are available (they speak little English, however).

At the southern tip of the island is the Savane des Pétrifications, with its petrified wood.

Historically interesting also are Diamond Rock and Trois Ilets, birthplace of the Empress Josephine.

Fort de France has two small museums and a public library where visitors may borrow books. The American Consulate has a reading-room.

Travelers may make arrangements in Fort de France to join one or all of the three guided tours of the island.

Sports include swimming, sailing, tennis, bicycling, submarine fishing, and hunting.

Physical Characteristics A mountainous island going from sea level to a height of 4,800 feet at Mount Pelée, a volcano that erupted in 1902 and destroyed the town of St. Pierre. Other mountains are the Pitons du Carbet, rising to 3,900 feet, Mount Balata, and Le Vauclin.

The island is 45 miles long and 20 miles wide, and has many rivers and springs. The coast is indented by bays affording anchorage for ships.

Martinique's dry season lasts from December to June, with occasional showers; its rainy season is from July to December. The annual average rainfall is about 87 inches.

Principal City The capital and principal city is Fort de France on the western coast, 9 miles from the Lamentin Aerodrome at Larienty. Fort de France harbor is well protected.

How to Get to Martinique

Sea: Alcoa Steamship Company; Canadian National Steamships (passenger freighters stop at Fort de France if there is cargo to deliver); French Line (fortnightly).

Air: Air France, Pan American World Airways, British West Indian Airways, Air Antilles, Cía. Dominicana de Aviación.

Entry Requirements All visitors must have a smallpox-vaccination certificate not more than 3 years old.

Citizens of the United States and Canada entering as tourists for a period of 2 weeks or less are exempt from passport and visa requirements if they have proof of citizenship containing their photograph, driver's license, and return or onward transportation.

Visitors from South America require an International Certificate of inoculation against yellow fever and smallpox.

The passports of persons entering Martinique for more than 2 weeks but less than 3 months must be visaed by the French Consul at the last port visited or last port of residence, except those of residents of Great Britain, Northern Ireland, Canada, British Colonies, and of United States citizens who possess a valid national passport.

Business Opportunities The principal types of business operating on Martinique are sugar factories, distilleries, pineapple-canning factories, fish-curing, beer-brewing, and pottery-making.

The hotel or resort business is not adequate to cope with the tourist trade. Regulations have been passed to encourage investment in tourism, such as reduction of income tax and exemption from certain other taxes for 10 years.

There are very few jobs available because of the large population and few industries.

Government In March 1946 Martinique was legally declared a Department of France. Laws existing in France also apply to Martinique except where special local laws provide otherwise. The Department is governed by a Prefect appointed by the State Ministry. A Council of 36 members creates, organizes, and governs local services, town board, medical assistance, and budget. Martinique is represented in Parliament in France by 3 deputies, 2 senators, and a counselor of the French Union.

Language and Nationalities The principal language is French. English is taught in the secondary classes of the high schools and in private institutions, but little English is spoken.

Ninety per cent of the population are native-born Negroes; about 2,100 are of French extraction, and the rest are Syrians, Italians, Arabs, Chinese, British, and Americans.

Banks, Currency Banks: Banque de la Martinique (Fort de France), Banque Nationale pour la Commerce et l'Industrie, Caisse Centrale de la France d'Outre Mer, Crédit Martiniquais.

The French franc is the monetary unit. 350 equal one U.S. dollar.

Exports and Imports

Principal exports: sugar, bananas, rum.

Principal imports: wheat flour, chemical fertilizers, codfish, textiles, foodstuffs.

Agriculture The economy of Martinique depends mainly on agriculture. The most important crops are sugar, bananas, and pineapple.

Flora and Fauna

Plants and trees: coconut, palm, evergreen, poirier, courbaril, mahogany (used for making furniture), flamboyant, cassia, cactus, bougainvillæa, hibiscus.

Birds: blackbird, swallow, dove, pigeon, sea birds.

Fish: redfish, jackfish, kingfish, tuna, shark, bonito. Shrimps (found only in the rivers), and river and crayfish are plentiful. Turtles are caught for food and their shells used for ornaments.

Churches The Roman Catholic Church is official, and 90 per cent of the population is Roman Catholic. Seventh Day Adventists are also represented.

Schools Nearly 150 elementary schools, with about 42,000 pupils, are scattered throughout the island. Fort de France has 2 secondary schools. Students who wish to study professions go to France when they have completed their schooling in Martinique. The Collège Technique in Fort de France has classes in handicraft; pupils are taught to work on wood, brass, and iron, to carve, paint, make earthenware and ceramics, to hand-paint pottery, and to embroider.

Hospitals and Health The Colonial Hospital and the Hospital Civil, and 2 clinics, St. Paul's and the Pasteur.

About 30 graduate dentists from the Dental School of Paris practice. Drink only boiled water and milk.

Architecture Many houses are built in the ancient French style with an entrance through a corridor and yard, stairs leading from the dining-room to the upper floors. There are a few modern buildings and several new bungalow colonies in suburbs.

Arts and Crafts Earthenware, ceramics, hand-painted pottery, embroidery, carvings.

Hotels

Name	*Rooms*	*Baths*	*Classification*	*Additional Information*
Lido (Fort de France)	14	6	E*	Private beach.
L' Impératrice (Fort de France)	50	50	E*	Elevator. In town, on Savane.
Berkeley (On road to St. Pierre)	14	Some	M*	Pension.

*American Plan E—expensive M—moderately expensive

***European Plan

Restaurants Chez Étienne, L'Auberge du Manoir, and the Lido Hotel offer excellent French cuisine and vintage wines.

MONTSERRAT

(*mŏnt′-sĕ̱-răt′*) *British West Indies*

LATITUDE: *16 deg. 45 min. N.* LONGITUDE: *62 deg. 10 min. W.*

POPULATION: *13,594* AREA: *32.5 sq. mi.*

CAPITAL: *Plymouth (2,200)*

Location Montserrat is in the Leeward Islands, 27 miles southwest of Antigua and 35 miles northwest of Guadeloupe.

Of Special Interest to Tourists (Electricity: no central supply) Montserrat has a few black sand beaches, as well as white. Visitors may swim, fish, play tennis, and watch cricket.

The chief attraction is lovely scenic drives. Cars may be rented to tour the hills and see the boiling springs on the south side of Chance Mountain.

Plymouth has a Government House, a little library, a movie, and the ruins of Fort Barrington and Fort St. George.

Physical Characteristics Montserrat is 11 miles long and 7 miles wide. It is of volcanic formation, very rugged and mountainous. Its highest elevation, Chance Mountain (2,999 feet), is an active volcano. Its hills are heavily forested.

The annual average rainfall is 62 inches and the average temperature is 82 degrees.

Principal City Plymouth, the capital and port of entry, lies on an open roadstead. It has a few grocery and drug stores, and one small department (drygoods) store.

How to Get to Montserrat

Sea: Alcoa and Canadian National lines; interisland motor launches from Antigua, St. Kitts, and St. Martin.

Entry Requirements Same as Antigua.

Business Opportunities Two cotton ginneries and two rum distilleries are in operation. The majority of the population is engaged in agriculture.

Government As one of the Presidencies of the British Leeward Islands group, Montserrat has its own Resident Commissioner and Executive and Legislative councils.

Language and Nationalities English is spoken. Ninety-five per cent of the population is of African descent.

Banks, Currency Royal Bank of Canada, Government Savings Bank. Monetary unit is the B.W.I. dollar, worth about 60 cents U.S.

Exports and Imports Principal exports: cotton lint, tomatoes, lime juice, vegetables, tamarinds.

Principal imports: wheat flour, sugar, fish, salt, meat (salted and pickled).

Agriculture Cotton, sugar, food crops, limes, and tomatoes are crops vital to the island's economy.

Flora and Fauna Similar to that on other Leeward islands.

Churches Church of England, Roman Catholic, Wesleyan, Seventh Day Adventist.

Schools There are 12 Government primary schools, a Roman Catholic primary school, and the Montserrat secondary school.

Hospitals and Health There are a small hospital, several doctors, one dentist. Drinking-water and milk should be boiled.

Hotels

Name	*Rooms*	*Baths*	*Classification*	*Additional Information*
Crescent Hill Hotel (Plymouth)	3	1	I*	Accommodations for only six guests.
Coconut Hill Hotel (Plymouth)	3	1	I*	Accommodations for only six guests.

*American plan I—inexpensive

PUERTO RICO

(*pwĕr′-tō-rē′-kō*) *United States West Indies*

LATITUDE: *between 18 deg. and 18 deg. 30 min. N.*

LONGITUDE: *between 66 and 67 deg. W.*

POPULATION: *2,210,703* AREA: *3,435 sq. mi.*

CAPITAL: *San Juan (224,205)*

Location Between Hispaniola and the Virgin Islands, Puerto Rico is 75 miles east of the Dominican Republic and 480 miles east of Cuba.

Of Special Interest to Tourists (Electricity: 110V AC)

Best buys are embroidered dresses, blouses, shirts, straw and fiber products, mahogany, and leatherwork.

Swimming at salt- and fresh-water pools and beaches all around the island.

Water skiing, fishing, golf, sailing, skeet- and trap-shooting, tennis, horseback riding, and dancing are among the activities that the visitor may participate in.

Cockfights, tennis matches, soccer, horse racing, baseball, and boxing may be seen.

Travelers may take part in the Government lottery with weekly drawings. There are several gambling casinos.

In addition to movies, a little-theater group gives plays in English, and performances are given by international ballet groups and theater troupes.

The museum, libraries, and most Government buildings are open to travelers, but are often closed from 12 noon until 2 p.m.

Sightseeing tours may be made by chartered plane as well as by car. Cars with or without chauffeurs may be rented. The tourist bureaus supply excellent road maps. Públicos are operated.

Old San Juan, dating back to 1508, has many historic sites and fine old buildings.

The National Rain Forest, El Yunque; the sugar central at Ensenada, where visitors are taken on a conducted tour; Mayagüez, the embroidery city; and the phosphorescent bay at Parguera are but a few of the interesting places to visit.

Coamo has hot springs and mineral baths.

Physical Characteristics On the western coast the mountains drop precipitously into the sea. The other coasts are bordered by plains varying in depth from 2 to 12 miles. Its highest mountain peaks are located in the central part, the highest, Cerro de Punta, being 4,390 feet above sea level.

The island's many rivers are not navigable, but are used for hydroelectric power and irrigation.

The average coastal temperature is 76.6 degrees. The mountain temperature is about 10 or 15 degrees lower.

Rainfall varies slightly according to location. It ranges from 55 to 75 inches a year on the north coast, 29 to 50 inches on the south coast. Averages taken over a 45-year period show that there are only 5 days a year in Puerto Rico without sun.

Principal City San Juan is the capital and principal port.

How to Get to Puerto Rico

Sea: Alcoa Steamship Company, Bull Insular Line, Lykes Bros. Steamship Co., Pope & Talbot Lines, Waterman Line, Royal Netherlands Steamship Company, Saguenay Terminals, and others.

Air: Eastern Air Lines, Pan American World Airways, Delta C. and S., Caribbean Atlantic Airlines, Cía. Dominicana de Aviación, Air France, British West Indian Airways, Iberia Air Lines.

Entry Requirements American citizens coming directly from the United States or the U.S. Virgin Islands are admitted without papers. United States immigration laws apply to Puerto Rico. Passports and visas are required.

Business Opportunities Puerto Rico is principally agricultural, although its industrialization is rapidly increasing. Manufacturing is increasing, and the island's exports now include such items as cottonseed oils, pharmaceuticals, furniture, and textiles.

The Puerto Rico Industrial Development Company, a Government-backed agency created in 1942, has aided financially or technically in establishing about 250 new industries.

The Tax Exemption Act of 1947 granted total property- and income-tax exemption until June 1959, with graduated taxes until 1962, to certain new businesses.

Government Puerto Rico is administered under the Organic Act of Puerto Rico of 1917, which granted U.S. citizenship to its natives. On July 3, 1950, the United States signed a bill granting Puerto Rico the right to draw up its own Constitution. The Governor is elected each 4 years and holds veto power over measures passed by the Insular Legislature. The Legislature consists of a Senate (19 members) and a House of Representatives (39 members). All are elected for a term of 4 years by popular vote.

Language and Nationalities The principal language is Spanish. English is taught in schools and is largely used commercially. Many natives can carry on simple English conversations.

About 2,000 continental Americans live in Puerto Rico. The rest of the inhabitants are native born.

Banks, Currency Banco de Ponce, Banco Popular de Puerto Rico, Bank of Nova Scotia, Chase Manhattan Bank, Credit Union Bank, Crédito y Ahorra Ponceño, First National City Bank of New York, Roig Commercial Bank, Royal Bank of Canada.

United States currency is used.

Exports and Imports

Principal exports: sugar products, refined and unrefined sugar, molasses, rum, fruits, nuts, tobacco, textiles, coffee.

Principal imports: food, merchandise, pork products, lard, dairy products, rice, wheat flour, dried beans, cigarettes, clothing, textiles, footwear, fertilizer, motor vehicles, tires, tubes, gasoline.

Agriculture Agriculture is the most important source of income and employment. Sugar cane, tobacco, coffee, fruits, and vegetables are raised.

Flora and Fauna Tropical plants, orchids, giant tree ferns, coconut palms.

Albacore, bonito, bonefish, dolphin, grouper, jack, kingfish, blue and white marlin, sailfish, snook, swordfish, tarpon, tuna.

Bahama duck, mallard, canvasback, Caribbean coot, blue heron.

Churches Roman Catholic, Baptist, Christian Science, Episcopal, Lutheran, Jewish, Methodist, Presbyterian.

Schools Elementary schools of 6 grades, junior high schools of 3 grades, senior high schools of 3 grades, public vocational schools, adult schools, summer and evening high schools, the University of Puerto Rico, and the University of St. Mary make up the school system.

Hospitals and Health Good hospitals, doctors, and dentists are available. Water is safe to drink. Climate is good for those suffering from hay fever.

Architecture Buildings of recent construction are ultra-modern. Many fine examples of early Spanish Colonial still stand.

Arts and Crafts The Puerto Rico Art Center (San Juan) holds exhibitions of local artists and of artists from neighboring Caribbean islands.

The little-theater group in San Juan puts on plays, ballets, and arranges for concerts and international artists to perform.

The paintings, ceramics, and sculpture of local artists may be purchased. Native tortoise-shell, straw, and embroidered articles are for sale.

Food Specialties

Arroz con pollo (rice with chicken).
Habichuelas (red beans).
Gandules (pigeon peas and pork).
Asopao (soupy form of rice with chicken, crab, or lobster).
Hallacas (mild—not hot—form of tamale with chicken or pork wrapped in banana leaves).
Pasteles (another version of tamale).
Tostones (plantains—large green bananas—sliced and fried).

Hotels

Name	*Rooms*	*Baths*	*Classification*	*Additional Information*
Condado Beach (San Juan)	180#	180	E***	Casino, restaurant, beach, pool, tennis.
Caribe Hilton (San Juan)	300#	300	E***	Casino, night club, beach, pool, restaurant.
Tropicana (San Juan)	15	15	M***	Casino, bar, restaurant, night club.
Kasablanca Hotel (San Juan)	12	12	M***	Restaurant, pool, beach privileges, roof garden.
La Rada (San Juan)	80#	80	M***	Pool, outdoor dining-terrace, water-ski school, dance studio, Le Rendez-vous restaurant.
Normandie Hotel (San Juan)	160	160	M***	Pool, beach, night club, restaurant.
Borinquen Country Club (Aguadilla)	21	21	M***	Beach, pool. Near bass-stocked lake.
Coamo Springs Hotel (Coamo)	50	Some	M*	Hot sulphur-water pool and baths. Riding, trap-shooting, movies.
La Parguera Guest House (Lasas)	15	6	I***	Swimming at Mata de la Gata Island. Night trips to phosphorescent bay.
La Palma (Mayagüez)	90 (15#)	Most	M* & ***	New wing recommended.
Melia Hotel (Ponce)	42	42	M***	Commercial. Fine stop-over spot for sightseeing.

#Air-conditioned   *American Plan   ***European Plan

E—expensive   M—moderately expensive   I—inexpensive

Restaurants Those listed are in addition to the hotel restaurants.

San Juan Area

Birds—at airport—bar, dining-room, coffee shop.
Café Palace.
Casino de Puerto Rico.
El Burrito.
El Manolete—dining, dancing, floor show on weekends.
El Nilo—native and American food. Open 24 hours a day.
La Estrella de Italia—Italian food.
La Mallorquina—good food. Opened 1848.
Las Guitaras—dinner music.
Mago's Saxony Steak House—steaks a specialty.
Mejico in Puerto Rico—Mexican dishes.
Piff Paff Pouf—dining, dancing, floor show.
Swiss Chalet—dinner music. Expensive, but superlative food.
Villa Firenze—Italian food.
Tropicana—gambling casino.
Hings—Chinese food.

Ponce Area

Playa de Isabel (out of town).

Mayagüez

La Sultana—Bullfighter décor in dining-room—soda fountain.
El Galeón—well-located seaside family restaurant, 8 miles south of town—carey en biftec (turtle steak).

SABA

(sä'-bä) Netherlands West Indies

LATITUDE: *17 deg. 38 min. N.* LONGITUDE: *63 deg. 14 min. W.*

POPULATION: *1,098* AREA: *5 sq. mi.*

CAPITAL: *The Bottom (500)*

Location Saba is 29 miles southwest of Sint Maarten, 19 miles northwest of Sint Eustatius, 40 miles northwest of Antigua, 120 miles southeast of St. Thomas.

Of Special Interest to Tourists Best buys are lace, drawn-linen work, embroidery.

Saba's unusual physical aspects are of the greatest interest to visitors. There are no beaches, and to reach the main village from the rocky landing-place the visitor must ride a jeep 800 feet up the only road. The other two villages are higher up the mountainside.

A hike up to the very top of the volcano past the village of Windwardside offers a view that is magnificent.

There are 533 stone steps from Ladder Bay to Bottom. Guide service is recommended for the climb to the top of the volcano.

Physical Characteristics Tiny Saba, with an area of only 5 mountainous square miles, is an extinct volcano rising abruptly 2,900 feet from the sea. It has no harbors and is surrounded by narrow rocky ledges. The only level section, 700 feet above sea level in the crater, has been made into a village.

The average temperature is 79 degrees, the average annual rainfall 43 inches. Nights are cool, sometimes cold.

Principal City The principal town, The Bottom, located in the volcanic crater, has a population of about 500 people. Clean, brightly painted wooden houses line its streets.

How to Get to Saba Saba must be reached by sea. There is no pier; ships anchor offshore. Passengers are taken ashore in small boats to Fort Bay or Ladder Bay. The *Antilia* from Curaçao connects with the island twice monthly.

Entry Requirements All visitors must have a return or through ticket to a destination outside the territory. United States citizens do not need a passport, but should have proof of citizenship and a smallpox-vaccination certificate not more than 3 years old.

Business Opportunities There is no industry on Saba. Most of the young male population goes off to work in the oil-refineries of Aruba and Curaçao, and some go to sea. The women spend most of their time making lace for sale locally and in Curaçao stores. Saba receives Government grants, and her prosperity is directly related to that of Curaçao and Aruba.

Government Saba, part of the Kingdom of the Netherlands, has an Administrator and 2 deputies, all under the jurisdiction of the Lieutenant Governor, who resides on Sint Maarten.

Language and Nationalities English is the principal language in the Netherlands Windward group, though Dutch is taught.

The population is about 60-per-cent white and 40-per-cent black.

Banks, Currency No banks. Monetary unit is the florin (fl.) or guilder, which is equal to 53 cents U.S.

Exports and Imports Lace is exported. Food and most articles necessary for life are imported.

Agriculture The soil is rocky. A limited amount of vegetables is raised. Some bananas are grown inside the crater lip. Agriculture is not an important factor in the economy of the island.

Flora and Fauna Tropical flowers and shrubs, mangoes, bananas, coconuts.

Donkeys, horses, sheep, goats, chickens.

Churches Anglican, Roman Catholic.

Schools Saba has 4 schools, with about 210 pupils.

Hospitals and Health There is a small Government hospital.

Architecture The Dutch influence is prevalent. Villages look as though transplanted from Holland. The houses are made of wood, painted, with shutters and red-tiled or shingle roofs.

Arts and Crafts Lace-making, drawn-linen work, embroidery.

Hotels There are no hotels. Saba has two Government guesthouses; one in The Bottom, with 4 bedrooms and 2 baths (3 meals), and one in

Windwardside, with 2 bedrooms and 1 bath (breakfast only). Charges are inexpensive.

It is wise to check in advance to learn whether accommodations are available, as guesthouses must give priority to Government officials.

Visitors may also be put up in private homes.

SAINT CROIX, VIRGIN ISLANDS

(sănt kroi') United States West Indies

LATITUDE: *17 deg. 42 min. N.* LONGITUDE: *64 deg. 48 min. W.*

POPULATION: *12,096* AREA: *84 sq. mi.*

CAPITAL: *Charlotte Amalie, St. Thomas (11,463)*

Location St. Croix is 60 miles east of Puerto Rico, 40 miles south of St. Thomas and St. John, and about 1,000 miles from the U.S. mainland.

Of Special Interest to Tourists (Electricity: 110V AC)

Best buys are silver, perfume, china, textiles, liquor, Danish glass, Virgin Island handicrafts, and sportswear.

Buses and taxis are available. Taxi-drivers act as guides, and the rates are set by the Chamber of Commerce.

Small drive-yourself cars can be rented by the day or week. A driver's license may be obtained at the Police office upon presentation of your present license. It is good for 30 days.

Bicycles may be rented.

A tour to Buck Island, 2 miles to the north, for a day may be arranged.

Fishing, spear-fishing, snorkeling, and boating excursions may be arranged.

A glass-bottomed boat is available.

Tennis may be played at the St. Croix Country Club (Frederiksted), the Tennis Club (Christiansted), and some of the hotels.

Horses may be rented. Hunting for doves, pigeons, and white-tailed deer is permitted in season. A non-resident license costing $15 can be obtained on the island.

Donkey races are very popular with visitors.

Cockfights may be seen, and horse racing takes place at the St. Croix Turf Club at Manning's Bay track in February and March. Polo games are also played here.

Libraries in Christiansted and Frederiksted may be used by visitors; a fee of $1 is charged.

The St. Croix Museum is in the public libary in Christiansted.

Interesting sights include Alexander Hamilton's mother's memorial and the store where he clerked as a young man; the Old Fort; the first church; Government House; and old sugar estates. Tours of houses and gardens may be arranged with the St. Croix Landmarks League in Frederiksted and the St. Croix Chamber of Commerce.

There are beaches at Cramer's Park, the St. Croix Country Club, the Frederiksted Beach Club, and on Buck Island.

Physical Characteristics The largest (28 miles by 10 miles) of the three U.S. Virgin Islands, it covers 84 square miles and has 12,096 inhabitants. It rises abruptly on the north and east. Mount Eagle rises to 1,165 feet. The southern coast consists of low-lying savannas and plains descending to 4 feet above sea level at Westend Saltpond.

The temperature average over a period of six years was 79.1 degrees. The annual average rainfall for the same period was 42.35 inches.

A few springs supply water. Rainwater is caught in cisterns for drinking. There are some artesian wells.

Principal City The two principal cities are Christiansted on the northeast shore (4,110) and Frederiksted on the west (1,925). They are 15 miles apart, connected by Centerline Road. Frederiksted harbor is an open roadstead; passengers and cargo are brought to shore in launches. It is near the Alexander Hamilton Aerodrome.

How to Get to St. Croix

Sea: Furness Bermuda Line, Alcoa Steamship Company, Bull Insular Line, Lykes Bros., Waterman Line, Delta Line.

Air: Caribbean Air Lines from Puerto Rico daily via St. Thomas; British West Indian Airways.

Entry Requirements United States citizens do not need passports, but must carry proof of citizenship for return to the United States. All other tourists require passports and visas.

Business Opportunities Travelers or others interested in setting up a business in the Virgin Islands are advised to make preliminary visits to study customs and island living to see if they would like it. The Christiansted or Frederiksted Chamber of Commerce and Tourist Board and an established lawyer should be consulted in order to get all possible information about the types of business already in existence and what new ones are needed.

Legislation has been passed to encourage new industry, promote tourism, and improve the economy. The main industries at present are tourism and the production of sugar and rum.

Government The Virgin Islands are an incorporated territory of the United States. Their Constitution, the Organic Act of the Virgin Islands (1936), set up the Virgin Islands as an insular possession of two districts: the Municipality of St. Croix, and the Municipality of St. Thomas and

St. John. The joint councils of the two municipalities enact legislation pertaining to the islands as a whole. The Governor and his assistant are appointed by the President of the United States and confirmed by the Senate. The seat of government for the islands is Charlotte Amalie (St. Thomas), the capital of the Virgin Islands (U.S.).

Language and Nationalities The language is English. Traces of Danish remain in street names, and a few people speak Danish. The population is made up of Americans of Danish, English, and Creole descent.

Banks, Currency Virgin Islands National Bank (Christiansted), New St. Croix Savings Bank.

United States currency is used.

Exports and Imports Sugar, rum, and cattle are exported.

Food, automobiles, electrical equipment, drugs, tires, hotel supplies, and bicycles are imported.

Agriculture Sugar, beets, cabbages, corn, cucumbers, lettuce, limas, onions, potatoes, and other familiar vegetables are raised.

Sugar production is essential to the economy.

Flora and Fauna Avocados, breadfruit, cashews, guavas, pomegranates, hibiscus, flamboyants, wild orchids, cacti, acacias.

Mongooses, cattle, horses, chickens.

Hundreds of varieties of fish, including dolphin, barracuda, sprat, herring, mullet, and Spanish mackerel.

Churches St. Croix is predominantly Roman Catholic; Lutheran, Anglican, Methodist, Baptist, and Presbyterian groups have congregations.

Schools Several parochial schools, and public grade and high schools are operating. Visitors planning to take their children and spend 3 or 4 months may enroll them in The Island School, a private day school, with grades from kindergarten through eighth.

Hospitals and Health Christiansted and Frederiksted both have hospitals. Doctors and dentists are available.

Architecture Danish influence is seen in the old peaked-roof houses. Many buildings have arcades over the sidewalks, thus permitting shopping while protected from the sun. Frederiksted has some Victorian buildings.

Arts and Crafts The Virgin Islands Co-operative in Christiansted is developing native handicraft. Embroidered items and articles made of woven straw may be found, as well as native paintings and wood carvings.

Hotels

Name	*Rooms*	*Baths*	*Classification*	*Additional Information*
Buccaneer (Christiansted)	37	37	E*	Private beach, tennis.
Hotel-on-the-Cay (Christiansted)	17	Some	E*	Private beach, tennis.
Club Comanche (Christiansted)	34	34	I* & ***	In town. Has 72-foot yawl.
Cruzan Club (Christiansted)	—	All	M*	Outskirts of town; has harbor view.
St. Croix by the Sea (Christiansted)	20	20	M*** & **	Pool.
La Grange Plantation House (Frederiksted)	35	25	M*	Inland; transportation to beach. Calypso.
Clover Crest (Frederiksted)	11	11	M*	Overlooks sea outside town. Pool.
Sprat Hall (Frederiksted)	10	Some	M*	Outside town. Beach, fishing, spear-fishing, riding, badminton.

*American Plan **Modified American Plan ***European Plan

E—expensive M—moderately expensive I—inexpensive

Restaurants and Night Clubs

The Henge Restaurant.

Plantation Night Club (Frederiksted)—bar, orchestra on Wednesdays and Saturdays, juke box.

Farchetti's (Christiansted)—bar, outdoor patio.

The Club Comanche and the Buccaneer have dancing on Saturday nights.

SAINT JOHN, VIRGIN ISLANDS

(United States West Indies)

LATITUDE: *18 deg. 22 min. N.* LONGITUDE: *64 deg. 45 min. W.*

POPULATION: 747 AREA: *20 sq. mi.*

CAPITAL: *Charlotte Amalie, St. Thomas (11,463)*

Location

St. John is 3 miles east of St. Thomas across Pillsbury Sound and 40 miles north of St. Croix.

Of Special Interest to Tourists Swimming at Caneel Bay, Cruz Bay, Trunk Bay, and Gallows Point, horseback riding, tennis, fishing (deep sea and spear), badminton, snorkeling, boating, and picnicking will occupy the traveler's time very pleasantly. This area is one of the finest yacht-cruising grounds in the world. It is possible to sail in a small boat east from St. Thomas among the Virgin Islands, both British and United States, and never be in open sea.

For exploring the island, guides are available with jeeps. There are old sugar-mill ruins, Indian inscriptions, an old fort, small settlements, and many fine views from the heights.

There is no night life.

Physical Characteristics Bordeaux Mountain rises to 1,277 feet. The terrain is mountainous and the slopes are covered with jungle growth.

The temperature averages 79 degrees, and the island is cooled by easterly trade winds. The annual rainfall is about 44 inches. September is the rainiest month.

Principal Cities Cruz Bay, the residence of the island's Administrator, is the principal town. It is on the southern point.

Coral Bay, 7 miles from Cruz Bay on the eastern shore, has a good harbor.

How to Get to St. John St. John has no airstrip; visitors must come by sea. Transportation from St. Thomas by motor launch is easily arranged; the trip takes about 40 minutes.

Entry Requirements Same as for St. Croix.

Business Opportunities See St. Croix regarding establishment of business.

St. John is the main source of supply for the bay leaves used in manufacturing bay rum.

Natives derive their living from farming, fishing, picking bay leaves, making charcoal, and weaving basketware. Some stock is raised for beef and dairy purposes.

Government See St. Croix.

Language and Nationalities See St. Croix.

Banks, Currency See St. Croix.

Exports and Imports Basketware and bay leaves are exported.

Food, machinery, wood, paper, chemicals, clothing, gasoline, and medicine are imported.

Agriculture A few truck farms raise garden vegetables.

Flora and Fauna Bay tree, flamboyant, palm, guava, sugar cane, lemon, lime, sapodilla, mahogany, turpentine.

Fauna is that of St. Croix, with less variety.

Churches See St. Croix.

Schools Education is compulsory between the ages of 6 and 15. There are public and parochial schools.

Hospitals and Health Cruz Bay has a clinic. St. Thomas (half an hour away) has a hospital.

Rainwater stored in cisterns is used for drinking, and must be boiled.

Arts and Crafts Native basket-weaving.

Hotels

Name	*Rooms*	*Baths*	*Classification*	*Additional Information*
Caneel Bay Plantation	45 (Some rooms are in 8 fully equipped cottages with maid service; meals at central dining pavilion)	45	E***	Beach, boats, fishing, spear-fishing.

***European plan E—expensive M—moderately expensive I—inexpensive

Name	*Rooms*	*Baths*	*Classification*	*Additional Information*
Trunk Bay Estate Guest Houses	10	4	M***	Swimming, boats, fishing, excellent cuisine.
Gallows Point (Cruz Bay)	3 houses with baths		M***	Swimming, snorkeling.
Ford Cottages	2 houses with baths		I***	

***European plan E—expensive M—moderately expensive I—inexpensive

Restaurants Trunk Bay Estate Guest Houses, Caneel Bay Plantation, and Mrs. Keating's Boarding House serve meals.

SAINT KITTS (SAINT CHRISTOPHER), NEVIS, ANGUILLA

(nee′-viss), (an-gwill′-uh) British West Indies

LATITUDE: *between 18 deg. 10 min. and 17 deg. N.*

LONGITUDE: *between 62 deg. and 63 deg. W.*

POPULATION: *51,044* AREA: *152 sq. mi.*

CAPITALS: *St. Kitts: Basseterre* *Nevis: Charlestown*
Anguilla: Road Bay

Location

St. Kitts is 45 miles west of Antigua.
Nevis is 2 miles southeast of St. Kitts.
Anguilla is 60 miles northwest of St. Kitts.
These three islands are part of the British Leeward Islands.

Of Special Interest to Tourists (Electricity: 230V AC)

Best buys: handmade baskets, hats, bags, embroidered work, tortoiseshell objects, and pottery made in Nevis.

Taxis, cars, bicycles, horses, fishing boats (tackle not provided), and launches may be rented.

Conaree Beach on St. Kitts is 2 miles from Basseterre and has bathhouses. Frigate Bay Beach, St. Kitts, is privately owned, but permission to use it can be obtained from the owner.

The best beach on Nevis is Pinneys.

The facilities of the St. Kitts Lawn Tennis Club are extended to travelers. Arrangements for a card may be made through the hotels.

Hunting trips may be arranged. A license for a gun must be obtained. (Shooting of migratory birds is permitted between July and September.)

Mountain-climbing interests many travelers. A trip to Mount Misery (4,314 feet) on St. Kitts takes a day. A car takes you to Belmont Estates, where you transfer to horseback up to 1,200 feet. The rest of the climb is made on foot. A descent into the crater can be made, but the climb out is strenuous.

Thirty miles of good roads make it possible to tour St. Kitts and see all the sights of interest, including Brimstone Hill Fortress completed in 1694, where you can view the neighboring Dutch island of Sint Eustatius from the top; the Basseterre sugar factory, which may be visited; and the country villages and churches. Pall Mall Square, Basseterre, has a pretty garden with tropical trees. St. George's Church, built by the French in 1670, destroyed by earthquake and fire and rebuilt several times, is of interest. A trip can be made by sailboat to Great Salt Pond. Horse races are held in August, and cricket and football may be seen.

Nevis offers boating, fishing, swimming, hiking, shooting, and some horseback riding. Carib Indian relics may be found. The ruins of the great houses; Alexander Hamilton's birthplace; Fig Tree Church; the thermal baths; pottery-making; and the scenic beauty are attractive to visitors.

Anguilla has no accommodations for overnight stays, but travelers sailing in near-by waters will enjoy spending a day picnicking on its beaches and exploring. It can be reached only by sea and is less than 2 hours from Marigot, St. Martin.

Physical Characteristics St. Kitts, 68 square miles, is very mountainous and of volcanic origin. It is 23 miles long and 5 miles at the widest point. Its highest peak is Mount Misery, 4,314 feet. The other outstanding landmark is Brimstone Hill, rising 750 feet from the flat land surrounding it. Average temperature is 79 degrees, and annual rainfall about 63 inches.

Nevis covers an area of 50 square miles. It is of volcanic origin and very mountainous. Its highest peaks are Nevis (3,596 feet) and Saddle Hill (1,432 feet). It is practically one large volcanic cone. Rainwater, and the Wingfield, Canyon, and Stonefort rivers supply water. The average temperature is 79 degrees, and the average annual rainfall about 53 inches.

Anguilla is a narrow strip of land 16 miles long by about 2 miles wide and only 23 feet high. It is covered by low-lying foliage and scrub vegetation. It has an area of 34 square miles. The average temperature is 78 degrees, and the average annual rainfall about 40 inches. Water supply is very limited because of the low rainfall.

Principal Cities St. Kitts: Basseterre (8,000), the capital. As a center for distributing goods to the near-by British, Dutch, and French islands, it is a very busy port.

Nevis: Charlestown, the capital and principal city, on an open roadstead.

Anguilla has no cities or towns, only a few settlements. Road Bay settlement is the capital.

How to Get to St. Kitts and Nevis Alcoa and Canadian National lines make stops. Large ships anchor offshore. Passengers and cargo are brought to land in lighters. A motor-launch service plies between St. Kitts and Nevis daily except Sundays. St. Kitts can be reached by air via British West Indian Airways, KLM (Royal Dutch Airlines), and Pan American World Airways.

Anguilla: Accessible only from the sea. Interisland boats make daily trips from St. Martin; a Government boat runs from Antigua.

Entry Requirements Same as Antigua.

Business Opportunities Chief industries are a sugar factory, a cornmeal factory, and a cotton gin. Raising sugar cane and sea-island cotton are the main occupations. The Hotel Ordinance, passed to encourage the building of hotels, also provides tax benefits.

Government St. Kitts, Nevis, and Anguilla form one of the four Leeward Islands Presidencies. Each island is administered by its own Commissioner or Administrator, aided by a Legislative and an Executive Council.

Language and Nationalities The population consists mainly of descendants of African slaves. The inhabitants speak English and a French patois.

Banks, Currency Barclays Bank (St. Kitts), Royal Bank of Canada (St. Kitts), Government Savings Bank (St. Kitts).

The monetary unit is the B.W.I. dollar (worth about 60 cents U.S.).

Exports and Imports

Principal exports: cotton, hides and skins, molasses, salt, sugar crystals.

Principal imports: wood and timber, flour, clothing, footwear, foodstuffs, cotton piece goods.

Agriculture

St. Kitts: sugar cane, sea-island cotton, copra.

Nevis: sea-island cotton, sugar cane, copra.

Anguilla: sea-island cotton.

Flora and Fauna Lily, rose, hibiscus, poinsettia, bougainvillæa, mahogany, coconut, royal palm, cabbage palm, palmetto, banana, plantain, fig, avocado, papaya, mango.

Monkey, dove, pigeon, blackbird, migratory birds.

Tarpon, bonefish, jack, yellowtail, parrot, etc.

Churches Anglican, Roman Catholic, Seventh Day Adventist, Methodist.

Schools In St. Kitts, 17 Government schools provide free education for children from 5 to 16. There are a Catholic school and 4 private schools.

Nevis has 10 Government schools (primary), 1 secondary, and 1 private school.

Anguilla has 5 Government primary schools.

Hospitals and Health St. Kitts has 2 hospitals, the Cunningham and the Alexander. Private doctors and dentists are available. In rural areas all water should be boiled. Mosquito nets are used at night.

Architecture Basseterre's houses are mainly wooden, but some are constructed of a grayish stone or of rough-hewn stone covered with plaster. The upper stories are wooden. In the rural districts almost all houses are of wood.

Arts and Crafts Straw hats, baskets, and bags are made by the natives. Some embroidered work and tortoise-shell jewelry is made. In Nevis, pottery is made.

Hotels—*St. Kitts*

Name	*Rooms*	*Baths*	*Classification*	*Additional Information*
New Hotel Royal (Basseterre)	10	4	I*	Sea front.
Shorty's Hotel (Basseterre)	5	2	M*	Bar, restaurant.
Kool Korner (Basseterre)	4	3	I*	In town.

*American Plan I—inexpensive M—moderately expensive

Restaurants The hotel restaurants and the Circus in Basseterre.

Hotels—*Nevis*

Name	*Rooms*	*Baths*	*Classification*	*Additional Information*
Austins by the Sea (Charlestown)	12	3	I*	On Pinneys Beach, has bar.
Sea View (Charlestown)	5	Some	I*	On beach.

*American Plan I—inexpensive

SAINT LUCIA

(sånt lū'-shĭ-a or lōō-sē'-à) British West Indies

LATITUDE: *between 13 deg. 43 min. and 14 deg. .07 min. N.*

LONGITUDE: *between 60 deg. 53 min. and 61 deg. .05 min. W.*

POPULATION: *84,812* AREA: *233 sq. mi.*

CAPITAL: *Castries (24,300)*

Location The most northerly of the Windward Islands, St. Lucia is 25 miles south of Martinique and 21 miles north of St. Vincent.

Of Special Interest to Tourists (Electricity: 230V AC-DC)
Best buys are native baskets, necklaces, and hats, English woolens, doeskins, linens, and liquor. Native crafts may be bought at the Home Industries on Bridge Street, at Castries Market, or from Mrs. W. E. Cox.

Fishing boats and cars may be rented. Taxis are available.

Beaches are at Vigie Point, Rat Island, Choc Bay, Reduit, and Pigeon Island. The private Vigie Club, Palm Beach Aquatic Club, and Pigeon Island Beach Club may be used by tourists. The Palm Beach Aquatic Club charges 50 cents for the use of the clubhouse and dressing-rooms.

St. Lucia's volcano, Soufrière, last erupted in 1776. It now emits hot vapor and gases and is a favorite tourist sight.

Experienced hikers will enjoy climbing Gros Piton and Petit Piton, two volcanic cones at the entrance of Soufrière Bay.

Historical sites include Fort Charlotte on Morne Fortuné, with a beautiful view of the harbor, and Fort Rodney on Pigeon Island, where the cote in which Admiral Rodney housed his carrier pigeons in 1782 is still intact.

A trip to Pigeon Island by motor launch will appeal to everyone. This tiny island has a unique thatch-roofed beach club, restaurant, and bar. The climb to Fort Rodney affords a fine view of St. Lucia. There is a guesthouse here, and arrangements to stay can be made with the owner, Mrs. Josette Legh Snowball.

The Church of the Immaculate Conception of Castries and specimens of Carib and Amerindian relics are interesting. The Carib Indian artifacts are at St. Mary's College in Vigie.

The Carnegie Library is located in the Botanical Gardens in George V Park. Tourists may borrow books and tour the gardens.

Sports-minded travelers will enjoy both tennis and spear-fishing.

Physical Characteristics This is a mountainous island of volcanic origin. It has one low-lying volcano, the Soufrière, with a large, bubbling crater lake. The highest peak is Mount Gimie (3,145). Gros Islet swamp, its lowest point, is several feet below sea level.

The annual rainfall averages about 80 inches. The temperature average is 78.5 degrees.

St. Lucia has many springs and small rivers from which drinking-water is derived.

Principal City Castries, with a population of 24,300, is the largest town. It is a mile from Vigie Airport, and within a 3-minute walk of the docks.

How to Get to St. Lucia

Sea: Canadian National, Alcoa, Harrison, and French lines make regular calls.

Air: British West Indian Airways calls regularly, linking St. Lucia with the International Airport at Trinidad.

Entry Requirements Same as Grenada.

Business Opportunities Principal businesses are the manufacture of rum and sugar from sugar cane, copra from coconuts, and the production of cocoa and agricultural produce.

An ordinance has been passed giving tax benefits to companies establishing new industries.

Available jobs are given to St. Lucians in preference to foreigners.

Government St. Lucia is a part of the British Windward Islands, which have an appointed Governor with headquarters in Grenada. Each island, however, has an appointed Administrator and retains its own institutions. The Administrator is assisted by a Legislative and Executive Council.

Language and Nationalities English is the principal language. A French patois is also spoken. The population consists mainly of British subjects of African descent, a few Lebanese, and Americans.

Banks, Currency Barclays Bank, St. Lucia Co-operative Bank Ltd.

The monetary unit is the British West Indies dollar (about 60 cents U.S.).

Exports and Imports

Principal exports: sugar, copra, cocoa, bananas, rum, bay rum, fruit.

Principal imports: clothing, machinery, medicines, foodstuffs, lumber, tobacco.

Agriculture

Agriculture is the staple industry of the island and provides employment for the majority of the inhabitants. Principal crops are sugar cane, cocoa, coconuts, bananas, and citrus fruits.

Flora and Fauna Lilies, roses, tropical flowers, poinsettias, oleanders, bamboo, wild palms, ferns.

Mongooses, manicous, agoutis.

Sandflies, mosquitoes, fireflies.

Boa constrictors, fer-de-lances.

Kingfish, tuna, dolphins, flying fish, jackfish, sardines. Turtles, lobsters, clams.

Churches St. Lucia is 90-per-cent Roman Catholic. Other denominations include Church of England, Wesleyan, Salvation Army, Seventh Day Adventist, and Baptist.

Schools

The 48 free primary schools receive grants from the Government. There are 2 secondary schools, one for boys and one for girls.

Hospitals and Health There are 4 hospitals, with 156 beds attended by 9 medical officers. Castries has 2 dentists.

Drink only boiled water and milk.

Arts and Crafts Pottery, baskets, needlework, native chairs, oil and watercolor painting, and hats are some of the local handicrafts.

Food Specialties Curries, chicken pelau, calaloo, and crab backs are featured in local restaurants.

Hotels

Name	*Rooms*	*Baths*	*Classification*	*Additional Information*
Hotel St. Antoine (Castries)	15	Some	M*	On slope of Morne Fortuné overlooking harbor.
The Villa (Castries)	4 suites, 5 double 8 single	4	M*	Overlooks harbor. Good food.
Blue Waters Hotel (Castries)	11 double, 1 single	Some	I*	On Vigie Beach. Specialty is sea food.

*American Plan. M—moderately expensive I—inexpensive

Restaurants

Billy's (Castries).
Blue Danube (Castries)—dancing to radio, occasional orchestra.
Minvielle & Chastanet's cafeteria (Castries).

SAINT THOMAS, VIRGIN ISLANDS

(United States West Indies)

LATITUDE: *18 deg. 20 min. N.* LONGITUDE: *64 deg. 55 min. W.*

POPULATION: *13,811* AREA: *32 sq. mi.*

CAPITAL: *Charlotte Amalie (11,463)*

Location

St. Thomas is 3 miles west of St. John, 40 miles north of St. Croix. Bermuda is 700 miles to the north.

Of Special Interest to Tourists Best buys are clothing, Calypso records, liquor, French perfume, Scandinavian silver and glass, native craft, Chinese jade, Mexican and Peruvian jewelry, English woolens, Italian linens, Indian silks and cashmere sweaters. (This is almost a free port; United States excise taxes and custom duties do not apply to imports to the Virgin Islands.)

Swimming at the many beaches (Magens, Morningstar, Lindbergh Bay), tennis, golf, riding, bicycles, horses, fishing, and hunting are all readily available.

A cruise of the harbor or to near-by islands for spear-fishing can be arranged.

A car can be rented to explore the island and visit the sugar plantations and the Jungle Garden.

Join a night-club tour to see the after-dark spots.

There are baseball, softball, and cricket games to watch.

Art exhibits are held occasionally at Berettas Center, and at Hotel 1829, Charlotte Amalie.

Planes can be chartered to see the island by air.

Physical Characteristics St. Thomas has rugged mountains, the high point being Crown Mountain (1,550 feet).

The average temperature is 79 degrees. September and October are very hot. Rain is slight, the annual average being only about 44.5 inches.

The easterly trade winds blow constantly and keep the island comfortably cool.

Principal City Charlotte Amalie, the largest town, is the capital of the three United States Virgin Islands.

How to Get to St. Thomas

Sea: Alcoa, Bull Insular, Lykes Bros., and Waterman lines.

Air: Pan American World Airways, Caribbean Atlantic Airlines, British West Indian Airways.

Entry Requirements Same as for St. Croix.

Business Opportunities See St. Croix regarding establishment of business.

St. Thomas produces cattle for beef and dairy purposes. It has 3 rum distilleries. A jelly, jam, and preserve business is being developed.

The St. Thomas Rural Co-operative produces local foodstuffs.

Government See St. Croix.

Language and Nationalities See St. Croix.

Banks, Currency See St. Croix.

Exports and Imports

Principal exports: rum, cattle, edible animal products, cane sugar, perfume, Virgin Islands handicrafts.

Principal imports: textiles, minerals, metals, machinery, drugs, clothes, alcohol, and articles for re-sale in free-port stores.

Agriculture Sugar, semi-tropical fruits and vegetables.

Flora and Fauna See St. Croix.

Churches Roman Catholic, Lutheran, Episcopal, Methodist, Seventh Day Adventist, Salvation Army, Christian Mission.

Schools Public-school system is under the Department of Education, with stateside standards. Antilles School is a private school: kindergarten through eighth grade.

Hospitals and Health Knud Knud Hansen Memorial Hospital in Charlotte Amalie. Doctors and dentists available. Tap water is safe to drink. Pasteurized milk is available.

Architecture Danish influence seen in the old forts and peak-roofed buildings.

Arts and Crafts Collections of locally executed paintings are exhibited for sale. Native baskets and Virgin Islands sport clothing are available.

Hotels

Name	*Rooms*	*Baths*	*Classification*	*Additional Information*
1829	13	Some	M**	Overlooks harbor.
Bluebeard's Castle Hotel (Charlotte Amalie)	48	48	E*	Dancing, private beach club, cottage cabañas.
Estate Constant (2.5 miles out of town)	34	34	E*	Transportation to private beach. Cabañas.
Higgins Gate (Charlotte Amalie)	12	Some	M* & ***	Popular for dinner by reservation. Liedown bar.
Hotel Flamboyant (3 miles out of town)	66	66	M*	Pool, dancing, tennis, beach, badminton.
Hotel Trade Winds (3 miles out of town)	40	40	I***	Near beach. Rooms have private sundecks.
Smith's Fancy (Charlotte Amalie)	12	12	M**	Overlooks harbor. Intimate atmosphere.
Mountain Top Hotel (high on Crown Mountain)	35	35	E*	Has beach club on private island. Excellent cuisine.
Virgin Isle Hotel (2.5 miles out of town)	125	125	E**	Beach, pool, dancing, tennis, Calypso, Sunday night buffet.

*American Plan　　**Modified American Plan　　***European Plan

E—expensive　　M—moderately expensive　　I—inexpensive

Restaurants and Night Clubs

The Patio (Charlotte Amalie)—taproom, bar, grill.

7 Queens (Charlotte Amalie)—bar and soda fountain.

The Gallery, Grand Hotel (Charlotte Amalie)—popular for lunch; bar; art exhibits.

Sebastians (on waterfront in Charlotte Amalie)—Calypso and piano entertainment at night.

The Magic Lamp (Charlotte Amalie)—bar.

Mike's—popular late spot. Good bar.

SAINT VINCENT

(*sănt vĭn'-sĕnt*) *British West Indies*

LATITUDE: *13 deg. 10 min. N.* LONGITUDE: *60 deg. 57 min. W.*

POPULATION: *71,000* AREA: *150 sq. mi.*

CAPITAL: *Kingstown (6,000)*

Location

St. Vincent is 21 miles south of St. Lucia, 100 miles west of Barbados, and 180 miles north of Trinidad.

Of Special Interest to Tourists (Electricity: 230V AC)

Best buys are sea-island cotton goods, local straw-work, and local rum.

Swimming, tennis, riding, mountain-climbing, spear-fishing, snorkeling, sailing, and fishing may be enjoyed.

Places to see include the Botanical Gardens, the oldest in the West Indies, where Captain Bligh's breadfruit tree stands; the public library, which houses some ancient Carib relics; Mount St. Andrew, overlooking Kingstown; Youngs Island, Mesopotamia Valley, Falls of Baleine; the Grenadine Islands; and the Soufrière volcano (4,048 feet).

Cricket matches are played in Victoria Park. The Aquatic Club has regular dances, as has the Sugar Mill Inn.

Visitors may go fishing with the men from the village of Layou for a small black whale.

Boats may be rented to visit the island of Bequia and the Falls of Baleine near the northern end of St. Vincent.

Bequia, Mustique, Mayreau, Canouan, and Union islands, with a total population of about 4,500, are dependencies of St. Vincent. They are part of the chain of islands known as the Grenadines. The Grenadines nearer Grenada are dependencies of that island.

Cars and taxis may be hired in Kingstown.

Physical Characteristics The terrain is mountainous, but roads are good. There is a fresh-water lake in the Soufrière crater. The valleys are long and fertile.

The average temperature is 80 degrees and the average annual rainfall is 95.71 inches, lighter along the coast than in the interior. St. Vincent has many rivers.

Principal City The ship's landing is near the center of Kingstown, the capital and principal city. About 6,000 people inhabit this city. It is 2.5 miles from Kingstown to the Villa Seadrome, the seaplane landing.

How to Get to St. Vincent

Sea: Canadian National, Alcoa, and Harrison lines. Passengers and cargo are transferred to launches to be brought ashore.

Air: St. Vincent Government Air Service from Barbados, Trinidad, Dominica, Martinique, St. Lucia, and Grenada.

Entry Requirements Passports are not required of British, Canadian, or United States citizens on a visit for a period up to 6 months. Proper identification, however, must be presented. Travelers from other countries require a valid passport bearing a British visa, and will be required to show a return ticket.

Landing-cards are issued to cruise-ship passengers, who may stay on the island without passports for the duration of the stay of their ship.

Business Opportunities The principal business is agriculture. There are several small factories.

Government St. Vincent is a Crown Colony of Great Britain with an appointed Governor assisted by a Legislative Council composed of a majority of elected members and an Executive Council composed of a majority of appointed members.

Language and Nationalities English is the principal language. An English-French patois is also spoken. The population consists mainly of British citizens of African descent, and British colonials.

Banks, Currency Barclays Bank, Co-operative Savings Bank.

The monetary unit is the British West Indies dollar, worth about 60 cents U.S.

Exports and Imports

Principal exports: arrowroot, cotton, sugar, peanuts, copra.

Principal imports: clothing, building materials, foodstuffs, gasoline, oil.

Agriculture The economy is principally agricultural. Arrowroot, sugar, coconuts, cassava, corn, bananas, and ground nuts are grown.

Flora and Fauna The foliage is semi-tropical and profuse.

Mongooses, manicous, moths, crapeau, iguanas.

Kingfish, snappers, dolphins, mackerel, cavali, groupers, sprats, a few turtles, lobsters (crayfish), river shrimp.

Churches Roman Catholic, Methodist, Anglican.

Schools Forty primary schools are in operation. Education in the primary schools is free.

Hospitals and Health The Colonial Hospital is in Kingstown. Doctors and dentists are available. The climate is healthful. Malaria and yellow fever are unknown. Water is good throughout the island.

Hotels

Name	*Rooms*	*Baths*	*Classification*	*Additional Information*
Sugar Mill Inn (above Villa Beach)	15	Some	M*	Swimming pool, transportation to Kingstown, Aquatic Club privileges.
Blue Caribbean (Kingstown)	20	Some	M*	In town.
Harbour Hotel (Kingstown)	6	1	I*	Pension type.
Olive's (Kingstown)	8	2	I*	Pension type.
South Bridge (Kingstown)	8	2	I*	
Sea View Hotel (Edinboro)	8	2	I*	
Sunny Caribee (Bequia Island)	9	Some	I*	

*American Plan M—Moderately expensive I—Inexpensive

Restaurants The Sugar Mill Inn, the Blue Caribbean Restaurant, the Aquatic Club—bar and snacks.

SINT (SAINT) EUSTATIUS

(sĭnt ŭ-stā'-shĭ-ŭs) Netherlands West Indies

LATITUDE: *18 deg. N.* LONGITUDE: *63 deg. W.*

This tiny (11 square miles) island is one of the Windward Islands of the Netherlands Antilles. It is 19 miles southeast of Saba.

Horseback riding and visiting the ruins of the old forts, the Dutch Reform church, and the Jewish synagogue are about all there is to offer tourists.

The terrain is hilly, rising in two volcanic cones; the highest peak, The Quill, reaches 1,950 feet. The temperature averages about 79 degrees and the annual rainfall average is 42 inches.

Oranjestad, the principal town, is on the western coast at the base of a mountain. It has an open roadstead.

The Government ship, the *Antilia*, stops by from Curaçao once a month. A plane from Sint Maarten flies in once a week. Private boats may be hired at Antigua or St. Thomas (U.S. Virgin Islands). The entry requirements are the same as those of Saba.

The main occupation of the less than 1,000 inhabitants is agriculture; farmers receive Government aid. They raise yams, onions, and some cotton. Dutch farmers have introduced mechanized farming.

Sint Eustatius is administered under the Lieutenant Governor at Sint Maarten. Its people speak English.

The Government Guest House has 4 bedrooms and 2 baths. Rates are very moderate.

SINT MAARTEN (SAINT MARTIN)

(Dutch: sĭnt; French: săn-mar′-tan″)
Netherlands-French West Indies

LATITUDE: *18 deg. N.* LONGITUDE: *63 deg. W.*

One of the Netherlands Windward group, Sint Maarten occupies almost half of the island on which it is located. The other portion is French, a dependency of Guadeloupe. Saba is 29 miles to the southwest, Sint Eustatius 19 miles to the south.

Tourists may cross freely to the French side of the island to buy liquor and perfumes, on which there is no import or excise tax.

The land area of the Dutch side is 16 square miles and the population is 1,533. Sint Maarten is hilly. Its highest peak is Mount Paradise (1,360 feet). The average temperature is 80 degrees; 42 inches of rain fall per year. The nights are cool. Water comes from wells, but in the dry seasons is fetched from springs in the valleys.

Philipsburg, the capital, is stretched out on a mile-long narrow sandbar between the Bay and Great Salt Pond. Two streets run the length of the sandbar. Juliana Airport is a 20-minute drive away.

KLM (Royal Dutch Airlines) operates a weekly service from Curaçao and St. Kitts. Chartered planes from Puerto Rico and St. Thomas also fly in, and Air France makes biweekly trips from Puerto Rico.

The *Antilia*, the new Government vessel (500 tons), has accommodations for about 18 cruise passengers. It leaves Curaçao once a month and makes stops at all the Netherlands islands and St. Kitts, taking about 10 days in all. It stops at Sint Maarten on both its outward trip and its return trip. The entry requirements are the same as for Saba.

Sint Maarten has a small salt industry, but fishing and agriculture are the chief occupations. Jobs are scarce, and most of the young men leave to work in the oil-refineries in Curaçao and Aruba.

A Lieutenant Governor, who is in charge of the three Netherlands Windward islands, administers Sint Maarten. Two deputies assist him. A representative is sent to the Central Government in Curaçao.

The people speak English and Dutch. There is a hospital with a Government physician.

The Little Bay Hotel has 24 bedrooms with private baths and some 2-room suites. It has a fine beach, central dining-room, and detached cottages. Prices are moderately high.

TOBAGO

(*tō-bä'-gō*) *British West Indies*

LATITUDE: *11 deg. 13 min. N.* LONGITUDE: *60 deg. 40 min. W.*

POPULATION: *32,600* AREA: *116 sq. mi.*

CAPITAL: *Scarborough*

Location

Tobago lies 21 miles northeast of Trinidad.

Of Special Interest to Tourists (Electricity: 115V AC)

Best buys are baskets, hats, and bags of straw, sandals, jewelry, and British imports.

Swimming at Store Bay, 8 miles west of Scarborough; Golden Grove Point private beach (get permission from Mr. Frank Latour at Golden Grove Estate); Mount Irvine Bay, 6 miles west of Scarborough; Little Back Bay, 6.5 miles west of Scarborough; Arnos Vale; and Man of War Bay Beach at Charlotteville.

Buses, taxis, and drive-yourself cars are available. A local license must be obtained from the police. There are many lovely drives around the island.

Horses and bicycles may be rented.

Fishing boats may be chartered.

A snorkeling expedition to Buccoo Reef to see the underwater life will be enjoyed by travelers of all ages. The trip is timed for low tide when the water is about knee high and the plant life, coral, crustaceans, mollusks, and fish may be clearly seen.

Visitors may also go lobster-fishing or play tennis and badminton.

Horse racing is held at Shirvan Park for 2 days in February or March and 2 days in October or November: pari-mutuel betting and sweepstakes.

Scarborough has a public library open to visitors. Its many centers throughout the island are served by book vans.

Travelers who want to see the bird-of-paradise island off Speyside will be taken by boat across the mile and a half of water. This island was bought by Sir William Inghram as a bird sanctuary, particularly for birds of paradise. Upon his death his sons presented it to the Government as a gift.

Physical Characteristics Volcanic in origin, Tobago's central mountain range rises to 1,890 feet. The island is 26 miles long by 7.5 miles at its widest point. Its lush vegetation is similar to that of Trinidad.

The average temperature ranges from 80 to 84 degrees. The annual average rainfall is 67 inches in the south and west, between 90 and 100 inches in the north.

Drinking-water is supplied by rivers and streams. The Hillsborough Dam provides water for Scarborough and the surrounding area.

Principal City Scarborough, the capital, is situated at the base of a hill at Rockly Bay. It is about 10 miles from Crown Point Airport, which is located at the southwest tip of the island.

How to Get to Tobago

Sea: Travelers must sail from Trinidad, a regular port of call for many large shipping lines. In addition, two Government-run coastal steamers, the *Trinidad* and the *Tobago,* ply between the islands three times a week. Once each fortnight the *Trinidad* circles Tobago, delivering and taking produce. This trip around Tobago takes three days and four nights and costs $17 without meals.

Air: British West Indian Airways flies into and out of Tobago daily from Piarco Airport, Trinidad; the flight takes half an hour.

Entry Requirements Same as Trinidad.

Business Opportunities Tobago is mainly occupied with agriculture. The Government is encouraging the development of new industries and, under the Aid to Pioneer Industries Ordinance, gives certain tax benefits to new businesses.

Government A ward of Trinidad, it is represented by its own elected member of the Legislative Council in Trinidad. It has its own local council and warden.

Language and Nationalities English is the principal language.

Only about 100 of the inhabitants are white, the majority being Negroes of African descent. There are a few East Indians.

Banks, Currency Barclays Bank in Scarborough.

The British West Indies dollar is the monetary unit, equal to about 60 cents U.S.

Exports and Imports

Principal exports: cocoa, copra, coconuts and coconut fiber, vegetables, livestock, poultry, lime oil, leaf tobacco.

Principal imports: foodstuffs, fuels and lubricants, chemicals, textiles, machinery, clothing, footwear, miscellaneous manufactured articles.

Agriculture The chief agricultural products are cocoa, limes, coconuts, and sugar. Agricultural co-ops have been organized to increase production and income.

Flora and Fauna Mountain immortelle, swamp immortelle, caraguan, cocoa, shack tree, saman, banyan, flamboyant, tulip tree.

Hibiscus, jasmine, moonflower vine, cocoa lily, spider lily, windflower, orchid, cactus.

Avifauna include the Tobago mockingbird, boat-tailed grackle, golden-eyed thrush, cornbird, blue tanager, Venezuelan house wren, bird of paradise.

124 varieties of butterflies.

Sailfish, tuna, albacore, barracuda, kingfish, wahoo, amberjack, dolphin, mackerel, angelfish, parrotfish. Crustaceans and mollusks may also be found.

Churches St. Andrew's Anglican, built in 1819. Methodist, Moravian, Roman Catholic, Plymouth Brethren, Seventh Day Adventist.

Schools Thirty-four primary schools, mainly run by churches with Government aid, Bishop's High School, a co-ed secondary school, and 5 domestic-science and handicraft centers in Scarborough comprise the school system.

Hospitals and Health Colonial Hospital at Scarborough. District nurses are stationed throughout the island, and an ambulance service is available. A mosquito-eradication campaign is going on. Water outside Scarborough should be boiled. Some pasteurized milk is available.

Hotels

Name	*Rooms*	*Baths*	*Classification*	*Additional Information*
Blue Haven (Scarborough)	26	26	E*	Beach and launch.
Arnos Vale Beach Hotel (Plymouth) (main house has 4 bedrooms; 2 cottages with 2 and 3 rooms, 1 cottage with 1 room)	23	23	E*	Beach barbecues, snorkeling, horses, boating, badminton.
Bacolet Guest House (Scarborough) (2 cottages)	35	Some	M*	Good beach.

*American Plan E—expensive M—moderately expensive

Name	*Rooms*	*Baths*	*Classification*	*Additional Information*
Hotel Robinson Crusoe (Scarborough)	20	20	E*	Beach, tennis, dancing Saturday night.
Castle Cove Beach Hotel (Scarborough) (2 cottages, 4 bedrooms)	9		M*	Chinese cuisine to order.
Alma Guest House	4	4	E*	In the hills—river bathing.

*American Plan E—expensive M—moderately expensive

Restaurants Only in hotels listed.

TRINIDAD

(trĭn′-ĭ-dăd) British West Indies

LATITUDE: *10 deg. 30 min. N.* LONGITUDE: *61 deg. 15 min. W.*

POPULATION: *558,300* AREA: *1,864 sq. mi.*

CAPITAL: *Port of Spain (111,380)*

Location Trinidad is the most southerly of the British West Indies. It is but 10 miles off the Paria peninsula of Venezuela. Tobago, its sister island, is 21 miles northeast. New York is 1,939 miles north.

Of Special Interest to Tourists (Electricity: 115V AC)
Best buys are East Indian jewelry, mahogany items, British silks, native paintings, linens, cottons, china and tableware, Irish linen, French perfumes and lingerie, English doeskin, tweeds, and cashmere sweaters, and Oriental curios from China and India. Groups of steel-band dolls make take-home gifts.

Swim at Maracas Bay, 14 miles from town, and picnic at the beaches at Toco, Manzanilla Point, and Mayaro Bay. There are hotel and club pools.

Taxis, drive-yourself cars, and buses are available. The railroad across the island makes several round trips each day.

Rugby, soccer, and cricket may be seen throughout the island. Other sports include tennis, golf, fishing, and hunting.

Calypso, dancing, music, and steel bands are fully described in the Trinidad chapter in the front of the book.

The drive over the skyline highway and return trip by The Saddle, the Botanical Gardens, Pitch Lake, and the Royal Victoria Institute Museum will interest visitors.

Physical Characteristics Trinidad is shaped like a short boot with an elongated toe. It is 50 miles long and 37 miles wide, with a total area of 1,864 square miles. The terrain is rocky and steep in some parts, with three mountain ranges running from east to west, the highest peak being El Cerro del Aripo (3,085 feet) in the northern range. A famous landmark is the grayish 109-acre Pitch Lake in La Brea.

The climate is tropical, with an average temperature of 84 degrees (74 at night). The average annual rainfall is 70 inches. The rainiest months are June through December.

The principal rivers are the Caroni, Ortoire, and Oropouche.

Principal City Port of Spain, population 111,380, is Trinidad's capital and most important city. This busy port handles thousands of ships each year. Located on the Gulf of Paria on the western coast, it is 12 miles west of Piarco Airport. West of Port of Spain in the gulf is the Cocorite seaplane area.

How to Get to Trinidad

Sea: Alcoa, American President, American Republic, Blue Star, Booth, Canadian National, Cunard, Elders and Fyffes, French, Harrison, Moore-McCormack, Norgulf, Nourse, Royal Mail, Royal Netherlands, Surinam, Argentine State, Grimaldi, and Venezuelan lines.

Air: Pan American World Airways, KLM (Royal Dutch Airlines), Línea Aeropostal Venezolana, Aerolíneas Argentinas, Aerovías Brasil, British West Indian Airways, St. Vincent Government Air Service, Air France, BOAC.

Entry Requirements United States, Canadian, and United Kingdom tourists with return tickets and proof of citizenship do not require passports if they intend to remain less than 6 months.

A currency declaration must be made on arrival, and visitors without special permission may not leave with more money than declared.

Business Opportunities Oil, asphalt, and agriculture are the most important industries. In order to promote the creation of new industries, the Aid to Pioneer Industries Ordinance was passed in 1950. It gives a 5-year holiday from import and income taxes plus generous depreciation allowances to approved new industries. The Government has also rented Crown lands at moderate fees for industrial purposes.

Government Trinidad is a Crown Colony ruled by a Governor appointed by the Queen. He is the Chairman of the 9-member Executive Council that assists him and a 27-member Legislative Council. Local affairs are handled by mayors and their councils.

Language and Nationalities English is spoken. The population is composed chiefly of English citizens of African descent, French, Spanish, Portugese, East Indians, and Chinese.

Banks, Currency

Banks: Barclays Bank; Canadian Bank of Commerce; Gordon, Grant & Co., Ltd.; Royal Bank of Canada; Trinidad Co-operative Bank, Ltd.; Bank of Nova Scotia.

Monetary unit is B.W.I. dollar, worth about 60 cents U.S.

Exports and Imports

Principal exports: bananas, grapefruit, petroleum, petroleum products, rum, unrefined sugar, cocoa, asphalt.

Principal imports: art silk fabrics, barytes, cars, cement, coal, chemicals, clothing, cotton fabrics, fish, footwear, lubricating oils, lumber, machinery, meat, medicine, milk, paints, paper, soaps, steel pipe, structural iron, tires and tubes, tobacco, trucks, wheat flour.

Agriculture Chief products are sugar, cocoa, coconuts, citrus fruits, and coffee. There are 8,000 acres devoted to citrus crops. These crops are important to the economic stability of the island.

Flora and Fauna Sugar cane, rice, cocoa, grapefruit, limes, bananas, herbs.

Immortelle tree, coconut palm, giant bamboo, and Samaan tree.

Begonias, zinnias, hibiscus, poui.

Churches and Temples Church of England, Baptist, Church of Scotland, Methodist, Presbyterian, Roman Catholic, Salvation Army, Seventh Day Adventist, Hindu, Mohammedan.

Schools There are 64 Government schools, 253 denominational primary and intermediate schools. The Imperial College of Tropical Agriculture 8 miles east of Port of Spain has its own experimental farm. The Colonial Microbiological Research Institute was opened in 1948.

Hospitals and Health Port of Spain has good hospitals and doctors.

The anti-malaria campaign has been very successful, and tourists need not sleep under mosquito netting in the hotels in Port of Spain; it is wise to take this precaution in hotels out of town.

The tap water in Port of Spain is safe to drink. Water in the country districts should be boiled.

Architecture The houses are a mixture of Spanish, French, Moorish, Chinese, Hindu, and Mohammedan. Many buildings have French-style iron balconies.

Arts and Crafts Because of the polyglot population, the handicrafts of many countries are found here. The silver jewelry is notable. Ivoryware, Indian sandals, Chinese linens, Indian saris, mandarin coats, and Chinese pajamas are obtainable. A sizable art colony produces primitive and modern paintings.

Food Specialties East Indian curries, calaloo, sans coche, and West Indian pepperpot stew.

Hotels

Name	*Rooms*	*Baths*	*Classification*	*Additional Information*
Bel Air (Piarco Airport)	33	Some	E***	
Bergerac (Port of Spain)	32	32	E*	Apartment hotel.
Bretton Hall (Port of Spain)	32	Most	M*	Modernized old mansion; pleasant dining-terrace.
Dundonald Hall (Port of Spain)	16	Some	M*	
Normandie Hotel (Port of Spain)	12	Some	M*	
Pan American Guest House (Piarco Airport)	52 (Air-conditioned)	52	E***	
Queen's Park Hotel (Port of Spain)	135	Some	E*	Largest and oldest; understaffed.

*American plan E—expensive M—moderately expensive
***European plan

Restaurants (All in Port of Spain)

Belvedere: Saturday-night dancing. Situated high on Lady Chancellor Hill overlooking port.

China Clipper: Chinese food.

Kimling: Chinese food.

Lotus: Chinese food. Good floor shows with Calypso singers and limbo dancers.

Miramar: downtown drinking-place. Good native shows.

Normandie Hotel: fine French cuisine. Dancing Fridays.

Rainbow Terrace: Chinese food, outdoor dining, dinner music, floor show nightly.

Tavern on the Green: American-style cooking.

Trinidad Country Club.

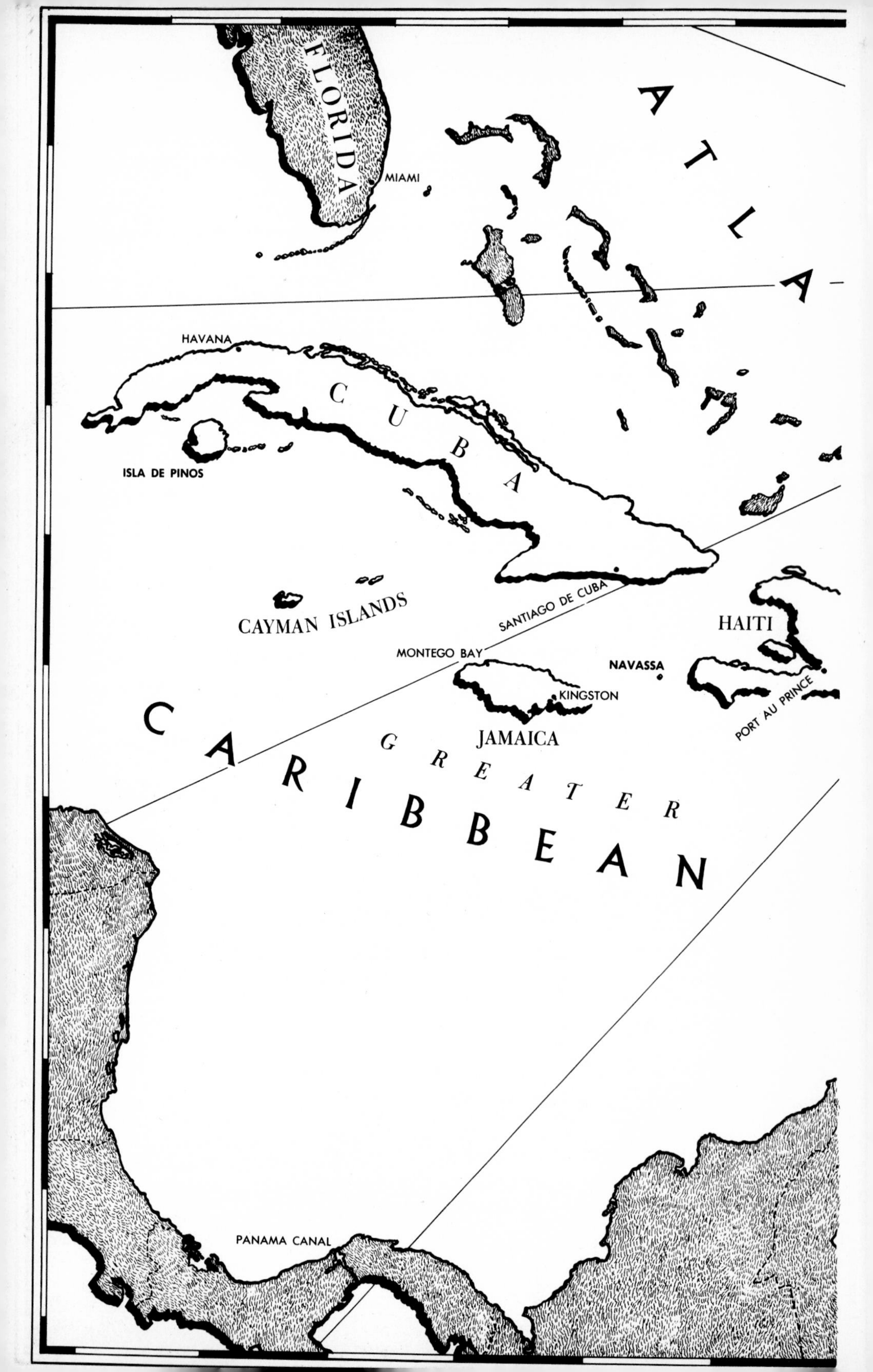
FLORIDA
MIAMI
ATLA
HAVANA
CUBA
ISLA DE PINOS
CAYMAN ISLANDS
SANTIAGO DE CUBA
HAITI
MONTEGO BAY
NAVASSA
KINGSTON
JAMAICA
PORT AU PRINCE
CARIBBEAN
GREATER
PANAMA CANAL

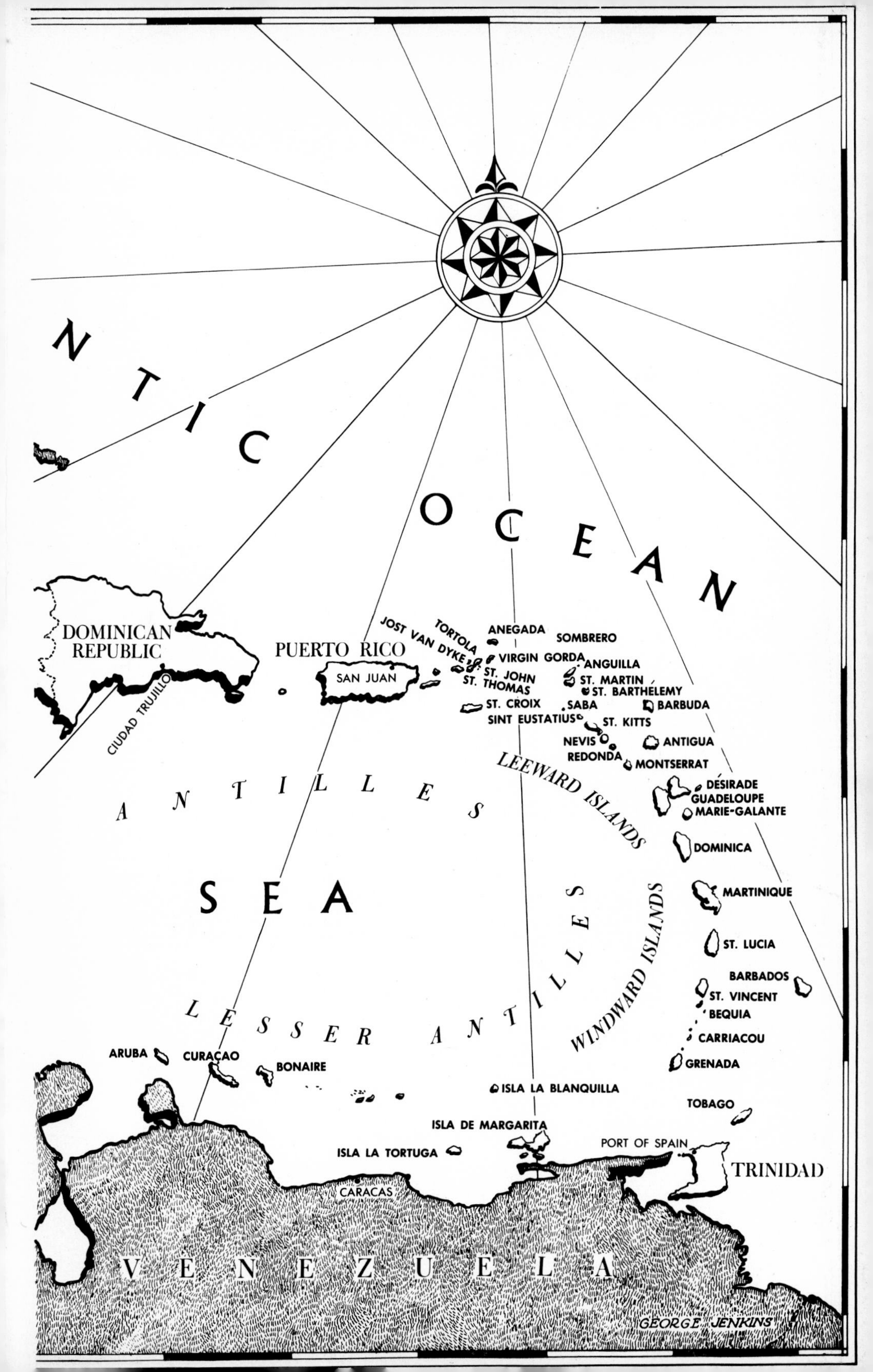
NTIC
OCEAN
DOMINICAN REPUBLIC
CIUDAD TRUJILLO
PUERTO RICO
SAN JUAN
JOST VAN DYKE
TORTOLA
ANEGADA
SOMBRERO
VIRGIN GORDA
ANGUILLA
ST. JOHN
ST. THOMAS
ST. MARTIN
ST. BARTHÉLEMY
ST. CROIX
SABA
BARBUDA
SINT EUSTATIUS
ST. KITTS
NEVIS
ANTIGUA
REDONDA
MONTSERRAT
LEEWARD ISLANDS
DÉSIRADE
GUADELOUPE
MARIE-GALANTE
DOMINICA
ANTILLES
SEA
MARTINIQUE
ST. LUCIA
WINDWARD ISLANDS
BARBADOS
ST. VINCENT
BEQUIA
CARRIACOU
GRENADA
LESSER ANTILLES
ARUBA
CURAÇAO
BONAIRE
ISLA LA BLANQUILLA
TOBAGO
ISLA DE MARGARITA
PORT OF SPAIN
ISLA LA TORTUGA
TRINIDAD
CARACAS
VENEZUELA
GEORGE JENKINS

A NOTE ON THE TYPE

The text of this book was set on the Linotype in Janson, a recutting made direct from the type cast from matrices made by Anton Janson. Whether or not Janson was of Dutch ancestry is not known, but it is known that he purchased a foundry and was a practicing type-founder in Leipzig during the years 1660 to 1687. Janson's first specimen sheet was issued in 1675. His successor issued a specimen sheet showing all of the Janson types in 1689.

His type is an excellent example of the influential and sturdy Dutch types that prevailed in England prior to the development by William Caslon of his own incomparable designs, which he evolved from these Dutch faces. The Dutch in their turn had been influenced by Garamond in France. The general tone of Janson, however, is darker than Garamond and has a sturdiness and substance quite different from its predecessors. It is a highly legible type, and its individual letters have a pleasing variety of design. Its heavy and light strokes make it sharp and clear, and the full-page effect is characterful and harmonious.

Composition by WESTCOTT AND THOMSON, INC., *Philadelphia, Pennsylvania. Lithography by* THE MURRAY PRINTING COMPANY, *Wakefield, Massachusetts. Bound by* H. WOLFF, *New York. Designed by* HARRY FORD.